Bombs, Bullets
and Bread

Bombs, Bullets and Bread

The Politics of Anarchist Terrorism Worldwide, 1866–1926

MICHAEL KEMP

McFarland & Company, Inc., Publishers

Jefferson, North Carolina

LIBRARY OF CONGRESS CATALOGUING-IN-PUBLICATION DATA

Names: Kemp, Michael, 1975– author.
Title: Bombs, bullets and bread : the politics of anarchist terrorism worldwide, 1866–1926 / Michael Kemp.
Description: Jefferson, North Carolina : McFarland & Company, Inc., Publishers, 2018 | Includes bibliographical references and index.
Identifiers: LCCN 2018030554 | ISBN 9781476671017 (softcover : acid free paper) ∞
Subjects: LCSH: Terrorism—History—19th century. | Terrorism—History—20th century. | Anarchism—History—19th century. | Anarchism—History—20th century.
Classification: LCC HV6431 .K425 2018 | DDC 363.32509/034—dc23
LC record available at https://lccn.loc.gov/2018030554

BRITISH LIBRARY CATALOGUING DATA ARE AVAILABLE

ISBN (print) 978-1-4766-7101-7
ISBN (ebook) 978-1-4766-3211-7

Front cover: Mug shot of French anarchist Émile Henry, 1894

Printed in the United States of America

*McFarland & Company, Inc., Publishers
Box 611, Jefferson, North Carolina 28640
www.mcfarlandpub.com*

Table of Contents

Preface   1

One. A People's Will   5

Two. Ghosts at the Feast   16

Three. The Emperor's Axe   37

Four. The Cook, the Blacksmith, the King
and the Weaver   50

Five. Machines Infernales   65

Six. The French Connection   79

Seven. The One-Armed Anarchist   106

Eight. An Outrage in the Park   120

Nine. A Carnival of Revenge   135

Ten. Museifu Shugi Banzai!   155

Eleven. Beneath a White Tower   178

Twelve. Teenage Wastelands   187

Chapter Notes   201

Bibliography   210

Index   217

BREAK—break it open; let the knocker rust;
Consider no "shalt not," nor no man's "must";
And, being entered, promptly take the lead,
Setting aside tradition, custom, creed;
Nor watch the balance of the huckster's beam;
Declare your hardest thought, your proudest dream;
Await no summons; laugh at all rebuff;
High hearts and youth are destiny enough.
The mystery and the power enshrined in you
Are old as time and as the moment new;
And none but you can tell what part you play,
Nor can you tell until you make assay,
For this alone, this always, will succeed,
The miracle and magic of the deed.
—John Davidson, "To the Generation Knocking
at the Door," December 1912

Preface

In his dissection of the British Empire, the travelogue *Following the Equator*, Mark Twain stated, "The very ink with which all history is written is merely fluid prejudice."[1] This aphorism has driven the creation of the volume before you.

Between the nineteenth and twentieth centuries a wave of terrorism was unleashed upon the globe. This surge was quickly ascribed to Anarchist proponents of the concept of "propaganda of the deed." In 1857, the Italian revolutionary and libertarian Socialist Carlo Pisacane published his *Political Testament*,[2] in which he argued that "ideas spring from deeds and not the other way around." The accepted wisdom is that the concept of direct action influencing social change, as originally envisioned by Pisacane, was embraced by Anarchist luminaries such as Mikhail Bakunin and was responsible for much of the carnage that followed. Between the 1860s and 1930s, supposed Anarchists were involved in a succession of bombings, assassinations, and attempted attacks through much of the world. Indeed, it is arguable that in public consciousness of the time, Anarchism was effective shorthand for terrorism, and to hold Anarchist political beliefs was to be a terrorist. During the peak of this first wave of propaganda of the deed, international newspapers, together with concerned readers, governments, and law enforcement officials, often described the attacks by supposed Anarchists as part of a global conspiracy. History, however, does not support this formidable myth.

Before continuing with this discussion, it is worth dissecting the use of the term *terrorism* itself. Originally stemming from the French *terrorisme*, which itself drew from the Latin verb *terrere* (meaning "to frighten"), the historical root lies with the Society of the Friends of the Constitution (or Jacobins, as they were more commonly known), which came to power in France in 1792. For the next two years, the Jacobin state, under the leadership of Maximilien Robespierre, unleased a wave of retribution against its opponents that included public executions, the formation of a powerful secret police force, and the restriction of human and political rights. These draconian measures were remembered by the French populace following Napoleon Bonaparte's rise to power, and the words *terrorist* and *terrorism* became terms of abuse. Initially, terrorism referred to the abuse of state power; however, these semantic roots have become gnarled and twisted in our modern age. Although there is little unified agreement on the definition of these terms, modern usage is directed toward actions or activities that utilize unlawful or extralegal intimidation or violence (typically against civilians) in pursuit of political aims, usually resulting in mass casualties or injuries. With the exception of a few instances in which civilians were attacked directly by Anarchists (most notably the attacks conducted by Émile Henry), the use of the word *terrorism* in the title of this book may seem somewhat

1

overstated. Typically the attacks engaged in by active proponents of propaganda of the deed belong to a history of terrorism that, in our own age of televised mass carnage, is forgotten. It can be argued that late nineteenth- and early twentieth-century Anarchists who engaged in attacks had more in common with the carefully meditated attacks of Hassan-i Sabbah and his Fedayeen, who were responsible for a series of assassinations (hence the word) in eleventh-century Persia (now Iran). The attacks detailed in this volume do not fit neatly into the original definition of terrorism as being representative of state actions or a modern definition of attacks that result in mass civilian casualties. Instead, they belong to a seemingly anachronistic definition, in which true political believers sought to generate widespread societal change through the use of force against the state (or the bourgeois members thereof).

A number of specific aims were foremost in my mind during the writing of this volume. Principally, I wished to remember the words of Twain and consider how the histories of the time period that this book examines have been constructed (and by whom). Typically, when considering the activities of supposed Anarchists and adherents of propaganda of the deed, historians have dwelled upon the acts themselves, not the actors. It is my humble hope that this book can help to fill this void. A cursory examination of some of the scant biographies of those responsible for terrorist outrages shows in many cases that those involved were not Anarchists at all. Rather, Anarchy was conflated with Socialism, Nihilism, Nationalism, and (in some cases) the actions of those suffering from mental or physical illness or those employed by police forces in the dual capacities of spy and agent provocateur. The major aim of this publication is to provide biographical data of the attackers to create a more complete picture that will allow for a deeper understanding of what, beyond their political beliefs, prompted their attacks.

Attacks by supposed Anarchists in the late nineteenth and twentieth centuries are often thought to have been limited to Europe and America. This is a fundamentally incorrect assumption. Attacks in Asia, Australia, Europe, the United States, and Russia are documented in this publication to provide an indicator of the international scope of Anarchist terrorism. It should be noted, however, that in preparing this book for publication, I have been forced to make difficult choices regarding what information to include. To my shame, I have not been able to include details on tertiary attackers or their actions that would further indicate the international nature of the threat. These include Anton Nilson, a militant Swedish Socialist and later Communist responsible for a ship bombing in 1908; Michele Angiolillo Lombardi, responsible for the assassination of the Spanish prime minister in 1897; Luigi Lucheni, who assassinated Empress Elisabeth of Austria in 1898; and Bhagat Singh, who bombed the Indian Central Legislative Assembly in 1929. Additionally, I do not provide details regarding the wave of bombings that swept through the United States in 1919 inspired by followers of the Italian Anarchist Luigi Galleani, the *Los Angeles Times* bombing of 1910, or organizations as diverse as the Guillotine Society and the Bonnot Gang, Japanese and French illegalists, the Revolutionary Insurrectionary Army of Ukraine, and Liu Shifu and the Chinese Assassination Corps. These and more have been left out of this publication for reasons of brevity, but also to allow for concentrated focus on those individuals who have been included. With the exception of some individuals familiar to students of this topic and the period of study, I have also attempted to provide biographical data about those actors and acts that typically are only included as passing sentences in other volumes. This book includes both new photographs and English translations of documents that have not been previously gathered together.

On the subject of materials, another aim of this book was to make available for the interested reader relevant documents pertaining to the individuals discussed. In writing this volume, I have drawn upon relevant historical documentation, manifestos, statements, interviews, and poetry and prose. A selection of these materials is provided in the hope that it will allow the reader to form a broader picture of the attackers under discussion.

Beyond the study of terrorism and history, the wave of attacks that occurred from the mid-nineteenth century onward is now largely forgotten. However, they remain extremely relevant to our own volatile age. The professionalism of both law enforcement responses and terrorist activities has advanced considerably from a time when heads of state and governments could arbitrarily stroll among their subjects with no security considerations. This book also seeks to highlight the circumstances of noteworthy attacks, many of which, for the modern reader, may appear to have been precipitated by security mechanisms that were either lax or derisible. This book owes much to the idea that history is prejudicial, and it is my contention that by failing to concentrate on the individual motivations, histories, and experiences of attackers, historians have sadly missed many factors that have allowed the fearful and often overwrought conflations of the past to continue.

One

A People's Will

During the latter part of 1869, a manifesto exploded in Russia, the shock waves of which were felt around the globe. Written by the Russian Nihilist and author Sergey Nechayev, the now infamous *Catechism of a Revolutionary* is one of the most radical books of its age, and it has proved hugely influential to Anarchist and revolutionary thought ever since (indeed, it was adopted by the prominent Black Panther Eldridge Cleaver[1] as a core element of his political philosophy). Subsequently embraced by one of the influential figures of the concept of propaganda of deed, Mikhail Bakunin, becoming "the credo of the International Brothers, a secret organization Bakunin formed in Italy,"[2] the *Catechism* is noteworthy for its call to total devotion to a revolutionary cause. The opening paragraph of the *Catechism*, which went on to influence Nihilists and Anarchists alike, is as follows:

> The revolutionary is a doomed man. He has no private interests, no affairs, sentiments, ties, property nor even a name of his own. His entire being is devoured by one purpose, one thought, one passion—the revolution. Heart and soul, not merely by word but by deed, he has severed every link with the social order and with the entire civilized world; with the laws, good manners, conventions, and morality of that world. He is its merciless enemy and continues to inhabit it with only one purpose—to destroy it.[3]

This absolutist and pronounced doctrine influenced revolutionaries of the time, and it continues to do so today.

One group that took much from the *Catechism* was the Russian organization Zemlya i Volya (Land and Liberty). Many members of Land and Liberty shared Bakunin's politics and held that Russian land (which was for the most part still ruthlessly controlled by the tsar and a corrupt aristocracy) should be handed to the Russian peasantry, and the state and ruling class structure should be dismantled for the benefit of society. In "June 1879 a split occurred at the Voronezh conference,"[4] and with the publication of the *Catechism*, Land and Liberty divided into two separate and oppositional political factions—namely, Black Partition and Narodnaya Volya (The People's Will). The former was largely ineffective at the time, and it rejected direct actions in favor of a wider socialist propaganda campaign among workers with a view to enacting social change through educative efforts and a rejection of terrorism. Narodnaya Volya was far more direct in its aspirations and actions, and, as revealed by David Rapoport, "The majority decided to adopt the 'terrorist struggle' and the assassination of the Tsar as their first goal, to achieve political and civil rights."[5]

One of the founding members of Narodnaya Volya was Alexander Kviatkovsky, who ironically was the son of a Russian aristocrat. Kviatkovsky was born in 1853, but by 1876 he had grown disenchanted with Russian society and had joined Land and Liberty. With the publication of the *Catechism*, Kviatkovsky helped establish Narodnaya Volya, in which he served as a member of the executive committee[6] and soon after was instrumental in forming an audacious idea: ridding Russia of the rule of the tsar required getting rid of Tsar Alexander II. Strange though it might seem to modern thinking, it was not just the belabored minority of the working class who were antagonized by the inefficiencies and monumental inequality of tsarist society. Many members of the Russian bureaucracy, the police and security forces, and the young aristocracy were openly appalled at the excesses of tsarist Russia. Indeed, many early Russian revolutionaries were either members of the aristocracy or educated members of the bourgeoisie, who dedicated not just their personal and familial fortunes but often their lives to the destruction of the tsarist state. As Steve Phillips somewhat understatedly states, "some of the more liberal members of the aristocracy recognized the need to modernize the country in order to maintain Russia's position as a great power."[7]

It was not just disaffected members of the aristocracy who found themselves at odds with tsarist Russia. Many members of the oppositional forces came from much humbler origins, including the peasantry. One such individual was Stepan Nikolayevich Khalturin.[8] Khalturin was the son of a peasant who was born in the village of Khalevinskaia (later Verkhnie Zhuravli), Orlov District, Viatka Province, on 2 January 1857. In 1871 he graduated from the Orlov District School, which, given his limited means, was no small feat in itself, and between 1874 and 1875 he attended the Viatka Technical School, where he became a qualified joiner and carpenter. During the latter part of 1875, like many of the rural peasantry before him, young Khalturin moved to St. Petersburg, then the imperial capital of Russia. Khalturin was one of those fortunate enough to benefit from the Emancipation Reform of 1861, which allowed some twenty-three million people to be emancipated from feudal serfdom and, in doing so, attain the rights of liberty they had so long been denied. "The reform of 1861, gave Russia a real opportunity to develop in a peaceful, evolutionary fashion."[9] The Russian peasant reform, coupled with an expanse of the Industrial Revolution, saw an influx of the former peasantry moving into St. Petersburg, and it soon developed into one of the largest industrial cities in Europe. Khalturin, as a carpenter, had skills that were of value to the process of industrialization, and he also found that he shared many political ideals with other revolutionary Narodniks (Russian populists who were a social consciousness

Stepan Nikolayevich Khalturin

movement involved in revolutionary agitation against the tsardom). As part of his contact with the Narodniks, Khalturin was often called upon to agitate various workers' groups, and he also helped supervise an underground workers' library and printing press.[10]

The year 1877 was an important one for Khalturin. In October of that year, he not only went underground (probably to avoid the Russian secret police) but also helped organize the factory strikes that occurred throughout St. Petersburg in 1878 and 1879 in opposition to some of the worst working conditions in Europe. By 1897, Khalturin had joined Narodnaya Volya and made contact with Alexander Kviatkovsky. Although Kviatkovsky and Khalturin were divided in terms of who should be the leading force of an uprising against the tsarist state (Kviatkovsky, like many members of Narodnaya Volya, believed that revolutionary activities should be led by the rural peasantry, while Khalturin, who had founded the Northern Union of Russian Workers in 1878, believed the city-based workers ought to be the leaders), they found agreement in an armed overthrow of the state.

The plan presented to Narodnaya Volya by Khalturin was a simple one: he would blow up the tsar. Thanks to his skill at carpentry, Khalturin had managed in 1879 to obtain employment at the tsar's Winter Palace under the assumed identity of Stepan Batyshkov.[11] His employment there had done nothing to diminish his revolutionary ire and frustration and, indeed, had only stoked it further. Constructed between 1754 and 1762, the Winter Palace consisted of "an impressive main imperial palace with more than 1000 halls and rooms"[12] serviced by a staff of nearly five hundred. The levels of ostentatious opulence were appalling considering that much of the Russian peasantry and the working classes lived in state of a poverty that was as grinding as it was absolute. After being furnished with dynamite from Kviatkovsky and other members of Narodnaya Volya, Khalturin slowly and carefully began to transfer the explosives to his lodgings in a cellar shared with other workers[13] on the Winter Palace grounds. The plan, once supplies had been gathered, was to position dynamite within a supporting wall that Khalturin had been tasked with repairing and plastering that was directly below the dining room of the tsar and his family.

The transfer of the dynamite to the palace was a long and laborious process, and it ultimately impacted not only Khalturin's mental health but also his physical well-being. One of the key components of dynamite, then as now, was nitroglycerine. Although nitroglycerine can be used to treat a variety of medical conditions, including heart disease and angina, it can also, with prolonged exposure, lead to poisoning. This is very likely what happened to Khalturin. Frequent skin contact with nitroglycerine caused a variety of symptoms, including a constant and persistent headache, hair loss, insomnia, and confused and muddled thinking. Quite apart from the potential poisoning, Khalturin was doubtless under mental strain as he "posed as a palace worker for four months"[14]— quite a significant period in which he had to keep his true identity and motives obscured. This may be one reason why Khalturin missed an opportunity to assassinate the tsar without recourse to explosives. During the period when he was transferring the dynamite to the palace, Khalturin found himself in the tsar's personal office making repairs to the furniture. Also present was the tsar himself. When questioned by members of Narodnaya Volya as to why he had not simply used his hammer to do more than merely repair furniture, Khalturin's response was that the tsar of Russia was "an old man and he had his back to me"[15] at the opportune time, and thus he would not have provided a fair match.

On the evening of 5 February 1880, Khalturin had set aside any ethical qualms he may have had about the use of his carpentry tools and was ready to act after months of preparation. On that fateful evening, Tsar Alexander II was due to dine with his family and his nephew by marriage, Prince Alexander of Battenberg (modern-day Bulgaria). Their repast was due to commence at 6:00 p.m. A few moments after 6:00 p.m., Khalturin lit a fuse with a ten-minute delay on the dynamite that was situated below the dining room, and then he casually left the Winter Palace for the last time.

Winters in Russia are brutal. In addition to the freezing temperatures, a frequent weather hazard is blizzards. One such blizzard occurred on the night of 5 February, delaying the arrival of Prince Alexander. He and his retinue arrived at the Winter Palace at 6:00 p.m. The dynamite packed beneath the dining room detonated shortly before 6:30 p.m. At that time neither Prince Alexander nor the tsar had reached the dining room, and the large explosion that rocked the Winter Palace failed to achieve its purpose. A late-running train and the Russian winter had prevented the assassination of the tsar. Sadly, several members of the household Finnish guard who had their quarters above the blast area were not as fortunate and suffered fatal injuries. Another forty to sixty members of the palace staff were gravely injured in the explosion. All told, the blast ended the lives of eleven people.[16]

Following the failed assassination of the tsar, the nitroglycerine poisoning that Khalturin had suffered prevented his rapid exit from St. Petersburg. Within a few months, however, he was well enough to travel, and he was in Moscow briefly helping spread propaganda (of the paper variety) to workers and denizens of the second-largest city in Russia.

After attempting to gain support for a workers' uprising, Khalturin found himself in Odessa. Here he and one of his colleagues from Narodnaya Volya killed the military prosecutor, General V. S. Strelnikov, who had been sent by tsarist forces to eradicate revolutionary activities within Odessa. Although Khalturin did not fire the fatal shot that killed the general, he was present on the scene dressed as a cab driver to provide a rapid exit for the actual assassin, Nikolai Zhelvakov.[17] Both assailants were quickly overpowered by the members of the crowd following the attack. The assassination had taken place in a crowded public park during the early evening as Strelnikov sat on a bench after his usual post-dinner walk, an area that was filled with other perambulators. Both Khalturin and Zhelvakov were arrested and provided false names, with Khalturin falling back on his familiar identity as Stepan Batyshkov. The connection to the Winter Palace bombing was overlooked by the tsarist security forces,

Dmitry Karakozov (Sputnik/Alamy Stock Photo)

and both Khalturin and Zhelvakov were promptly tried and convicted of the attack on Strelnikov. Following an order from Alexander III, they were both hanged in Odessa on 22 March 1882.

At the time of his execution, neither the tsarist security and intelligence forces, or indeed the Russian people, knew that Khalturin was the failed bomber of the Winter Palace from two years earlier. A year prior to the execution, Andrei Zhelyabov was arrested (in connection to another failed assassination attempt on the tsar), and he died in prison in 1884, taking the identity of the palace bomber to his grave. Slowly following the Bolshevik revolution, however, the identity of the Winter Palace bomber became apparent, and Khalturin served as a propaganda tool in his own right for helping to establish the place of the worker (and not just the peasant) in Russian revolutionary politics.

Khalturin's attempt to assassinate the tsar was not the first, nor would it be the last. The earliest attempt was made on 4 April 1866 by a young revolutionary by the name of Dmitry Vladimirovich Karakozov. Karakozov was born in the town of Kostroma, situated at a confluence of the Volga and Kostroma rivers, on 4 November 1840. Although allegedly born into a family of minor nobility like Kviatkovsky, little is known of Karakozov's life. One fact that has been established, however, is that he was the cousin of Nikolai Ishutin. Like Alexander Berkman was later to be, Ishutin, who was born only months before his cousin on 15 April 1840 in Serdobsk, was an ardent reader later in life of *What Is to Be Done?* by Nikolai Chernyshevsky, and he would subsequently claim that there had only ever been three great men in human history: "Jesus Christ, Saint Paul and Nikolai Chernyshevsky."[18] Inspired by the hero of the novel, Ishutin obtained a job on a Volga steamboat from which to foment revolution. Ishutin, who would later be described as a "hunchbacked youth, nicknamed 'the General,'"[19] was one of the first Russian utopian Socialists; however, he also advocated violence and was to be a major influence in the life of his younger cousin.

Although nothing is known of Karakozov's early schooling, by the time he was in his twenties, like his cousin, and perhaps even on his recommendation, Karakozov had read Chernyshevsky and come to despise his privileged background and the harsh reality of Russia of this period wherein "one class sucks another's blood."[20] He had also been expelled from two universities—Kazan in 1861 for "participation in the disturbances there"[21] and Moscow in 1865 for failure to pay his tuition fees. Following his expulsion from Moscow University, Karakozov was affected by depression, and "in the winter of 1865–66 he was taken ill and spent two months in the university infirmary. He was suffering from an intestinal disease, but he came to believe that his ailment was mental. He imagined that his days were numbered."[22] Despite this somewhat dismissive judgment, it is entirely possible that Karakozov was actually verging on suicide, and, indeed, some historians have determined his later actions to be those of a "disturbed and possibly suicidal young man and not the culmination of a real conspiracy."[23]

According to accepted historical understanding, in 1865, Ishutin formed his Organizatsiya (Organization),[24] which he hoped would help drive Russia toward a more equal social basis. When first established, the Organization sought to engage in peaceful alternatives, and it was involved in the dissemination of peaceful propaganda, as well as establishing "a co-operative bindery and a dressmaking establishment."[25] In January 1866, the Organization ruptured to the point that a smaller body by the name of Hell was formed. As highlighted by Adam Ulam, "members of [Hell] would devote themselves exclusively to terror: assassination, armed robbery, blackmail, of the rich, etc."[26] Although thus may all sound like student posturing, members were committed, and, as Paul Avrich notes, "one member even considered poisoning his own father and giving his inheritance to the cause."[27] Given the family connection, it was subsequently believed that Karakozov was part of his cousin's schemes.

Following his recovery from the sickness prompted by his expulsion from Moscow University, Karakozov vanished in February 1866, leaving behind a suicide note.[28] He did not commit suicide, however, and would later claim to his concerned peers that he had been to visit a monastery. Following his return from his mysterious (and possibly monastic) location, Karakozov openly discussed regicide, which made his peers, even those within the Organization, concerned. Although "a morose, self-centered youth, deaf in one ear, whose grey eyes were set in a lean, sickly face,"[29] when discussing the removal of the tsar from Russia, Karakozov became noticeably animated. Karakozov was to disappear again, and by spring 1866 he was resident in St. Petersburg. During his travels, Karakozov had prepared a manifesto, titled Друзьям-рабочим (To Friends-Workers). He distributed his handwritten proclamation to friends and strangers alike, hoping that within it they would find a call to revolt. Karakozov even went as far as mailing a copy of his manifesto to the then governor of St. Petersburg, complete with, as Ana Siljak notes, his preemptive confession that "I have decided to destroy the evil Tsar, and to die for my beloved people."[30] The message was lost in the mail, however, and the governor received no advance notification of Karakozov's plans. On 4 April 1866, Karakozov put those plans into action.

The Summer Garden was personally designed by Tsar Peter in 1704 and situated next to the Summer Palace. This large park in the heart of St. Petersburg became one of the most frequented and evocative promenades for the bourgeoisie. It was known that Tsar Alexander II frequently chose to walk its environs, and his personal security was lax. For a potential assassin, it would make a perfect location at which to attack. On the morning of 4 April 1866, Tsar Alexander had enjoyed one of his regular strolls and was leaving the gardens with his small retinue. Karakozov saw him coming and seized his chance. He dashed toward the tsar and raised his hand to fire. The double-barreled pistol he had selected for the assassination discharged one of its bullets, but his aim was awry. According to the historical record, just before the bullet could be discharged, Ossip Komissarov, a peasant-born hatter's apprentice who had been emancipated by the peasant reform of 1861, and who had seen Karakozov approach, had "struck at the man's hand and the bullet embedded itself in the pavement."[31] As pointed out by Avrahm Yarmolinsky, however, this rescue presents a "rather questionable story,"[32] allowing the tsar known as the liberator of the serfs to be saved providentially by a liberated serf.

Rather than take his second shot, Karakozov took a quick glance at the tsar's guards that were swarming toward him and ran. He was quickly wrestled to the ground by the pursuing guards and his pistol removed. Guards noted that in the process of fleeing, and while being flung to the ground, Karakozov had struggled to keep a hand in his pocket at all times. Carefully they extricated his hand and found that his pocket contained morphine and strychnine to kill himself, in addition to prussic acid to disfigure his face—a tactic promoted to members of Hell when seeking to escape from the forces of law and order following a successful assassination. Also in his pockets was a crumpled copy of his manifesto, which read, in part, "I have long been tormented by the thought and given no rest by my doubts why my beloved simple Russian people have to suffer so much! ... Why next to the eternal simple peasant and laborer in his factory and workshop are there people who do nothing—idle nobles, a horde of officials and other wealthy people, all living in shining houses? I have looked for the reason for all this in books, and I have found it. The man really responsible is the Tsar ... the Tsar is the first of the nobles. He never holds out his hand to the people because he is himself the people's worst enemy."[33]

Following his arrest, Karakozov was transferred to the Peter and Paul Fortress, where one of his boyhood idols, Chernyshevsky, had himself been detained in 1862. Here, under forceful questioning, he implicated thirty-five other members of his cousin's Organization, and then he turned to Russian Orthodoxy for solace. As noted by Yarmolinsky, Karakozov "showed signs of mental derangement, which the authorities chose to disregard. For hours he was on his knees in prayer."[34] His prayers went unheeded, however, and his trial began later that year. As noted, the Karakozov's co-defendants included "thirty-five people, some of them mere boys,"[35] and although twenty-five of them were to be released without charge, ten alleged conspirators faced lengthy terms of hard labor. One of these was Nikolai Ishutin, and he was to die, aged only thirty-eight, in Kara katorga some thirteen years later. Karakozov himself was sentenced to death by hanging, which was enacted in St. Petersburg on 3 September 1866.

Following the execution of Karakozov, there were numerous other attempts on the life of Tsar Alexander II. The son of a Polish nobleman, Antoni Berezowski, attempted to assassinate the tsar on 6 June 1867 when he was in attendance at the Paris World Fair. With the motivation of attempting to free his native Poland from Russian imperial rule, Berezowski had purchased and adapted a two-shot pistol. Unfortunately for Berezowski, his attempts at improving the weapon had affected its structural integrity, and the pistol misfired, which resulted in grave injuries to the horse of a cavalryman but not to the tsar. Berezowski was subsequently sentenced to lifelong hard labor in New Caledonia, where he died in 1916. On 20 April 1879, Tsar Alexander was fired on five times by a thirty-three-year-old ex-student by the name of Alexander Soloviev. The tsar of all the Russias escaped the would-be assassin's bullets by running in a zigzag pattern, and Soloviev was quickly detained before being executed by hanging on 28 May 1879. Later that year, in December, members of Narodnaya Volya sought to blow up the tsar in transit while he was returning from vacation on a train. They missed, damaging only the tracks. Respite was brief for Tsar Alexander, however, as on 13 March 1881 members of Narodnaya Volya (including Nikolai Rysakov, Ignacy Hryniewiecki and Ivan Emelyanov) were finally able to assassinate him using a variety of explosives thrown into his carriage. Finally, the Nihilists had got their man.

The actions of Karakozov and Khalturin are representative of a wider struggle against the oppressive reign of Tsar Alexander II over a nearly fifteen-year period. Inspired by Nihilism, these two individuals represented sectors of society that were both opposed to tsarist rule. Originally a serf, Khalturin was one of the first to utilize dynamite as a weapon against civilians; Karakozov, the dropout son of minor aristocracy, was the first to fire on the Russian monarch. Although their backgrounds were vastly different—one from poverty, the other from the bourgeoisie—their motivations were similar, and both hoped that the removal of a ruler would lead to an improvement in social conditions through mass revolution. In this sense, they are both evocatively illustrative of propaganda of the deed, and their actions would resonate with generations of later revolutionaries.

Catechism of a Revolutionary (Sergey Nechayev)

Source: Marxists Internet Archive, https://www.marxists.org/subject/anarchism/nechayev/catechism.htm (accessed January 2017)

The Duties of the Revolutionary Toward Himself

1. The revolutionary is a doomed man. He has no personal interests, no business affairs, no emotions, no attachments, no property, and no name. Everything in him is wholly absorbed in the single thought and the passion for revolution.

2. The revolutionary knows that in the very depths of his being, not only in words but also in deeds, he has broken all the bonds which tie him to the social order and the civilized world with all its laws, moralities, and customs, and with all its generally accepted conventions. He is their implacable enemy, and if he continues to live with them it is only in order to destroy them more speedily.

3. The revolutionary despises all doctrines and refuses to accept the mundane sciences, leaving them for future generations. He knows only one science: the science of destruction. For this reason, but only for this reason, he will study mechanics, physics, chemistry, and perhaps medicine. But all day and all night he studies the vital science of human beings, their characteristics and circumstances, and all the phenomena of the present social order. The object is perpetually the same: the surest and quickest way of destroying the whole filthy order.

4. The revolutionary despises public opinion. He despises and hates the existing social morality in all its manifestations. For him, morality is everything which contributes to the triumph of the revolution. Immoral and criminal is everything that stands in its way.

5. The revolutionary is a dedicated man, merciless toward the State and toward the educated classes; and he can expect no mercy from them. Between him and them there exists, declared or concealed, a relentless and irreconcilable war to the death. He must accustom himself to torture.

6. Tyrannical toward himself, he must be tyrannical toward others. All the gentle and enervating sentiments of kinship, love, friendship, gratitude, and even honor, must be suppressed in him and give place to the cold and single-minded passion for revolution. For him, there exists only one pleasure, one consolation, one reward, one satisfaction—the success of the revolution. Night and day he must have but one thought, one aim—merciless destruction. Striving cold-bloodedly and indefatigably toward this end, he must be prepared to destroy himself and to destroy with his own hands everything that stands in the path of the revolution.

7. The nature of the true revolutionary excludes all sentimentality, romanticism, infatuation, and exaltation. All private hatred and revenge must also be excluded. Revolutionary passion, practiced at every moment of the day until it becomes a habit, is to be employed with cold calculation. At all times, and in all places, the revolutionary must obey not his personal impulses, but only those which serve the cause of the revolution.

The Relations of the Revolutionary Toward His Comrades

8. The revolutionary can have no friendship or attachment, except for those who have proved by their actions that they, like him, are dedicated to revolution. The degree

of friendship, devotion and obligation toward such a comrade is determined solely by the degree of his usefulness to the cause of total revolutionary destruction.

9. It is superfluous to speak of solidarity among revolutionaries. The whole strength of revolutionary work lies in this. Comrades who possess the same revolutionary passion and understanding should, as much as possible, deliberate all important matters together and come to unanimous conclusions. When the plan is finally decided upon, then the revolutionary must rely solely on himself. In carrying out acts of destruction, each one should act alone, never running to another for advice and assistance, except when these are necessary for the furtherance of the plan.

10. All revolutionaries should have under them second- or third-degree revolutionaries—i.e., comrades who are not completely initiated. These should be regarded as part of the common revolutionary capital placed at his disposal. This capital should, of course, be spent as economically as possible in order to derive from it the greatest possible profit. The real revolutionary should regard himself as capital consecrated to the triumph of the revolution; however, he may not personally and alone dispose of that capital without the unanimous consent of the fully initiated comrades.

11. When a comrade is in danger and the question arises whether he should be saved or not saved, the decision must not be arrived at on the basis of sentiment, but solely in the interests of the revolutionary cause. Therefore, it is necessary to weigh carefully the usefulness of the comrade against the expenditure of revolutionary forces necessary to save him, and the decision must be made accordingly.

The Relations of the Revolutionary Toward Society

12. The new member, having given proof of his loyalty not by words but by deeds, can be received into the society only by the unanimous agreement of all the members.

13. The revolutionary enters the world of the State, of the privileged classes, of the so-called civilization, and he lives in this world only for the purpose of bringing about its speedy and total destruction. He is not a revolutionary if he has any sympathy for this world. *He should not hesitate to destroy any position, any place, or any man in this world.* He must hate everyone and everything in it with an equal hatred. All the worse for him if he has any relations with parents, friends, or lovers; *he is no longer a revolutionary if he is swayed by these relationships.*

14. Aiming at implacable revolution, the revolutionary may and frequently must live within society will [*sic*] pretending to be completely different from what he really is, for he must penetrate everywhere, into all the higher and middle-classes, into the houses of commerce, the churches, and the palaces of the aristocracy, and into the worlds of the bureaucracy and literature and the military, and also into the Third Division and the Winter Palace of the Czar.

15. This filthy social order can be split up into several categories. The first category comprises those who must be condemned to death without delay. Comrades should compile a list of those to be condemned according to the relative gravity of their crimes; and the executions should be carried out according to the prepared order.

16. When a list of those who are condemned is made, and the order of execution is prepared, no private sense of outrage should be considered, nor is it necessary to pay attention to the hatred provoked by these people among the comrades or the people. Hatred and the sense of outrage may even be useful insofar as they incite the

masses to revolt. It is necessary to be guided only by the relative usefulness of these executions for the sake of revolution. Above all, those who are especially inimical to the revolutionary organization must be destroyed; their violent and sudden deaths will produce the utmost panic in the government, depriving it of its will to action by removing the cleverest and most energetic supporters.

17. The second group comprises those who will be spared for the time being in order that, by a series of monstrous acts, they may drive the people into inevitable revolt.

18. The third category consists of a great many brutes in high positions, distinguished neither by their cleverness nor their energy, while enjoying riches, influence, power, and high positions by virtue of their rank. These must be exploited in every possible way; they must be implicated and embroiled in our affairs, their dirty secrets must be ferreted out, and they must be transformed into slaves. Their power, influence, and connections, their wealth and their energy, will form an inexhaustible treasure and a precious help in all our undertakings.

19. The fourth category comprises ambitious office-holders and liberals of various shades of opinion. The revolutionary must pretend to collaborate with them, blindly following them, while at the same time, prying out their secrets until they are completely in his power. They must be so compromised that there is no way out for them, and then they can be used to create disorder in the State.

20. The fifth category consists of those doctrinaires, conspirators, and revolutionists who cut a great figure on paper or in their cliques. They must be constantly driven on to make compromising declarations: as a result, the majority of them will be destroyed, while a minority will become genuine revolutionaries.

21. The sixth category is especially important: women. They can be divided into three main groups. First, those frivolous, thoughtless, and vapid women, whom we shall use as we use the third and fourth category of men. Second, women who are ardent, capable, and devoted, but whom do not belong to us because they have not yet achieved a passionless and austere revolutionary understanding; these must be used like the men of the fifth category. Finally, there are the women who are completely on our side—i.e., those who are wholly dedicated and who have accepted our program in its entirety. We should regard these women as the most valuable or our treasures; without their help, we would never succeed.

The Attitude of the Society Toward the People

22. The Society has no aim other than the complete liberation and happiness of the masses—i.e., of the people who live by manual labor. Convinced that their emancipation and the achievement of this happiness can only come about as a result of an all-destroying popular revolt, the Society will use all its resources and energy toward increasing and intensifying the evils and miseries of the people until at last their patience is exhausted and they are driven to a general uprising.

23. By a revolution, the Society does not mean an orderly revolt according to the classic western model—a revolt which always stops short of attacking the rights of property and the traditional social systems of so-called civilization and morality. Until now, such a revolution has always limited itself to the overthrow of one political form in order to replace it by another, thereby attempting to bring about a so-called revo-

lutionary state. The only form of revolution beneficial to the people is one which destroys the entire State to the roots and exterminated all the state traditions, institutions, and classes in Russia.

24. With this end in view, the Society therefore refuses to impose any new organization from above. Any future organization will doubtless work its way through the movement and life of the people; but this is a matter for future generations to decide. Our task is terrible, total, universal, and merciless destruction.

25. Therefore, in drawing closer to the people, we must above all make common cause with those elements of the masses which, since the foundation of the state of Muscovy, have never ceased to protest, not only in words but in deeds, against everything directly or indirectly connected with the state: against the nobility, the bureaucracy, the clergy, the traders, and the parasitic kulaks. We must unite with the adventurous tribes of brigands, who are the only genuine revolutionaries in Russia.

26. To weld the people into one single unconquerable and all-destructive force—this is our aim, our conspiracy, and our task.

Two

Ghosts at the Feast

Following the brutal suppression of the Paris Commune of 1871, France was a fractured state. The memory of the events that followed the spontaneous revolt, which left thousands dead and exiled, left a deep scar in the French consciousness and heavily influenced relationships between the working class and the bourgeoisie. Overt political activities were banned, trade unions became illegal, and even political moderates were forced to operate outside the bounds of unjust laws. Prior to the events of 1871 France had a long history of Individualist Anarchism, but it was arguably the state repression that followed the fall of the Commune that led to the rise of an often forgotten branch of propaganda of the deed: illegalism.

Individualist Anarchism had a pronounced history on French soil prior to the events of 1871. As early as 1849, one of the participants in the French revolution of 1848, Anselme Bellegarrigue, was calling for a rejection of much of Proudhon's thought and an embrace of solipsistic acts of civil disobedience. Although his career in France was cut short by his immigration to the United States in 1852, and he has largely been forgotten by history, the ideas of Bellegarrigue were to take hold following the Commune. These ideas were bolstered by the work of Max Stirner, most tellingly *The Ego and Its Own* (*Der Einzige und sein Eigentum*), which was published in 1844. In this work, Stirner critiques humanism, liberalism, and concepts of collectivism in favor of an amoral (although not inherently immoral) egoism. For Stirner, the ego presents a possibility of freedom, and the egoist can move beyond morality in the pursuit of fulfilling their wants and necessities. It was the egoism of Stirner, fused with the earlier philosophies espoused by Proudhon and now-little-known actors such as Bellegarrigue, that gave rise to the concept of propaganda of the deed. Illegalism was just one element of this broader concept, which embraced the ego in pursuit of political ends. By seeking reclamations and expropriations from the moneyed classes, its adherents aimed to demonstrate not only that their individual desires could be obtained beyond capitalism but also that, in meeting such needs, the process of revolutionary change would be escalated by example. For modern readers, it may seem unlikely that a mixture of justifiable rage about the suppression of the Commune, the restrictions put in place regarding political assembly, and the philosophy of individualism led to a situation in late twentieth-century France that reverberated, and arguably continues to reverberate, globally. One of the principal adherents of the philosophy of illegalism was a young Frenchman, Marius Jacob, a one-time potential priest, teenage pirate, and, later, successful politically motivated burglar.

Alexandre Marius Jacob (better known as Marius Jacob) was born on 29 September 1879 in Marseille. By the time of his birth, Marseille was a thriving metropolis, but a fractured one. Between 1880 and 1911, the city experienced no less than 237 strikes. Many thousands of workers were routinely unemployed, and the wages of the area were far below the French national average of the period. The economic gap between rich and poor was vast. Unfortunately, Marius was at the time of his birth (and throughout most of his life) toward the latter end of that scale.

Marius' father, Joseph Leon Jacob, started out as a cook with a shipping company; however, when he met his future wife, Marie Elisabeth Berthou, he secured employment in a bakery near the docks of Rue Fontaine-Rouviere in Marseille. Marie Berthou, who was married at the age of eighteen, secured a loan from her family in order for her and Joseph to open a bakery; unfortunately, domestic bliss escaped them. According to accounts provided by Bernard Thomas, "Alexandre-Marius grew up as best he could between this unsatisfied Amazon of a mother and this emasculated father."[1] Living in an

Alexandre Marius Jacob

abusive home where his restless father regularly beat his mother, Marius' best moments were when his father's drinking companions and ex-shipmates would visit and between drinks regale the youngster with tales of "exotic ports of call in strange-sounding islands…. Java, Borneo, Celebes, Fiji, Sumbawa—where, inevitably, apocalyptic typhoons blew, while lovely halfbreeds devised lascivious belly dances for their exclusive benefit."[2] For a child raised in an abusive home environment, these seafaring tales must have provided refuge for his spirit, as a calm inlet provided solace from the typhoons in the tales. Between 1882 and 1884 his parents tried unsuccessfully to expand the ranks of the Jacob family; however, their efforts were to prove in vain (Marius had three siblings, Andre, Toussaint, and Joseph Marius, all of which died within days and months of their birth), which likely created additional stress within the family and may also explain why Marie doted on Marius throughout his life and why, as Marius would remember later, his father sank into alcoholism.[3]

Marius Jacob attended a fee-paying Christian Brothers school and was a serious and dedicated student. He apparently was also susceptible to many of the underlying lessons, and as an eight–year-old he had declared that he wanted to become a priest, earning derision from his secular father. When he was eleven and a half, Jacob was granted permission to sit his school certificate. It was expected that he would go on to obtain his diploma and potentially further down an academic path; however, the bakery had begun to suffer from not only lack of customers but also his father's frequent drinking bouts, and Jacob was forced to seek employment rather than pursuing academia further.

Jacob secured employment as a cabin boy on a ship by the name of *Tibet*, which set sail with him as part of the crew on 22 February 1890. He soon discovered that a life on the open waves was not as glamorous as his father and his former shipmates had claimed. Indeed, life as a cabin boy was brutal and tedious for the most part. In addition to being servants for the ship's crew and passengers, cabin boys (who were typically slightly older than Jacob) endured casual beatings and abuse. The duties of a cabin boy largely centered on the activities of sweeping, cleaning, waiting, and being a general dogsbody. This drudgery, coupled with regular beatings and crew quarters that were far from comfortable or commodious, may have helped dispel some of the romance of the sea. Following several voyages on the *Tibet*, Jacob was able, at the tender age of twelve, to sign on with the *Ville de la Ciotat* in the capacity of trainee helmsman. Not only was this position better paid, but this ship also took him as far away as the Seychelles and Sydney. His time aboard the ship did not last long, however, and according to Bernard Thomas he may have been a target for sexual assaults. The following year, aged thirteen, he had signed on as crew on board the *Armand-Behic*. As soon as the ship reached Australian shores, Jacob absconded at Sydney with little more than a few pennies in his pockets and the clothes on his back.

After surviving as best he could in Sydney, eventually Jacob was persuaded to sign on with a whaling ship. Unfortunately for Jacob, but fortunately for historians and lovers of a good yarn, the ship and crew was focused not on the pursuit of whales but on other ships. According to Thomas, Richard Parry,[4] and a number of other biographers, Jacob had inadvertently signed on with a crew of pirates. The Australian coast of the 1890s may not seem like an immediately obvious location for piracy, but, as Stephen Gapps reveals, it had a long history dating back to 1629.[5] Although, according to Thomas, Jacob was only present on two piratical expeditions, he learned the invaluable lesson that not only did crime pay but, unlike what he may have absorbed during his Christian Brothers education, the wages were not death—at least not for him. It was perhaps during this time that Jacob learned other lessons. There is strong evidence to suggest that some of the ships Jacob had signed on for during his period at sea were actively engaged in the transport and poor treatment of economic emigrants. As Alain Sergent highlights, "At the age when most kids were still in petticoats tied to their mother or had never left their hometown, Alexander learned to consider one of the most sordid aspects of the exploitation of man by man…. And, between slaves and merchants, unconscious instruments of those, these indifferent or cruel sailors still added to the suffering of pitiful emigrants."[6]

As soon as the piratical crew docked in Sydney, Jacob again absconded, sickened by some of the abuses he had witnessed on board ship. Jacob did not remain on solid ground for long, though, and soon signed on to the English vessel *Prince of Albert*, bound for Liverpool before heading home to Marseilles. Here he was promptly arrested for his desertion from the *Armand-Behic*. It is not certain how long his detention lasted, but for a thirteen-year-old, even one who had traveled around the globe aboard various ships, it cannot have failed to have a negative impact. Thanks in no small part to the appeals of his mother, Jacob was released and took to the sea for the next several years. Jacob's career as a mariner was interrupted when he contracted "the fevers"[7] in Dakar. This was in all probability malaria, but, whatever the root cause of this mysterious illness, it would have a lasting impact on the still adolescent Jacob. From his sickbed, Jacob discovered literature, or, more specifically, the novel *Ninety-Three* by Victor Hugo. Later described as "a striking example of the epic of national freedom,"[8] this tale of revolutionary derring-do outlines a vision of a society based on sexual equality, individual liberty, and, tellingly, limited government.

Eventually recovered from his illness, Jacob soon found himself part of the political milieu of Marseilles. Abandoning the sea, he found employment at the Juge print works in the Rue de la Republique as an apprentice compositor. As part of his work at Juge, Jacob became a skilled compositor and, thanks to his interest in politics (including a burgeoning interest in Anarchism), was soon typesetting for a local paper, *L'Agitateu*. By 1896, Jacob was a youthful would-be revolutionary, and his actions at *L'Agitateu* and throughout Marseilles had not been overlooked by the local police. It was at around this time that Jacob first ran afoul of the state's legal forces when he was "set up by an agent provocateur who procured explosives then snitched."[9] Following his arrest, the supposed informant, identified as Lecca,[10] was not seen in Marseilles again. At the age of seventeen, Jacob found himself the victim of a police conspiracy and sentenced to six months' imprisonment for manufacturing explosives, which commenced on 1 September 1897. It would not be his last spell of imprisonment.

Following his release from prison on 11 February 1898, Jacob found that the police had not forgotten him during his detention. A regular attendee of Anarchist meetings in Marseille, Jacob's attendance and increasing radicalism may have been driven by political idealism, anger at the state that had falsely accused and imprisoned him, or the fact that the police insisted on contacting his prospective employers to discuss his criminal record. Additionally, he was suspected of a number of small burglaries. By this time, Jacob was one of the most reputed and targeted of the residents in Marseilles. He was, for example, able to obtain employment with a local pharmacist in 1899; however, following a visitation from a police inspector Favre (as documented by Jean-Marc Delpech), Jacob was within a month unemployed. Far from dampening his revolutionary ardour, his false imprisonment and constant harassment from the police since his release only made Jacob more confrontational.

Shortly before the meeting between the pharmacist and the police inspector, Jacob met Rose Roux. According to the account provided by Thomas,[11] Rose and Jacob became deeply attached to each other and, indeed, just prior to his loss of employment at the pharmacy, moved into a furnished room together in Marseilles. What Thomas fails to mention, however, is that Rose was fifteen years older than twenty-year-old Jacob (this age difference is substantiated by Delpech[12]). Rose had a troubled life prior to meeting Jacob, and following a spell as the companion of a full-time gambler and part-time Anarchist burglar by the name of Clarenson, she had also resorted to working as a part-time prostitute, as many working-class women left in dire economic straits were called upon to do. Although the age gap was significant, Rose and Marius were deeply in love, by all accounts, and had Inspector Favre not intruded on their nascent domestic bliss, perhaps they would have settled down to a life of domesticity and been forgotten to history.

Starting in 1899, Jacob engaged in the activity that was to make him infamous in the history of radical politics—namely, burglary. On 1 April (or 31 March, depending on which account is accepted) 1899, Jacob, along with a comrade from his Marseille rabble-rousing, Arthur Roques, and a recently released convict by the name of Morel, broke into the shop of a local pawnbroker. As Delpech and Sergent reveal, however, this was no simple smash and grab. Indeed, the robbery was conducted with the complicity and assistance of the pawnbroker and his staff at the Petit-Saint-Jean establishment. Being the oldest, and thus most credible for the purposes of the robbery, Roques claimed to be a police inspector, accompanied by his clerks, Morel and Jacob, sent to search the premises of the pawnbroker for evidence related to a case of homicide. Strangely, valuable evidence that included "jewels, watches, earrings, candelabras, bonds, policies, plate, and cutlery"[13] was discovered when Jacob was left alone with the pawnbroking ledgers and produced a matching list of suspicious materials. The gang was able to pack up a variety of high-value materials into a collection of suitcases, also provided by the pawnbroker. A young clerk was placed in handcuffs, suspected of facilitating the exchange of stolen goods, and placed into a taxi with Jacob. While the "inspector" and his clerk made their escape with the evidence in a second taxi, Jacob escorted the clerk in handcuffs to the Marseilles courthouse, where he was made to sit on a bench to be attended to by a judge. It was only as the courthouse was closing that the concierge noted the (doubtless distraught) pawnbroker's clerk and involved actual police inspectors, by which point Jacob, Roques and Morel, along with the purloined goods, had long since departed. From Marseille, Jacob and Roques made their way to Spain and successfully divested themselves of their haul.

Between March and June 1899, Jacob and Roques roved between France and Spain, conducting a string of burglaries. Some of these produced significant returns (including 30,000 francs from the home of a notary in Aix); others, however, were not nearly as successful. After breaking into the unoccupied country home of the counts of Cassagne, Jacob was unable to breach the security of their strongbox, and so, in a fit of pique, he left a note on their sideboard that read, "You are lucky, filthy aristocrat, that we had not enough time: otherwise your strongbox would be much lightened by now. Until the next time. Let us hope it may go better."[14] He signed his missive "Attila."

Ultimately Jacob's luck ran out, and in June 1899 the French police issued a warrant for his arrest. By 29 June he had been arrested in Toulon owing to the confession of Morel (and others) about his involvement in the pawnshop robbery. Briefly detained in Toulon, Jacob was subsequently transferred to Aix prison. From his arrest onward, Jacob feigned madness. Indeed, according to the account provided by Thomas, he went so far as to kiss the face of the Aix prison warden and declare him the messiah. Jacob's act was convincing, however, and rather than facing the five-year sentence that had been imposed at the time of the warrant being issued, a jury declared on 29 June 1899, at the Aix-en-Provence assizes, that Jacob should be transferred to the Mont Perrin asylum in Marseilles for observation.

Being detained in a nineteenth-century asylum was far from a pleasant experience; however, Jacob's luck again held. He was fortunate enough to become friends with a male nurse in the asylum by the name of Marius Royères. Unlike many in the working class, Royères was sympathetic to Anarchism, and he also knew a number of people with whom Jacob shared a passing acquaintance in Marseilles. It was Royères who actively helped assist Jacob in not only exaggerating his symptoms but also ensuring that he was transferred to a padded cell near the perimeter of the prison. On the night of 18 April 1900, the reason for the transfer, and Jacob's increasingly erratic and violent behavior (he would attempt to bite anyone who came near him), became clear.

With the help of external accomplices who breached the security of the asylum and were able to get ropes to the windows of Jacob's cell, which were then broken, Jacob made good his escape. Who these accomplices were and the scope of their involvement is a topic of some dispute. According to Thomas, they were expressly hired by Marie and Joseph Jacob to help liberate their son. In the account provided by Sergent, the accomplices were able to pass a gun to Jacob with which he threatened the asylum director, who heard the window of his cell break. According to Delpech, however, it was actually the nurse Royères who was instrumental in ensuring that asylum staff members were in the right place at the right time. Realistically, it may well be the case that it was a combination of external entities (including, perhaps, Rose Roux and Jacob's comrades in the radical community of Marseilles), in addition to the sympathies of Royères, that led to Jacob's escape. Whoever was responsible for facilitating and ensuring his escape could not be established by the police, and Jacob found himself out of the asylum and on the run.

The day after escaping the asylum, Jacob arrived (in the guise of a joiner by the name of Jean Concorde, with the papers to match his new identity) at the house of an Anarchist contact by the name of Saurel in the coastal city of Sète. Following a burglary in Sète in which the second home of a lawyer from Montpellier by the name of Torquebiau was targeted, Jacob traveled to Paris at the start of 1901. Here he formed the idea of Les Travailleurs de la Nuit (The Night Workers), which was to be an organized and self-funding Anarchist group of robbers devoted to the expropriation of property and capital.

Between 1901 and 1905, Jacob and a small band of friends and acquaintances that included Rose's previous lover Clarenson, Rose herself (who was now the lover of Jacob), and the male nurse Royères carried out more than 150 burglaries throughout France, Belgium and Germany. As highlighted on the blog of the Libertarian Creative Workshop,[15] it is entirely possibly that Jacob and his band of Night Workers also targeted properties as far afield as Egypt and North Africa. In Paris, Jacob assumed the identity of Georges Escande, an antiquarian, and he frequently could be found at the Café Mugniez, which was then a haunt for radicals of all political types, from royalists to Anarchists. Jacob and his Night Workers predominantly targeted the homes of the wealthy, such as the Countess de Melun and the queen of Belgium, as well as religious sites such as a church in Brumetz and the cathedrals in Tours and Le Mans. Indeed, as pointed out by George Woodcock, Jacob made it a point of pride only to engage in robberies against those elements of society that were not productive; once, when he realized that his gang had chosen to attempt to burglarize the house of the noted writer Pierre Loti, they left without taking anything.[16] Typically the robberies followed a nonviolent pattern, with goods being removed by stealth, not force, and occasionally angry proclamations being left in a prominent position by "Attila" or one of the gang.

One of the criticisms leveled at Jacob is that, in essence, the burglaries that he performed with the assistance of others were bourgeois in nature. By choosing to focus on property and its corollary, money, Jacob risked falling victim to the acquisitive force that governed much of society. However, propaganda of the deed focused upon attacks against symbols. By repeatedly relieving the rich and the clerical of their material assets, Jacob was attacking not only his victims but also the concept of wealth itself. As Jacob himself would later write, "Theft is the restitution, the regaining of possession. Instead of being cloistered in a factory, like in a penal colony; instead of begging for what I had a right to, I preferred to rebel and fight my enemy face to face by making war on the rich, by attacking their goods."[17] In addition, the funds raised by Jacob and the Night Workers did not provide luxuriant lifestyles for themselves but were often distributed among the Anarchist community of the period, helping to purchase ink and paper for periodicals, as well as food and lodging for those individuals who had fallen on hard times.

Unlike many criminals of the time, all of those associated (however loosely) with Jacob held down employment in one form or another. As Delpech highlights, their ranks included "nurses, bailiffs clerk, waiter or typographer, sculptor, florist and even circus acrobat."[18] Additionally, they had at their disposal a range of outfits that included ecclesiastical and military dress, in addition to tuxedos and fashionable outfits favored by the bourgeoisie. Many of Jacob's companions were armed with Browning revolvers in the event that they had to defend themselves. Over the course of a three-year period, the gang committed multiple burglaries on an almost industrial scale using both cunning and planning. They encountered some setbacks, such as on 14 May 1902, when Roques was sentenced to ten years' hard labor, but the vast majority avoided arrest and detection, and those who did not avoided providing injurious confessions. However, on the night of 21 April 1903, the gang's luck began to run out in earnest.

The day before the night that was to be the undoing of Marius Jacob, he and a member of the extended gang, Leon Pélissard, traveled to Abbeville to meet Felix Bour. Bour was born in Paris on 13 May 1881 and raised by his grandmother. Just as with Jacob, Bour had been a religious youth and had served as an altar boy. After obtaining his certificate of study, he started work as a weaver. Following his military service, when he became disenchanted with religion and the state, Bour met Jacob at an Anarchist meeting in Paris and soon formed a connection to the adventurous and slightly older man. Due to both his age and his looks, Bour was given the nickname "little blond" or "kid" by Jacob and his confederates.[19] For a while, Jacob lived with Rose, his mother, and Bour at an apartment in Rue Leibniz.

On the day in question, Bour had been in Abbeville for a few days and had already scouted a number of locations for the gang's consideration. In keeping with their typical modus operandi, Bour had gained entry to a number of properties in the surrounding area and, rather than making off with loot, had left strips of paper situated in both doors and windows. The logic of the gang, which had thus far managed to avoid arrest, was that if such markers were left undisturbed, the occupants of the property were absent, and they would have sufficient time to secure and transport any valuables that they could find. As they had so many times before, the gang soon found a seemingly unoccupied property belonging to a widow named Tilloloy in Le Saint Pierre in Abbeville.

As revealed by both Delpech and the French National Archives,[20] Jacob and his gang couldn't have picked a worse location. Upstairs neighbors, disturbed by the noise of a broken window, were quick to rouse from their slumbers. While a man who lived upstairs made his way to the nearby police station, Jacob and his accomplices, having been warned by the lookout Bour, made their way at speed in the direction of Pont Remy. Situated in Picardy, Northern France, Pont Remy was on the Longueau–Boulogne railway line, and it allowed for moderately rapid access to Boulogne. The unlucky trio eventually reached Pont Remy at around 2:00 a.m. after trudging through the early morning fog and attempted to find a local hotel. Finding none open (or willing to open their doors in the early hours to a trio of strange men), they sought refuge at the local train station. After waiting at the station and engaging the station master in conversation, the trio were able to find a local café that opened at 5:00 a.m., where they could rest and regroup following a disappointing and aborted robbery.

The repast and relaxation were short lived, however. At 6:00 a.m. a police brigadier by the name of Auquier and a constable named Pruvost arrived at the Gare de Pont-Rémy station, where they found Jacob, Pélissard and Bour waiting to board the first morning train to Boulogne. Upon sighting the police, chaos broke out. Bour was first to flee, pursued by Pruvost, who was shot twice in the abdomen and then stabbed twice between the shoulders for good measure. Meanwhile, Auquier attempted, with the assistance of a station official (perhaps the same station master with whom the trio had spent a few hours), to wrestle with both Jacob and Pélissard; for his efforts, the brigadier was shot in the stomach and stabbed twice. The shooting of Pruvost was to prove fatal; however, Auquier did not suffer mortal wounds. With both members of the police pursuit bleeding, the trio split up and went their separate ways, with Jacob heading to Airaisne, making his way down the railways tracks and cutting across fields.

The shooting of two police officers marked a descent into violence from which Jacob and his accomplices never recovered. Up until this point, all their robberies had been exceedingly well planned and executed, with the theft of property being an act of symbolic rather than physical violence. Although Jacob and his compatriots routinely went about their business armed, it had not been necessary up until the events in Abbeville to utilize their weapons. The police were quick to respond to this outrage, and they soon picked up Jacob's trail owing to the heavy rainfall that did little to obscure the tracks of his escape. On the morning of 23 April 1903, the mastermind behind more than 150 expropriations found himself in police custody.

Between his arrest in 1903 and his eventual trial in Orléans on 24 July 1905, the police made numerous arrests of those associated with Jacob, including both his mother Maria and his lover Rose (his mother was acquitted of all charges at trial; Rose, however, fared much worse and was sentenced to five years in prison, where she later died in 1907). In total, twenty-three supposed members of Jacob's Night Workers faced prosecution. Jacob and Bour were sentenced to hard labor for life in the Salvation Islands penal colonies. Another fourteen members of the extended gang were found guilty and sentenced to more than one hundred years of cumulative imprisonment. In December 1904, several months prior to the trial, a twice-monthly Anarchist journal began publication in Amiens. Titled *Germinal*, it sought to build support for Jacob and the rest of his gang. The sentences ultimately handed down demonstrate that it did not prove entirely successful.

Following public pressure, most of which came from his mother, Jacob was eventually released from prison on 30 December 1927. Although he had been transferred to French soil in 1925, Jacob had spent the previous twenty years in the penal colonies, seeking to escape repeatedly, although these attempts were not nearly as numerous as those of Clément Duval (as shall be discussed later in this chapter). Following his release, Jacob married Pauline Charron and published his memoirs, never once disavowing his earlier actions. Unrepentant and largely unbowed to the end, Jacob committed suicide by morphine overdose on 28 August 1954, not wishing to experience the indignities and infirmities of a protracted old age.

A figure of inspiration for Marius Jacob and later illegalists can be found in the life and actions of fellow Frenchman Clément Duval. Surprisingly, for a figure who played such a seminal role in the development of illegalism as a politically inspired movement, and an outgrowth of Anarchist propaganda of the deed, historians know very little about Duval. Those details that are known are contested, disputed, and (at the time of this writing) muddied. Duval was born in 1850 in France. The exact location and date of his birth are, however, contested. L'Éphéméride Anarchiste puts his date of birth at 11 March 1850 in Paris[21]; however, this information is disputed by Marianne Enckell, historian, archivist, and one of the few authorities on Duval, who, although she places the birth of Duval in March 1850, shifts the location to the Cérans Foulletourte district of Sarthe.

Clément Duval

Little is known of Duval's life until his next appearance in the pages of history in 1870. As documented elsewhere in this book, the Franco-Prussian War commenced in earnest in July 1870 following the political posturing that had resulted from the Austro-Prussian War of 1866. It was a conflict that was to prove bloody and acrimonious and have a lasting impact on revolutionaries throughout Europe, including the young Duval. In 1870, aged twenty, he joined the 5e Corps d'Armée under the leadership of General Pierre Louis Charles de Failly. Life in the French army for an ordinary infantryman such as Duval during the Franco-Prussian War was particularly harsh. Disease was rife, and food supplies were scarce, French troops being fueled by jingoism more than bread. General de Failly also had a miserable war. On 6 August 1870 the French army was crushed at Bitche and Beaumont before being encircled near the Belgian frontier at Sedan. Popular opinion held General de Failly responsible for this failure, although he likely bore no more blame than any other French commander. Regardless, de Failly was captured by the Prussians at Sedan on 2 September 1870. It is not clear if Duval was also captured, but at some point during the war he contracted smallpox. His health was further affected when he was severely wounded by a mortar bomb, forcing him to spend several months in the miserable conditions of a French military hospital. According to his own recollections as presented in court, Duval during his time in the military obtained the rank of colonel; however, he was soon demoted owing to insubordination.[22]

According to Paul Albert[23] (many of whose claims are disputed by Marianne Enckell[24]), Duval returned to Paris in 1873 a man broken in body by the war. According to Paul Simons, however, Duval spent the following ten years attempting to recover from his physical wounds, with four of those being spent in hospitals.[25] Before leaving for the front, Duval had married in Paris, although no records of this marriage can be found. Albert claims that in his absence Duval's father had died and his young wife had engaged in an affair. Duval was thus forced into the position of being the sole breadwinner for a family that was falling apart. These circumstances, coupled with arthritis, rheumatism, and possibly other health conditions that would not typically have affected a twenty-three-year-old, left him in a precarious situation. Unfortunately, it is impossible to determine the scope and impact of these conditions owing to the confusion that lies at the heart of any discussion concerning Duval. It is unknown what Duval's family background was or whether he had siblings or children to support (some accounts have stated that he did indeed have a son). There is even a pronounced confusion as to what his primary occupation was before he subsequently turned to the activities that were to make him infamous. Alexandre Skirda describes him as a "mechanic and thief"[26]; elsewhere he is described as a "locksmith,"[27] an "iron worker,"[28] and even somewhat unbelievably as a "jewel thief."[29] In nineteenth-century France, Duval could easily have been all three at one time or another. Owing to the injuries sustained during the Franco-Prussian War, Duval essentially became unemployable. As a result, the broken man rapidly became a desperate one. Then as now, desperation proved to be the mother of invention.

In 1878 Duval was jobless and doubtless hungry; driven by the same desperation and poverty that were so familiar to many of his peers, he turned to crime. According to his own account, he had at this point a wife and two children to support, and "no money and no bread in the house."[30] Although only an Anarchist in spirit at this juncture, Duval decided that he had a right to exist, job or no job. On a visit to the Bois de Boulogne, Duval passed a station (possibly Porte Dauphine), and when the station master was distracted, he reached into the cash box and retrieved eighty francs. This was far from a windfall, and Duval soon found that the money he had acquired was quickly spent on medical costs and providing for his family. Having found his first foray into criminality both successful and trivial to achieve, if not profitable, Duval decided to repeat it. He made the classic neophyte criminal mistake of returning to the scene of his earlier crime and attempting to repeat it. Unfortunately, this time around the station master on duty was sharper eyed than on the previous occasion, and Duval soon found himself detained in police custody.

At the time of Duval's arrest the French legal system was particularly severe in nature. Although he had not been in trouble with the law previously, the attempted crime was one that did not involve violence, and its inception had arisen from penury, the law courts dealt with him harshly. Still suffering from the medical issues that were to plague him for the rest of his life, Duval was confined to the Mazas prison for a year. Prison de Mazas was the main prison for Paris and, ironically, had been opened in the year of Duval's birth in 1850, when it was inaugurated on 19 May. When it first opened, Mazas was considered a model prison; however, for the inmates life within its walls was bleak. In keeping with concepts of prison at the time, inmates were held in single cells (6.5 feet by 6.5 feet) and kept in complete isolation day and night. With furnishings that consisted of a hammock, a stool, a table, and a small water can, it was a watchful place devoid of any industry other than silent brooding.[31] It was possibly in this French version of the panopticon that Duval not only further developed his political ideas but also nurtured his sense of injustice at the circumstances that had led him here.

Although he had been drawn into crime by poverty caused by ill health and lack of regular employment to support his family, on his release from Mazas in 1879 Duval discovered that his family had abandoned him. Now practically destitute and bereft of his family connections, Duval may well have faced an unfortunate and probably short future had he not been able to secure employment at the Choubersky workshops,[32] which manufactured and sold portable heating systems and stoves. Sadly, this bout of employment did not last, and Duval found himself crippled by the rheumatism that had first affected him when serving in the Franco-Prussian War. Unemployed for thirteen months, Duval drifted desperately from hospital to hospital, reduced to penury.

Paris in the 1880s was awash with progressive and revolutionary groups. Though badly documented now and largely forgotten, they undoubtedly helped inspire Marius

Jacob and his Night Workers and, indeed, later generations of illegalists. Some of these groups were overt in their criminality; others were nothing more than discussion and social groups where like-minded individuals could share their troubles. However, they were all perceived as belligerent threats to the French state. As Alvan Sanborn details,[33] these groups often had inflammatory names: for example, Les Enfants de la Nature, La Panthere de Batignolles, Les Gonzes Pailus du Point-du-Jour, La Jeunesse Anti-Patriotique de Belleville, Le Drapeau Noir, Les Quand Meme, La Revolte des Travailleurs, Le Cercle Internationale, La Torpille, Le Groupe Libertaire, Les Formats, Le Reveil, Les Resolus, L'Emancipation, Les Anti-Travailleurs, Les Indomptables, Les Sans-Patrie, Les Amis de Ravachol, Les Occurs de Chene, La Dynamite, Terre et Independence, Les Indignes, La Vipere, Le Glaive, and Les Parias de Charonne. To pick just a few from this selection, polite French society would certainly have been appalled by groups with such names as the Black Flag, the Revolt of the Workers, the Friends of Ravachol, the Dynamite, and Earth and Independence.

At some point in 1880, Duval made contact with La Panthere de Batignolles (the Panther of Batignolles). In *A Proust Dictionary*,[34] Maxine Vogely describes La Panthere de Batignolles as "a Parisian club active during the 1880s. It was an anarchist group which sometimes met on the rue de Levis in the quarter of Paris called 'les Batignolles.'" According to Victor Serge,[35] Duval was the leader of La Panthere de Batignolles; however, while he may indeed have served in a leadership role for a brief period, this was not the case in 1880. Membership of such groups and associations was nebulous at best; however, in addition to Duval, the Anarchist writer Georges Darien (pseudonym for Georges Hippolyte Adrien) and Joseph Tortelier[36] were known members. Owing to the clandestine nature of such groups, their full membership and range of activities will probably never be known. On 23 November 1884, members of La Panthere organized a meeting at the Salle de la Réunion in Paris that occasioned violent clashes with the police.[37] Perhaps owing to the involvement of Duval, their actions went further than occasional brawls with gendarmes.

In March 1883, La Panthere de Batignolles and other groups from the northern suburbs of Paris gathered at a demonstration of the unemployed led by the famed Communard Louise Michel and the rabble-rousing Anarcho-Syndicalist Emile Pouget. As part of the protest organization, arson attacks against the property interests of the bourgeoisie were threatened in posters that adorned the gates of factories. The French state did not respond well to such threats from the urban poor and dispossessed, and following altercations with the police, the then fifty-four-year-old Michel was detained forcibly by the gendarmes and subsequently sentenced to six years' imprisonment (this sentence was commuted the following year to allow her to attend to her dying mother). Pouget attempted to free Michel from the less than gentle clutches of the police and was in turn arrested and sentenced to eight years. Pouget, however, was not eligible for an early release and served the entirety of his sentence. According to Duval's later memoirs, he was arrested and imprisoned for forty-eight hours in 1883, for the crime of "rebellion against police officers,"[38] an incident that may have occurred during the March protest. Arrests and violence aside, on the day of the demonstration several bakeries were ransacked so that, at least for a while, the mass unemployed of late nineteenth-century Paris could eat. The violence of the day and the threats that had played a part in the heavy-handed response by the forces of law and order were not to be forgotten by either La Panthere de Batignolles or Duval.

Following the protest, a series of arson attacks ravaged the suburbs of Paris. As discussed by Albert,[39] these targets included many places in which the workers were routinely expected to be employed for fourteen hours a day for little more than starvation wages. Although the nineteenth century had seen an explosion in the number of employment opportunities, for many these jobs included long hours, grueling conditions, and enforced penury. The working conditions for many of the urban poor, and the disparity between the often indolent bourgeoisie and those employed to make their necessities and trinkets, were a driving force in radicalization, which ultimately led to an improvement in working conditions that some today in the developed world are fortunate enough to benefit from. Between 1883 and 1886, fires raged at, respectively, a piano factory, the Omnibus Bastille-St. Ouen, the firm of Belvalette de Passy, a furniture workshop owned by a Rothschild, and (perhaps most suspiciously of all) the Choubersky workshops where Duval had found brief employment. Duval and La Panthere de Batignolles did not take credit for these incidents, but as many of these establishments had some connection to the group's members, it does not take a substantive leap to assume that the group may have had some involvement in some or all of the arson attacks.

During the period that arson attacks were inflicted on a variety of factories, workshops, and establishments that routinely abused their workers, it is highly likely that Duval resorted to crime. As stated previously, the range of illnesses that had resulted from his brief military career made sustained bouts of employment problematic. It was not just for reasons of disability, however, that Duval turned to crime, as would later be revealed during his somewhat sensational trial, the results of which would reverberate through the Anarchist movement and are still hotly contested today. It seems likely that by the time of his trial Duval was an experienced and proficient housebreaker who utilized the profits of his endeavors to survive. Unfortunately for Duval, his criminal career, however influential it was to become, was brief.

On the night of 4 October 1886,[40] Duval and an accomplice named Turquais used what skills he had acquired following his release from prison to break into a mansion situated on Rue Montceau in Paris. The property was ordinarily occupied by a Madame Herbelin and her niece, Madeleine Lemaire, in addition to their staff. As Duval made his way into the house, he found it empty, as all the inhabitants were on vacation. What Duval may or may not have known at the time was that Madeleine Lemaire was then one of the most renowned female painters in France. Famed for her paintings of flowers, she was a close friend of Marcel Proust and had been given the sobriquet "Empress of the Roses" by French dandy, art collector, and aesthete Robert de Montesquiou. Lemaire was very much of the establishment and a darling of the leisured bourgeoisie; indeed, this may have been why Duval chose to target her property. Upon gaining entry to the house, Duval wasted no time in stripping it of jewels and silverware to the value of 15,000 francs. According to testimony that he was later to give at trial, Duval was more than satisfied to disappear back into the night with his haul; however, Turquais had other ideas. Little is known of Turquais, and he was never arrested; however, as Duval stated at his trial, it was that individual who decided that their exit from the property needed a more fiery conclusion. Ignoring Duval's objection that the house would make suitable and luxurious accommodations for numerous families following the inevitable revolution, Turquais lit two fires and left the property with Duval in tow.

Stealing 15,000 francs worth of property and burning down the mansion of a famous painter naturally attracted the attention of the gendarmerie, and they were keen to focus their inquiries on the Anarchists and radicals who made up much of Paris. Like London, Paris was a nexus for revolutionary movements at the time, with immigrants from around Europe and beyond living in the city. Unlike London, which allowed for the mostly free assembly of radicals from across the globe (for purposes of international monitoring rather than the vaunted British sense of fair play) with the implicit understanding that attacks were not to be committed on British soil, the Parisian police were typically far more active and repressive in their measures. As part of their inquiries, the gendarmerie rapidly recovered jewelry belonging to Lemaire from a fence favored by Anarchists. The fence was quick to point the finger of blame at an individual by the name of Houchard. As with the mysterious Turquais, little is known to history of Houchard, save for Duval's testimony Houchard sold a brooch that was subsequently identified as belonging to Lemaire to the voluble fence. What the police knew, however, was that Houchard was acquainted with a fellow Anarchist by the name of Didier and an older ex-convict by the name of Duval.

Sometime in October, the police trailed Houchard and Duval to the home of Didier. Among their number were a Sergeant Rossignol and a constable by the name of Pelletier. Seeing the suspects enter the premises, the police followed suit. Upon gaining entry, Didier's wife identified Duval to Rossignol and Pelletier, who attempted to remove him from the property so he could be questioned by their nearby captain (some accounts put the number of police in the area as high as twenty[41]). As the gendarmes made their way into the street with Duval, the prisoner resisted. In the tussle that followed, Sergeant Rossignol yelled out, "I arrest you in the name of the law!" Not to be outdone, Duval responded with a line that was later to make him infamous—"I kill you in the name of freedom!"—and produced a long-bladed knife. Duval was able to stab the unfortunate police sergeant a number of times (some accounts say eight times; however, according to the later memoir composed by Duval, it was only twice) before falling on him in the scuffle. According to Duval, "Officer Pelletier right away took advantage of my fall by grabbing me by my throat and private parts; and Rossignol was able to get hold of my right thumb and bite it."[42] Following this rather inglorious end to the brawl, Duval, Didier, and Houchard were all arrested and charged with arson, robbery, and the attempted murder of Rossignol.

Just as with so much of Duval's life, there is confusion as to when his trial began. According to Albert,[43] the trial commenced on 11 February 1887 and concluded the following day. This timing is disputed by Robert Hunter,[44] who places the trial date one month earlier, between 11 January and 12 January 1887. What is known of the trial is that it was short (as was to be expected of French jurisprudence at the time) and controversial, and it would have far-reaching consequences. Duval was defended by Fernand Labori, who would go on to have a storied career. In this, one of his first cases, Labori attempted to provide a rationalization for his client's activities, which unfortunately met with little success. Labori would later defend Auguste Vaillant (who would toss a largely ineffectual bomb in the French Chamber of Deputies on 9 December 1893) and also the ill-fated Captain Alfred Dreyfus, who would find himself a victim of French antisemitism.

Duval used his trial to defend his right to steal to in order to survive, an argument that was vociferously disputed by the presiding judge, Bérard Des Glajeux. As part of his defense strategy, in addition to allowing his client to discuss expropriation with an increasingly irate judge, Labori called two character witnesses who knew Duval closely, Ricois and Bronsin (presumably part of the La Panthere de Batignolles), but they failed to provide meaningful assistance. Both witnesses refused to take the oath, not even after a recess was granted to discuss their refusals. Both men (including the partially deaf sixty-nine-year-old gunsmith, Bronsin) were charged the exorbitant sum of one hundred francs for their refusal to declare the oath and loyalty to the court and the French state. Worse was yet to come for Duval, however: on the day after his trial had started, the fractious judge declared that Duval had been sentenced to death without the necessity of the plaintiff in the case (Madeleine Lemaire) presenting any testimony. Duval's co-defendants, Didier and Houchard, fared better and were both released. As Duval was led from the court to be transferred to La Roquette Prison, he shouted, "Long Live Anarchy!" to the public gallery that was filled with not only idle spectators but also members of the French Anarchist community.

Duval's trial followed a familiar pattern with regard to those accused of politically inspired crimes (particularly those associated with propaganda of the deed). Justice was not only swift but also, in many cases, largely absent. Many working-class defendants knew that the odds of success in the legal system were not in their favor and that their only hope for avoiding harsh sentencing lay in contrition and appeals to the mercy of the court system. Even in such scenarios, depending largely upon the mood of the courts (and, more specifically, the presiding judge), they were unlikely to receive clemency. The legal system was largely utilized as a cudgel, and personal bravery was required to stand against it. Duval displayed such courage, and this was not overlooked; as Hunter reveals, "eight days afterward, on January 23, an indignation meeting against the condemnation of Duval was organized by the anarchists, at which nearly 1,000 were present."[45] In addition to mass protest against Duval's conviction, Labori appealed the case, but his appeal was nullified. It was probably only because of the growing protests and involvement of public figures such as Louise Michel that Duval had his death sentence commuted on 29 February 1887 by Jules Grévy, then president of the French Republic (Grévy himself would be forced to resign in December 1887, following the involvement of his son-in-law, Daniel Wilson, in the selling of Legion of Honor awards), to deportation and hard labor for life in the prison camps of French Guiana.

After spending miserable months in La Roquette Prison, Duval was transported on 25 March 1887 from Toulon to begin his sentence in the penal colony of Cayenne in French Guiana. This archipelago of attrition stretched over several islands of the Îles du Salut group and consisted of Île Royale, Île Saint-Joseph, and the infamous Île du Diable (Devil's Island). Royale was mostly utilized as a reception area for all prisoners, Saint-Joseph for the purposes of solitary confinement and punishment, and Diable for political prisoners. During his time in the French penal colonies, Duval was to spend time in all of these locations. Life in the penal colonies was, for many, worse than death, as the Dry Guillotine was a notoriously harsh and punitive environment. As detailed by René Belbenoît,[46] and largely fictionalized by Henri Charrière in the seminal *Papillon*, the penal colony was an environment built upon retribution rather than rehabilitation. This was no different for Duval, who documented his experiences in *Outrage: An Anarchist Memoir of the Penal Colony*.

During his time in the penal colonies, Duval never maintained the political beliefs that had led to his internment, and he formed a number of relationships with his fellow political prisoners. He also made a number of abortive escape attempts (by most accounts twenty) and endured the worst conditions that French Guiana could throw at him. On the night of 21 October 1895, the revolt known as the St. Joseph Massacre began, which involved both Duval and his fellow illegalist, Vittorio Pini. During this incident, guards got drunk and fired on the prisoners, who included many Anarchists. By the end of their extralegal rampage, eleven prisoners (including the young accomplice of Francois Ravachol, Simon) had been shot and their bodies dumped into the shark-infested seas. For Duval, it was just one more indignity among many.

As documented by Paul Simpson,[47] Duval finally gained his freedom on the night of 14 April 1901 (after spending fourteen years in the penal colonies). Along with eight other prisoners, Duval was able to make his escape in a flimsy canoe. After encountering storms and successfully evading the authorities, Duval and his compatriots washed up on the shores of Dutch Guyana, from which Duval somehow made his way successfully to New York (probably overland via Puerto Rico). At the time of this publication, details of this daring escape have yet to be translated into English, as they appear to have been lost from the original manuscript (according to the account provided by Marianne Enckell). Upon arriving in New York in 1903, Duval composed his memoirs with the assistance of Luigi Galleani, one of the leading figures of propaganda of the deed in the United States, and these were published in the Italian Anarchist weekly *Cronaca Sovversiva* (Subversive Chronicle) starting in 1907. Following the publication of his memoirs and his support from the Italian Anarchist community, Duval lived peacefully for the most part in Brooklyn, New York, until his death at the age of 85 on 29 March 1935.

Clément Duval is often cited as being one of the inspirational figures behind *Papillon*, and although his stubborn defiance in the penal colonies was doubtless inspiring (if far more politically overt than those of Charrière), it left him in part a broken man. Before his imprisonment, Duval had been badly affected by injuries sustained on behalf of the French state, and these conditions were further compounded by his tenure in the harsh conditions of the Dry Guillotine. His criminality was initially spurred by poverty; it was only following his initial imprisonment that he began to develop a political explanation for his illegal activities. In this sense he was similar to Marius Jacob but stood apart from the likes of Vittorio Pini and later Jules Bonnot, who were also highly influential with regard to not only illegalism but also the later wave of expropriation activities that were to surge across Latin America and be resumed by diverse radical political groups from the 1960s onward.

In most histories of illegalism, Vittorio Pini becomes little more than a footnote; however, his actions were just as significant as those of his French peers. Pini became so infamous that he served as the model for the born criminal to illustrate the theory of "criminality arising from anarchy,"[48] as detailed by the father of modern criminology, Cesare Lombroso. Pini was born on 12 December 1859 in the town of Reggio nell'Emilia (also known as Reggio Emilia) to Anna Mazzucchi and Mario Vittorio. According the Franco Serantini Library,[49] Pini had an inauspicious start in life. His father, Mario, was a partisan who had fought alongside Giuseppe Garibaldi, but, like many Italians of the period, the family lived in extreme levels of poverty. Although part of a large family, Pini witnessed the deaths of six of his brothers and also of his father, who died in a hospice charity (the causes of these deaths are lost to history but were probably the result of poverty, hunger, and disease). By the age of twelve, Pini had left full-time schooling and began work as a printer's apprentice. Following a brief apprenticeship, Pini was soon engaged in the printing of a newspaper with strong Republican tendencies (of which his father would doubtless approved), and it was here that he reportedly became interested in the politics that were to shape much of his later activities. In 1876, aged seventeen,

Pini moved to Milan and took part in the six-month print workers' strike. To support himself during this period, Pini briefly became a clerk for the district court of Milan and was also a fireman. In the latter role he acquitted himself well, saving a family from a burning house. In 1886, Pini, like many of his peers, immigrated to Paris in an attempt to improve his precarious economic circumstances.

It was in Paris that Pini's nascent political leanings began to crystallise. Although he had been exposed to penury and the economic injustices of Italian life of the period, it was in Paris, while working as a shoemaker, that Pini first encountered the privations of the urban Parisian poor (which were especially pronounced in the expatriate communities) and read the works of Peter Kropotkin. Within a matter of months, Pini had evolved into an Individualist Anarchist (like many of his peers in exile) and had established (along with fellow emigres Luigi Parmeggiani, Alessandro Marocco, Giacomo Merlino, and Caio Zavoli) the "Gruppo Intransigente." This group was dedicated to expropriation and committing robberies to further its revolutionary aims, and Pini was undoubtedly "the wild man of the group."[50] By 1887, the group had committed enough robberies to finance the publication of a few issues of radical newspapers—namely, *Il Ciclone* (*The Cyclone*, Paris, one issue, September 1887) and *Il Pugnale* (*The Dagger*, Paris, 2 issues, April and August 1889). The group was far from reserved when it came to publicly declaring its ideology; indeed, the masthead of *Il Ciclone* was "Expropriation, Dagger, Dynamite." As Nunzio Pernicone reveals,[51] the contents of the publications were no less inflammatory; as stated in the pages of *Il Ciclone*, "enough with organization and dictators, and instead of wasting our time serving as foot-stools for these scoundrel mystifiers, let us occupy ourselves with chemistry, making bombs, dynamite, and other explosive materials that must be used for the destruction of the stinking and ruling bourgeoisie."[52] The Gruppo Intransigente did not just reserve its actions for the French capital, however. As discussed elsewhere in this book, nineteenth-century London was a hothouse for political radicals from throughout Europe. In 1888 authorities in London were told that Pini and his peers were "more dangerous as a group of thieves than as a political group."[53] Unfortunately, this assessment was to prove a flawed one.

In October 1888, Pini published a manifesto titled "Manifesto degli anarchici in lingua italiana al popolo d'Italia" (Manifesto of the Anarchists in the Italian Language to the People of Italy) in response to the calls of Celso Ceretti, an ex-Garibaldino and former internationalist who rejected the actions of Pini and his peers and called for a union of the Latin races to avert potential armed conflict between Italy and France. Along with Camillo Prampolino, Ceretti was viewed by Pini and the members of Gruppo Intransigente as a politically divisive figure whose activities only helped to support the bourgeoisie and distract from social revolution. By February 1889, their ire had turned to action, and Pini and Parmeggiani returned to Italy to deal with this supposed threat. On 13 February 1889, Ceretti was violently attacked and stabbed several times by Pini and Parmeggiani in Mirandola, resulting in his death. Several days later, on 16 February, Pini and Parmeggiani were intercepted by the police as they traveled to Reggio Emilia to assassinate Prampolino. Following a shootout with the carabinieri, Parmeggiani fled to London, while Pini made good his escape to Paris.

The liberty of the latter was not to last long, however, and on 19 June 1889 Pini was arrested by the French police in no small part thanks to the testimony of Carlo Terghazi, who, in addition to being a recent convert to the group, was a police agent. During his trial, which took place between 4 November and 5 November, Pini was keen to assume sole responsibility for the death of a political rival in addition to providing justifications for theft and robbery that were in keeping with those of other illegalists of the period. His defense, however, fell on deaf ears, and Pini was sentenced to twenty years' hard labor in the French penal colonies that were also home to Duval. Like Duval, Pini made repeated escape attempts, and on one occasion he got as far as neighboring Suriname. Here, however, he was wounded by a gunshot in his leg and soon returned to the penal colonies. Subsequent escape attempts also met with failure, and Pini died of sickness in Cayenne on 8 June 1903.

The history of illegalism and Individualist Anarchism is marked by the three figures detailed in this chapter, but what started as a nineteenth-century phenomenon continued well into the twentieth century. The later actions of La Bande à Bonnot, Peter the Painter, Octave Garnier, and even the Guillotine Society in Japan illustrate that what began as a localized and largely French idea spread quickly and globally. Indeed, the idea of rationalized expropriation in support of political aims and agendas is arguably still prevalent in all axes of the political spectrum. However, for many associated with nineteenth-century Anarchism, illegalism was ultimately a flawed idea. In addition to fostering individualist rather than collectivist actions in response to capitalism, by engaging in acts of criminality (as determined by the state) those who engaged in such actions were actually fully embracing capital in pursuit of their goals. Through engaging in actions that could ultimately result in death, one of the major critiques of illegalist activities is that, in essence, they were little more than nihilistic exhibitions of ego. Indeed, some of those who had once engaged in such actions would later repudiate them, as Marius Jacob himself did when, in 1948, he stated, "I don't think that illegalism can free the individual in present-day society.... Basically, illegalism, considered as an act of revolt, is more a matter of temperament than of doctrine."[54] Illegalism was arguably a central component of propaganda of the deed, providing as it did an alternative for those seeking to move beyond the constraints and demands of capitalism. It continues to provide a heady cocktail for those impacted by unjust economic systems (as shown by the recent Yomango movement in Spain). The tactics of direct reappropriation of wealth, however, do little to address the fundamental disparity that wealth creates, and this failure arguably is the fatal weakness that has always resided at the core of illegalism and its actors.

Why I Was a Burglar (Marius Jacob)

Source: Jean Maitron, *Histoire du mouvement anarchiste en France* (Paris: Societé universitaire d'editions et de librairie, 1951), as referenced by the Anarchist Library, https://theanarchistlibrary.org/library/marius-jacob-why-i-was-a-burglar; translated by Mitch Abidor (2005)

Messieurs:
You now know who I am: a rebel living off the products of his burglaries. In addition I burned down several hotels and defended my freedom against the aggressions of the agents of power.

I laid bare to you my entire existence of combat: I submit it as a problem for your intelligence.

Not recognizing anyone's right to judge me, I don't ask for either pardon or indulgence. I don't go begging to those I hate and hold in contempt. You are the stronger. Dispose of me as you wish; send me to a penal colony or the scaffold. I don't care! But before going our separate ways let me tell you one last thing.

Since you primarily condemn me for being a thief it's useful to define what theft is.

In my opinion theft is a need that is felt by all men to take in order to satisfy their appetites. This need manifests itself in everything: from the stars that are born and die like beings, to the insect in space, so small, so infinite that our eyes can barely distinguish it. Life is nothing but theft and massacre. Plants and beasts devour each other in order to survive.

One is born only to serve as feed for the other. Despite the degree of civilization or, to phrase it better, perfectibility to which he has arrived, man is also subject to this law, and can only escape it under pain of death. He kills both plants and beasts to feed himself: he is insatiable.

Aside from objects of alimentation that assure him life, man also nourishes himself on air, water, and light. But have we ever seen two men kill each other for the sharing of these aliments? Not that I know of. Nevertheless these are the most precious of items, without which a man cannot live.

We can remain several days without absorbing the substances for which we make ourselves slaves. Can we do the same when it comes to air? Not even for a quarter of an hour. Water accounts for three quarters of our organism and is indispensable in maintaining the elasticity of our tissues. Without heat, without the sun, life would be completely impossible.

And so every man takes, steals his aliments. Do we accuse him of committing a crime? Of course not! Why then de we differentiate these from the rest? Because the rest demand the expending of effort, a certain amount of labor. But labor is the very essence of society; that is, the association of all individuals to conquer with little effort much well-being. Is this truly the image of what exists? Are your institutions based on such a mode of organization? The truth demonstrates the contrary.

The more a man works the less he earns. The less he produces the more he benefits. Merit is not taken into consideration. Only the bold take hold of power and hasten to legalize their rapine.

From top to bottom of the social scale everything is but dastardy on one side and idiocy on the other. How can you expect that penetrated with these truths I could have respected such a state of things?

A liquor seller and the boss of a brothel enrich themselves, while a man of genius dies of poverty in a hospital bed. The baker who bakes bread doesn't get any; the shoemaker who makes thousands of shoes shows his toes; the weaver who makes stocks of clothing doesn't have any to cover himself with; the bricklayer who builds castles and palaces wants for air in a filthy hovel. Those who produce everything have nothing, and those who produce nothing have everything.

Such a state of affairs can only produce antagonism between the laboring class and the owning, i.e., do-nothing, class. The fight breaks out and hatred delivers its blows.

You call a man a thief and bandit; you apply the rigor of the law against him without asking yourself if he could be something else. Have we ever seen a *rentier* become a burglar? I admit that I've never known of this. But I, who am neither *rentier* nor landlord, I who am only man who owns just his arms and his brains to ensure his preservation, had to conduct myself differently. Society only granted me three means of existence:

work, begging, or theft. Work, far from being hateful, pleases me: man cannot do without working. His muscles and brain possess a sum of energy that must be spent. What I hated was sweating blood and tears for a pittance of a salary; it was creating wealth that wouldn't be allowed me.

In a word, I found it hateful to surrender to the prostitution of work. Begging is degradation, the negation of all dignity. Every man has a right to life's banquet.

The right to live isn't begged for, it's taken.

Theft is the restitution, the regaining of possession. Instead of being cloistered in a factory, like in a penal colony; instead of begging for what I had a right to, I preferred to rebel and fight my enemy face to face by making war on the rich, by attacking their goods.

Of course I understand that you would have preferred that I submit to your laws; that as a docile and worn out worker I would have created wealth in exchange for a miserable salary, and when my body would have been worn out and my brain softened I would have died on a street corner. Then you wouldn't have called me a "cynical bandit," but an "honest worker." Using flattery, you would even have given me the medal of labor. Priests promise paradise to their dupes. You are less abstract: you offer them a piece of paper.

I thank you for so much goodness, so much gratitude, messieurs. I'd prefer to be a cynic conscious of my rights instead of an automaton, a caryatid.

As soon as I took possession of my consciousness I gave myself over to theft without any scruples. I have no part in your so-called morality that advocates the respect of property as a virtue when in reality there are no worse thieves than landlords.

Consider yourselves lucky, messieurs, that this prejudice has taken root in the people, for this serves as your best gendarme. Knowing the powerlessness of the law, of force, to phrase it better, you have made them the most solid of your protectors. But beware: everything only lasts a certain time. Everything that is constructed, built by ruse and force, can be demolished by ruse and force.

The people are evolving every day. Can't you see that having learned these truths, conscious of their rights, that all the starving, all the wretched, in a word: all your victims, are arming themselves with jimmies and assaulting your homes to take back the wealth they created and that you stole from them?

Do you think they'll be any more unhappy? I think the contrary. If they were to think carefully about this they would prefer to run all possible risks rather than fatten you while groaning in misery.

"Prison … penal colonies … the scaffold," it will be said. But what are these prospects in comparison with the life of a beast made up of all possible sufferings.

The miner who fights for his bread in the earth's entrails, never seeing the sun shine, can perish from one minute to the next, victim of an explosion; the roofer who wanders across the roofs can fall and be smashed to pieces; the sailor knows the day of his departure but doesn't know if he'll return to port. A good number of other workers contract fatal maladies in the exercise of their métier, wear themselves out, poison themselves, kill themselves to create for you. Even gendarmes and policemen—your valets—who, for the bone you give them to nibble on, sometimes meet death in the fight they undertake against your enemies.

Obstinate in your narrow egoism, do you not remain skeptical in regard to this vision? The people are frightened, you seem to be saying. We govern them through fear and repression. If he cries out we'll throw him in prison; if he stumbles we'll deport him to the penal colony; if he acts we'll guillotine him! All of this is poorly calculated, messieurs, believe you me. The sentences you inflict are not a remedy against acts of revolt. Repression, far from being a remedy, or even a palliative, is only an aggravation of the evil.

Collective measures only plant hatred and vengeance. It's a fatal cycle. In any case, since you have been cutting off heads, since you have been populating the prisons and the penal colonies, have you prevented hatred from manifesting itself? Say something! Answer! The facts demonstrate your impotence.

For my part I knew full well that my conduct could have no other issue than the penal colony or the scaffold. You must see that this did not prevent me from acting. If I gave myself over to theft it was not a question of gain, of lucre, but a question of principle, of right. I preferred to preserve my liberty, my independence, my dignity as a man rather than to make myself the artisan of someone else's fortune. To put it crudely, with no euphemisms: I preferred to rob rather than be robbed!

Of course I, too, condemn the act through which a man violently and through ruse takes possession of the fruits of someone else's labor. But it's precisely because of this that I made war on the rich, thieves of the goods of the poor. I too want to live in a society from which theft is banished. I only approved of and used theft as the means of revolt most appropriate for combating the most unjust of all thefts: individual property.

In order to destroy an effect you must first destroy the cause. If there is theft it is only because there is abundance on one hand and famine on the other; because *everything* only belongs to *some*. *The struggle will only disappear when men will put their joys and suffering in common, their labors and their riches, when all will belong to everyone.*

Revolutionary anarchist, I made my revolution. Vive l'anarchie!

For Germinal, to you, to the cause.

A Letter from Mazas Prison (Clément Duval, Mazas Prison, 24 October 1886)

Source: https://michaelshreve.wordpress.com/duval-clement/ (accessed: February 2017)

Companions,

Although I am not well known to you, you know that I am an anarchist. I am writing this letter to you to protest against the insanities that must have leaked out about me in particular and about the anarchists in general in all different kinds of newspapers which joined together to say, when I was arrested, that I was an ex-convict and had already been convicted of theft. As if you could call someone a thief who was a worker who had nothing but misery whereas for me theft does not exist except in the exploitation of man by man, in short, in the existence of everyone who lives at the expense of the producing class.

Here is why and how I committed the offense that they call theft. In 1870 I was, like so many others, stupid enough to go and defend the property and privileges of others; but I was 20 years old. From the war I brought back two wounds and rheumatism— a terrible sickness that has already cost me four years in the hospital. After serving as cannon fodder, I served as a guinea pig for the gentlemen of science. They made me take more than a kilo of sodium salicylate, which drastically weakened my eyesight. Proof is that at 36 years old I am wearing glasses and the bosses do not like that.

So, in 1878 I got out after three months in the hospital. I started working again for eight days; I got sick again; I stayed home for a month. I had two children and my companion got sick as well. No money and no bread in the house. Even though I was not part of the anarchist movement, which did not exist or was very small at the time (the study of sociology had not ended and it was still only in an embryonic state, plus they had not yet cut off the heads of anarchists to spread it), I had already, long before, freed myself of the prejudices that block the minds of the masses, an enemy of all authority.

I was an anarchist in heart, in love with what was beautiful, grand, generous, revolting against all abuses and injustices. From this fact I recognized the undeniable right that nature gave to every human being: the right to exist. An opportunity presented itself. With no qualms I put my hand in a stationmaster's cash box. I took my hand out with 80 francs. 80 francs does not go far when you have nothing—medicine is expensive.

Therefore, I decided to go back and visit the stationmaster's cash box, telling myself, "So what? The company steals enough from its employees. I who have absolutely nothing can very well take a little of its surplus." What a bad idea because I was arrested there and sentenced to a year in prison. I am not embarrassed by this conviction, I take full responsibility. When society refuses you the right to exist, you have to take it and not help it along, which is cowardice.

There, companions, is the exact truth of my conviction. No companion knew about it, so I took sole responsibility for my actions and whoever takes advantage of human stupidity to try to discredit such a just and noble idea as the one that the anarchists defend, trying to dump on the whole of it the faults and wrongs (if faults and wrongs they are) of one of its defenders, is a cretin who trembles before the strict logic of the anarchist idea.

I thought that these explanations might be necessary for the anarchist companions, so I would appreciate it if you would include my letter in the next issue of *Révolté*.

Three

The Emperor's Axe

The Paris Commune, the revolutionary government that seized control of the French capital for a few months in 1871, had a profound impact upon the history, geography, and politics of much of the world, particularly Northern Europe. The commune (and the reaction to it) led in no small part to the Franco-Prussian War, and it had a lasting impact on both France and Germany beyond military conflict. One of the commune's most pertinent side effects is that, even following a Prussian victory, it led to Otto von Bismarck developing a vitriolic hatred of any party or individual within the German state (which would subsequently to become an empire) that held political views that were anything other than stolidly conservative in nature.

Following the defeat of the French in 1871, the treaty of Frankfurt, and the establishment of the German Empire (and Bismarck's appointment as its first chancellor), Bismarck described anarchists and socialists alike as "this country's rats [which] should be exterminated,"[1] and he sought to suppress democratically elected parties such as the Social Democrats. As Bismarck and other agents of the state attempted to restrict political thought within the empire, many Germans began to despise the emperor, Wilhelm I, as well as his appointed chancellor and a Germany that was fast becoming deeply iniquitous, divisive, and restrictive.

On the afternoon of 11 May 1878, the eighty-one-year-old emperor and his forty-year-old daughter, Princess Louise of Prussia (upon whom he had lavished attention from birth, much to the detriment of her only brother and the subsequent emperor of Germany, Frederick III), were taking their customary afternoon drive in an open-topped carriage when shots rang out; shouts were raised, and the smell of gunpowder hung in the air. The would-be assassin was a twenty-one-year-old who, for the most part, has largely been forgotten by history; he was the first of a number of Anarchists to attempt regicide in a very brief amount of time.

Emil Heinrich Max Hödel (sometimes spelled "Hoedel") was born on 27 May 1857 in Leipzig. Little is known of his early life other than the accounts published by Ernest Vizetelly[2] and in *Volksblatt*.[3] Details about Hödel's father, a man named Lehmann are not available, though it is known that Hödel was illegitimate; his mother subsequently another man and assumed his name (again, the circumstances of this marriage and the details of the wider Hödel family have been lost to history). Statements from his mother and step-father following the events of May 1878 describe young Max Hödel as an irascible child who was frequently both argumentative and rude. The same can be said of many other children, especially those from fractured or abusive home environments, and it may be worth considering such claims as being the product of a right-wing press seeking to establish a causal link between such behaviors and subsequent attempted regicides. The juvenile Hödel may not have been too innocent, however, as he was detained at age twelve by the police for a succession of thefts. In keeping with the brutality of German justice of the time, Hödel was allegedly whipped and then detained until the age of 14 in the Zeitz reformatory. The reformatory environment of 1869 was doubtless unwelcoming for any child, no matter how irascible, and the Moritzburg in Zeitz was both an hour away from Leipzig and an imposing and sullen edifice to encounter.

Hödel used his time in the reformatory to his advantage and commenced training as a plumber (some reports, most notably Vizetelly's, claim that he was a tinsmith). He continued in his chosen occupation when he left the reformatory environment, up until he left Leipzig in 1875 at the age of 18. For the next year, Hödel traveled and worked as a journeyman plumber through the German Empire, visiting Berlin, Bayern, Frankfurt, and Cologne prior to returning to Leipzig in 1876. During his time in Berlin, Hödel supplemented his income as a plumber by selling papers on behalf of Adolf Stoecker's Christian Social Party. In addition, Hödel also sold papers on behalf of the Social Democratic affiliated, National Liberals party most notably, *The Torch*. Although only a minor party affiliate, Hödel found himself attending a congress in Hungary and subsequently in Vienna, Austria, in 1877. During his time in Vienna in April 1878, Hödel was formally expelled from the Social Democrats in Leipzig for handling funds dishonestly. In all probability, this was because he chose to retain some of the payments he had received for selling papers on the party's behalf.

Prior to 1878, very few on the German left affiliated themselves openly with Anarchist thought and action, and although Hödel had some casual contact with Johann Most, it seems unlikely that the then deputy of the Social Democratic Party serving as a representative to the Reichstag would have taken much interest in a young and itinerant paper seller and plumber. During this period, Hödel had begun to reject constitutional Socialism and was actively concerned with ideals more in keeping with those favored by Anarchism. Indeed, at a public meeting at Metz on 28 March 1878, Hödel stated that "the military is quite unnecessary, that the people could govern themselves even at all without kings and princes." A few days later, he declared at another public meeting, "We need no emperor, no king, and no government." For the Social Democrats who played an active part in German government of the day, albeit with a small number of delegates to the Reichstag, the latter statement must have been particularly unwelcome (especially when considered in the context of Bismarck's repeated attempts to suppress the party).

During April 1878, Hödel left Leipzig, ostensibly to travel to Dresden and

Emil Heinrich Max Hödel

Bohemia; instead, he found his way to Berlin. During this time Hödel allegedly purchased a music box with money he reportedly stole from his mother in Leipzig and played it around the bars of Berlin. In addition to the limited income he could earn as a casual busker, Hödel was, until his formal published dismissal from the Social Democrats on 9 May (two days before his attempted regicide), selling papers on the party's behalf in Berlin. Hödel's living conditions during his time in Berlin are something of a mystery, but it is known that he visited a photography studio on or around 6 May. The photographer, Dietrich, would subsequently testify at Hödel's trial that Hödel had claimed during their sitting that although he was not presently of interest to anyone, the photographer should retain the negatives to mass produce his image, as he would soon send an "electric spark through the world." History remains unclear as to whether Dietrich chose to take this advice.

Wilhelm I was a man of routine. Although in his eighties, the German emperor believed in regular constitutionals (albeit of the horse-drawn variety), and he could usually be found in his carriage on Unter den Linden at some point during most afternoons. At around half past three on Saturday, 11 May 1878, he and his daughter were ensconced in their carriage about halfway between the Brandenburg Gate and the Royal Palace. Near the Russian Embassy, Hödel waited for the carriage to pass before raising a revolver he had purchased sometime prior and taking his shot. Seeing his shot go wide, Hödel tried firing a second time. During this brief window of time, Princess Louise had fainted and the octogenarian emperor apparently rose to his feet and asked, "Are those shots for me?" (which seems in retrospect to be a staggeringly odd response). The observations of the emperor aside, Hödel soon found himself an object of interest for many of the pedestrians present on the Unter den Linden that afternoon. A spectator grabbed Hödel by the neck, but he quickly twisted away. Being pursued by several spectators, including a coachman who was on the carriage that had been fired at, Hödel turned and shot wildly at his pursuers. According to the account provided later by Vizetelly, one of the pursuers was so badly beaten by Hödel that he died some days later of internal injuries. This allegation is not borne out by other accounts, which claim that Hödel fired two wild shots (both of which missed) before throwing aside the revolver and being captured on Schadowstrasse, where he was beaten prior to the police interceding.

Following his arrest (and probably multiple beatings), Hödel was bought rapidly to trial. In July 1878, his behavior in court was described as being contrary in nature; indeed, when his sentence was handed down, Hödel allegedly turned to his counsel and stated, "Thank you for any defense; it helps me nothing." Although not the first attack against a monarch in recent German memory, Hödel's attempt and subsequent detention was a major media event at the time. Owing the vitriol of the press (and, indeed, of Bismarck), very little attempt was made to prepare a defense for Hödel, and the court reaction was predictable. On 10 July 1878, the Prussian State Court sentenced Hödel to death for the crime of high treason. This sentence was subsequently carried out at the Lehrter Strasse prison on 16 August 1878. The executioner, Julius Krautz (who would later be described as Germany's most famed executioner), was new to the job and forced by necessity to borrow an axe with which to behead Hödel. Reports of the time indicate that Hödel stripped to the waist and sneered at the spectators of his death as Krautz decapitated him with his borrowed axe and earned his first fee of 300 marks.

Following the botched assassination attempt by Hödel in May, life mostly reverted back to its normal state within the imperial household. Despite the attempt on his life, the Wilhelm I stuck to his routine of an afternoon procession in an open-topped carriage with no additional security mechanisms in place. This would prove to be a serious mistake, as mere weeks following Hödel's attack, on Sunday, 2 June, Wilhelm found his body peppered with shot and covered in blood and rapidly being driven back to the Imperial Palace.

The perpetrator behind this second attempted regicide was Karl Eduard Nobiling. Born in Kolno near Birnbaum in the then Prussian Province of Posen in 1848, Nobiling had a very different upbringing from that of Max Hödel. Nobiling was born into a stable home, with his father being a tenant of the local manor. Little is known of his early life apart from statements made by an ex-classmate of his, a Mr. Lambeck (who subsequently became a Cologne municipal junior high school teacher), in an issue of *Volksblatt*.[4] Lambeck described the young Nobiling as showing "very little zeal throughout his student career. If he could write a work, he did it certainly. Nevertheless, he rose regularly from class to class. His good memory and especially his clear and thrilling mind could cope with all the work with ease. It completely lacked soul." It is worth remembering that *Volksblatt* was a weekly publication that definitely lacked any Republican zeal and was on the right side of the political spectrum, and Lambeck's memory may well have been influenced by the events of the day. He did, however, describe Nobiling as academically successful and gifted with a sardonic, if cynical, mind.

Karl Eduard Nobiling

Nobiling's early academic promise was borne out when he later commenced university studies in political science and agriculture at the University of Halle and Leipzig University. Combining both work and study, Nobiling was also employed at the Statistical Office in Dresden before submitting his doctoral thesis ("Contributions to the History of the Rural Economy of the Saalkreise of the Province of Saxony") in Leipzig in 1876. During his student years and his time in Dresden, Nobiling may have come into contact with Social Democrats and the wider Socialist movement; however, history has never been able to successfully confirm this intersection.

Following his graduation as a doctor of philosophy, Nobiling moved to Berlin in October 1877. He changed accommodations frequently and was not active among radical circles or present at any meetings during this period. Finally, in January 1878, Nobiling rented rooms on the second floor of No. 18 Unter den Linden. Unlike Hödel, who had to support himself as best he could as a part-time busker and paper seller, Nobiling was able to pay his rent from private means and with the income he earned from contributions to scientific journals of the day. One innocent motivation for Nobiling's move to Berlin, beyond the city being an academic and cultural center, was that his mother and at least one of his siblings were in the city at the time. Following the death of Nobiling's father (details of which are scant), his mother had remarried and was now resident in Berlin. Whether from a sense of family duty or pursuit of his career, the positioning of Nobiling's rooms would prove fateful.

Max Hödel's attempted assassination of Wilhelm I in May was a major event within Germany and Europe as a whole. The motivations of the attacker were the talk of the media and private conversation, and, according to the accounts provided by Vizetelly, Nobiling was well aware of the incident. According to unnamed acquaintances, Nobiling took no small satisfaction in Hödel's failure, finding him insufficient for accomplishing such a seismic task as regicide. Indeed, it may have been this failure that prompted Nobiling's later actions rather than any higher political goals or motivations.

The morning of 2 June 1878 found Nobiling sitting at his desk composing a number of notes indicating that his landlady and laundress should be paid from money that could be found in one of the desk drawers. Also upon the desk were a loaded revolver and a double-barrel shotgun loaded with coarse shot. Other than settling his accounts, Nobiling's actions during the morning of 2 June are unknown to history. His activities in the afternoon would, however, be recorded in far greater detail. As two o'clock neared, Nobiling was positioned in a chair by a window on the second floor overlooking the Unter den Linden. As the imperial carriage passed directly beneath his window, Nobiling raised the shotgun and fired both rounds at the emperor, who at that point was returning a salute from the spectators. Eighteen pieces of shot were embedded in Wilhelm's helmet, with a further thirty slamming into his face, head, hands, arms, and back. Falling back into the carriage, Wilhelm was raced back to the Imperial Palace, bleeding profusely and already presumed dead by many observers at the scene of the shooting.

As the carriage containing the bloodied, yet still breathing, emperor sped away, the crowd on Unter den Linden surged toward number 18. Police agents and random observers quickly identified the window from which the shots had been fired and raced upstairs toward Nobiling. As they burst into his rooms and neared his desk, an innkeeper by the name of Holt was fired upon and injured. More of the crowd surged into the room, only to see Nobiling place the revolver at his temple. Although Nobiling had time to discharge the weapon, the bullet that slammed into his temple did not prove immediately fatal, and he was left with a fractured skull before being overpowered by the mob that had raced into his room. Nobiling quickly lapsed into unconsciousness before being carried away by the police for interrogation. During this time, the emperor had been returned to his palace and hastily examined by his doctors. Far from being fatally wounded, as the crowd had initially suspected, Wilhelm would eventually recover from his injuries.

Over the following weeks, Nobiling lapsed in and out of consciousness. At various points he was lucid enough to be visited by both his mother and his sister, as well as to be interrogated not just by the police but also by the presiding judge in his case. One purpose of the interrogations was to establish whether Nobiling was part of a conspiracy plotting to murder the emperor and, indeed, if his actions and those of Hödel were linked. As highlighted at the beginning of this chapter, Otto von Bismarck was famed for his vitriolic hatred of both Anarchists and Socialists, and he saw conspiracy everywhere. This paranoia was soon infused into both the police and the judiciary of the period. Yet, despite the overriding desire for a provable conspiracy, none was ever found; in the few moments of lucidity that Nobiling had, he claimed that he had acted alone, without the support of a wider web of conspirators. His attempt on Wilhelm's life was motivated, according to his own admissions, by his precarious financial position coupled with a response to the actions of Hödel and his belief that his was the more fitting hand to end imperial rule. According to reports in *Volksblatt*, Nobiling had also sought to kill the emperor "because he considered it beneficial for the welfare of the state, to eliminate the head of state." Following the attempted assassination, Nobiling sought (unsuccessfully) to commit suicide. The mechanism by which he made his attempt and his reasons for doing so (presumably because he had a bullet lodged in his skull and thus was in physical agony) have been lost to history; however, his efforts were fruitless. Nobiling, unlike Hödel, would not survive to face German imperial justice. On 10 September 1878, after surviving three months with a fractured skull, Nobiling died from meningitis owing to an infection caused by the bullet still embedded in his body.

Although unconnected, the actions of Hödel and Nobiling had a significant impact on the German psyche, and the reaction to the separate assassination attempts was swift. The Reichstag was dissolved on 11 June 1878. Following elections at the end of June, the Socialists, whose numbers in the Reichstag had been growing, lost three of their twelve seats. Worse was to come, however, when the first of the Anti-Socialist Laws was enacted on 19 October 1878. Owing to the actions of Hödel and Nobiling (despite their different political beliefs—Hödel was perhaps closer to being an Anarchist, whereas Nobiling was more aligned politically with Socialist Republicans), and the furor that was whipped up by the populist press, Bismarck had the opportunity he had been waiting for. Although the Anti-Socialist Laws did not specifically outlaw the Social Democrats, the enacted legislation did effectively cripple the party and many other left-leaning organizations within Germany at the time. The new legislation banned any organization or meeting seeking to promote Socialist or Anarchist ideas, principles, or aims; trade unions were also outlawed throughout Germany, and forty-five newspapers had their presses smashed and were forced to close. Even as late as 1888, some ten years after the Anti-Socialist Laws were enacted, they were still being utilized, and Bismarck sought to expel all suspected or proven Socialists or Anarchists from Germany. The wave of repression that followed the assassination attempts stifled debate (parliamentary or otherwise) and led to a state of siege and, indeed, state-sponsored terrorism throughout imperial Germany. It is in the context of this repression unleashed by Bismarck that the events of 1885 and the actions of a typesetter who would later be known as the "Father of Germany Anarchy" perhaps be considered.

Friedrich August Reinsdorf was born on 31 January 1849 in Pegau, a small town some eleven miles from Leipzig. Between 1604 and 1605, Pegau had been one of the municipalities within Germany that had hosted witch trials (and the inevitable executions that followed them). Centered initially around a Benedictine monastery, Pegau was a prosperous place at the time of Reinsdorf's birth (the major occupations being boot and shoemaking, along with the manufacture of felt and metal wares), and although the monastery had been dissolved in 1539, it was still a provincial and highly religious town. Reinsdorf was the oldest son of the shoemaker, Friedrich August Reinsdorf, and his wife, Emilie Christinae; eleven more siblings eventually joined the family. Young Reinsdorf attended the local elementary school and trained as a typesetter for the print industry. By 1865, at the age of sixteen, Reinsdorf had graduated from his academic training and commenced the wanderings across Germany that would be a major factor in his life. It is not known whether this youthful tour across Germany influenced his political thinking, or if Reinsdorf was already questioning the social and political conditions within Prussia at the time. Doubtless he had experienced these conditions early enough, with all the major industries within Pegau being strictly piecework in nature, and the gap between owners and producers abundantly clear. With eleven children to feed, his father probably had to work long hours in brutalizing conditions to stand any hope of providing food. Whether it was youthful experiences or something that happened during his travels as a journeyman typesetter, by 1870 Reinsdorf had made a decision that was to have long-lasting ramifications for his life.

As discussed elsewhere in this chapter, the Franco-Prussian War commenced in 1870, and Reinsdorf, whom Max Schütte[5] claims was already imbued with hatred for the Prussian state, moved to Switzerland to escape the carnage. In Switzerland, Reinsdorf was active in the trade union "Typographia" and began to attend meetings of the International Workingmen's Association and other Social Democrat organizations. Having developed his oratorical skills during his earlier wanderings, he was often called upon to speak at such meetings. During his time in Geneva, and later in Zurich, Reinsdorf met such revolutionary luminaries as Johann Becker (one of the central figures in the Baden Revolution and a long-time friend of both Karl Marx and Friedrich Engels), Peter Kropotkin, and Mikhail Bakunin. Probably as a result of his speeches and contacts, Reinsdorf was of understandable interest to the police of Switzerland, as well as the German spies who operated in Switzerland, and it was probably during this period that he adopted his later nom de guerres: Steinberg, Bernstein and Gfeller.

By August 1874, Reinsdorf had moved back to Germany and was working in Leipzig under the name of Bernstein. He soon found himself in trouble again, however, and was denounced as an Anarchist thanks to his fiery and impassioned speeches at Social Democratic meetings. As a result, Reinsdorf soon found himself unemployed. Now in his twenties, Reinsdorf cut an imposing figure, but, in addition to being unemployed, he was suspected of being a spy or agent provocateur by those involved in the Social Democratic movement in Leipzig. It is not known whether August Reinsdorf and Max Hödel crossed paths in Leipzig, but they certainly moved in similar circles. Following the attacks by Hödel and Nobiling in 1878, much of the German Social Democratic movement sought to disavow the two would-be regicides. Reinsdorf, however, was vociferous and energetic in defense of their actions, having been introduced to the concept of propaganda of the deed some years earlier, prior to the death of Bakunin in 1876. Following the attacks, police pressure mounted in Leipzig, and thanks to the emergency laws, detentions and arbitrary arrests became a common aspect of life. To escape arrest, Reinsdorf traveled back to Switzerland, a flight made all the

Friedrich August Reinsdorf

more necessary after he was questioned by the police in connection to the attack by Hödel and subsequently released without being charged.

During his time in Switzerland, Reinsdorf reconnected with Johann Most. Most had first encountered Reinsdorf in 1876 in Berlin, and the two had found that they shared similar revolutionary viewpoints. In 1878, Reinsdorf was officially invited to contribute to Most's publication, *Freiheit* (Freedom), which was then published in London, and he actively did so, contributing a number of theoretical treatises on anarchism. Reinsdorf's stay in Switzerland was not to be a long one, however, and he was forced to return to Germany after an assault charge was brought against him. Again his departure proved timely, and he was charged in absentia to three and a half years of penal servitude. The year 1879 found Reinsdorf in Berlin, where he published a clandestine Anarchist newspaper, *Der Kampf*. However, before a single copy could be distributed, the Berlin police raided the apartment in which the paper was being printed and destroyed not only the copies but also the presses on which they were made. Reinsdorf was not arrested in the police raid, although a number of his compatriots were. In the summer of 1880, Most attended a congress near Wyden castle in Zurich for Social Democratic groups within Germany. Thanks to the split that occurred between Communist and Anarchist thought (and Most's own fervor for the latter), he soon found himself formally expelled from the party, and Reinsdorf was once more accused of being an agent of the state, paranoia among German radicals of the time being particularly pronounced owing to the wave of repression unleashed by Bismarck following the failed assassinations some years earlier.

By 1880, Reinsdorf had found a temporary home in Berlin under the alias of Gfeller. It was during this time period that he may have formulated a plot to blow up the Reichstag in response to the Anti-Socialist Laws. In the early part of 1881, Reinsdorf was arrested, according to testimony provided by the police informer and spy Neumann. No materials relevant to any proposed bombing were recovered, and although he was found to be in possession of a dagger and a false passport, Reinsdorf only served a few months in detention before being summarily expelled from Berlin in June 1881. Later that month, Reinsdorf was back in Leipzig before being expelled on 28 June 1881. Following his expulsion by the police in two cities, Reinsdorf traveled to his hometown of Pegau. There, he was arrested on charges of stealing dynamite; however, Reinsdorf managed to evade arrest when the individual from whom the dynamite had been stolen could not positively identify him as the thief. This was not the last time that dynamite was to play an important role in Reinsdorf's life. From Pegau, Reinsdorf traveled to Nancy in France, where he obtained work before leaving for Paris and, subsequently, London.

London in the 1880s, although less repressive than Continental Europe, still had enough of a police presence and foreign agents to make even the most hardened of activists uncomfortable, and 1883 found Reinsdorf back in Germany in the small town of Elberfeld (now a municipality of the city of Wuppertal), again using an assumed identity (this time that of Johan Penzenbach). At this time, an opportunity for Reinsdorf to put into action what he had been proposing in print for years presented itself. A new monument was set to be unveiled and inaugurated in the Niederwald landscape park on 28 September 1883. This monument would commemorate the victory over France in the Franco-Prussian War and had been constructed at an estimated cost of one million gold marks. Dominating a broad hill on the right bank of the Rhine, the monument was to be inaugurated by the aging Wilhelm I (now eighty-six), with Bismarck and many members of the aristocracy and government in attendance. For Reinsdorf, it proved an attractive target for an attempted regicide.

In Elberfeld, Reinsdorf organized a series of meetings in the homes of Wilhelm Weidenmüller, the shoemaker Karl Holzhauerm, the typesetter Emil Kuchler and the weavers Rudolf Palm and Karl Bachmann. During these meetings, discussions of social justice and workers' rights turned to discussions of insurrectionary activities. Sadly for Reinsdorf, one of the attendees, Palm, was a police agent in the employ of the local police commissioner, Gottschalk. The latter was doubtless informed when Reinsdorf and his compatriots obtained a cache of dynamite that was subsequently buried in a local wood. Initially the group may have planned on utilizing the dynamite on the Sedantag (Day of Sedan). This semi-official memorial holiday occurred annually on 2 September to commemorate the victory in the 1870 battle of Sedan. A time of triumphalism for the ruling classes, Sedantag was never recognized officially and was largely derided by the working classes. Regardless of the disdain that the members of the group (and many of their peers) felt for the "celebration," the plan to detonate explosives at this event was quickly disregarded owing to the potential for injury to innocent civilians.

The group had no such compunctions regarding their next explosive attempt. On the night of 4 September 1883, one of the members, Bachmann, was sent out to visit the restaurants of Elberfeld where the bourgeoisie gathered. He was equipped with a small tin that contained a crude bomb constructed of bullets, shrapnel, and a small dynamite charge. Initially, Bachmann had planned to detonate the device at a beer hall, but, finding the hall crowded (and not with the bourgeoisie for whom the bomb was intended), he headed to the Willemsensche casino in Wuppertal. Here he quickly secreted the device in a hole cut in the floor of the casino and made his escape. Luckily for those in the casino, the device was poorly constructed and failed to detonate correctly, resulting in no damage beyond waiters spilling a few glasses of beer. As such, the bombing was assumed by many in Wuppertal and Elberfeld to be nothing more than a joke gone awry. It is not known whether Palm informed the police of this attack; however, following the explosion, Bachmann was provided with funds by Reinsdorf and beat a hasty retreat to Luxembourg.

The bad luck continued: On 8 September, Reinsdorf was admitted to the St. Joseph Hospital in Elberfeld with a serious injury to his shin. The official story given at the time of admission was that he had injured himself while crossing a railway line; however, it is more than likely that his injuries were sustained while experimenting with the creation of explosive devices that actually detonated. During his convalescence, the idea of bombing the Niederwald Monument became fixed in Reinsdorf's mind.

While in the hospital, Reinsdorf was visited regularly by Emil Kuchler. Little is known of Kuchler other than that he was born on 9 November 1844 in Krefeld (a town on the banks of the Rhine). According to Hugo Friedländer,[6] Kuchler was, like Reinsdorf, a typesetter; indeed, they may have been colleagues at some point. Kuchler was actively involved in Reinsdorf's plot, having helped to gather the funds to acquire the dynamite. During one of their frequent visits together, it was suggested that, rather than Reinsdorf and Kuchler planting the device, this task should be carried out by Franz Reinhold Rupsch, a young saddler's apprentice who had attended meetings of the Reinsdorf circle. At the time of the attack, Rupsch was barely twenty years old (he was born in 1863). He was also single and, unlike Kuchler, did not have any dependents (Kuchler was the father of six young children). Initially the plan was for Rupsch to take sole responsibility for planting the device, owing to his lack of attachments and dependencies, but also because of the group's limited financial means. In a quirk of fate (or possible direct police involvement), the group received an unexpected windfall when Palm contributed 40 marks to the cause. It was then decided that Kuchler would go with Rupsch and observe the planting of the device.

On 26 September 1883, Kuchler and Rupsch retrieved the dynamite from the woods where it had been secreted and made their way toward Assmannshausen and the Niederwald Monument. As night fell on 27 September, the two conspirators hid the dynamite in a drainage pipe that ran beneath the only road leading to the monument. Before leaving the hospital, both Kuchler and Rupsch had been told by Reinsdorf to purchase a waterproof fuse; however, they trailed almost thirty feet of the cheaper non-waterproof fuse wire they had purchased instead from the drainage pipe to a nearby tree that they had marked. Unfortunately, the 50 pfennigs that Kuchler and Rupsch had saved by opting for the fuse wire ultimately proved costly, as the night saw a heavy and constant rainfall that saturated both the fuse and the dynamite.

The following day, on 28 September, the economically minded Kuchler and Rupsch returned to the tree near the Niederwald Monument. Kuchler acted as lookout for the royal party (albeit without Bismarck in tow). On seeing their approach, he signaled Rupsch. However, despite repeated efforts (and probably much swearing and sweating), Rupsch could not get the damp fuse to light as the emperor and his guests made their way toward the monument. The hapless duo waited for the end of the dedication ceremony and tried again as Wilhelm departed, only for the farce to continue, as the fuse yet again failed to light. Having failed in their efforts to detonate the dampened dynamite, Rupsch and Kuchler retrieved it from the drainage pipe and considered their next move. According to local rumor, the emperor and his party (including princes and politicians) would attend a concert at the Festhalle at Rudesheim that evening, so Kuchler and Rupsch moved themselves and the dynamite there. Working quickly, they positioned the dynamite next to the kitchen area of the Festhalle and lit the fuse. At some point on the journey, both the fuse and the dynamite had dried out, and the resulting explosion shook the Festhalle. Although all the glassware in the kitchen shattered in the explosion and a bartender by the name of Lauter temporarily lost his hearing, nobody attending the concert was hurt. As for the emperor, he was in Weisbaden, almost twenty miles from the Festhalle at Rudesheim. Following the explosion, Rupsch and Kuchler returned to Elberfeld after pawning Kuchler's watch to pay for the return trip.

Reinsdorf was still in the hospital during the unsuccessful bombing, probably expecting major news to arrive. The press at the time did not mention either the explosion at the Festhalle or, as Reinsdorf had hoped, news of a regicide at the Niederwald Monument. Latter historians can only imagine the annoyance and stress he must have felt at the failure caused by a 50-pfennig fuse and the vagaries of the German weather. Toward the end of October 1883 (some accounts claim 21 October, others 23 October), Reinsdorf was discharged from the hospital. On the evening of 29 October, a large explosion significantly damaged the Frankfurt Police Headquarters Building; however, no casualties were sustained, as the building was unoccupied. Authorities at the time were keen to blame the recuperated Reinsdorf for the attack, but he successfully established that he had not been in Frankfurt (or, indeed, anywhere near its vicinity) at the time of the explosion. Following his release from the hospital, Reinsdorf had obtained a job in Elberfeld working for a book printer (using the alias Pelzenbach). On 27 October he claimed illness and made his way to the industrial town of Barmen, where Kuchler and Rupsch had deposited the dynamite that left over from their abortive attempt at regicide.

Following recovery of the dynamite, Reinsdorf made his way toward Weisbaden. His original plan was to detonate an explosion at the central train station; however, he discarded this idea owing to the potential injury that could be caused to innocent women and children. From Weisbaden, Reinsdorf traveled to Hannover before moving on to Hamburg, again using the alias Pelzenbach; in Hamburg he was admitted to the hospital on 7 November, suffering from tuberculosis. Reinsdorf had suffered frequent spells of ill health, most relating to tuberculosis, and his attempts at propaganda of the deed may have been motivated in part by his illness; perhaps he believed that the time available to him in which to make an impact upon an unjust society was limited. He was discharged from the hospital on 9 January 1884; however, the earlier explosion in Frankfurt had created problems for Reinsdorf, and he was detained by the police on 11 January. Although Reinsdorf protested his innocence and again proved that he had been in Bremen at the time of the explosion, he remained in police custody. During his detention, his co-conspirators—Karl Rheinbach, Karl Bachmann, Emil Kuchler, August Töllner, Karl Holzhauer, Fritz Söhngen and Franz Reinhold Rupsch—were rounded up by the police. One name conspicuous by its absence from this list was the weaver, Palm.

Following their arrest and detention, news of the conspiracy against the emperor at the Niederwald Monument slowly began to circulate in the press. In May 1884 the Anti-Socialist legislation was renewed, with an added amendment in June of that year making it illegal to manufacture, possess, sell, or import dynamite without a license from the police. Explosives had granted Anarchists and the dispossessed an opportunity to strike back against the German state, and the state was keen to address this vulnerability. Unwarranted possession of dynamite now carried a sentence of ten years up to life imprisonment, with the death penalty for any use of dynamite that resulted in the loss of life.

It was not until 15 December 1884 that the trial of Reinsdorf and the other conspirators commenced in Leipzig. It would be a short affair. Reinsdorf and the others faced fourteen judges and were accused of instigating the bombing of the Willemsensche casino in Wuppertal, the attack on the Frankfurt Police Headquarters, the Festhalle explosion and the attempt against Wilhelm I at the Niederwald Monument. The evidence against them was damning; chief among the fifty-four witnesses was the police spy, Rudolf Palm (who subsequently secured work in a lucrative post as an overseer in the workhouse at Brauweiler). Throughout the trial, Reinsdorf sought to shield his co-accused, who actually (in the case of Kuchler and Rupsch) assisted the prosecution by providing much of the damning testimony themselves. Additionally, throughout the trial Reinsdorf used his time on the stand to vigorously cross-examine witnesses and was frequently warned about his language and remarks. When questioned by the presiding judge as to what he understood Anarchism to represent, Reinsdorf responded, "A society in which every person can develop to the fullest extent of his abilities. In order that this may be accomplished no-one should be burdened with excessive labour; want and misery should be banished from the world; every form of force should cease to be; all forms of ignorance and superstition should be eliminated from the world."[7]

Despite Reinsdorf's rhetoric, the judgment against him and his co-defendants came quickly. On 22 December 1884, three of the defendants—Reinsdorf, Rupsch, and Kuchler—were sentenced to death. Karl Bachmann received nine years in prison. Karl Holzhauer was convicted of high treason with ten years' imprisonment for aiding and abetting, while the other three defendants—Karl Rheinbach, Fritz Söhngen and August Töllner—were acquitted of all charges. On 6 February 1885, Rupsch had his sentence commuted to life imprisonment, partly owing to his youth, but also because his testimony had assisted the state in developing a stronger legal case against Kuchler.

On 7 February 1885, Reinsdorf and Kuchler were executed at the Halle prison, with Reinsdorf being the first to face the executioner's axe. Following a meal of bouillon, beef-steak, butter cakes and wine (as well as the cigar that followed), Reinsdorf was led to the execution block at 7:00 a.m. After stripping to his waist, Reinsdorf was placed into position. As the executioner raised his axe, Reinsdorf shouted out, defiant to the last, "I die for humanity, down with barbarism, long live anarchism!" Kuchler, who had been watching the proceedings from his cell, was marched next to the execution block. His final words were more prosaic than his compatriot's: "I die an innocent man, my poor wife, my poor children." The executions of Reinsdorf and Kuchler were not the end of the violence, however, and in September 1885 Holzhauer's body was found hanging in his cell, the ten-year sentence the court had imposed being too much for him to bear.

During the course of his reign over a unified Germany, Wilhelm I faced a number of assassination attempts, none of which were successful. The corresponding reaction from a conservative and reactionary government was to impose fundamentally undemocratic laws that only stoked the justifiable rage of the German working class. Just as the Anti-Socialist Laws sought to erase Anarchism from Germany, some German Anarchists sought to destroy the state by removing its figurehead. Ultimately it was to prove a costly, bloody, and pointless endeavor for both factions.

Action as Propaganda (Johann Most)

Source: The Anarchist Library, https://theanarchistlibrary.org/library/johann-most-action-as-propaganda (accessed November 2016); originally published in Freiheit, 25 July 1885

We have said a hundred times or more that when modern revolutionaries carry out actions, what is important is not solely these actions themselves but also the propagandistic effect they are able to achieve. Hence, we preach not only action in and for itself, but also action as propaganda.

It is a phenomenally simple matter, yet over and over again we meet people, even people close to the center of our party, who either do not, or do not wish, to understand. We have recently had a clear enough illustration of this over the Lieske affair…

So our question is this: what is the purpose of the anarchists' threats—an eye for an eye, a tooth for a tooth—if they are not followed up by action?

Or are perhaps the "law and order" rabble, all of them blackguards extraordinary, to be done away in a dark corner so that no one knows the why and the wherefore of what happened?

It would be a form of action, certainly, but not action as propaganda.

The great thing about anarchist vengeance is that is proclaims loud and clear for everyone to hear, that: this man or that man must die for this and this reason; and that at the first opportunity which presents itself for the realization of such a threat, the rascal in question is really and truly dispatched to the other world.

And this is indeed what happened with Alexander Romanov, with Messenzoff, with Sudeikin, with Bloch and Hlubeck, with Rumpff and others. Once such an action has been carried out, the important thing is that the world learns of it from the revolutionaries, so that everyone knows what the position is.

The overwhelming impression this makes is shown by how the reactionaries have repeatedly tried to hush up revolutionary actions that have taken place, or present them in a different light. This has often been possible in Russia, especially, because of the conditions governing the press there.

In order to achieve the desired success in the fullest measure, immediately after the action has been carried out, especially in the town where it took place, posters should be put up setting out the reasons for the action in such a way as to draw from them the best possible benefit.

And in those cases where this was not done, the reason was simply that it proved inadvisable to involve the number of participants that would have been required; or that there was a lack of money. It was all the more natural in these cases for the anarchist press to glorify and explicate the deeds at every opportunity. For it to have adopted an attitude of indifference toward such actions, or even to have denied them, would have been perfectly idiotic treachery.

"Freiheit" has always pursued this policy. It is nothing more than insipid, sallow envy which makes those demagogues who are continually mocking us with cries of "Carry on, then, carry on" condemn this aspect of our behavior, among others, whenever they can, as a crime.

This miserable tribe is well aware that no action carried out by anarchists can have its proper propagandist effect if those organs whose responsibility it is neither give suitable prominence to such actions, nor make it palatable to the people.

It is this, above all, which puts the reactionaries in a rage.

Four

The Cook, the Blacksmith, the King and the Weaver

Italy in 1849 was in crisis. Citizens in Lombardy had ceased both smoking and playing the lottery to deny the attendant tax revenues to the then ruling Austrians. Across the country insurrectionary activities were on the rise, and a wave of revolution was beginning to swell. Into this environment, on 19 February 1849, a child was born in Salvia di Lucania. This small town and community in the province of Potenza in southern Italy was sometimes referred to as Salvia, after the sage plant (*Salvia officinalis*). Years later, however, the town would be forced to change its name to Savoia di Lucania after the arrest of its newest arrival: Giovanni Passannante.

Passannante was the youngest of ten children born to Pasquale and Maria Fiore. Four of his siblings died at an early age, but young Giovanni would go on to play an important role in Italian history. Like many in rural Italy at the time, the Passannante clan was poor, barely scratching out a living from the land that surrounded them. As a young child, Giovanni seriously burned his hand, leaving him with a lifelong injury,[1] which for a child born into rural poverty could well have been a death sentence. According to Giuseppe Galzerano, the familial poverty was so pronounced as to require Giovanni to start work rather than school; indeed, at the same time that he was attending school at the age of six (the only year it is believed that he attended) he was also forced to beg for subsistence.[2] Giovanni was subsequently employed in a variety of jobs, including both shepherd and general laborer.

Possibly as a result of the grinding poverty at home, Giovanni Passannante moved to the town of Vietri di Potenza, where he found employment as a dishwasher, prior to moving on to the city of Potenza itself. Here he found employment, albeit as a dishwasher and kitchen scullion at the Croce di Savoia hotel. His self-taught reading skills sadly did not impress the hotel management, and he was sacked for spending his time reading books and newspapers.[3]

It may have been at the Croce di Savoia that Passannante first met Giovanni Agoglia, a retired captain who had served in the Royal Italian Army during the Napoleonic Wars and was also a former resident of Salvia. It may have been this fact, coupled with Passannante's intellectual curiosity and physical handicap, that piqued the older man's interest. For whatever reason, Agoglia was to have a significant impact on Passannante's life. When Agoglia left Potenza to take up residence in Salerno, he took the now jobless Passannante with him and gave the younger man an annuity to allow for him to continue his schooling. Like many Italians of the age, Passannante was fervently Catholic, and he spent much of his spare time reading the Bible. As he grew older, however, he shifted his attentions to newspapers and magazines and was particularly interested in the writings of Giuseppe Mazzini.

Mazzini was an Italian journalist, politician, and activist for a unified Italy, and a central figure in the Italian revolutionary movement. Born in Genoa to a wealthy university professor father and a mother filled with religious fervor, Mazzini was accepted into university at a mere fourteen years old. Here he trained in law before graduating in 1826 and practicing as a lawyer for the poor. Following early legal troubles, Mazzini was exiled to Geneva, Switzerland, in 1831. After attempting to form a number of organizations, and the attendant insurrections in favor of a unified Italy in France (which resulted in arrest and exile), Mazzini found himself in London in 1840 prior to organizing attempted revolts in Italy in 1843, 1848, 1849 and indeed until his death of pleurisy in Pisa in 1872. Throughout his life, Mazzini was a staunch Italian nationalist and republican who envisioned a free and independent Italy. Mazzini steadfastly refused to compromise his ideals and, unlike other nationalists (such as Giuseppe Garibaldi), refused to swear oaths of allegiance to the House of Savoy. Perhaps oddly, given his republicanism, Mazzini was also staunchly opposed to Marxism and Communism, and he decried the Paris Commune.[4] Karl Marx was not impressed and described Mazzini's ideas as "nothing better than the old idea of a middle-class republic."[5] In other interviews, Marx would go further still, calling Mazzini "that everlasting old ass."[6] Mazzini's legacy was to prove significant to Italian politics, inspiring both those on the right, such as Mussolini, and those on the left, including the anti–Fascist Mazzini Society that was formed by Gaetano Salvemini and other Italian exiles in the United States in 1939. For the young Passannante, the "old ass" would also be a highly influential figure.

Giovanni Passannante

During his time in Salerno, Passannante had begun attending meetings of pro–Mazzini groups (*filomazziniani*). At one of these meetings he crossed paths with Matteo Melillo. Unlike Passannante, Melillo was the son of Italian landowners and, as a result, had not known youthful privations, but the two young men were the same age and had the same interest in a unified Italy; indeed, Melillo was a founder of the Youth Association of Progress and a familiar face in pro–Mazzini and internationalist organizations in Salerno.[7] On the night of 15 May 1870, Passannante had his first brush with the Italian legal system. He, Melillo and another republican, Onofrio Pacelli (who was originally from Ricigliano, near Salerno, and then aged 39), were arrested for posting revolutionary proclamations. Oddly, these proclamations had not been composed by the older Pacelli, or even the more politically active Melillo, but by the 21-year-old Passannante. Perhaps aware of an imminent uprising in Calabria, Passannante's postings called for an uprising in Salerno against the existing government as well as raging against the monarchy and the papacy. Perhaps just as damning, Passannante had in his possession at the time of his arrest a copy of Mazzini's newspaper, *Il popolo d'Italia*. As punishment for his late-night poster campaign (and probably because he was the author of the proclamations), Passannante received a sentence of three months for subversion, with his co-defendants Melillo and Pacelli only being imprisoned for one month. In addition to being convicted and imprisoned for subversion, Passannante was accused of plotting violent attacks. According to the deposition of another tenant of Passannante's building, he was actively learning French and plotting to assassinate Napoleon III (the nephew of Napoleon I and then president of the French Second Republic), accusing him of being the "cause of impediment to the implementation of the Universal Republic."[8] From a one-time child beggar born into poverty to a teenage kitchen scullion, Passannante had developed his political outlook to the point of writing insurrectionary proclamations and allegedly plotting attacks against foreign heads of state in pursuit of an Italian Republic.

The year 1870 would also prove monumental for the rest of Italy. In September of that year, King Victor Emmanuel II of the House of Savoy sent Count Gustavo Ponza di San Martino to Rome. In the recent past, Garibaldi had been unsuccessful in conquering Rome, largely owing to the papal reliance on French troops. The purpose of this diplomatic mission by San Martino was to offer Pope Pius IX a peaceful resolution to the issue of Italian unification. According to reports at the time, Pius did not greet the arrival of Victor Emmanuel's emissary (or, indeed, the potential unification of Italy) with much enthusiasm. Throwing the correspondence from the king on a nearby table, the pope allegedly proclaimed in anger that "I am no prophet, nor son of a prophet, but I tell you, you will never enter Rome!"[9] Pius XI was correct in understating his powers of prophecy, as, on 2 October 1870, Rome was finally taken following a brief siege later in September, and it officially became part of the newly minted Kingdom of Italy as of 9 October 1870. After decades of bloody conflict, the Italian government had all but deposed the papacy and Napoleon III and, in doing so, created a unified Italy.

These seismic shifts in the Italian political landscape had little impact on those who were forced to endure poverty regardless of the machinations of the nascent state and monarchy. This was certainly true for Passannante. Following his release from detention in Salerno, Passannante was kept under surveillance by the prefecture before returning to his hometown of Salvia, where he was able to secure casual employment in exchange for room and board. Prison may well have proved a seminal event in young Passannante's life, as in September 1870, around the same time that Pius XI was making his inaccurate proclamations, Passannante was composing a will.[10] This document he left with his illiterate parents and sister, along with a copy of the New Basilicata newspaper of 23 March 1871, which contained news of the Paris Commune, as well as writings that Passannante had composed about both Garibaldi and Mazzini. After a few months in Salvia, Passannante returned to Salerno. The sojourn in the town of his birth may have had as much to do with visiting his parents and putting his affairs in order as with allowing time for the heat to die down in Salerno. With the eyes of the prefecture now elsewhere, Passannante was able to secure work as a cook in a textile factory belonging to the August Engler family. He also joined the Workers' Association of Pellezzano, a mutual aid society dedicated to improving the lot of the working poor. Although he became disenchanted with the financial management of the organization and ultimately left, it was probably while he was a member there or at the Mutual Aid Society of Workers (which he joined later) that Passannante was able to secure the funds necessary to open the restaurant Trattoria del Popolo. Unfortunately, the nascent business venture was forced to close in December 1877, owing to Passannante putting his ideals before his business and providing free meals for the poor.

Following the collapse of the restaurant, Passannante moved to Naples in June 1878. Naples was a thriving port city, and for an experienced cook it provided all manner of employment opportunities that may not have been available in the rest of Italy. In Naples, Passannante was able to find casual work as a cook, though often on an insecure basis, and he was frequently forced to change employers. He also had to rely on small loans from friends to make ends meet and became part of a Libertarian group by the name of Universal Republic. Although he was only in Naples for what was to be a limited time, Passannante had to share rooms with three others. For many people, this position may have seemed concerning. However, Passannante was a committed internationalist with a deep hatred of those who wallowed in wealth while the majority of people lived in the miserable conditions so pronounced in nineteenth-century Italy.

In January 1878, King Victor Emmanuel II, who would come to be known as the "Father of the Fatherland," died in Rome, and his son Umberto (who adopted the title Umberto I of Italy rather than Umberto IV of Savoy) ascended to the throne. Umberto would later be described by some as "a colorless and physically unimpressive man, of limited intellect,"[11] and a "comparatively pallid character."[12] As a young man, Umberto had served briefly in the Italian wars of independence and, following his engagement to the Austrian Archduchess Mathilde, who died as a result of accident, married his blonde and bejeweled first cousin, Margherita. Even at the start of his reign, Umberto was an anathema to many. He had secured his kingship at the age of thirty-four and exhibited many of the typical excesses of a young monarch. The levels of disparity between the rich and the poor in Italian society had become bloated and pronounced during the nineteenth century. The youthful working experience of Passannante was far from unusual at the time, and death by starvation was a very real possibility for many. Wealth was secured in the hands of the monarchy and the ruling business and administrative classes, and for many Italians, including those who had fought and died for a unified Italian republic, this level of economic division was sickeningly absolute.

Disregarding the poverty of much of the Italian people, Umberto, following his father's death and his own assumption of the throne, decided to conduct a lavish tour of his new kingdom, accompanied by his wife and their son, Victor Emmanuel, the prince of Naples. As part of his grand tour, Umberto planned to travel to Naples in November 1878. Prior to his arrival, however, there was a wave of attacks and subsequent state reprisals. On 9 February, a bomb was thrown by Emilio Capellini into a procession honoring the late King Victor Emmanuel II as it passed near Uffizi in Florence, injuring several of the marchers. A week later in Livorno forty-eight rusted bombs were found (or potentially planted) by the police in the home of an internationalist. Later that year, in May and June, Emperor Wilhem I of Germany survived the assassination attempts enacted by Karl Nobiling and Max Hödel (as detailed in the previous chapter). Although unconnected to events in Italy, for the Italian authorities these attacks spoke of a widespread Anarchist conspiracy and necessitated a crackdown. This belief was further reinforced by the discovery of a manifesto allegedly written by the Romagnole Federation. It read, "Arise, arise against the oppressors of Humanity: all the kings, emperors, presidents of republics, [and] priests of all religions that are the true enemies of the people. Destroy with them all the judicial, political, civil, and religious institutions!"[13]

The crackdown, when it came, was quickly enacted, and throughout September and October 1878, police in Florence and Naples arrested Anarchists, radicals, internationalists, and indeed anyone who could be perceived as a threat to the countrywide tour of the new monarch. One of those missed in the police roundup was Passannante. A few days prior to the king's visit to Naples, a protest was organized by typographers Luigi Felico and Thaddeus Ricciardi. This demonstration was violently interrupted by the police, and a number of individuals (including Pietro Cesare Ceccarelli, Francesco Saverio Merlino, Francesco Gastaldi, and Giovanni Maggi) were arrested for distributing revolutionary leaflets. It was doubtless hoped that these arrests in Naples would mark the end of the protests.

The days before Umberto I was due to arrive in Naples, accompanied by his wife Margherita and Prime Minister Benedetto Cairoli, had not just been fraught from the perspective of the protestors. The city council was also having heated debates owing to the high costs incurred by the planned visitation.[14] Regardless, the city council had assumed the costs, and the royal visitation was scheduled for 17 November. Passannante arose early from his temporary lodging on 16 November and made his way into the twisting medieval streets of Naples. Here he was able to sell his jacket and use the proceeds to purchase a three-inch penknife. At some point during the day he also found some red cloth and wrapped the knife within its folds. Probably chilled by the sea air, Passannante returned to his lodgings for the night.

The following day, Umberto I and his retinue began their triumphant procession through the streets of Naples. Along the route, supplicants lined up and presented their pleas to the royal couple and the prime minister. Among the crowd lining the route was Passannante, waiting for an opportune time to approach the carriage as it passed by. As the carriage and its escort reached Largo della Carriera Grande, Passannante saw his chance. Approaching the carriage as if he, too, was a supplicant in search of royal aid, Passannante withdrew his blade and, with the red cloth trailing behind him, lunged at the monarch with a cry of "Death to the king, long live the Universal Republic, Viva Orsini!"[15] Fortunately, Umberto was able to deflect the lunging Passannante, receiving only a minor cut on the arm. Margherita was also quick to react, throwing a bouquet of flowers that she had been holding in Passannante's face and shouting, "Cairoli! Save the king!"[16] Dutifully, Prime Minister Cairoli grabbed Passannante by the hair but was slashed on the leg for his efforts. The abortive attempt on the life of the monarch was quickly subdued in earnest when a captain of the Italian cuirassiers, Stefano De Giovannini, struck Passannante on the head with his saber. Bleeding from a head wound, Passannante was rapidly subdued and arrested as the procession rolled on.

News of the attempted regicide spread quickly in Italy, and the following day, 18 November, thankful monarchists organized countrywide demonstrations to celebrate the would-be assassin's failure. In Florence, as a procession passed along the Via Nazionale, a bomb was thrown into the assembled crowd, killing three spectators (two men and a girl) and wounding more than ten others. The following day, police in Florence arrested fifty-eight suspects. On the night of 18 November, a barracks in Pesaro was also attacked and there were clashes with the police in Bologna, Genoa and Pesaro. It seemed for a while that Passannante's failed attack had released the genie of discontent from its bottle.

As the press subsequently reported, the attempted regicide of Umberto I "caused the utmost excitement and indignation"[17] throughout Italy. The poet Giovanni Pascoli, speaking at a Socialist meeting in Bologna, allegedly read his "Ode to Passannante." This poem was immediately destroyed after the reading, with only the stanza "Con la berretta d'un cuoco faremo una bandiera" (With the cook's cap, we'll make a flag) surviving. Pascoli himself would deny ever having written such an ode, calling it "the most famous and misquoted non-existent poems of Italian literature"[18]; however, this claim is disputed by eyewitness accounts from Gian Battista Lolli, the secretary of the Socialist Federation of Bologna.[19] On 15 April 1879, the French Anarchist Paul Brousse was expelled from Switzerland after a conviction for publishing an article in *L'Avant-Garde* that celebrated Passannante's attack against the king[20] (as well as the attacks against Wilhelm I). By the end of 1878, even Pope Leo XIII had become involved. In an encyclical titled *Quad apostolici muneric*, issued on 28 December, the pope railed against the "deadly pestilence that winds through the innermost recesses of society and brings it to the extreme danger of ruin" in addition to "the sect of those who, with diverse and barbarous names, call themselves socialists, communists, and nihilists."[21] The Italian press was keen to focus on Passannante as being known for his bad character before the assassination attempt. Verona's *L'Arena* and Milan's *Corriere della Sera* described him as a known bandit who had allegedly killed a woman in the past, and a lithograph published in Turin went even further, reporting that his father was a mobster (cammorist).[22]

Things were not just bad for Passannante, however. Many in the Italian parliament blamed Prime Minister Cairoli's liberal policies for the near assassination of Umberto I, the bombing in Florence, and the civil unrest that had bubbled up since the attack. Parliamentary leaders on both the right and the left demanded more repressive powers to face down the challenges posed by the unruly urban poor of Italy. On 11 December, the Cairoli government lost a vote of confidence in the Italian parliament, and Cairoli, who had only a few weeks earlier wrestled with the would-be assassin, was forced to resign as Italian prime minister. (It is not known whether he limped when leaving.)

Even before Passannante's trial could begin, the Italian state had already commenced its reprisals. Following Passannante's arrest in Naples, police had traveled to his hometown and searched his parents' lodgings. Finding seditious literature (which none of his family could actually read), the police had searched in vain for a conspiracy. Unable to find one, the entire family (with the exception of one brother) was declared insane and interred in the asylum at Aversa. When the trial commenced on 6 March 1879, Passannante's defense was headed up by Leopoldo Tarantini, though he was far from a popular choice. Indeed, according to the Italian Anarchist Francesco Merlino, Tarantini acted primarily as "a second accuser."[23] To no one's surprise, on 7 March, Passannante was given the mandatory death sentence for attempted regicide. Perhaps concerned about the dissent this verdict might precipitate, or possibly seeking to live up to his reputation and nickname of "Il Buono" (the Good), King Umberto commuted Passannante's sentence to life imprisonment on 29 March. As it transpired, perhaps death would have been more humane.

Following sentencing, Passannante was transferred to Portoferraio on the island of Elba, situated off the coast of Tuscany. Here he was interred in a cell that was below sea level and pitch dark, with no toilet facilities and no room in which to stand. The prisoner was to be held in complete isolation and constantly chained. In this environment, Passannante rapidly developed scurvy, his skin becoming discolored because of the absence of light and his eyes growing perpetually weaker. Allegedly he was also routinely tortured, his cries being audible to sailors that passed the island, and his mental condition deteriorated so severely that he began to consume his own feces.[24] After ten years, the parliamentarian Agostino Bertani and the journalist Anna Maria Mozzoni were able to visit Passannante in the hellhole of Portoferraio. News of his condition shocked Italians, and he was transferred to the Montelupo mental hospital in Fiorentino after having been adjudged insane. Having been left mostly blind and irreversibly mentally damaged by the Italian state, Passannante still displayed some of his youthful fervor. Visited by the lawyer and Tuscan deputy Giovanni Rosadi a few years following his transfer, Passannante was asked whether he recognized his guest. Keeping his eyes closed, Passannante declared, "We all know each other, because we are all brothers."[25]

Having scratched a monarch and nicked a prime minister, Passannante died, crippled in mind and body, on 14 February 1910, aged sixty. Unfortunately, his indignities were not yet at an end. Following his death, Passannante was beheaded. It is not known who authorized this action and, indeed, what happened to the postmortem body (one lurid account claimed that the body was fed to wild pigs). Passannante's brain, however, was preserved in formaldehyde and retained in Montelupo until 1935, when it was transferred to the Criminal Museum in Rome, where it was on display for more than seventy years in a sealed case labeled *criminale abituale* (habitual criminal). It took many years and repeated protests before the brain of Passannante was secretly buried in his hometown of Savoia di Lucania[26] on 10 May 2007.

Although assumed by the popular press (and, indeed, later historians) to have been an Anarchist, Passannante was actually far from it. However, he may well have been part of the radical Italian milieu, as were many of the urban poor. At his trial, and by his own admission, Passannante confessed to being motivated not by Anarchist thought or conspiracy but by the nascent Italian republican state's betrayal of its people. Another individual who was perhaps motivated by personal poverty, desperation and anger at the disparity between rich and poor in nineteenth-century Italy was Pietro Umberto Acciarito.

Acciarito was born on 27 June 1871 (and named after the royal personage with whom his fate would be so intertwined) in the small town of Artena in the Lazio region of Italy. His father, Camillus, was a sometime janitor, but the impoverished agricultural landscape of rural Italy failed resolutely to provide opportunity enough to feed a family. Like many others at the time, the young Acciarito and his family joined the flood of humanity moving from the country to the cities, eventually settling in Rome. There had briefly been an increase in the availability of employment in Rome, which had drawn many people to the city, but by the 1880s a collapsing economy had all but destroyed the construction sector on which so many of the rural poor had been forced to rely. Many formerly poor rural families became poor urban families, with no tangible assistance being supplied by the Italian state. Partially as a result of this situation, and as a result of deportations of the jobless construction workers from Rome to their native provinces, a major May Day protest was planned in Rome for 1891. On the afternoon of 1 May, thousands of protestors gathered in the Piazza di Santa Croce in Gerusalemme. Unfortunately for the flag-waving radicals and the many hundreds of unemployed who had gathered in the piazza, they were surrounded by hundreds of soldiers and mounted cavalry. After an incendiary and impromptu speech by the Tuscan Anarchist Galileo Palla, the mood of the crowd turned violent, as did that of the surrounding soldiers. The demonstrators quickly discovered that righteous ire and improvised weaponry were no defense against bullets and the repeated cavalry charges made through the town square. By the end of the day, several hundred protestors were injured, with an unknown number of fatalities,[27] and in the weeks that followed there were mass arrests throughout Rome. Historians do not know whether Acciarito was present at the May Day protest, but given that he was a twenty-year-old who largely worked as a casual blacksmith, and the protest took place in the same town where he resided, it seems likely that he was there. Seeing the wave of violence unleashed by the military, and the indignation of a desperately poor and unsupported crowd, may well have influenced his later life and actions.

According to Nunzio Pernicone, who remains one of the few historians to focus at all on the life of Acciarito,[28] by 1895 Acciarito's luck may have been changing. He received (from a now unknown source) news of a job offer for a blacksmith with the Bank of Naples. Sadly, as he discovered after arriving in the coastal city, all was not as it seemed. The Bank of Naples employed sub-contractors and was financially irregular, to say the least. Indeed, it had a nasty habit of not paying its workers at all. Following a series of complaints about non-payment, Acciarito was eventually sacked for good in February 1897. The bank must have paid him something at some juncture, however, as he was able to rent a small blacksmith shop in Naples. Sadly for Acciarito, this shop was soon forced to close, and he was also forced to forego his marriage to a local girl, Pasqua Veneraba, owing to a lack of customers in an economy caught in a downward spiral. Unfortunately, the economic situation was not the only thing that was in a downward spiral; Acciarito was, by all accounts, lapsing into a deep and resentful depression himself. Indeed, soon after the forced closure of his workshop, Acciarito was forced to sell all of his tools, upon which he had relied for many years. Following the sale, Acciarito was visibly depressed, and acquaintances in his neighborhood heard him muttering that the government must provide for the poor and "that he intended to kill a big shot or himself."[29] Concern was so pronounced about Acciarito's mental state and potential actions that his father reported him to the local police. They promptly issued an arrest warrant; however, Acciarito managed to avoid detection and arrest by taking up temporary residence in a hotel with Pasqua.

Prior to the issuance of this warrant, Acciarito had not been either of interest to or in trouble with Italian legal authorities. Indeed, his only legal problem had been an arrest in 1893 when he was detained for carrying a dangerous weapon (this later turned out to be an awl that he was using as part of a design course he attended during one of his frequent bouts of unemployment). Despite claims that were to be made later, Acciarito had limited contact with either Anarchist or Socialist groups at the time, and his only real commitment was signing a manifesto issued by Errico Malatesta's *L'Agitazione*. Indeed, as Pernicone points out, many "believed Acciarito's devotion to anarchism was entirely inadequate, and often chided him for devoting more time to his girlfriend than to the movement."[30] At this point in his life, Acciarito sounds like many working-class young men throughout history: interested in the rebel chic of a cause but predominantly interested in the friendships they could provide (and, of course, in women).

By April 1897, Acciarito was still evading the police, and his thoughts had turned much darker than some of his former comrades and "serious" revolutionaries could have envisioned. Reading the local newspapers, Acciarito discovered that his namesake, King

Umberto, would be attending the derby races to be held outside Rome on 22 April 1897. On 20 April, Acciarito saw his father for what was to be the last time, and he said as much. His father asked if he intended to emigrate and received only the reply that he would be attending the races. Showing remarkable foresight, and no doubt alarmed by the conclusions that he had reached, Acciarito's father again informed the police, this time advising them that an attack against the king was imminent. The police do not seem to have believed that this represented a genuine threat, and no arrest warrant or additional security was in place for the royal outing to the races.

At 2:00 p.m. on 22 April, King Umberto was making his way in his carriage along Porta San Giovanni with his aide-de-camp, Emilio Ponzo Vaglia. The carabinieri assigned to protect the carriage and its occupants were 650 feet behind them, accompanied by a member of the king's bodyguard. As the carriage drew level with him, Acciarito leaped forward, pulling from his pocket a homemade knife, and lunged. King Umberto was able to evade the blade of the prospective assassin, and before Acciarito could attempt a second strike, the forward momentum of the carriage threw him to the ground. Here he was quickly detained by the somewhat lax police detail. Showing somewhat unbelievable stoicism, the king is alleged to have turned to Vaglia and remarked that such incidents were "risks of the trade" before proceeding as planned to his outing to the races.

Following the attack by Passannante, the Italian government, disregarding all available evidence, had been keen to place the blame for the attempted regicide on the Anarchist community. A wave of arrests, reprisals, and repression had been unleashed following the earlier incident, and this pattern was repeated after Acciarito's attack. Following the incident, the police were quick to arrest several leading Anarchists, Socialists, and unruly republicans, as well as an acquaintance of Acciarito, Romeo Frezzi, who was apparently guilty of committing no other crime than possessing a photograph of Acciarito. After several days of questioning (which in Italy at that time probably amounted to little more than torture), the unfortunate Frezzi was declared dead. At the end of the first investigation that was conducted into his death, it was declared that Frezzi had committed suicide by running repeatedly into the wall of his cell. A secondary investigation was conducted in which it was claimed that Frezzi had actually died of a stroke. Later still, a third investigation concluded that he had committed suicide by jumping twenty feet. None of this was particularly convincing, and it seems likely that the carabinieri were overenthusiastic in their questioning and beaten Frezzi to death. This supposition led to mass protests against police brutality in Rome, and there may well have been more than a kernel of truth to those claims, as the officials responsible for Frezzi's detention and interrogation were quickly transferred to other posts.

Following the scandal that was unleashed by Frezzi's untimely death, Acciarito was rushed to trial, starting at the Rome Court of Assize on 28 May 1897. Unfortunately for those branches of the Italian state arguing that there existed a wide-ranging Anarchist plot to assassinate the monarch, this theory was quickly discounted by Acciarito's testimony when he assumed all responsibility, giving as the reason for his attack:

> I committed it because of poverty, like one who commits suicide because of poverty, turns brigand, or joins the criminal underground. Responsibility for the poverty in which the workers live belongs to the bourgeois classes who starve the workers. The working people are dying of hunger while millions are spent on Africa and on the horse races. Seeing such things causes bad blood. The King is the father of this country; therefore, when the country is in poverty, the father of the country must provide. They say he gives charity. What does five dollars of charity do! Afterward everything returns as

before. We want work, we young men need work, but instead we poor wretches are dying of hunger. I know that I hate all the idle rich. I know that after working hard I was compensated with hunger and treated like a criminal. I did not know if I shall kill a King, the Pope, or someone else. I was incredibly enraged; I saw the King and struck at him to vent my feelings.[31]

Acciarito's trial concluded a day after it had started, on 29 May, and the verdict was a foregone conclusion. He had by his own admission attempted regicide and, like Passannante before him, was sentenced to life imprisonment. On hearing his sentence, Acciarito proclaimed, "Today for me, tomorrow the bourgeois government. Long live anarchy! Long live the social revolution!" His proclamation aside, the sentence was to be enacted in the same conditions and in the same location—namely, Portoferraio—that Passannante had faced. Just as with Passannante, Acciarito was held in strict solitary confinement, and he, too, slipped into madness. Acciarito was later transferred to Montelupo, where he died at the age of seventy-two on 4 December 1943. Following his death, Acciarito was, again like Passannante, dissected and autopsied, and the eugenicists who did so declared that his skull revealed a predisposition to murder.

An observer of the events surrounding the life of Umberto I may have expected that following two attempts on his life, and the attendant waves of repression that they unleashed, he would have made more overt attempts to win over the loyalty and appreciation of the poor. Unfortunately, this was far from the case, due in no small part to not only Umberto's pronounced sense of entitlement but also the vagaries of nature. In addition to an assassination attempt against the king, 1897 saw a catastrophic wheat harvest. From more than 3.5 million tons in previous years, the wheat harvest was diminished by upward of a ton. Import duties were also increased by the Spanish-American War of 1898. Global events and a harvest failure thus led to an increase in the cost of a stable diet for the poor, and it was not long before protests commenced in earnest, demanding "bread and work" throughout the country. In the southern Italian city of Bari, 2,000 protestors (according to news reports of the time) "attacked the tax office, devastated the public gardens, and then proceeded to make an assault upon the Town Hall and prison."[32] Events turned even more violent in Naples when the police fired upon and killed several protestors. On 5 May 1898, a general workers' strike was called to protest the rising cost of bread that was leaving many hungry. In the town of Pavia in Lombardy, police fired on the crowd, killing the son of a deputy from Milan. The following day the workers at the Pirelli factory in Milan walked out of work and began a protest, circulating literature denouncing the recent events. Demonstrations also broke out in Florence and Livorno, resulting in a number of deaths when police again fired upon protestors. On the same day, the Italian government declared martial law and a state of siege in Lombardy, and the Italian general Fiorenzo Bava-Beccaris, who had a long and storied career, was dispatched to Milan. Infantry, cavalry and artillery were also dispatched at speed, and by the time he arrived the general had upward of 45,000 troops at his disposal.

On 7 May, some 60,000 people took to the streets, protesting the cost of wheat and bread. Spreading from the working-class districts of Milan, they converged throughout the day on the city center. Bava-Beccaris deployed his troops in the central square of Milan, the Piazza del Duomo, determined to drive the strikers back. Seeing the crowds approaching, Bava-Beccaris ordered his troops to fire on the protestors, and he also ordered artillery to fire into their ranks. According to government sources, some 80 demonstrators were killed, with more than 450 injured. The demonstrators themselves claimed that 400 people were killed and more than 2,000 wounded. The *New York Times* split the difference, claiming that 300 people had been killed, with 1,000 injured.[33] Whatever the ghoulish mathematics, by the time the smoke had cleared and the cannons had quieted, the streets around the Duomo were drenched with civilian blood. Bava-Beccaris was not yet finished, however. On 9 May, artillery was used to smash open the walls of a monastery in the Porta Monforte district in Milan. Bava-Beccaris may have truly believed that the monastery was a nest of radical demonstrators; however, as reported in the press at the time,[34] the inhabitants included monks and the poor and needy who had been waiting for food and alms. The death toll from this single artillery assault was initially reported as being 80 but soon grew to hundreds. Following these events, ad-hoc tribunals were established and some 1,500 people were sentenced to prison. In one of the most egregious of these imprisonments, a founder of the Socialist Party of Italy, Filippo Turati, was sentenced to twelve years for helping to instigate the rioting. In fact, he had been distributing literature seeking to calm and diffuse the growing unrest and violence.

Given that Bava-Beccaris had fired cannons on protestors and monks alike, and set up what were essentially extrajudicial trials, it would not be unreasonable to expect that his actions would inspire a negative response from the Italian state and its head, King Umberto I. In actuality, the response was quite the reverse. In June 1898, Bava-Beccaris was awarded the Great Cross of the Order of Savoy (*Grande Ufficiale dell'Ordine Militare die Savoia*) medal by Umberto. Rather than seeking to punish a general who had overseen one of the worst massacres in nineteenth-century Italy (one that would only be surpassed by the actions of German occupation troops in Sant'Anna di Stazzema and Marzabotto in 1944), Umberto rewarded him. This action created justifiable outrage in Italy and beyond.

Among the Italian expatriate community in Paterson, New Jersey, news of the Milanese bread massacre caused outrage. One particular individual who expressed anger at the massacre, and the monarch who had watched it happen, was Gaetano Bresci. Bresci was born on 10 November 1869 in Coiano, a district in the Tuscan city of Prato. His father, Gaspare Bresci, and mother, Maddalena Godi, were, according to all accounts, not as poverty-stricken as Passannante had been, but they were hardly members of the middle class, though they did in all likelihood own property.[35] By the time Bresci was in his teens, he was already a political prisoner. As an apprentice silk weaver, he gradually grew politicized due to the treatment that was inflicted on many of his peers. According to some reports,[36] by the age of fifteen, Bresci was a member of an unnamed Anarchist group in Prato, and in 1892 he was sentenced to 15 days in jail for contempt and insubordination to the police. At age twenty-three, Bresci was classified as a "dangerous anarchist." How this impacted his weaving career is not clear, but, after a brief stint in Milan,[37] Bresci was exiled to the island of Lampedusa under special measures introduced by the then Italian prime minister, Francesco Crispi, in 1895.

Unlike many of his peers, Bresci was fortunate in that his time on Lampedusa was limited, and he received a formal amnesty in 1896. Upon his repatriation to the Italian mainland, Bresci was able to find work at a wool factory, Michele Tisi & Co. Here, according to Arrigo Petacco,[38] Bresci acquired the nickname of the "Dandy" owing to the attention he gave to his dress and his frequent visits to barbers and restaurants. Bresci also regularly practiced with a pistol he had managed to acquire. Another of his preferred pastimes, as with many other young men then and now, was engaging in affairs with his female co-workers. Petacco suggests that Bresci may have fathered a child with a female co-worker by the name of Maria. Perhaps to avoid the responsibilities of fatherhood, or for broader political reasons, Bresci decided to immigrate to the United States. He borrowed some thirty pounds from his family, allegedly giving some money to Maria for the care of his child, before setting sail for America. Bresci arrived on Ellis Island on 8 February 1897 on board the ship *Columbia* from Genoa[39] along with twenty-five other passengers.

New York in the latter part of the nineteenth century could be brutal for recently arrived unskilled immigrants, as indeed it had always been. Fortunately for Bresci, although he was a new arrival, he had a number of distinct advantages. At some point prior to leaving for the United States, Bresci had taught himself English, and, unlike many who arrived with nothing but a few possessions and limited savings, he also had a number of contacts already settled in Paterson, New Jersey.[40] Paterson was known as "Silk City," and out of just over a hundred thousand people living there by the time of Bresci's arrival, more than ten thousand were skilled Italian weavers. Given his profession, and his knowledge of some of the other residents of the city, it was almost inevitable that Bresci would move to Paterson. Before he did, however, Bresci first settled in New Hoboken, where he met (and possibly married[41]) an Irish immigrant, Sophie Kneiland, with whom he was to have two children, Madeleine and Gaetanina.

At the time of Bresci's arrival, Paterson was already forming strong workers' organizations to combat the conditions that many faced in the mills.[42] It did not take long for Bresci to become involved. According to reports that were published several years later,[43] Bresci became part of the Gruppo diritti all' esistenza (Right to Existence) Anarchist organization, regularly attending its Wednesday meetings, and was also one of the founders of the Italian-language Anarchist paper, *La Questione Sociale*. Bresci was employed in the silk mills of Paterson (including the Hamil and Booth silk mill) and was comparatively wealthy, earning some $15 a week. He was also clearly committed to the cause, inasmuch as he was able to, according to Emma Goldman, lend $150 to *La Questione Sociale* during a critical period. Many who write about Bresci assume that he must have been a fulltime firebrand, but although he was a skillful propagandist, he was also a young father who probably enjoyed the plentiful beer that accompanied the discussions of social problems at the weekly meetings he attended.[44] Perhaps he would have remained engaged in politics but largely lost to history were it not for the Bava-Beccaris massacre of 1898 (discussed earlier in this chapter).

The news of the events in Milan spread quickly through the Italian community in the United States, and Bresci was particularly affected. According to Sophie, Bresci wept and cursed the "murderer king" and his role in the events in Milan.[45] This allegation is further supported by statements made by Bresci himself: "When in Paterson I read about the events in Milan where even cannon were used [against the protesters], I wept from anger and I prepared myself for revenge…. Besides avenging the victims, I also wanted to revenge myself, forced, after a very difficult life to emigrate."[46] In May 1900, Bresci approached *La Questione Sociale* and asked for the return of his $150. He used the repaid loan to purchase a Hamilton and Booth revolver[47] and a one-way ticket back to Italy.

Immediately after returning to Italy, Bresci returned to Prato, where he studiously practiced with his new revolver much as he had done before leaving for Paterson. After staying with his sister in Castel San Pietro Terme, he finally made his way to Milan. While there, Bresci learned that Umberto I was due to attend a gymnastics competition in Monza before attending an awards ceremony for the sports society Forti e Liberi. The monarch would be staying in his nearby palace, Villa Reale Monza, for the duration of

July. Bresci traveled from Milan to Monza and soon found a room on Via Cairoli, near the train station, where he waited for his opportunity to come.

Sunday, 29 July 1900, had been a sweltering day. More than 2,000 spectators had crowded into the outdoor sports complex to watch the gymnastics competition. Umberto I set off on the sparsely protected route (later reports indicated that there may have been as few as ten carabinieri lining the route between the palace and the sports field[48]) at approximately 9:30 p.m., arriving to distribute the medals at 10:00 p.m. The field and crowds were illuminated by electric arc lights, casting shadows in which unseen threats could hide. After awarding medals to the winning athletes, the king returned to his carriage, and overexcited members of the crowd surged forward from their seats, blocking its departure. From three rows back in the crowd, Bresci stood on his seat, some twelve feet away from Umberto, and raised his 32-caliber revolver. In rapid succession, he fired four shots at the monarch, all of which slammed into his body. As the king collapsed backward, bleeding profusely and past medical help, Bresci was wrestled to the ground by angry members of the crowd before being retrieved from what could have devolved into an impromptu lynching by the marshal of the carabinieri, Andrea Braggio. Bresci allowed himself to be arrested without a struggle, pausing only to state, "I did not kill Umberto. I have killed the King. I killed a principle."[49] Bresci had finally succeeded where both Passannante and Acciarito had failed.

The fate that befell Bresci was no less brutal than that faced by the earlier would-be regicides. Following a swift trial in which he was defended by the lawyer Francesco Saverio Merlino, Bresci was convicted of the murder of Umberto I and sentenced to life imprisonment in Santo Stefano prison on the desolate and isolated Pontine Islands. Here he was to be held in a special cell measuring 10 feet by 10 feet, devoid of all furnishings and with his feet constantly shackled. On 22 May 1901, Bresci was found hanged in his spartan cell, with the word "Vengeance" carved into the wall.[50] Whether Bresci acted alone in both the assassination of Umberto and his own death is contested to this day. The likelihood is that given Italian jurisprudence during this period, and the severity of the offense for which he was convicted, prison guards may well have been responsible for his demise.

The actions of Passannante, Acciarito and Bresci eventually led to the death of Umberto I and influenced many other disciples of propaganda of the deed. Although Bresci's actions were derided in a 2 August editorial of the official Italian socialist newspaper, *Avanti!*, as those of a "criminal madman,"[51] they undoubtedly served as an inspiration for some (most notably Leon Czolgosz), and he is still remembered both in his home of Prato (where a street was named after him in 1976) and in a number of memorials. The Italian monarchy of the late nineteenth and early twentieth centuries oversaw an economically fractured society and even rewarded massacres. It can come as no major surprise that those Italians influenced by thinkers such as Errico Malatesta decided to take action, however brutal, in response to the brutality that they faced.

Marsh-Bloom (Voltairine de Cleyre)

Source: The Anarchist Library (Voltairine de Cleyre, "Collected Poems," 1901), https://theanarchistlibrary.org/library/voltairine-de-cleyre-collected-poems (accessed March 2017)

To Gaetano Bresci

Requiem, requiem, requiem,
Blood-red blossom of poison stem
Broken for Man,
Swamp-sunk leafage and dungeon-bloom,
Seeded bearer of royal doom,
What now is the ban?

What to thee is the island grave?
With desert wind and desolate wave
Will they silence Death?
Can they weight thee now with the heaviest stone?
Can they lay aught on thee with "Be alone,"
That hast conquered breath?

Lo, "it is finished"—a man for a king!
Mark you well who have done this thing:
The flower has roots;
Bitter and rank grow the things of the sea;
Ye shall know what sap ran thick in the tree
When ye pluck its fruits.

Requiem, requiem, requiem,
Sleep on, sleep on, accused of them
Who work our pain;
A wild Marsh-blossom shall blow again
From a buried root in the slime of men,
On the day of the Great Red Rain.

Alla stazion di Monza (At the Station of Monza—Anonymous)

Source: Anti-War Songs, https://www.antiwarsongs.org/canzone.php?id=55504& lang=en (accessed March 2017)

Alla stazion di Monza	At the station of Monza
arriva un tren che ronza	comes a message buzzing
hanno ammazzato il re	They killed the king
colpito con palle tre	He's hit by three balls.
Bruceremo le chiese e gli altari,	We'll burn the churches and altars,
bruceremo i palazzi e le regge	we'll burn the palaces and holds
con le budella dell'ultimo prete	with the entrails of the last priest
impiccheremo il papa e il re	We will hang the pope and the king.
Rivoluzione sia, guerra alla società,	Revolution is, war on society,
rivoluzione sia, guerra alla società.	revolution is, war on society.
Piuttosto che vivere, che vivere così,	Rather than live, than to live like this,
meglio morire per la libertà,	better to die for freedom,
meglio morire per la libertà.	better to die for freedom.
E il Vaticano brucerà	It will burn the Vatican
E il Vaticano brucerà	It will burn the Vatican
E il Vaticano brucerà	It will burn the Vatican
con dentro il papa	with the pope inside.
E se il governo si opporrà	And if the government will oppose

E se il governo si opporrà
E se il governo si opporrà
rivoluzione!
Rivoluzione sia, guerra alla società,
rivoluzione sia, guerra alla società,
piuttosto che vivere, che vivere così,
meglio morire per la libertà,
meglio morire per la libertà.

And if the government will oppose
And if the government will oppose
revolution!
Revolution is, war on society,
revolution is, war on society,
rather than live, than to live like this,
better to die for freedom,
better to die for freedom.

Five

Machines Infernales

Nineteenth-century France was a deeply iniquitous society. The Industrial Revolution had mutated into a lengthy depression, and the situation within France was even more pronounced. Having been defeated in the Franco-Prussian War (19 July 1870–10 May 1871), France was required, as part of the reparations to Germany, to pay the sum of $250 million. This disaster was followed by the global crash of 1873. Although the economic depression seemed to lift in 1880 (at least in the United States), the Paris Bourse crash of 1882 precipitated the worst financial crisis within the French economy in the nineteenth century. Frequent diseases affecting both silk and grapes caused even more financial chaos. Into this turmoil in the small town of Saint-Chamond, upper Loire, François Claudius Koenigstein (who would later come to be labeled the "King of the Anarchists"[1]) was born on 14 October 1859.

The young François was the son of a Dutch father, Jean Adam Koenigstein, and a French mother, Marie Ravachol.[2] This family was like numerous others in France during this period, inasmuch as they were practically destitute. Many families were not only financially poor but also fragmented. When François was eight years old, his father left Saint-Chamond, possibly in pursuit of work or possibly to escape the burdens of a common-law wife and children. Although Koenigstein was a laminator by trade, he had also previously been arrested and briefly imprisoned for assaulting a works foreman, and troubles with the law may have precipitated his departure. Whatever his reasons for leaving, he never returned; as a result, François took his mother's maiden name in his eighth year and was forced to seek employment to support himself, his mother and his siblings. From that point on, he would be known as Ravachol, and it was this name that would become tightly bound up with the history of propaganda of the deed in France and beyond.

The town of Saint-Chamond was during this period a place of coal mines, steel, iron and glass works, as well as silk and ribbon factories. An industrial town, it provided many employment opportunities (though usually poorly paid) even for eight-year-olds like young François Ravachol. Following the departure of his father, Ravachol was able to secure employment as a dyer's assistant in the silk and ribbon factories of his hometown. Such employment may have provided him with a basic knowledge of chemistry that would prove very useful to him in the future. During this time, his younger sister died and his older sister gave birth to an illegitimate child. When Ravachol was eighteen, he read a copy of *Le Juif Errant* (The Wandering Jew), an 1844 novel written by Eugène Sue.[3] This bleak tale of cholera and Jesuit corruption led Ravachol to lose faith in religion.

Like many working-class young men of the period, Ravachol began to embrace Anarchist politics, and he started attending meetings and joining labor groups seeking to organize and improve working conditions within the heavily industrialized factories of France. As a result of his nascent political activities, Ravachol lost his position as a dyer's assistant. Although he had some skills as an accordion player and was able to utilize these to play "at a few small festivals to earn a little money,"[4] this was far from a reliable or well-paid position. To address that problem, Ravachol set himself to, in his own apparently misspelled words, "making false money, a means not very lucratif and but dangerous."[5] The reasons for his subsequent actions become even more apparent in a final statement published after his execution: "What can he who lacks the necessities when he's working do when he loses his job? He has only to let himself die of hunger. Then they'll throw a few pious words on his corpse. This is what I wanted to leave to others. I preferred to make of myself a trafficker in contraband, a counterfeiter, a murderer and assassin."[6]

Ravachol's next foray into criminality was a dramatic and venal one. According to the account provided by Ernest Vizetelly,[7] Ravachol committed a string of crimes, starting with a double murder. (It is should be borne in mind that, in addition to being an author, Vizetelly was a journalist and experienced war correspondent. When his book was first published, Anarchists were the boogeymen of Europe (sometimes with valid reason), and it is perhaps worth considering the wider influence of society as well as the sometimes sensationalist nature of journalism at the time when discussing Vizetelly's account. That said, Vizetelly may well have had closer access to source materials that have subsequently been lost.)

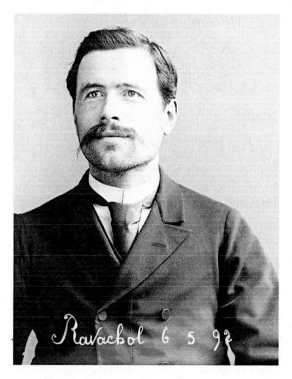

François Claudius Koenigstein, a.k.a. Ravachol

On the night of 29 March 1886, the twenty-seven-year-old Ravachol, according to Vizetelly, walked the several miles from the industrial heart of Saint-Chamond to the small village of La Varizelle. This village was the home of eighty-six-year-old Monsieur Rivollier and his elderly female servant, Mrs. Fradel. Rivollier was, according to local gossip, possessed of considerable wealth, something that Ravachol himself was not. Perhaps inspired by politics, desperation, or psychosis, Ravachol pried open a window of Rivollier's house and soon found himself in the octogenarian's bedroom. Raising the hatchet he had used to gain access to the house above his head, Ravachol bought it down upon that of his victim, "kill[ing] him by splitting his skull."[8] The servant, Mrs. Fradel, heard a disturbance and, peering into the bedroom, saw the scene of carnage within. Sensibly, she fled screaming from the scene. However, she was no match for Ravachol, who soon caught up with her outside the house, killing her before she could raise the alarm. Returning to the house, he searched it, and then he calmly returned to the lodging he shared in Saint-Chamond with his then partner, Mademoiselle Rulhiere. The exact sum he obtained from this double murder has been lost to history; however, according to Mademoiselle Rulhiere, it was a small amount. Following the brutal crime, the local gendarmerie searched the area. The investigation, such as it was, resulted in the arrest of four or five suspicious characters (probably passing itinerant workers) who were all subsequently interrogated and released. It should be noted that Ravachol never admitted to this crime and spent much of his trial both publicly and privately denying it.

For the next five years, Ravachol worked in a variety of jobs, all of which he lost. In May 1891, he found himself without either a job or any money. A fortnight following the May Day protest in Fourmies, at which troops fired on textile workers seeking an eight-hour working day, resulting in the deaths of nine people and the injury of at least thirty more,[9] a ghoulish opportunity presented itself to Ravachol. In the spring of 1891 the Countess de la Rochetaille had died and was interred between the towns of Saint-Étienne and Saint-Chamond in the cemetery of Saint Jean de Bonnefond. According to local gossip, the countess had been buried while bedecked in her not inconsiderable collection of jewelry. For an opportunist criminal with no income, and a belief that it was immoral for the bourgeoisie to retain their wealth in death when the poor had none while alive, this situation presented an intriguing possibility.

Sometime during the night, Ravachol set off from Saint-Chamond and made the slow 4.5-mile walk to the cemetery. He traveled light, bringing with him only the few tools he could carry unobtrusively. Reaching the barred gates of the cemetery, Ravachol scaled the walls and headed toward the grave of the Countess de la Rochetaille. Using the tools he had brought with him and his brute strength, Ravachol removed the stones that covered the coffin and broke it open. He searched for the jewelry that was supposedly interred with the corpse, but all he found was a small religious medallion affixed to the countess's body on a ribbon around her rapidly decaying neck. Ravachol tore the ribbon from the corpse's neck and flung it and a small wooden cross aside, and then he left the cemetery as silently and unseen as when he had arrived.

Owing to his failure to secure any jewelry during his attempt at grave robbing, Ravachol was by June 1891 probably in dire financial straits. These may have led to the murder he did ultimately confess to, that of the so-called hermit of Chambles, a small village situated on the outskirts of Saint-Étienne. At this time Ravachol may have been working in the casual capacity of an accordionist in Saint-Étienne, and it was possibly in this capacity that he heard of the hermit. Jacques Brunel was known to locals as a reclusive figure. Since 1840 he had lived in a hillside cabin above Chambles and received food and clothing from the surrounding residents. He was known to be frugal in his spending habits, and so it was assumed that, as his food, drink, and clothing were all provided by others, he might well possess significant cash reserves.

On the morning of 19 June 1891, Ravachol took a train to Saint-Victor-sur-Loire and set out on foot to nearby Chambles. He was spotted on the road by a passing girl, to whom he reportedly gave a penny. Unaware of Ravachol's approach, Jacques Brunel was inside his cabin recovering from a morning of gardening. Ravachol gained entry to the hermit's cabin (probably through a cellar) and, in doing so, woke him from his slumbers. Seeing the hermit lying in the corner on his disorganized pallet bed, Ravachol produced a fifty-franc note. One of the sources of income that Brunel was known to have at this time was saying prayers for the passing public. It should be remembered that France at this time was a highly religious and, to some extent, superstitious place, and, for a believer, having prayers imparted by a supposedly pious hermit who had rejected the trappings of civilization could potentially elevate the impact of such prayers. Ravachol requested that Brunel say such prayers for him, with the proviso that he was only willing to pay twenty francs and thus would require change from the fifty-franc note. Brunel denied having any money to give Ravachol and attempted to rise from his bed. Seeing the distrust (and probably shock at finding a stranger in his house) on Brunel's face, Ravachol launched himself at the elderly hermit. Having first stuffed a handkerchief into the hermit's mouth, Ravachol held Brunel down, strangling him with his own pillow, until the hermit ceased his feeble struggling.

Following the murder of Brunel, Ravachol searched the cabin from top to bottom. Eventually, he found what he was looking for: in a cupboard, in a cooking pot, under the hermit's bed, and in a loft, Ravachol discovered a variety of gold, silver, and copper coinage in excess of 25,000 francs. After stuffing his pockets with as much gold and silver as he could carry, he calmly left the cabin and returned to the nearby railway station. Following an omelet and wine at the station café, a satiated Ravachol returned to the cabin and began the laborious task of sorting the hermit's treasury. Realizing that there was more present than could be carried away, Ravachol left his victim, his money, and other assorted valuables and clothing he had gathered up in his search of the property before returning the following day with a bag with which to carry the coinage away. On his return trip, Ravachol also bought with him his mistress, La Rulhiere. Following the removal of goods from Brunel's cabin, Ravachol returned to Saint-Étienne. It was later on the afternoon of 20 June that Brunel's body was found by one of the residents of Chambles.

The violent murder and robbery of a pious ninety-two-year-old hermit was a shock to the residents of Chambles and the surrounding area, but, with canvassing, the local gendarmerie were quickly able to determine a suspect. As Vizetelly notes, Ravachol "had been noticed on his journeys backwards, and forwards"[10] to the small town and to the train station that served it, and on 27 June 1891 he was arrested at his home, as was La Rulhiere and two local traders in stolen goods, Pierre Crozet and Claude Fachard. While being transferred on foot to the Saint-Étienne police station, the group was interrupted when a drunken stranger crashed into them. While the police were distracted by the drunk, Ravachol took the opportunity to slip away. It remains a mystery whether the drunk who allowed Ravachol to make good his escape was an actual stranger or an accomplice working in tandem. After allowing such a distraction to facilitate an escape, the commissioner of the local gendarmerie, Teychené, was both penalized and removed from the district. La Rulhiere,[11] Crozet and Fachard were also removed from the district when they received sentences of seven-, five- and one-year imprisonments, respectively. As for Ravachol, he had seemingly disappeared.

A few days following Ravachol's escape, a pair of handcuffs similar to the one he had been wearing while the police dealt with a passing drunk was recovered atop a pile of coal in a Saint-Étienne coal shed. Following this discovery, the hat and coat that Ravachol had been wearing when he had escaped police custody were found on the banks of the Rhône near Lyons, together with a supposed suicide note that read, "Comrades, not wanting to be allowed to play bourgeois justice ... I decided to end my life. I only regret one thing: not having had time to put the money in a safe place so that the propaganda would have benefited at least.... Goodbye to all, and long live anarchy!"[12] As France was soon to learn, Ravachol's supposed suicide was a ruse, and sadly his body would not wash up on the shores of the Rhône any time soon.

Following his escape from the gendarmerie and faking his own death, Ravachol found himself at the home of Jus-Beala and Mariette Soubert in Saint-Étienne. He was by all accounts[13] still present in Saint-Étienne when a murder occurred on 27 July 1891. On the Rue de Roanne, Madame Marcon ran an ironmonger's shop with her forty-six-year-old daughter. At around 10:00 p.m., two men entered the shop; after purchasing a shoemaker's hammer, they used it to bludgeon the daughter and her mother, who was sleeping in the room at the rear of the shop. Although Ravachol and Jus-Beala were presumed to be involved in this murder, with Soubert acting as lookout, their involvement was never categorically proven. Indeed, Soubert and Jus-Beala were subsequently exonerated of the attack, and Ravachol (who was far from shy about admitting to his transgressions) always denied his involvement. Additionally, the motivation for the violent murder of the two women seems to have been robbery, and it is very unlikely that Ravachol would have required any additional funds following the brutal murder of Brunel, the Chambles hermit.

Wanted for murder in Saint-Étienne (the authorities were rightly suspicious of his supposed suicide), Ravachol left town with Soubert and Jus-Beala in tow and soon found himself in the northern suburb of Paris, Saint-Denis, under the assumed identity of Louis Leger. Here Ravachol would form a group with Soubert, Jus-Beala, and an eighteen-year-old apprentice Simon (also known as "Biscuit" or "Cookie" for reasons that are lost to history) and embark on a bombing campaign that would gravely concern the Parisian bourgeoisie of the day.

The May Day protest in Fourmies, which left protestors dead in 1891, was not the only strife upon which Parisian Anarchists were focused. In addition to the grinding economic conditions of the time, and the lack of legal rights and protections, a number of other state actions had helped to foster discontent. In 1891 a protest occurred in the Levallois commune of Paris, timed to coincide with other actions throughout France. Upward of thirty demonstrators sought to parade from Levallois-Perret in Clichy. Following the protest, at around 3:00 p.m. on 1 May 1891, a decision was made by the gendarmerie to attempt to seize the red flag that the protestors had marched behind. People started shoving, and shots were fired. When the smoke lifted, there were no casualties (unlike in Fourmies), but the police had arrested three supposed anarchists—namely, Henry Louis Decamps, Charles Augustus Dardare, and Louis Leveillé, the latter of whom had been shot and injured in the protest. Following their detention, Decamps, Dardare, and Leveillé were transferred to the police station, where, like many protestors before them, they were severely beaten.[14]

Initially largely ignored by the Anarchist press, and overshadowed by the Fourmies protest, the clash at Clichy soon started to circulate as a major topic of interest owing to the response not only of a violent police force but also of an equally violent and brutal judiciary. At the trial of Decamps, Dardare and Leveillé, the advocate General, Léon Bulot, called for the death penalty for the defendants. Although this was ultimately ruled against, the trio did receive sentences that ranged between three and five years in prison. The treatment of the accused, from beating to sentencing, was widely published in Anarchist newspapers of the time such as *The Revolt*, and Ravachol would certainly have been aware of these events, in addition to the French state's ongoing repression of dissenters (including members of the Paris Commune of 1871), and, indeed, he would later justify his subsequent actions as being enacted "'to avenge,' he said, 'the abominable violences committed against our friends, Decamps, Leveille, and Dardare.'"[15]

On the night of 7 March 1892, Ravachol and his group constructed a crude bomb consisting of dynamite and iron debris in a pot. The initial plan was to detonate the device outside the police station at Clichy where, only a few months earlier, officers had shot, detained, and beaten Decamps, Dardare and Leveillé. For reasons that are lost to history, this attack was not carried out, and the group instead turned its attention to the prosecutors of the unlucky trio. Sometime during the early hours of 11 March 1892, Ravachol could be found on the Boulevard Saint-Germain opposite the darkened house that belonged to the individual in charge of the Clichy prosecution case, Edmond Benoît. Armed with a pistol and a pot filled with fifty sticks of dynamite and iron debris, which had been transported across Paris under the skirts of Mariette Soubert, Ravachol broke into Benoît's house. Leaving the crude bomb on the second-floor landing, Ravachol and his group withdrew into the night as the bomb exploded, causing widespread property damage (including destroying the staircase it had been placed on) but failing to injure anyone.

Obviously a bomb being detonated in the heart of Paris in the home of a prosecutor caused an uproar in both the press of the day and the public consciousness. Another bombing came only days later, when, on the night of 18 March, a device exploded at the Lobau Barracks, behind the Hotel-de-Ville. Like the earlier attack against the home of Benoît, the explosion caused widespread property damage but did not result in any casualties. Initially, Ravachol and his associates were blamed for this detonation as well, but ultimately they were found to be innocent of this attack, which had been carried out by another Parisian Anarchist (a carpenter by trade named Meunier) operating independently of Ravachol. However, it was not long before another bomb blast woke the people of Paris from their sleep, and this explosion was certainly the doing of Ravachol.

Following the first attack against Edmond Benoît, Ravachol and his young accomplice, Simon, created a much more potent bomb than the one they had initially used. Rather than being carried in a pot and consisting of fifty sticks of dynamite, this device could be carried in a valise and was approximately double the capacity of the first explosive device. They intended to utilize this new bomb against Advocate General Bulot, who had sat in judgment of (and called for the death penalty for) Decamps, Dardare and Leveillé. Before the device could be detonated, however, an informant led the gendarmerie to arrest Simon. Ravachol, as he had before, managed to evade arrest, and the plan was still in motion. On the morning of 27 March 1892, Ravachol stood outside No. 39 in the Rue de Clichy, where he knew that Bulot kept an apartment. However, Ravachol could not be sure which apartment in the bourgeois apartment building belonged to the judge, so, in keeping with his earlier methodology, he left the device on the second-story landing, lit it, and promptly left the scene.

The first explosion caused by Ravachol had created some property damage; the second explosion caused No. 39 to be reduced to its foundations. Amid the smoke and rubble, miraculously nobody was killed. There is some debate as to whether the explosion resulted in any injuries (Mitch Abidor disputes the account of Vizetelly), but it does not take a huge leap to conclude that if a crowded building is reduced to rubble, injuries of some sort may occur. Numerous reports put the number of injuries at six or seven, some allegedly serious in nature. Following the bomb blast, Ravachol calmly made his way to a restaurant owned by a Monsieur Very on Boulevard Magenta. The concept of an Anarchist bomber relaxing in a restaurant following a successful attack is perhaps somewhat disingenuous, so it is worth clarifying that Very's establishment was a mixture of wine shop and restaurant in the most basic sense of the word. It was perhaps closer to a café than an epitome of formal dining.

Monsieur Very operated his restaurant in conjunction with his wife, Mademoiselle Lhérot, whose brother would prove instrumental in Ravachol's downfall. On that fateful morning, Lhérot, working as a waiter, engaged in a conversation about military service with Ravachol, who (never one to miss an opportunity for propaganda) spoke to him about Anarchism. In the course of the conversation, Ravachol imparted news about the explosion that had only hours before devastated much of Rue de Clichy, along with details of the earlier attack on Boulevard Saint-Germain that were largely unknown at the time. Although not initially suspicious, Lhérot noted a scar on Ravachol's hand. When a police description circulated of Ravachol, including the scar on his left hand, Lhérot took notice. "Three days later, Ravachol returned to dine in the same place. The waiter by then had seen a newspaper description of Ravachol, and instead of going to get the first course, he went to see the patron, who returned with the police."[16] The gendarmerie were finally able to detain and arrest Ravachol, although doing so was allegedly arduous inasmuch as, according to contemporary reports, it required ten men to control him. Unlike their colleagues in Saint-Étienne, the Parisian gendarmerie were not distracted by passing drunks, and Ravachol soon found himself detained in police custody.

Barely four weeks after his imprisonment, Ravachol was due to stand trial at the Paris Assizes, along with several other defendants, including the unlucky Simon, on 26 April. The court was heavily guarded and largely surrounded by the gendarmerie, with police escorts for the judge, jurors, and legal counsel. The reason for this increased level of security was simple, if troubling. Since the arrest of Ravachol, Lhérot had regaled all visitors to Very's restaurant with his part in the now infamous defendant's arrest. The evening prior to the commencement of the trial, an explosion tore through the restaurant, resulting in the death of the proprietor, Monsieur Very, and one of his patrons, Hamonod. The boastful waiter, Lhérot (who was in all probability the intended victim of the bombing), survived, and the two bombers, who were part of Ravachol's circle, Meunier and Francois, made good an escape to London (albeit a temporary one, as they were extradited in 1894).

Once the defendants had been escorted to the dock, Ravachol, Jus-Beala, Simon, and Mariette Soubert found themselves facing down the powers of the French state and the witness testimony of Ravachol's one-time mistress Chaumentin. Ravachol was keen to assume personal responsibility for the bombing campaign that had preceded his arrest, and he denied the involvement of the other defendants. For Jus-Beala and Mariette Soubert, this proved a useful legal strategy, and they were subsequently acquitted and released. However, Ravachol and his young apprentice, Simon, were both sentenced to life sentences. For Simon, this was to prove his undoing, as he was subsequently killed in an uprising at the penal colony to which he was transported. However, Ravachol—for the time being—had managed to escape with his life.

Ravachol was still very much of interest to the Parisian authorities, and he found himself in the dock of the Assize Court at Montbrison on 21 June (with both Jus-Beala and Mariette Soubert) to face charges for the string of murders and robberies highlighted elsewhere in this chapter. Once again he found himself confronted with a former mistress, this time in the form of La Rulhiere, "at the sight of whom he shed tears, whilst she for her part declared that she still loved him, and had accused him wrongly before the accusing magistrate."[17] The defendants denied all charges, with the exception of Ravachol, who accepted legal responsibility for both the robbery of Countess de la Rochetaille's grave and the murder of the hermit of Chambles (whom he claimed had only been murdered when a simple burglary was discovered). Again, luck was with Jus-Beala and Mariette Soubert, and they were charged only with having sheltered Ravachol, thus receiving light sentences. In a packed courtroom filled with fifty members of the press, as well as Ravachol's sister, Josephine, and brother, Henri Koenigstein, the judge decreed that Ravachol was to be executed. The press took furious notes, Josephine fainted, and Ravachol, appearing both calm and controlled, declared chillingly that he knew he would be avenged prior to exclaiming "Vive l'Anarchie!" as he was removed from the dock.

Ravachol's execution was scheduled for 11 July 1892, and he passed his time in jail awaiting it largely without incident. He refused visitations from the prison chaplain and also refused to appeal for clemency. At 3:00 a.m. on 11 July, Ravachol was awakened from what witnesses reported as a deep sleep and transported to the place of public execution, on the corner of the Rue du Palais de Justice and Rue des Prisons: a crossroads named "Place des Prisons." While being transported, the prison chaplain attempted to engage Ravachol in confession; instead of piety, he was greeted with a ribald and singing Ravachol, who declared, "If you want to live a happy life, hang your boss, and cut the priests in two." In the early light of dawn, Ravachol found himself face down on the guillotine at 4:00 a.m. As the blade fell, Ravachol made what was to be his final proclamation, "Vive l'Re—" (presumed by history to be "Vive l'Revolution!"), only to have it interrupted as the blade sliced through his neck.[18]

Ravachol's death did not end the troubles of the French state. In the wake of his execution, a series of bombs were detonated across Paris by those seeking to emulate his actions. For some in the French Anarchist community, Ravachol achieved an almost messianic status; indeed, he was subsequently described as a "violent Christ" by Victor Barrucand in the 24 July 1892 edition of *The Endehors* (included in the literary supplement of *Le Révolté*, August 1892). Not everyone was enamored with Ravachol and his actions, however; in the January 1892 edition of *Le Révolté*, Peter Kropotkin (a co-founder of the journal) decried the divisive figure of Ravachol. His campaign of bombings and violence was, according to Kropotkin, only fit for opéra bouffe (a form of late nineteenth-century French operetta, many of which were produced at the Théâtre des Bouffes-Parisiens and often featured overwrought heroines and cape-wearing villains[19]) and consideration by the bourgeoisie of the day. The Italian Anarchist Francesco Saverio Merlino, who would later go on to provide a legal defense for Gaetano Bresci, went further, disavowing Ravachol and stating that "his explosions lose their revolutionary character because of his personality, which is unworthy to serve the cause of humanity."[20] As Alex Butterworth notes, however, the fact that Ravachol "went to the guillotine for the murder of an ancient hermit did nothing to hinder his lionization, and the anarchism that he preached until the very moment the blade fell was immediately taken up by myriad other voices."[21]

Ravachol remains today a deeply divisive figure. He is lauded by some, and his actions excused as a reaction to the gross economic injustices of his age. For others, he remains an example of a moustache-twirling villain suitable only for a bourgeois understanding of Anarchist actions. Arguably, Ravachol was neither a Christ-like figure nor a cartoon villain. In actuality, he was dangerous, destructive, and politically naïve. These, however, were not traits unique to him. In many ways, Ravachol was both emblematic and a product of the dangerous, destructive, and iniquitous age in which he lived. Just as his homicidal actions were inexcusable and the loss of innocent lives shocking, so, too, was the economic system of nineteenth-century France that shaped him and so many of his ilk. Ravachol's true significance comes not in his bombs, his murders, his execution, or even his ego, but rather in his status as an angry, dispossessed product of an angry, dispossessed state.

My Principles (Ravachol)

Source: *Un saint nous est né*, edited by Philippe Oriol (Paris: L'équipement de la pensée, 1992), as referenced by Marxists Internet Archive, https://www.marxists.org/reference/archive/ravachol/1892/principes.htm (accessed December 2016); translated by Mitchell Abidor

While in prison, this document was dictated to the police by Ravachol. It remained unpublished until the historian Jean Maitron found it in the Paris Police Archives in 1964.

The above named, after having eaten his fill, spoke to us as follows:

"Messieurs, it is my habit, wherever I am, to do propaganda work. Do you know what anarchism is?"

We answered "No" to this question.

"This doesn't surprise me," he responded. "The working class which, like you, is forced to work to earn its bread, doesn't have the time to devote to the reading of pamphlets they're given. It's the same for you.

"Anarchy is the obliteration of property.

"There currently exist many useless things; many occupations are useless as well, for example, accounting. With anarchy there is no more need for money, no further need for bookkeeping and the other forms of employment that derive from this.

"There are currently too many citizens who suffer while others swim in opulence, in abundance. This situation cannot last; we all should profit by the surplus of the rich; but even more obtain, like them, all that is necessary. In current society, it isn't possible to arrive at this goal. Nothing, not even a tax on income, could change the face of things. Nevertheless, the bulk of workers think that if we acted in this way, things would improve. It is an error to think this way. If we tax the landlord, he'll increase his rents and in this way will arrange for those who suffer to pay the new charges imposed on them. In any event, no law can touch landlords for, being the masters of their goods, we can't prevent them from doing whatever they want with them. What, then, should be done? Wipe out property and, by doing this, wipe out those who take all. If this abolition takes place, we have to also do away with money, in order to prevent any idea of accumulation, which would force a return to the current regime.

"It is in effect money that is the cause of all discord, all hatred, of all ambitions; it is, in a word, the creator of property. This metal, in truth, has nothing but an agreed upon price, born of its rarity. If we were no longer obliged to give something in exchange for those things we need to live, gold would lose its value and no one would seek it. Nor could they enrich themselves, because nothing they would amass could serve them in obtaining a better life than that of others. There would then no longer be any need of laws, no need of masters.

"As for religions, they'd be destroyed, because their moral influence would no longer have any reason for existence. There would no longer be the absurdity of believing in a God who doesn't exist, since after death everything is finished. So we should hold fast to life, but when I say life I mean life, which does not mean slaving all day to make the bosses fat and, while dying oneself of hunger, become the authors of their well-being.

"Masters aren't necessary, these people whose idleness is maintained by our labor; everyone must make himself useful to society, by which I mean work according to his ability and his aptitude. In this way, one would be a baker, another a teacher, etc. Following this principle, work would diminish, and each of us would have only an hour or two of work a day. Man, not being able to remain without some form of occupation, would find his distraction in work; there would be no lazy idlers, and if they did exist, there'd be so few of them that we could leave them in peace and, without complaint, let them profit from the work of others.

"There being no more laws, marriage would be destroyed. We would unite by inclination, and the family would be founded on the love of a father and mother for their children. For example, if a woman no longer loved he who she had chosen as a companion, she could separate from him and form a new association. In a word, complete freedom to live with those we love. If in the case I just cited there were children, society would raise them, that is to say, those who will love the children will take them in charge.

"With this free union, there will be no more prostitution. Secret illnesses would no longer exist, since these are only born of the abuse of the coming together of the sexes; an abuse to which women are forced to submit, since society's current conditions oblige them to take this up as a job in order to survive. Isn't money necessary in order to live, earned at whatever cost?

"With my principles, which I can't in so little time lay out in full detail, the army will no longer have any reason to exist, since there will no longer be distinct nations; private property would be destroyed, and all nations would have joined into one, which would be the Universe.

"No more war, no more disputes, no more jealousy, no more theft, no more murder, no more court system, no more police, no more administration.

"The anarchists have not yet gone into the details of their constitution: the mileposts alone have been laid out. Today the anarchists are numerous enough to overthrow the current state of things, and if that hasn't yet happened, it's because we must complete the education of the followers, give birth in them to the energy and the firm will to assist in the realization of their projects. All that is needed for that is a shove, that someone put themselves at their head, and the revolution will take place.

"He who blows up houses has as a goal the extermination of all those who, by their social standing or their acts, are harmful to anarchy. If it was permitted to openly attack these people without fearing for the police, and so for one's skin, we wouldn't set out to destroy their homes though explosive devices, which could kill the suffering classes they have at their service at the same time as them."

Ravachol's Forbidden Speech

Source: Marxists Internet Archive, https://www.marxists.org/reference/archive/ravachol/1892/forbidden-speech.htm (accessed December 2016); translated by Mitchell Abidor

On trial for murder after a series of bombings, Ravachol attempted to give the following speech, not to deny his guilt, but to accept and explain it. According to contemporary accounts, he was cut off after a few words, and the speech was never delivered. He was guillotined shortly afterwards.

If I speak, it's not to defend myself for the acts of which I'm accused, for it is society alone which is responsible, since by its organization it sets man in a continual struggle of one against the other. In fact, don't we today see, in all classes and all positions, people who desire, I won't say the death, because that doesn't sound good, but the ill-fortune of their like, if they can gain advantages from this. For example, doesn't a boss hope to see a competitor die? And don't all businessmen reciprocally hope to be the only ones to enjoy the advantages that their occupations bring? In order to obtain employment, doesn't the unemployed worker hope that for some reason or another someone who *does* have a job will be thrown out of his workplace. Well then, in a society where such events occur, there's no reason to be surprised about the kind of acts for which I'm blamed, which are nothing but the logical consequence of the struggle for existence that men carry on who are obliged to use every means available in order to live. And since it's every man for himself, isn't he who is in need reduced to thinking: "Well, since that's the way things are, when I'm hungry I have no reason to hesitate about using the means at my disposal, even at the risk of causing victims! Bosses, when they fire workers, do they worry whether or not they're going to die of hunger? Do those who have a surplus worry if there are those who lack the basic necessities"?

There are some who give assistance, but they are powerless to relieve all those in need and who will either die prematurely because of privations of various kinds, or voluntarily by suicides of all kinds, in order to put an end to a miserable existence and to not have to put up with the rigors of hunger, with countless shames and humiliations, and who are without hope of ever seeing them end. Thus there are the Hayem and Souhain families, who killed their children so as not to see them suffer any longer, and all the women who, in fear of not being able to feed a child, don't hesitate to destroy in their wombs the fruit of their love.

And all these things happen in the midst of an abundance of all sorts of products. We could understand if these things happened in a country where products are rare, where there is famine. But in France, where abundance reigns, where butcher shops are loaded with meat, bakeries with bread, where clothing and shoes are piled up in stores, where there are unoccupied lodgings! How can anyone accept that everything is for the best in a society when the contrary can be seen so clearly? There are many people who will feel sorry for the victims, but who'll tell you they can't do anything about it. Let everyone scrape by as he can! What can he who lacks the necessities when he's working do when he loses his job? He has only to let himself die of hunger. Then they'll throw a few pious words on his corpse. This is what I wanted to leave to others. I preferred to make of myself a trafficker in contraband, a counterfeiter, a murderer and assassin. I could have begged, but it's degrading and cowardly and even punished by your laws, which make poverty a crime. If all those in need, instead of waiting *took*, wherever and by whatever means, the self-satisfied would understand perhaps a bit more quickly that it's dangerous to want to consecrate the existing social state, where worry is permanent and life threatened at every moment.

We will quickly understand that the anarchists are right when they say that in order to have moral and physical peace, the causes that give birth to crime and criminals must be destroyed. We won't achieve these goals in suppressing he who, rather than die a slow death caused by the privations he had and will have to put up with, without any hope of ever seeing them end, prefers, if he has the least bit of energy, to violently take that which can assure his well-being, even at the risk of death, which would only put an end to his sufferings.

So that is why I committed the acts of which I am accused, and which are nothing but the logical consequence of the barbaric state of a society which does nothing but increase the rigor of the laws that go after the effects, without ever touching the causes. It is said that you must be cruel to kill your like, but those who say this don't see that you resolve to do this only to avoid the same fate.

In the same way you, *messieurs* members of the jury, will doubtless sentence me to death, because you think it is necessary, and that my death will be a source of satisfaction for you who hate to see human blood flow; but when you think it is useful to have it flow in order to ensure the security of your existence, you hesitate no more than I do, but with this difference: you do it without running any risk, while I, on the other hand, acted at the risk of my very life.

Well, *messieurs*, there are no more criminals to judge, but the causes of crime to destroy! In creating the articles of the Criminal Code, the legislators forgot that they didn't attack the causes, but only the effects, and so they don't in any way destroy crime. In truth, the causes continuing to exist, the effects will necessarily flow from them. There will always be criminals, for today you destroy one, but tomorrow ten will be born.

What, then, is needed? Destroy poverty, this seed of crime, in assuring to all the satisfaction of their needs! How difficult this is to realize! All that is needed is to establish society on a new basis, where all will be held in common and where each, producing according to his abilities and his strength, could consume according to his needs. Then and only then will we no longer see people like the hermit of Notre-Dame-de-Grace and others, begging for a metal whose victims and slaves they become! We will no longer see women give up their charms, like a common piece of merchandise, in exchange for this same metal that often prevents us from recognizing whether or not affection is sincere. We will no longer see men like Pranzini, Prado, Berland, Anastay and others who kill in order to have this same metal. This shows that the cause of all crimes is always the same, and you have to be foolish not to see this.

Yes, I repeat it: it is society that makes criminals and you, jury members, instead of striking you should use your intelligence and your strength to transform society. In one fell swoop you'll suppress all crime. And your work, in attacking causes, will be greater and more fruitful than your justice, which belittles itself in punishing its effects.

I am nothing but an uneducated worker; but because I have lived the life of the poor, I feel more than a rich bourgeois the iniquity of your repressive laws. What gives you the right to kill or lock up a man who, put on earth with the need to live, found himself obliged to take that which he lacks in order to feed himself?

I worked to live and to provide for my family; as long as neither I nor my family suffered too much, I remained what you call honest. Then work became scarce, and with unemployment came hunger. It is only then that the great law of nature, that imperious voice that accepts no reply, the instinct of preservation, forced me to commit some of the crimes and misdemeanors of which I am accused and which I admit I am the author of.

Judge me, *messieurs* of the jury, but if you have understood me, while judging *me* judge all the unfortunate who poverty, combined with natural pride, made criminals, and who wealth or ease would have made honest men.

An intelligent society would have made of them men like any other!

La Ravachole

Source: Marxists Internet Archive, https://www.marxists.org/reference/archive/ravachol/la-ravachole.htm (accessed December 2016); translated by Mitchell Abidor

Sung to the tune of the song of the French Revolution, la Carmagnole—the chorus of which ends: "Long live the sound of the cannon"—La Ravachole set the spirit of the anarchist Ravachol to music.

> In the great city of Paris,
> There are well-fed bourgeois,
> There are the poor,
> Who have an empty stomach:
> The former are greedy,
> Long live the sound, long live the sound,
> The former are greedy,
> Long live the sound
> Of the explosion!
>
> Let's dance the Ravachole
> Long live the sound, long live the sound
> Let's dance the Ravachole
> Of the explosion!
>
> Ah ça ira ça ira ça ira
> All the bourgeois will taste the bomb
> Ah ça ira ça ira ça ira
> We'll blow up all the bourgeois
> We'll blow them up!
>
> There are sell out magistrates,
> There are big-bellied financiers,
> There are cops,
> But for all these scoundrels,
> There's dynamite,
> Long live the sound, long live the sound,
> There's dynamite,
> Long live the sound,
> Of the explosion!
>
> There are the feeble-minded senators,
> There are the rotten deputies,
> There are the generals,
> Murderers and executioners,
> Butchers in uniform,
> Long live the sound, long live the sound,
> Butchers in uniform,
> Long live the sound
> Of the explosion!

… … …
Ah, goddamit, it's time to put an end to this,
We've moaned and suffered long enough,
No half-way war,
No more cowardly pity,
Death to the bourgeoisie!
Long live the sound, long live the sound
Death to the bourgeoisie!
Long live the sound
Of the explosion!

Six

The French Connection

In the early hours of 5 February 1894, the prefect of the Parisian police, Monsieur Lepine, made his way through the still empty streets of the French capital. His destination was the Place de la Roquette in the eleventh arrondissement, and his purpose was to ensure that the expected demonstrations could not occur. At this same time, the workers were busy at La Roquette Prison. Screws had been tightened, ropes secured, and edges sharpened. After a final inspection from Monsieur Louis Diebler, the state executioner, it was agreed that the guillotine was ready for its grisly purpose. As reported by the press of the time, at "6:45 o'clock the gas lights in the vicinity of the prison began to pale,"[1] and the expectant crowd of seven or eight hundred that had been denied a glimpse of the guillotine thanks to the efforts of Lepine and the gendarmerie grew silent. The only sounds were the marching feet of the twenty-five heavily armed members of the mounted guards as they formed two columns on either side of the heavy wooden prison door leading to the base of the guillotine. Inside, away from the unfolding events that 1,200 people were now attempting to get a view of from adjoining streets and the rooftops of houses, the prisoner Auguste Vaillant stirred in his sleep, waking fully as a prison guard inserted a key into the lock of his cell. His arrival signaled the last few moments of Vaillant's life, and one of the many executions to be performed in nineteenth-century France.

Auguste Vaillant was born on 27 December 1861 in Mézières (later to become Charleville-Mézières when a suspension bridge across the River Meuse was built to join the two communities) in the Ardennes region of northeast France. According to contemporary accounts,[2] his mother, Josephine Rouyer, had been seduced by an unnamed town gendarme. The arrival of Auguste signaled the departure of his mother's paramour, and he abandoned both the boy and his mother to their fates when Vaillant was around ten years old. Little is known of Vaillant's early childhood beyond this early trauma. He was fortunate enough to secure employment as an apprentice pastry cook, but the limited wages he received were insufficient to support his needs, and, as John Merriman states, "he was let go when he got hungry one day and made a cake for himself."[3] Following this incident, at the age of twelve, an aunt with whom Valliant had been living placed the boy on a train to Marseilles.

Unfortunately, she had neglected to purchase a ticket for him, and he was arrested. By this time, his absent father was working as a gendarme on the island of Corsica, and Vaillant was able to secure one last service from him when he paid the fine of sixteen francs.

Released by the authorities in Marseilles, Vaillant now found himself alone, and desperately hungry. He was frequently required to beg and steal food, leading to a number of arrests. Somehow he managed to survive, drifting around France, moving from Marseilles to Paris and even Algeria. During this period Vaillant was able to secure a variety of low-paid jobs, including general laborer and grocer's assistant. At the age of seventeen, Vaillant was arrested for dining in a Parisian restaurant and being unable to pay for the meal he had consumed. Even as a healthy young man, Vaillant had discovered that the wages paid to the working classes of France and the instability of employment did not lead to financial security. It may have been this realization that initially drew him to Socialism.

Auguste Vaillant

By 1885, aged 24, Vaillant was living on Rue Ordener in Paris. Here he found employment as a sales representative for breweries servicing local hostelries. He was also the secretary of the committee of the eighteenth arrondissement of the Socialist Revolutionary Union.[4] He earned little at the time, with barely enough funds to survive, and his knowledge of politics was still largely nascent. According to Charles Malato, "he was not yet acquainted with Proudhon, Karl Marx, Spencer and Kropotkin, the great sociologists; he had only read and repeatedly re-read some popular pamphlets which he purchased for a few sous, and which fertilized his eager brain with ideas as yet unknown to him."[5] Two years later, Vaillant became part of Les Egaux de Montmartre. Originally founded in the working-class northern suburbs of Paris near Saint-Denis, Les Egaux de Montmartre was a Socialist club, but it grew closer to Anarchism as the political situation in France became more volatile. In addition to Vaillant, the club was frequented by Ravachol (whose actions are detailed in the previous chapter) and the Belgian individualist Jean Pauwels.

By September 1890, Vaillant had left Paris for Algeria, where he had secured work in a quarry. This employment, like many jobs that had gone before it, did not last long, and Vaillant would later make his way to the Chaco region of Argentina. Here by some means, according to Ernest Vizetelly, he was able to secure "a concession of 150 acres of land with which he hoped to prosper."[6] According to accounts provided by Malato, this venture was not the lasting success Vaillant may have hoped for when he left his position in Algeria, and he soon found that he was subject to usurious rental terms by the land owners. During his tenure in Argentina, he helped establish an Anarchist journal by the name of *La Liberte* that "may account in a measure for the difficulties in which Vaillant at last found himself."[7] After three years abroad that reduced Vaillant to penury, he was once again back in Paris.

Little is known of Vaillant's actions upon his return to France, and it is unclear whether he remained in the country for long. According to later statements provided to the press by his wife Marchal, Vaillant "passed three months in America teaching school."[8] Research conducted for this publication did not discover any immigration records for this period relating to Vaillant, but his journey back to France from Argentina could conceivably have involved a temporary halt in the United States in order to recoup some of the financial losses he had suffered in Chaco (or, indeed, just to raise the cost of the return fare). By 1893, however, Vaillant had returned from his travels in Argentina (and possibly the United States). Back in Paris, Vaillant found accommodations in Montmatre and married Marchal. Although the young couple's circumstances were bleak, with Vaillant forced to change employment often thanks to the caprices of the market, they were soon joined by a daughter, Sidonie. Following the birth of his daughter, Vaillant secured employment as a leather worker, but his economic circumstances did not improve. As Merriman relates, when Vaillant asked the factory foreman for a raise, as he had a wife and child to support, the reply was brusque: "I don't give a damn about your wife. I hired you."[9] For Vaillant, the rapaciousness of French society and employers and the sheer insecurity of working conditions would serve as motivators for his future actions.

At some juncture in 1893, continued poverty forced Vaillant and his young family to take up residence at the Hotel de l'Union in the Choisy-le-Roi district in the southeastern suburbs of Paris. The small room was split between Vaillant and the first cousin of his wife. Lacking the funds to pay rent for a home of his own, and suffering frequent hunger pangs, Vaillant was still working as a leather worker, producing bags and accessories for the idle rich. He was also politically active, serving as secretary of the bibliothèque philosophique pour l'étude des sciences naturelles (philosophical library for the study of the natural sciences), which was dedicated to advancing knowledge of science, sociology, and politics. Driven by frustration, hunger, and a life that had been forced to be both itinerant and unstable—as well as anger at the execution of his one-time fellow club member, Ravachol—Vaillant decided it was time for action rather than continued debate.

In November 1893, Vaillant borrowed the sum of twenty francs from the wife of the French Anarchist Paul Reclus and fellow Anarchists who were engaging in burglaries to support the cause. He used these funds to rent a room on Rue Laguerre in the fourteenth arrondissement. Here he constructed a small homemade bomb that was composed of green powder, small tacks, and cotton wool soaked in sulfuric acid. By design, the device was intended to injure and scare, rather than to kill. Although an inexperienced bomb maker, Vaillant, like many of his peers, possessed enough practical knowledge of chemistry to be able to determine the difference between a lethal device and a non-lethal one. Although his room in the Rue Laguerre was seldom slept in, according to later reports, it provided enough space, secrecy, and peace for Vaillant to focus on the creation of his bomb. In addition to designing the device, Vaillant used his small flat to select the target of his attack: the French Chamber of Deputies (la Chambre des deputes). Established in 1814, the chamber was home to the French National Assembly.

On the afternoon of 9 December 1893, Vaillant left his small, cramped room on Rue Laguerre and began his journey across Paris to the Palais Bourbon in the seventh arrondissement. By the time he had arrived, the afternoon winter sun bounced off the ripples of the Seine. Days before, Vaillant had obtained a pass for the public gallery. Making his way past a guard at the entrance, Vaillant ascended the stairway to the public gallery and took his seat overlooking the deputies. His intent, according to contemporary reports,[10] was to target the deputies—specifically, Charles Dupuy, who had been appointed president of the Council of Deputies earlier in the year by the loathed French president Sadi Carnot. At approximately 4:00 p.m., Vaillant was sitting in the public balcony next to an unnamed woman. As the deputies went about the business of government, Dupuy rose to his feet; so, too, did Vaillant. The woman sitting next to him saw him produce his homemade device from his pocket, and as he drew back his arm to fling it at Dupuy, she reached for it, and the device spiraled downward. In a flash of light, the bomb exploded, creating panic and confusion. As the smoke cleared, it became clear that multiple deputies had been injured. The unnamed woman who had deflected the bomb had contusions on her arm, and a deputy by the name of Guillotier suffered a fractured skull that later required surgery. Despite the mass of confusion, Dupuy's voice boomed above the chaos: "Messieurs, la séance continue!" (Gentlemen, the meeting continues!)

Vaillant's attack had caused more fear than harm; however, during the course of carrying out his plan, he had also inadvertently harmed himself. Following the attack, Vaillant sought treatment for his wounds at the Hôtel-Dieu de Paris, the central Parisian hospital. He presented himself at the hospital with a significant wound to his nose and minor lacerations to the rest of his body, including cuts to his hands that appeared to have been blackened by gunpowder. In light of the events at the Chamber of Deputies, medical staff were suspicious of his injuries. In response to the attack, the Parisian police sought inspiration in their files.[11] In these records, it was noted that the name of Vaillant featured prominently among the Anarchists of Paris. Reacting to the suspicions of the hospital staff that had been passed along, the police traveled to Vaillant's bedside and secured his full confession only a day after the attack. However, this version of events, which features an incompetent bomber and a seemingly well-orchestrated law enforcement response swinging immediately into effect, is questioned by Bernard Thomas.[12] In his view, the police had employed agent provocateurs to commission Vaillant in the planning of the attack or in the preparation and materials of his device. As a result, it was known to them when the attack would occur, and Dupuy was likewise aware that such an attack would be carried out using a non-lethal device. The attack, as argued by Thomas, also served the interests of the state in terms of its later response.

Two days following Vaillant's attack, and one day after his arrest, the Chamber of Deputies introduced the first of what would come to be known pejoratively as the *lois scélérates* (villainous laws), described by Clyde Thogmartin "as the most serious challenge to press freedom."[13] On 29 July 1881, the French government had introduced the law of freedom of the press, which sought to determine the limits of acceptable printed speech. According to this legislation, direct provocation to criminality, such as a direct call to revolt or murder, in the press would be considered criminal in nature. In the amendment proposed following Vaillant's bombing, indirect provocation or apologist responses to illegality would be declared unlawful. On 12 December 1893, this amendment (which could lead to seizure of assets, arrest, or even preventative arrest of those suspected of potentially breaching the law) was passed by 413 votes to 63. This was the first specific response made by the French state to the supposed Anarchist threat. Less than a week later, on 15 December 1893, a second law, concerned with *associations de malfaiteurs* (association of wrongdoers), was proposed. This law specifically targeted Anarchist groups and permitted the arrest and indictment of members and sympathizers alike, unless they were willing to provide details of their association to the police and thus position themselves as viable informants. The Chamber of Deputies passed this amendment into law on 18 December, but they were not yet finished with legislative changes. The third law was proposed and voted into existence on 28 July 1894, and it concerned *pour réprimer les menées anarchistes* (to quell anarchist schemes). This legislation specifically sought to target French Anarchists, and in its wake hundreds of workers were arrested, resulting in a wave of repression that led to widespread and lengthy prison terms and deportation orders. Although this legislation was only rigorously applied by the French state for less than a year (most controversially in the Trial of the Thirty, at which French intellectuals, journalists, and radical publishers were dragged into the dock), it remained an ever present threat and was only repealed from French law in 1992.

After spending the Christmas period in the bleak setting of La Roquette Prison, Vaillant's trial commenced on 11 January 1894. He was represented by Fernand Labori, who had defended the illegalist Duval seven years earlier (and who would go on to defend the unfortunate Alfred Dreyfus). Unfortunately for Vaillant, the defense that could be provided was limited, as the trial concluded on the same day that it began. Vaillant was not prepared to endure his sentence with no defense, however, and, in a number of exchanges with Presiding Judge Caze,[14] he stated that his attack was intended to publicize the conditions the working and unemployed poor were subjected to in fin-de-siècle Paris and that he had neither killed nor indeed intended to kill with his actions. Despite Labori's request to the jury to "not be intimidated by the suggestion that unless Vaillant shall be executed society is doomed," they pronounced Vaillant guilty. As Caze read out his death sentence, Vaillant was led from the courtroom with a defiant cry of "Long live Anarchy!"

Acting on Vaillant's instructions, Labori did not lodge a legal appeal. Public sympathy concerning the events of Vaillant's life and his family circumstances, however, was pronounced, and not just among the Anarchist or Bohemian communities. The conservative newspaper *Le Figaro* called for a reprieve and began a subscription to benefit Sidonie, Vaillant's daughter. One of the deputies who had been wounded in the attack, Abbe Lemire, circulated a petition that was signed by sixty of her colleagues, seeking clemency on Vaillant's behalf. Even the aristocracy became involved when the Duchess of Uzes offered to adopt Sidonie. However, Vaillant refused this offer, instead authorizing the adoption of his daughter by fellow Anarchist Sebastian Faure, who would later go on to be a defendant in the Trial of the Thirty.

Despite the outpouring of public emotion regarding the case of Vaillant, Dupuy refused to compromise, and French President Sadi Carnot refused all requests for pardon. Clemency declined and popular public opinion ignored, at 7:10 a.m. on 5 February 1894, Vaillant was led from the closed door of La Roquette Prison, past lines of guards, toward the guillotine. As he neared the base of the scaffold, he yelled out, "Death to bourgeois society! Long live Anarchy!"

Following his execution, Vaillant's remains were transferred to a marked plot in the Ivry cemetery. As described by Vizetelly, within twenty-four hours "the cemetery keepers discovered on Vaillant's grave a little pyramid inscribed: Labor improbus omnia vincit (great labor overcomes everything) as well as a card bearing the words 'Glory to thee, I am only a child, but I will avenge thee.'"[15] In addition to anonymous visitors, Vaillant's grave attracted protestors, and the government was forced to respond. On February 13,[16] an order was issued forbidding anyone to visit the grave of Vaillant, and police were stationed to ensure that this dictate was followed. Even in death, Vaillant was in conflict with the state, and the cards and inscriptions left on his windswept grave would prove to be prescient.

Three days prior to Vaillant's execution by the French state, an explosion ripped through the fashionable Café Terminus. Situated near the terminus railway station of Gare Saint-Lazare in Paris, Café Terminus occupied the ground floor of the Hotel Terminus. Constructed some twenty years previously, the hotel attracted a mixture of business travelers and the bourgeoisie, who utilized it as a base for their expeditions and outings around Paris. The café beneath the hotel was a stylish affair and, although it only had a small stage, attracted a broad range of wealthy patrons. Just after 8:00 p.m., a slender young man entered the café. Taking a seat by the stage, he ordered a glass of beer and sipped it slowly. As the small orchestra commenced performing the popular tunes of the period at 8:30 p.m., he signaled a waiter and ordered a second glass of beer and a cigar. By 9:00 p.m. a crowd of some 350 patrons had gathered in the café, and the young man had paid his bill. He stood up and headed toward the door to the street. Opening it, he withdrew a bomb from his coat pocket and lit it using the nub of a cigar that he still had between his lips. Casually he opened the door and threw the device into the midst of the crowded café. The device "struck on the electric lights and then, falling on a marble table, exploded."[17] The young man's actions had been noted by a waiter before the bomb fell, and he promptly chased after the bomber, soon joined by a gendarme and a railway worker as the young man bolted through the Paris streets. For Émile Henry, the chase had commenced.

Émile Henry did not fit the popular image of what Paul Avrich describes as the "the wild-eyed, depraved anarchist"[18] common in fin-de-siècle France. A serious youngster,

Émile Henry

he would mature into a serious young man with an intellectual bent and a passion for social justice. He was also, conversely, responsible for "indiscriminate attacks on ordinary civilians"[19] that would not be out of place in our own volatile modern age. For those who still remember his actions, Émile Henry has become little more than a historical metaphor for the bloodletting of modern terrorists, rather than a reflection of the emaciated poor of his own time. But, as Émile was himself to claim in his own defense, his actions were driven in no small part by the belief that "the whole of the bourgeoisie lives by the exploitation of the unfortunate, and should expiate its crimes."[20] His actions were also motivated by a fervent reaction against the French state that had executed Ravachol and would imminently do the same to Vaillant. How a studious young man made the decision to indiscriminately bomb civilians can perhaps be better understood by examining the past that bought him to such actions.

Émile Henry was born on 26 September 1872, in the Sant Martí de Provençals district of Barcelona, into a political household. His father, Sixte-Casse Henry (known as Fortuné), was a former Communard, poet, and journalist. In his youth, Émile's father had been part of Parisian literary society, and when the Commune was founded, he was elected as a representative for the tenth arrondissement. Fortuné had also spent time in prison in both 1862 and 1863 for his political organizing. Following his release from prison in February 1863, Fortuné turned his back on literary circles and found employment as a leather worker and shoemaker. In 1867 he married a young dressmaker, Rose Caubet, who came from French Catalonia. That same year Fortuné, along with Louise Michel and Marguerite Tinayre, established the Société des équitables de Paris,[21] a workers' education cooperative. During the existence of the Commune, Fortuné was known for his desire to negotiate with Versailles. He was one of the Commune's last defenders, and as troops gathered in the streets and began to execute Parisian civilians during the Bloody Week of May 1871, he made his escape to Zaragosa, and then on to Barcelona, where Rose, along with the couple's older son, Jean August-Charles Fortuné Henry (who had been born in August 1869 and would, like his younger brother, later go on to be an Anarchist), had already taken refuge. Fortuné's earlier desire to negotiate with Versailles was not appreciated, and he was sentenced in absentia to death for sedition and insurrection. Fortuné prospered in Spain, and by the time of his son Émile's birth he had secured employment as the manager of a mine and mercury plant in Bayarque near Almería. Despite his history as a revolutionary and poet during the time of the Commune, Fortuné became a respectable member of the Spanish working classes, although one who pined for a return to France.

Young Émile was precociously intelligent, and, as revealed by Merriman, he "did so well on the obligatory examinations given in the primary school of Sant-Marti-de-Provensals that he was awarded a certificate of merit, proclaiming that the boy had demonstrated 'a great proof of his hard work and talent.'"[22] On 11 July 1880 the French Senate passed a general amnesty for Communards, with the exception of those who had been found guilty of arson or assassination,[23] and Fortuné and his young family were able to return to France, where he secured employment as a secretary for his friend, Dr. Edmond-Alfred Goupil (or Goupy). Sadly, Fortuné was not to enjoy his return from exile for long, and he died on 28 May 1882 in Paris of mercury poisoning (in all probability caused by the fumes that had permeated so much of the Spanish factory in which he had been a manager). For eight-year-old Émile, the loss of his father and his tales of revolutionary adventures as a Communard must have come as a psychic shock.

With the primary breadwinner of the household deceased, Émile's family was plunged into penury. Although his mother Rose had several wealthy relatives and the family of Fortuné included a sister who had married a marquis, the young widow found herself in no position to seek their assistance. Indeed, as pointed out by Merriman, Rose would later claim that her sons were "abandoned by those in our family who could have helped them. There was no humiliation that they were not made to suffer."[24] Although the family was forced to claim public assistance from the Paris council, eventually the marquise and the rest of Fortuné's extended family began to take an interest in the fate of his widow and sons, and it was Émile who was to benefit both financially and emotionally from their concern. In 1884, at the age of twelve, Émile began attending at the Jean-Baptiste-Say school in the sixteenth arrondissement. This institution had a reputation for preparing pupils for admission to the Grandes écoles, prestigious centers of learning from which graduates largely continued on to join the professional classes of France. Émile was accepted into the Jean-Baptiste-Say school on a half scholarship, with the residual tuition fees being met by his aunt, the marquise. Émile excelled academically and exhibited no behaviors that caused alarm among his peers or the academic staff; indeed, one of the latter would later describe him as "a perfect child, the most honest one can meet."[25]

Following the completion of his studies, Émile sat and successfully passed the rigorous oral and written examinations for the École Polytechnique, then a hotbed for engineering and science scholars. According to Malato,[26] the primary reason that Émile was ultimately unable to attend the school was owing to the "vindictive temper of a professor." During one of the preparatory lectures, one of Émile's peers released a stink bomb. For reasons that are lost to history, Émile was suspected of carrying out this sophomoric prank, and when he refused to confess or assign blame to the responsible party, he was expelled before his education could begin in earnest. Although he was the nephew of a marquise, and his family status had improved in the years since his father's death, Émile's expulsion may have been a result of class-based elitism rather than other factors. For the seventeen-year-old Émile, this setback would arguably prove to be one of the defining episodes of his youth.

Cast out of education, Émile was in need of employment if he was to survive. Relief came by way of his uncle, Jean Bordenave, an engineer who requested that Émile accompany him to Venice on business. As his later testimony was to reveal,[27] this was a well-paid position for the period, and in Italy he earned 100 francs a month. After a few months, Émile unceremoniously left Venice and his uncle behind. The reason for his departure, as outlined by Merriman, may have been that as part of his employment his uncle wished him to "undertake secret surveillance of the workers."[28] Under questioning later, Émile was to remain close lipped on this subject, but it must have been another blow, albeit one that may have been caused by political conscience as opposed to cruel circumstance. Back in Paris, he was jobless and sought solace by moving into the home of his older brother, who was then residing near the Saint-Martin canal. Here, after several months of unemployment, Émile secured a position in a store selling fabrics.

For a few years, Émile, always well dressed and quite at odds with the radicals with whom he would later relate, got by in a variety of jobs. According to Malato, it was during this period that Émile began to explore spiritualism, perhaps seeking to contact the father he doubtless missed. But this intellectual exploration did not last long, and Émile "rebelled against the frauds he discovered; he left the Spiritualists, though he did not discontinue his investigations."[29] By 1891, however, Émile was more concerned with earthly matters. His older brother, known as Fortuné, had by this time made the transition from Socialism to Anarchism (a transition that Émile would soon make himself) and had begun to associate with a young couple, the Gautheys, both of whom were committed Anarchists. According to the account provided by Merriman, Émile experienced a jolt of unrequited love for Madame Élisa Gauthey. Although he lavished his attentions on her and sought to woo her with his poetry (he had by this juncture gained a reputation for being as poetic as his late father), the capricious Élisa did not return his affections. It was during this period that Émile in all probability broke ties he had formed in Parisian Socialist circles. His brother had similarly commenced as a Socialist orator, but as police repression increased, his politics veered toward not reconstruction of the state through Socialist voting blocs but its destruction to allow for the creation of an equitable society in its stead. As the younger Fortuné led, so his intense and well-dressed brother followed.

Toward the end of 1891, Émile became liable for military conscription and was called upon to join the French infantry in September 1893. Persuading a German friend to post a letter to his mother from Berlin, Émile claimed that he had secured employment in Germany and had no intention of either returning to France or serving in the military of a state for which he felt increasing rancor. Although the postmark may have been believable, his declaration failed to move the military, which declared Émile as a deserter in 1892. It was during this period that Émile was to fully immerse himself in the Parisian Anarchist milieu.

On 2 May 1892, a meeting was held in which Fortuné, who was fast gaining a reputation as a fiery speaker in support of the Anarchist cause, praised the recently imprisoned Ravachol. A disturbance broke out, and the police informers (who were frequently present at such meetings) took note of Fortuné's words. The following day his rooms were raided by the Parisian police, who, after a thorough search, arrested his brother Émile. Following several days in custody, Émile was released; however, this brush with the brusque law enforcement of the period may have hardened his resolve. By July, Émile had secured employment as an apprentice watchmaker, a position that was to come back to haunt him; indeed, as Vizetelly highlights, "it was afterwards asserted that he did so with the express object of studying a branch of mechanics which he might utilize in preparing a really effective infernal machine."[30] Émile's tenure as a horologist was not a protracted one, and within a few months he was able to secure employment with a Monsieur Duboy, a decorative sculptor, as a secretary, at the recommendation of his Anarchist comrade and sometime burglar Ortiz. It was during this period that Émile also contributed to *L'En Dehors* (The Outside), an Anarchist journal operated by one of the most colorful Individualist Anarchists, Zo d'Axa (real name: Alphonse Gallaud de la Pérouse). Zo d'Axa was, in the words of Jules Bertaut, "a sort of Socialist condottieri, a dandy, a rake, and a natural adventurer."[31] Originally a cavalryman in the French military, Zo d'Axa would go on to be the editor of an ultra–Catholic newspaper in Italy, a missionary who seduced any women to whom he was attempting to minister, and eventually an Anarchist when he was pursued through Europe for allegedly insulting the virtue of the empress of Germany. By 1891, he had established *L'En Dehors*, which would go on to publish Émile's work in the company of articles by Jean Grave, Albert Libertad, and Octave Mirbeau, among others.

By August 1892, the attentions of Zo d'Axa, Fortuné, and the rest of the Parisian Anarchists (including Émile) turned toward an industrial conflict that was occurring in the town of Carmaux, to the north of Toulouse. Carmaux was formerly an agricultural center, but by the end of the nineteenth century it was renowned for two industries: the production of glass and coal mining. In the latter industry, an industrial dispute commenced that was to become hotly debated within Anarchist and Socialist circles.[32] A local miner, Calvignac, was elected town major of Carmaux thanks in no small part to his colleagues. He was later dismissed from his employment, as his mayoral duties were said to be impinging upon his work. In addition, a number of shop stewards were dismissed. The miners began a strike calling for their reinstatement as well as an improvement on the all but starvation wages they were paid. Not only were the mine owners intransigent, refusing to negotiate, but they also called in the French military, which unleashed a wave of repression, violence, and arrests. Nine miners were arrested when they peaceably entered the offices of the mine director, Humblot. For Socialists, the conflict in Carmaux illustrated the strength of organized labor; for Anarchists such as Émile, it illustrated labor's failure, as workers remained unpaid, falsely imprisoned, and exposed to brutalization. Even before the strike, mining in France during this period was an exceedingly dangerous occupation, with regular deaths and financial hardship caused by unemployment in response to downturns in the demand for coal. For Émile, whose father had worked in mines, the exploitation of the miners, their frequent deaths, and the spiraling company profits unleashed a wave of anger that was to have deadly consequences.

Émile decided to take action, and he conducted a reconnaissance of the Carmaux mining company offices located in Paris. Located in the elegant and luxurious surroundings of Avenue de l'Opera, Émile found that the "company offices were located on the mezzanine. And the rest of the building was populated with the rich: 'a wealthy milliner, and banks, and so on.' There would be no innocent victims."[33] Following his review of the building, Émile returned to his temporary lodgings and drew upon his previous love of science and engineering to construct a reversal bomb in a small iron pot that would explode if jarred or otherwise turned. Although unstable in the extreme, and dangerous for the assailant as well as the intended victim, the device would finally allow Émile to take the kind of action that many had spoken about since the arrest of Ravachol amid the growing wave of Anarchist propaganda of the deed in France.

On 8 November 1892, Émile left his employer's offices to carry out a series of errands. Returning to his lodgings, he retrieved the bomb and, ensuring that he remained unseen, delivered it to the doorstep of the Carmaux mining company before rapidly returning to work. An iron pot wrapped in a paper would today be an unusual sight, but in nineteenth-century Paris it was an alarming one. The immediate reaction of Raymond Garin, the office clerk who discovered the device, is unknown. The police were promptly called, and in their company the device was transferred to the nearby police station of the first arrondissement situated on Rue des Bons-Enfants. Moments after arriving, the device detonated, killing the gendarmes Etienne Fomorin, Marc Reaux, Henri Pousset and Charles Troutot in addition to the hapless Raymond Garin. The explosion ripping through a central Parisian police station attracted instant attention, and the station sub-brigadier Emile Henriot was one of the first to reach the scene of carnage. The blood, smoke, and scattered limbs claimed another victim as Henriot collapsed to the ground by what remained of his unfortunate colleagues, suffering a fatal heart attack. News reached Émile that same afternoon of the explosion; by the following day, after having borrowed some money from fellow Anarchists, he made his escape to London.

Little is known of the time that Émile spent on the other side of the English Channel, but he joined a thriving expatriate Anarchist community in London. Like many others (including Armand Matha, the manager of *L'En Dehors* and a primary suspect in having removed evidence from Émile's apartment following his arrest), he spent his days at the Autonomie Club. Here he was remembered as being a defender of propaganda of the deed, and, according to Hermja Oliver, "his presence and propaganda in London cannot fail to have exerted influence among the French anarchists."[34] Émile must have made quite an impression, as the London-based Anarchist journal *The Torch* (established in 1894 by W.M. Rossetti, brother of the famed pre–Raphaelite painter Dante Gabriel Rossetti), which in March 1895 had decried violence within Anarchism, in July of that year published an article by the Dutch Anarchist Alexander Cohen in which Émile was described as "charitable, self-sacrificing and kind."[35,36] *The Torch* was also quick to condemn British authorities' extradition of Meunier (who had allegedly attacked the Café Very in reprisal for Ravachol's arrest, as detailed in the previous chapter) and his accomplice Jean-Pierre Francois, "another bomber and friend of Émile Henry."[37]

By 1893 Émile had returned to France, and he was determined to avenge the execution of Ravachol and the arrest of Vaillant. According to Merriman[38] (who has provided the most exhaustive overview of Émile's activities and life to date), on 15 December, Émile approached the watchmaker shop where he had previously been employed as an apprentice in search of employment. No work was available for him, and although he attempted to sell his previous employer a watch, it was worth nothing, as the minute hand was missing from the clock face. For Émile himself, time was also running out. Paris, like London, was awash with informers and undercover police, and it was inevitable that in such an environment, Émile would come to their attention. As the brother of a noted Anarchist speaker, the son of a known radical, and no shrinking violet in his defense of propaganda of the deed, it had not gone unnoticed that he had vanished without warning following the attack against the Carmaux mining company offices. His presence back in the French capital was almost certainly noted with interest, and those tasked with investigating Parisian Anarchists were probably pondering what his next actions would be. They would not have to wait long to find out.

For many Anarchists, the arrest and execution of Ravachol had proved a defining event. Although Ravachol's actions were doubtless abhorrent (the murder of an unarmed elderly hermit is hardly defensible regardless of the economics surrounding the act), for many state's actions were equally offensive. The arrest of Vaillant, who had been motivated by poverty (and who had carried out an attack that may have been deliberately non-fatal in nature), coupled with the introduction of villainous laws, had only served to inflame further bad feeling. The actions of the French state in seeking to suppress what would later prove to be nonexistent global Anarchist conspiracies resulted in a groundswell of opposition and anger. Émile Henry would shortly unleash his anger upon the bourgeois world that had caused many of those around him to either be imprisoned or, when they protested the gross social and economic inequalities of the age, lose employment opportunities, thus forcing them to choose between stealing and starving.

By December 1893, Émile had taken up residence in a small flat at the Villa Faucheur.[39] Here he lived humbly under the assumed name of Louis Dubois and started creating a number of bombs that he could later use. Indeed, as revealed in his later courtroom testimony,[40] even though his rooms had, following his arrest, been broken into, they still contained enough explosive materials to produce between twelve and fifteen separate devices. By 12 February 1894, Émile was ready to enact the first of what he may have envisioned as many attacks, a decision that drew him to the Café Terminus. Following the detonation of his bomb in the café (which injured as many as thirty people, some of them gravely, and resulted in the death of a patron by the name of Ernest Borde[41]), Émile fled the scene. He was initially chased though the Parisian streets by a waiter named Tissier and an office worker named Martinguet. As the chase intensified and a policeman by the name of Poisson joined in, Émile turned and fired the revolver he had brought with him (he also had what would turn out to be a knife dipped in poison). The bullet missed Poisson while grazing the unfortunate Tissier; still the pursuit continued. More Parisians and gendarmes joined the frantic dash, and Poisson drew closer. Again Émile turned and fired at Poisson at close range, and although the policeman was slightly injured, eventually the crowd was able to subdue the agitated bomber.

Although he initially refused to provide his name and was not carrying any identification at the time of his arrest, following a few days in detention, Émile told the guards (with whom he had struck up a rapport) who he was; his identity was subsequently confirmed by undercover agents working within the police force. However, the motivation behind his actions would not become apparent until his trial commenced on 27 April 1894.

As with other trials of Anarchists who had preceded him, Émile's time in court was limited. Although he was defended by Maître Nicolas Hornbostel, such defense as could be provided was muted, as the lawyer was "immeasurably less eloquent than Émile."[42] Émile himself would prove to be contentious in his eloquence. He frequently objected to the questioning of the prosecutor, Bulot, and used the trial as a justification for his actions at the Café Terminus. When questioned by the presiding judge in the trial about his mysterious actions in 1893 and warned to be aware of how his silence could potentially be used against him, Émile replied with understanding of what was to befall him: "I don't care. I don't have to beware of my silence. I know full well that I'll be condemned to death."[43]

The press was quick to pick up on the French state's fears that the actions of Auguste Vaillant and Émile Henry, far from being completely unlinked, were elements in a global Anarchist plot. Indeed, the *New York Times* would report that "it is believed now that the outrage committed by Emile Henry at the café of the Hotel Terminus, on Monday night, when twenty-four persons were injured by the explosion of a bomb thrown by him, was part of a vast Anarchist conspiracy."[44] According to this theory, Émile's actions were planned in London, and twenty-two of his peers from his time at the Autonomie Club were abroad in Europe waiting to commit further attacks. The existence of this shadowy cabal of Anarchist terrorists was to prove fallacious, and, as highlighted throughout this book, although adherents of propaganda of the deed may have shared similar motivations, they were ultimately driven by their own individual histories.

Speaking in his own defense, Émile provided the justification for his actions, which had as much to do with the state's reaction to nonexistent conspiracies as it did with the actions of some of his peers:

> The bomb in the Café Terminus is the answer to all your violations of freedom, to your arrests, to your searches, to your laws against the Press, to your mass transportations, to your guillotinings. But why, you ask, attack these peaceful café guests, who sat listening to music and who, no doubt, were neither judges nor deputies nor bureaucrats? Why? It is very simple. The bourgeoisie did not distinguish among the anarchists. Vaillant, a man on his own, threw a bomb; nine-tenths of the comrades did not even know him. But that meant nothing; the persecution was a mass one, and anyone with the slightest anarchist links was hunted down. And since you hold a whole party responsible for the actions of a single man, and strike indiscriminately, we also strike indiscriminately.[45]

Despite his defense and the limited capabilities of his lawyer, the death sentence was unsurprisingly imposed by the presiding judge at 7:40 p.m. on the evening of 28 April. Émile met the sentence with defiance and, as reported by the press, shouted, "Courage, Comrades! Vive l'Anarchie!"[46]

In the early morning hours of 21 May 1894, Émile was led from his cell in La Roquette Prison toward the guillotine that was still manned by Louis Diebler, who had previously executed Vaillant. As he neared the scaffold, Émile yelled through the morning fog, "Long live Anarchy!" At 4 a.m. he was forced head first into the guillotine and the blade fell. Even Émile's death was to prove controversial, however. On 22 May, the press reported[47] that a Doctor Benoit, who had examined the postmortem body at the École de médecine, had declared that, in his professional opinion, Émile had been dead before the guillotine blade had fallen. According to his examination, rather than a steel blade being the cause of death, Émile had actually died of syncope, or a fatal loss of consciousness caused by a decrease in blood flow to the brain caused by stress and low blood pressure. Further investigation by Benoit was prevented, however, when the government returned what was left of Émile to his family for burial in the Montparnasse Cemetery. If the French state had hoped that executing Émile would deter further attacks, it was to be sorely disappointed. Just as the imprisonment and execution of Vaillant proved a motivator for Émile Henry, the death of the latter would likewise have a lasting impact on the security of not just France but also Europe as a whole.

On the night of 24 June 1894, in the Grand Théâtre at Lyon, the crowd was for the most part already seated, although many were growing increasingly restive. The great and good of Lyon were awaiting the start of Racine's *Andromaque*. Competition for tickets had been fierce, but this performance was one of the events at which to be seen that season in Lyon, so it would doubtless be worth the investment. Although the tragic retelling of Greek mythos was not to the taste of all the audience members, there were some among them who were aggrieved at the delay in the start of the performance. However, the guests of honor (and the reason for the hefty competition for tickets) had not yet arrived.

At approximately 9:15 p.m., two men dashed to the theater entrance and shouted that the president of France, Marie François Sadi Carnot, had been killed. Although not all the theatergoers heard the interruption, "news spread swiftly to the rear seats of the theatre, and thence passed like a wind over the great audience."[48] Some of the more hysterical audience members cried out in alarm; however, the majority were more cynical and refused to believe that such an incident had occurred. Surely it was a prank of the worst kind? The fears and suspicions of the crowd were temporarily allayed when two figures entered the presidential box; however, such hopes as may have been raised were soon dashed. Rather than Carnot, the theatergoers were now confronted with the sight of Monsieur Rivaud, the prefect of Lyon, in the company of Deputy Chaudrey. Between sobs, the former announced gravely that the president of France had been assassinated.

The murder of Carnot was the first assassination of a French head of state since 1610 (when Henry III had been stabbed by the fanatical Catholic, Jacques Clément, who had disguised himself as a priest for the occasion), but it was not entirely unexpected. For many, Carnot had become a hated figure thanks in no small part to his refusal to pardon Ravachol, Vaillant, and Henry, in addition to his introduction of laws directed at suppressing the supposed Anarchist threat. Such a scare was doubtless helpful to Carnot and the government, as it served to pull attention away from the Panama Scandal of 1892. The Panama Canal Company had collapsed that year, taking with it more than $300 million of thousands of individual investors' capital. As Eugen Weber highlights, "The Panama Scandal was a Republican debacle. Over a hundred deputies, senators, ministers, and ex-ministers were implicated in the company's dishonest and demeaning shenanigans."[49] Bribery and corruption were rampant, and for Carnot and others in the government the agitation by Anarchist adherents of the philosophy of propaganda of the deed served a highly useful political purpose. Carnot's campaign against the French Anarchists earned him their everlasting ire, and, as highlighted by Merriman, "the holy grail of those anarchists inclined to violence was the assassination of President Sadi Carnot."[50] As was revealed on that fateful evening in the theater, someone had achieved this aim.

The day of 24 June had started well for President Carnot. He was in Lyon to attend the Exposition universelle, internationale et colonial (Universal, International and Colonial Exposition) held at the Parc de la Tête d'Or. Connected to the city of Lyon by three tram lines, the exposition consisted of a number of pavilions containing exhibits of French triumph and progress, as well as a metal dome some 720 feet in diameter and 180 feet in height. In addition to being treated to a tour of the sites (which ironically included a workers' exhibit), Carnot had dined at a banquet held in his honor by the Lyon Chamber of Commerce at the Palace of the Bourse, Place des Cordeliers. Here he had indicated that he would not seek a second term, having survived the political ramifications of the Panama scandal, and that elections would be held at the end of the year. Carnot's announcement was greeted with enthusiasm, not because those in attendance held him in as much contempt as did many of the scandal's victims or the Anarchists, but because he had chosen to retire seemingly at the zenith of his popularity with the bourgeoisie. Carnot "left the Chamber of Commerce banquet, given in his honor, a little after 9pm and walked to his carriage, which was waiting at the Place de la Bourse."[51] From there

Sante Geronimo Caserio

the carriage proceeded down the Rue Sainte-Bonaventure and then via the Rue de la République toward the theater. With Carnot in the carriage were Brigadier General Leon Borius, former head of the military house of the president of the Republic; General Nicolas Joseph Voisin, military governor of Lyon; and the mayor of Lyon, Dr. Antoine Gailleton. As the carriage pulled slowly onto the Rue de la République, a young man stepped out from the crowds lining the street. In his hand he was holding what appeared to be a bundle of papers, presumably a petition of some kind for the attention of Carnot or his advisors. Before any of the outriders could react, the young man had jumped on the running board of the carriage, produced a knife from within the folds of the papers he was carrying, and plunged it deep into the body of Carnot, who slumped backward with a cry. The president of France was mortally wounded, as his assailant, Sante Geronimo Caserio, yelled defiantly.

Many of the details of Caserio's life are disputed; however, what is known is that he was born in the small Italian town of Motta Visconti, situated in the Lombardy region, on either 7 September or 8

September 1873. According to some accounts, his father was named Antonio,[52] while in others he is called Giovanni.[53] All those researchers and historians who have concerned themselves with Caserio (and they have not been plentiful) agree that his mother was Martina Broglia. Young Sante was born into a large family of six older brothers living in an environment of poverty, as was endured by many among the Italian rural poor. In his youth, Caserio's father had been a boatman on the Ticino River in northern Italy during the summer months, and in the harsh Italian winters he scraped by as a woodsman. The boy Sante was supposedly given the middle name of Geronimo in tribute to the Apache leader and medicine man who was a stoic figure of resistance to the U.S. and Mexican states. The reason behind giving such an unusual middle name to the youngest addition to the family is not known, but Caserio's later actions certainly lend credence to the argument that he was appropriately named.

Life for the Caserio clan was tough; with so many mouths to feed, there was frequently not enough food to go around. For this reason, in 1884, an eleven-year-old Sante was forced to travel to Milan in search of employment. This was not the first job he had held; as outlined by the Franco Serantini Library,[54] Sante Caserio had previously been employed as the assistant to a shoemaker in his native Motta Visconti. After apprenticing with wine merchants (the duties of which probably consisted of little more than being a general dogsbody), Caserio was able to secure a position in 1886 as an apprentice in the Tre Marie (Three Marys) bakery. The following year, his father, who was still residing with the rest of the family in their hometown, unexpectedly died. The official cause of his death, as with many others during this period, was pellagra. This disease, which can kill in less than five years, is caused by a chronic vitamin deficiency owing to a lack of variety in diet. For the rural poor, diets during the nineteenth century were extremely limited, consisting of little more than corn. It was this lack of dietary variation, coupled with the harsh life of a workingman, that led to the early death of Caserio's father. Separated from his family, and with no parental support network in Milan, life for Caserio must have been difficult.

Though by all accounts a hard worker, Caserio was only semi-literate. The fact that he had achieved any literacy at all was due in no small part to his attendance at a primary school in Motta Visconti, where he was taught by the poet Ada Negri. Widely published in her native Italy and abroad in the United States during her lifetime, Negri now is a largely neglected literary figure. Before her brief flirtation with Fascism, Negri had long been concerned with injustice, being described by Emma Goldman as "the ardent poetess of revolt."[55] During his time in Motta Visconti, Caserio was also exposed to religion and, according to news reports that appeared when he had achieved his later infamy, was "worthy of representing St. John, in a sheepskin gown, in the religious processions."[56] Although in his teens he would lose his religious devotion, Caserio would soon find a new cause more in keeping with the views of his one-time primary school teacher.

The behavior patterns of young apprentices in the nineteenth century would perhaps be shocking for many modern readers. These young teenage boys and girls, operating with no parental oversight and enduring harsh working conditions, frequently engaged in alcohol-fueled gambling sessions when not attempting to get one another into bed. Caserio, however, had different aspirations, although he was by no means as unique as many historians have posited. As Fausto Buttà reveals in his sweeping history of Milanese Anarchism, many of those detained by the legal authorities for engaging in Anarchist circles were between the ages of fourteen and seventeen, and numerous young people at the time were exposed to Anarchist ideas through the pamphlets and leaflets that were distributed throughout Milan. These began to multiply following the events of 1891 at the Piazza di Santa Croce. As discussed elsewhere in this book, on 1 May 1891 authorities in Rome had attacked a crowd of unemployed workers gathered for a demonstration using cannon and mounted guards, leaving many dead and wounded in their authoritarian wake. For the eighteen-year-old Caserio, this event would prove integral to his later actions and identity.

During this period, it is likely that Caserio met Pietro Gori. Gori was an Italian lawyer, journalist and Anarchist poet who had previously spent time in prison for organizing a May Day protest in Livorno when he was a student. By 1891, he was settled in Milan and had begun publishing his *L'amico del popolo* (Friend of the People) newspaper, which had the high honor of having all of its twenty-seven issues seized by the police. In all likelihood, Caserio met Gori in the Anarchist club of Via Santa Sofia, which was populated by the young Milanese radicals of the day (including Caserio's friend, Antonio Caspani, who found occasional employment flyposting on the club's behalf). Caserio clearly made an impression on the more seasoned Gori:

> One morning in the winter I saw him near the Chamber of Labor in Milan, he was handing out propaganda pamphlets and bread to the unemployed workers. He had bought the pamphlets as well as the bread with his own savings. I never saw him even a bit drunk, which was quite unusual among poor people, and he also smoked very little. As concerns juvenile vices, he was a puritan. One night he scolded a few friends of his who were coming out of a brothel: "How can you abuse these poor women, buying their flesh and love?" and as one of those guys, an opportunist, said: "At least we relieve a little of their misery with our money," Caserio went in, gave one lira to one of the women, who looked at him in wonder, and went away without speaking. One day I asked him: "You're a nice young boy, why don't you make love?" "I used to," he answered, "but since I married the anarchist idea I've stopped going around with women, and now I'd like to find a partner for life, as I would like her to be." He rented a flat where he used to give hospitality at night to all the homeless comrades in Milan. It was a real campsite, whereas he was at work at the bakery all night.[57]

Gori was not alone in his praise of Caserio; in 1947, toward the end of his life, his one-time friend and comrade, Caspani, described Caserio as follows:

> Tranquil young man, sensitised to the misery of this society made up of the corrupted and the corruptors, where the most insolent richness is next to the worst misery. Caserio was affected by the sight of beggars, and moved to tears, told me: "If I were a mendicant, I would beg with a knife in my hand." As a baker's boy he was able to provide some loaves of bread to feed some of his unemployed comrades. In this matter he was peculiar. A comrade did not need to humiliate himself in asking; Caserio understood and provided bread to those who were hungry. In Caserio's opinion, a comrade was a brother, someone like him and someone else's need was his own need.[58]

By 1892, Caserio had found the cause he would dedicate the rest of his short life to, and he would approach it with the same zeal he had once applied to the religious processions that had filled his youth in Motta Visconti. Initially Caserio joined some like-minded youngsters who had formed an Anarchist group by the name of Porta Romana; however, he soon grew dissatisfied with them and formed his own rival group, Porta Genova. Caspani's later recollections reveal that the headquarters of this group was situated in a small garret flat in Corso Genova 17; Caserio had rented this apartment with the limited funds he had and decorated it with chairs, cheap oil lamps, and a red and black flag sporting the words "Penniless-Communist-Anarchist Group." Gori and his associates had long been under police surveillance, but it was Caserio's actions as part of Porta Genova that would bring him to the attention of the carabinieri. On 26 April 1892, Caserio was arrested for the first time; his offense was distributing an antimilitarist message addressed to the soldiers of Santa Prassede barracks in Milan. As with the garret room for Porta Genova, Caserio likely paid for the printing of this simple pamphlet using his own limited funds. It is not known whether any of his fellow group members were arrested, or if Caserio was merely in the wrong place at the wrong time and grew overzealous with the wrong soldier. At his trial he was defended by his old friend Pietro Gori; in the end, he was sentenced to a twelve-month prison sentence for the distribution of seditious materials. After serving eight months, Caserio was released; however, he subsequently found that he had been conscripted by draft into the army that he had only months before been protesting. Rather than acquiesce to the force of the Italian military, Caserio used what little money he could gather from friends and acquaintances and fled to Switzerland. In Milan he was officially declared a deserter, with all the lasting ramifications of such a sentence. Barely into his nineteenth year, Caserio had transformed from apprentice baker into political exile on the run.

Initially Caserio moved to Lugano in southern Switzerland, which was far enough across the border for him to avoid arrest but close enough that the majority of city residents spoke Italian. In Lugano, Caserio was able to obtain work in a bakery and recover from his flight from Italy and the conditions he had doubtless endured while imprisoned. However, his recuperation (or perhaps his employment) did not last long, and Caserio was soon on the move again, first to Lausanne and then to Geneva, where he was briefly detained by the Swiss police. It was perhaps this incident that caused Caserio to enter France in July 1893, spending a few weeks in Lyon before moving on to Sète (known as Cette until 1928), an unpretentious port town in southern France. As highlighted by Barbara Stefanelli, Sète at the time of Caserio's arrival had "a strong anarchist tradition ... Caserio met other comrades but kept in touch with the Italian groups and received anarchist papers."[59] In Sète, Caserio was again able to find employment as a baker, this time in the Viala bakery, and, as required by law, he registered with the local police as a militant Anarchist. Caserio risked deportation by this admission, but, in what has to be classified as a grave misjudgment, the then prefect of Hérault (of which Sète is part) stated, "Quant à Caserio, the je ne crois pas dangereux" (as for Caserio, I do not think him dangerous).[60] In addition to receiving Italian papers in Sète, Caserio attended the Café du Gard (then a hotbed for local French Anarchists) and learned of the executions of both Auguste Vaillant and Émile Henry. In June 1894, Caserio heard of President Carnot's plans to attend the exposition in Lyon, which were widely publicized in the press, and began to consider vengeance.

On the morning of Saturday, 23 June, Caserio went as normal to his job at the bakery. Following a quarrel that he may have instigated, he resigned, and by 10:00 a.m. he was on the streets of Sète with twenty francs' back pay in his pocket. Sometime later on that fateful morning he was in the shop of Monsieur Guillaume, a sometime gunsmith who sold Caserio a five-franc knife. Purportedly made from Toledo steel, it was a showy as well as inevitably deadly blade, "the hilt of which was of copper gilt and the scabbard of velvet, in black and red stripes."[61] By the afternoon, Caserio was in attendance at the Café du Gard and let it be known that he intended to travel to Lyon, a claim that was not initially believed. Although the journey from Sète to Lyon was a lengthy one, his comrades should have been less skeptical, as by 3:00 p.m. he had begun his journey. During the afternoon and evening of 23 June Caserio traveled by train until he reached Avignon, where he was forced to sleep on a bench for the night. The following morning he had a choice between traveling directly to Lyon or going to Vienne by train. If he traveled to the former, he would be forced to spend his remaining twelve francs on the cost of a ticket, leaving nothing for food. A train to Vienne would only cost nine francs and thus leave him enough for basic sustenance. Caserio decided on the latter option, as he would need his strength. After eating a meal of bread in Vienne, and purchasing a paper that contained the program of the president's activities in Lyon (in which he wrapped his newly purchased knife), Caserio began the six-hour hike toward his target in the summer rain.

By 9:00 p.m., Caserio had reached Lyon and plunged his blade into the president of France. According to the account of his actions provided by Stefanelli, once the deed was done, Caserio "still had time to find a way through the crowd, but instead he ran in front of the coach shouting: 'Long live Anarchy! Long live the Revolution!'"[62] The first assassin of a French head of state in almost three centuries was easy to subdue, and he was soon dragged away to the police station at Rue Molière, as President Carnot was driven at speed toward the palace of prefecture, where, despite the ministrations of the medical professionals of Lyon, he was soon declared dead. As news of the assassination broke (along with the identity of the assassin), Italian businesses were attacked throughout France.

Caserio's trial began in Lyon on 2 August 1894 and, as with so many other Anarchist trials, concluded the following day. Presided over by Judge Breuillac, and with Attorney General Folchier acting as prosecutor, Caserio provided no defense, nor did he request one; his only statement to the court prior to being sentenced was that he had acted alone and had no accomplices. Following a thirteen-minute deliberation, the jury returned a verdict of guilty at 12:18 p.m. on 3 August. Only after the presiding judge imposed a sentence of death did Caserio, as reported by the press of the day, display any response: "As the sound of the Judge's voice ceased Caserio pulled himself together— for a moment he was almost limp—and in a feeble voice exclaimed: 'Vive la revolution!'"[63] Following formal sentencing, a court-appointed translator read out a document that Caserio had provided. Originally banned from publication or circulation by the court, this message was later published by Emma Goldman in *The Psychology of Political iolence*,[64] and it provides insight into Caserio's motivation. In his statement (which is provided at the end of this chapter), Caserio highlighted not only the social inequalities of his day and the pellagra that claimed the lives of so many (including his father) but also the legislation imposed by Carnot, and the execution of Vaillant, before concluding that the members of the jury should "take care, for men reap what they have sown."

Following the announcement of his sentence, Caserio was detained until 16 August 1894. At 4:50 a.m. Caserio was led from his cell at the Prison Saint-Paul in Lyon, his arms bound behind him. As he reached the scaffold on which sat the guillotine, and "the attendants seized him to lay him under the knife, he struggled fiercely to free himself. At 4:55 o'clock all was ready. Caserio shouted 'Courage Comrades!' 'Long Live Anarchy!' The knife fell at 5 o'clock precisely."[65] The short life of Sante Geronimo Caserio was ended by a guillotine operated by Louis Diebler, the same man who had executed both Vaillant and Henry.

The trio of Vaillant, Henry and Caserio not only had a lasting influence on the history of Anarchism in France and propaganda of the deed but also directly impacted legislative frameworks intended to address the threats that these men posed. Although their actions were not indiscriminate, inasmuch as their targets were deliberately chosen, it can be said that the state's repressive legal and extralegal actions escalated their actions and fueled their rage. What had begun with a non-lethal attack against the seat of the French government spiraled rapidly into a number of attacks that ultimately left civilians dead and France without a head of state. Although the trio's actions were interlinked, their motivations were different. Auguste Vaillant was desperate and poverty stricken, and although he was fueled by the theories of propaganda of the deed (and possibly police agents), his intention was to highlight not only his own conditions but also those of the urban poor as a whole. Émile Henry was the most intellectually gifted of these three attackers, and he used his intellect to fuel his fanaticism. By turning his weapons against the urban bourgeoisie, one might argue that Henry sought to highlight the disparity between those who could dine in leisure and those who, mere streets away, were only concerned with where their next meager meal was coming from. In purposefully targeting civilians, Henry emerges from history as a thoroughly modern individual. His passion and youth were arguably skewed to allow him to commit acts that were just as reprehensible as those of a negligent state. Henry failed to spark a revolution, but he was successful in pushing the state to unleash a wave of repression against his fellows. Sante Caserio remains the enigma of the three. Although raised in poverty and enduring much the same plight that afflicted many of his peers from the working class, his trajectory is, at first glance, peculiar. However, when one considers that he was effectively forced into exile and imprisoned for political activism, in addition to being required to endure the tumult of capitalism at a young age, his cold rage becomes more understandable.

Desperation, retribution, and rage are perhaps the best descriptors for the actions of Vaillant, Henry and Caserio. Although their actions failed to reshape French society for the better and led to the introduction of a range of laws that were oppressive in the extreme, they were to prove influential to other individuals of the period; indeed, in the case of Henry, the effects and impacts of fatal terrorist attacks against civilians is something that humanity still has to endure.

Courtroom Speech (Auguste Vaillant)

Source: Emma Goldman, *Anarchism and Other Essays*, as referenced by the Anarchist Library, https://theanarchistlibrary.org/library/auguste-vaillant-courtroom-speech (accessed March 2017)

Gentlemen, in a few minutes you are to deal your blow, but in receiving your verdict I shall have at least the satisfaction of having wounded the existing society, that cursed society in which one may see a single man spending, uselessly, enough to feed thousands of families; an infamous society which permits a few individuals to monopolize all the social wealth, while there are hundreds of thousands of unfortunates who have not even the bread that is not refused to dogs, and while entire families are committing suicide for want of the necessities of life.

Ah, gentlemen, if the governing classes could go down among the unfortunates! But no, they prefer to remain deaf to their appeals. It seems that a fatality impels them, like the royalty of the eighteenth century, toward the precipice which will engulf them, for woe be to those who remain deaf to the cries of the starving, woe to those who, believing themselves of superior essence, assume the right to exploit those beneath them! There comes a time when the people no longer reason; they rise like a hurricane, and pass away like a torrent. Then we see bleeding heads impaled on pikes.

Among the exploited, gentlemen, there are two classes of individuals. Those of one class, not realizing what they are and what they might be, take life as it comes, believe that they are born to be slaves, and content themselves with the little that is given them in exchange for their labor. But there are others, on the contrary, who think, who study, and who, looking about them, discover social iniquities. Is it their fault if they see clearly and suffer at seeing others suffer? Then they throw themselves into the struggle, and make themselves the bearers of the popular claims.

Gentlemen, I am one of these last. Wherever I have gone, I have seen unfortunates bent beneath the yoke of capital. Everywhere I have seen the same wounds causing tears of blood to flow, even in the remoter parts of the inhabited districts of South America, where I had the right to believe that he who was weary of the pains of civilization might rest in the shade of the palm trees and there study nature. Well, there even, more than elsewhere, I have seen capital come, like a vampire, to suck the last drop of blood of the unfortunate pariahs.

Then I came back to France, where it was reserved for me to see my family suffer atrociously. This was the last drop in the cup of my sorrow. Tired of leading this life of suffering and cowardice, I carried this bomb to those who are primarily responsible for social misery.

I am reproached with the wounds of those who were hit by my projectiles. Permit me to point out in passing that, if the bourgeois had not massacred or caused massacres during the Revolution, it is probable that they would still be under the yoke of the nobility. On the other hand, figure up the dead and wounded on Tonquin, Madagascar, Dahomey, adding thereto the thousands, yes, millions of unfortunates who die in the factories, the mines, and wherever the grinding power of capital is felt. Add also those who die of hunger, and all this with the assent of our Deputies. Beside all this, of how little weight are the reproaches now brought against me!

It is true that one does not efface the other; but, after all, are we not acting on the defensive when we respond to the blows which we receive from above? I know very well that I shall be told that I ought to have confined myself to speech for the vindication of the people's claims. But what can you expect! It takes a loud voice to make the deaf hear. Too long have they answered our voices by imprisonment, the rope, rifle volleys. Make no mistake; the explosion of my bomb is not only the cry of the rebel Vaillant, but the cry of an entire class which vindicates its rights, and which will soon add acts to words. For, be sure of it, in vain will they pass laws. The ideas of the thinkers will not halt; just as, in the last century, all the governmental forces could not prevent the Diderots and the Voltaires from spreading emancipating ideas among the people, so all the existing governmental forces will not prevent the Reclus, the Darwins, the Spencers, the Ibsens, the Mirbeaus, from spreading the ideas of justice and liberty which will annihilate the prejudices that hold the mass in ignorance. And these ideas, welcomed by the unfortunate, will flower in acts of revolt as they have done in me, until the day when the disappearance of authority shall permit all men to organize freely according to their choice, when every-one shall be able to enjoy the product of his labor, and when those moral maladies called prejudices shall vanish, permitting human beings to live in harmony, having no other desire than to study the sciences and love their fellows.

I conclude, gentlemen, by saying that a society in which one sees such social inequalities as we see all about us, in which we see every day suicides caused by poverty, prostitution flaring at every street corner,—a society whose principal monuments are barracks and prisons,—such a society must be transformed as soon as possible, on pain of being eliminated, and that speedily, from the human race. Hail to him who labors, by no matter what means, for this transformation! It is this idea that has guided me in my duel with authority, but as in this duel I have only wounded my adversary, it is now its turn to strike me.

Now, gentlemen, to me it matters little what penalty you may inflict, for, looking at this assembly with the eyes of reason, I can not help smiling to see you, atoms lost in matter, and reasoning only because you possess a prolongation of the spinal marrow, assume the right to judge one of your fellows.

Ah! gentlemen, how little a thing is your assembly and your verdict in the history of humanity; and human history, in its turn, is likewise a very little thing in the whirlwind which bears it through immensity, and which is destined to disappear, or at least to be transformed, in order to begin again the same history and the same facts, a veritably perpetual play of cosmic forces renewing and transferring themselves forever.

Defence Speech (Émile Henry)

Source: *Gazette des Tribunaux*, 27–28 April 1894, as referenced by https://www.marx ists.org/reference/archive/henry/1894/defence-speech.htm (accessed March 2017); translated by George Woodcock

It is not a defence that I present to you. I am not in any way seeking to escape the reprisals of the society I have attacked. Besides, I acknowledge only one tribunal -myself, and the verdict of any other is meaningless to me. I wish merely to give you an explanation of my acts and to tell you how I was led to perform them.

I have been an anarchist for only a short time. It was as recently as the middle of the year 1891 that I entered the revolutionary movement. Up to that time, I had lived in circles entirely imbued with current morality. I had been accustomed to respect and even to love the principles of fatherland and family, of authority and property.

For teachers in the present generation too often forget one thing; it is that life, with its struggles and defeats, its injustices and iniquities, takes upon itself indiscreetly to open the eyes of the ignorant to reality. This happened to me, as it happens to everyone. I had been told that life was easy, that it was wide open to those who were intelligent and energetic; experience showed me that only the cynical and the servile were able to secure good seats at the banquet.

I had been told that our social institutions were founded on justice and equality; I observed all around me nothing but lies and impostures.

Each day I shed an illusion. Everywhere I went, I witnessed the same miseries among some, and the same joys among others. I was not slow to understand that the grand words I had been taught to venerate: honour, devotion, duty, were only the mask that concealed the most shameful basenesses.

The manufacturer who created a colossal fortune out of the toil of workers who lacked everything was an honest gentleman. The deputy and the minister, their hands ever open for bribes, were devoted to the public good. The officer who experimented with a new type of rifle on children of seven had done his duty, and, openly in parliament, the president of the council congratulated him! Everything I saw revolted me, and my intelligence was attracted by criticism of the existing social organization. Such criticism has been made too often for me to repeat it. It is enough to say that I became the enemy of a society that I judged to be criminal.

Drawn at first to socialism, I was not slow in separating myself from that party. I have too much love of freedom, too much respect for individual initiative, too much repugnance for military organization, to assume a number in the ordered army of the fourth estate. Besides, I realized that basically socialism changes nothing in the existing order. It maintains the principle of authority, and, whatever self-styled free-thinkers may say about it, that principle is no more than the antiquated survival of faith in a superior power.

Scientific studies gradually made me aware of the play of natural forces in the universe. I became materialist and atheist; I came to realize that modern science discards the hypothesis of God, of which it has no need. In the same way, religious and authoritarian morality, which are based on false assumptions, should be allowed to disappear. What then, I asked myself, was the new morality in harmony with the laws of nature that might regenerate the old world and give birth to a happy humanity?

It was at this moment that I came into contact with a group of anarchist comrades whom I consider, even today, among the best I have ever known. The character of these men immediately captivated me. I discerned in them a great sincerity, a total frankness, a searching distrust of all prejudices, and I wanted to understand the idea that produced men so different from anyone I had encountered up to that point.

The idea—as soon as I embraced it—found in my mind a soil completely prepared by observation and personal reflection to receive it. It merely gave precision to what already existed there in vague and wavering form. In my turn I became an anarchist.

I do not need to develop on this occasion the whole theory of anarchism. I merely wish to emphasize its revolutionary aspect, the destructive and negative aspect that brings me here before you.

At this moment of embittered struggle between the middle class and its enemies, I am almost tempted to say, with Souvarine in Germinal: "All discussions about the future are criminal, since they hinder pure and simple destruction and slow down the march of the revolution...."

I brought with me into the struggle a profound hatred which every day was renewed by the spectacle of this society where everything is base, everything is equivocal, everything is ugly, where everything is an impediment to the outflow of human passions, to the generous impulses of the heart, to the free flight of thought.

I wanted to strike as strongly and as justly as I could. Let us start then with the first attempt I made, the explosion in the Rue des Bon-Enfants. I had followed closely the events at Carmaux. The first news of the strike had filled me with joy. The miners seemed at last to have abandoned those useless pacific strikes in which the trusting worker patiently waits for his few francs to triumph over the company's millions. They seemed to have entered on a way of violence which manifested itself resolutely on the 15th August 1892. The offices and buildings of the mine were invaded by a crowd of people tired of suffering without reprisals; justice was about to be wrought on the engineer whom his workers so deeply hated, when the timorous ones chose to interfere.

Who were these men? The same who cause the miscarriage of all revolutionary movements because they fear that the people, once they act freely, will no longer obey their voices; those who persuade thousands of men to endure privations month after month so as to beat the drum over their sufferings and create for themselves a popularity that will put them into office: such men—I mean the socialist leaders—in fact assumed the leadership of the strike movement.

Immediately a wave of glib gentlemen appeared in the region; they put themselves entirely at the disposition of the struggle, organized subscriptions, arranged conferences and appealed on all sides for funds. The miners surrendered all initiative into their hands, and what happened, everyone knows.

The strike went on and on, and the miners established the most intimate acquaintance with hunger, which became their habitual companion; they used up the tiny reserve fund of their syndicate and of the other organizations which came to their help, and then, at the end of two months, they returned crestfallen to their pit, more wretched than ever before. It would have been so simple in the beginning to have attacked the Company in its only sensitive spot, the financial one; to have burnt the stocks of coal, to have broken the mining machines, to have demolished the drainage pumps.

Then, certainly, the Company would have very soon capitulated. But the great pontiff's of socialism would not allow such procedures because they are anarchist procedures. At such games one runs the risk of prison and—who knows?—perhaps one of those bullets that performed so miraculously at Fourmies? That is not the way to win seats on municipal council's or in legislatures. In brief, having been momentarily troubled, order reigned once again at Carmaux.

More powerful than ever, the Company continued its exploitation, and the gentlemen shareholders congratulated themselves on the happy outcome of the strike. Their dividends would be even more pleasant to gather in.

It was then that I decided to intrude among that concert of happy tones a voice the bourgeois had already heard but which they thought had died with Ravachol: the voice of dynamite.

I wanted to show the bourgeoisie that henceforward their pleasures would not be untouched, that their insolent triumphs would be disturbed, that their golden calf would rock violently on its pedestal until the final shock that would cast it down among filth and blood.

At the same time I wanted to make the miners understand that there is only one category of men, the anarchists, who sincerely resent their sufferings and are willing to avenge them. Such men do not sit in parliament like Monsieur Guesde and his associates, but they march to the guillotine.

So I prepared a bomb. At one stage the accusation that had been thrown at Ravachol came to my memory. What about the innocent victims? I soon resolved that question. The building where the Carmaux Company had its offices was inhabited only by bourgeois; hence there would be no innocent victims. The whole of the bourgeoisie lives by the exploitation of the unfortunate, and should expiate its crimes together. So it was with absolute confidence in the legitimacy of my deed that I left my bomb before the door to the Company's offices.

I have already explained my hope, in case my device was discovered before it exploded, that it would go off in the police station, where those it harmed would still be my enemies. Such were the motives that led me to commit the first attempt of which I have been accused.

Let us go on to the second incident, of the Café Terminus. I had returned to Paris at the time of the Vaillant affair, and I witnessed the frightful repression that followed the explosion at the Palais Bourbon. I saw the draconian measures which the government decided to take against the anarchists. Everywhere there were spies, and searches, and arrests. A crowd of individuals were indiscriminately rounded up, torn from their families, and thrown into prison. Nobody was concerned about what happened to the wives and children of these comrades while they remained in jail.

The anarchist was no longer regarded as a man, but as a wild beast to be hunted everywhere while the bourgeois Press, which is the vile slave of authority, loudly demands his extermination.

At the same time, libertarian papers and pamphlets were seized and the right of meeting was abrogated. Worse than that: when it seemed desirable to get one comrade completely out of the way, an informer came and left in his room a packet which he said contained tannin; the next day a search was made, on a warrant dated the previous day, a box of suspicious powders was found, the comrade was taken to court and sentenced to three years in gaol. If you wish to know the truth of that, ask the wretched spy who found his way into the home of comrade Mérigeaud!

But all such procedures were good because they struck at an enemy who had spread fear, and those who had trembled wanted to display their courage. As the crown of that crusade against the heretics, we heard M. Reynal, Minister of the Interior, declare in the Chamber of Deputies that the measures taken by the government had thrown terror into the camp of the anarchists. But that was not yet enough. A man who had killed nobody was condemned to death. It was necessary to appear brave right to the end, and one fine morning he was guillotined.

But, gentlemen of the bourgeoisie, you have reckoned a little too much without your host. You arrested hundreds of men and women, you violated scores of homes, but still outside the prison walls there were men unknown to you who watched from the shadows as you hunted the anarchists, and waited only for the moment that would be favourable for them in their turn to hunt the hunters.

Reynal's words were a challenge thrown before the anarchists. The gauntlet was taken up. The bomb in the Café Terminus is the answer to all your violations of freedom, to your arrests, to your searches, to your laws against the Press, to your mass transportations, to your guillotinings. But why, you ask, attack these peaceful café guests, who sat listening to music and who, no doubt, were neither judges nor deputies nor bureaucrats? Why? It is very simple. The bourgeoisie did not distinguish among the anarchists. Vaillant, a man on his own, threw a bomb; nine-tenths of the comrades did not even know him. But that meant nothing; the persecution was a mass one, and anyone with the slightest anarchist links was hunted down. And since you hold a whole party responsible for the actions of a single man, and strike indiscriminately, we also strike indiscriminately.

Perhaps we should attack only the deputies who make laws against us, the judges who apply those laws, the police who arrest us? I do not agree. These men are only instruments. They do not act in their own name. Their functions were instituted by the bourgeoisie for its own defence. They are no more guilty than the rest of you. Those good bourgeois who hold no office but who reap their dividends and live idly on the profits of the workers' toil, they also must take their share in the reprisals. And not only they, but all those who are satisfied with the existing order, who applaud the acts of the government and so become its accomplices, those clerks earning three or five hundred francs a month who hate the people even more violently than the rich, that stupid and pretentious mass of folk who always choose the strongest side—in other words, the daily clientele of Terminus and the other great cafés.

That is why I struck at random and did not choose my victims! The bourgeoisie must be brought to understand that those who have suffered are tired at last of their sufferings; they are showing their teeth and they will strike all the more brutally if you are brutal with them. They have no respect for human life, because the bourgeoisie themselves have shown they have no care for it. It is not for the assassins who were responsible for the bloody week and for Fourmies to regard others as assassins.

We will not spare the women and children of the bourgeois, for the women and children of those we love have not been spared. Must we not count among the innocent victims those children who die slowly of anaemia in the slums because bread is scarce in their houses; those women who grow pale in your workshops, working to earn forty sous a day and fortunate when poverty does not force them into prostitution; those old men whom you have made production machines all their lives and whom you cast on to the waste heap or into the workhouse when their strength has worn away?

At least have the courage of your crimes, gentlemen of the bourgeoisie, and grant that our reprisals are completely legitimate.

Of course, I am under no illusions. I know my deeds will not yet be understood by the masses who are unprepared for them. Even among the workers, for whom I have fought, there will be many, misled by your newspapers, who will regard me as their enemy. But that does not matter. I am not concerned with anyone's judgment. Nor am I ignorant of the fact that there are individuals claiming to be anarchists who hasten to disclaim any solidarity with the propagandists of the deed. They seek to establish a subtle distinction between the theoreticians and the terrorists. Too cowardly to risk their own lives, they deny those who act. But the influence they pretend to wield over the revolutionary movement is nil. Today the field is open to action, without weakness or retreat.

Alexander Herzen, the Russian revolutionary, once said: "Of two things one must be chosen: to condemn and march forward, or to pardon and turn back half way." We intend neither to pardon nor to turn back, and we shall always march forward until the revolution, which is the goal of our efforts, finally arrives to crown our work with the creation of a free world.

In that pitiless war which we have declared on the bourgeoisie, we ask for no pity. We give death, and we know how to endure it. So it is with indifference that I await your verdict. I know that my head is not the last you will cut off; yet others will fall, for the starving are beginning to know the way to your great cafés and restaurants, to the Terminus and Foyot. You will add other names to the bloody list of our dead.

You have hanged in Chicago, decapitated in Germany, garrotted in Jerez,—shot in Barcelona, guillotined in Montbrison and Paris, but what you will never destroy is anarchy. Its roots are too deep. It is born in the heart of a society that is rotting and falling apart. It is a violent reaction against the established order. It represents all the egalitarian and libertarian aspirations that strike out against authority. It is everywhere, which makes it impossible to contain. It will end by killing you.

Courtroom Statement (Sante Geronimo Caserio)

Source: Emma Goldman, *The Psychology of Political Violence*, as referenced by Marxists Internet Archive, https://www.marxists.org/reference/archive/goldman/works/1917/political-violence.htm (accessed March 2017)

Gentlemen of the Jury! I do not propose to make a defense, but only an explanation of my deed.

Since my early youth I began to learn that present society is badly organized, so badly that every day many wretched men commit suicide, leaving women and children in the most terrible distress. Workers, by thousands, seek for work and cannot find it. Poor families beg for food and shiver with cold; they suffer the greatest misery; the little ones ask their miserable mothers for food, and the mothers cannot give it to them, because they have nothing. The few things which the home contained have already been sold or pawned. All they can do is beg alms; often they are arrested as vagabonds.

I went away from my native place because I was frequently moved to tears at seeing little girls of eight or ten years obliged to work fifteen hours a day for the paltry pay of twenty centimes. Young women of eighteen or twenty also work fifteen hours daily, for a mockery of remuneration. And that happens not only to my fellow countrymen, but to all the workers, who sweat the whole day long for a crust of bread, while their labor produces wealth in abundance. The workers are obliged to live under the most wretched conditions, and their food consists of a little bread, a few spoonfuls of rice, and water; so by the time they are thirty or forty years old, they are exhausted, and go to die in the hospitals. Besides, in consequence of bad food and overwork, these unhappy creatures are, by hundreds, devoured by pellagra—a disease that, in my country, attacks, as the physicians say, those who are badly fed and lead a life of toil and privation.

I have observed that there are a great many people who are hungry, and many children who suffer, whilst bread and clothes abound in the towns. I saw many and large shops full of clothing and woolen stuffs, and I also saw warehouses full of wheat and Indian corn, suitable for those who are in want. And, on the other hand, I saw thousands of people who do not work, who produce nothing and live on the labor of others; who spend every day thousands of francs for their amusement; who debauch the daughters of the workers; who own dwellings of forty or fifty rooms; twenty or thirty horses, many servants; in a word, all the pleasures of life.

I believed in God; but when I saw so great an inequality between men, I acknowledged that it was not God who created man, but man who created God. And I discovered that those who want their property to be respected, have an interest in preaching the existence of paradise and hell, and in keeping the people in ignorance.

Not long ago, Vaillant threw a bomb in the Chamber of Deputies, to protest against the present system of society. He killed no one, only wounded some persons; yet bourgeois justice sentenced him to death. And not satisfied with the condemnation of the guilty man, they began to pursue the Anarchists, and arrest not only those who had known Vaillant, but even those who had merely been present at any Anarchist lecture.

The government did not think of their wives and children. It did not consider that the men kept in prison were not the only ones who suffered, and that their little ones cried for bread. Bourgeois justice did not trouble itself about these innocent ones, who do not yet know what society is. It is no fault of theirs that their fathers are in prison; they only want to eat.

The government went on searching private houses, opening private letters, forbidding lectures and meetings, and practicing the most infamous oppressions against us. Even now, hundreds of Anarchists are arrested for having written an article in a newspaper, or for having expressed an opinion in public.

Gentlemen of the Jury, you are representatives of bourgeois society. If you want my head, take it; but do not believe that in so doing you will stop the Anarchist propaganda. Take care, for men reap what they have sown.

Seven

The One-Armed Anarchist

The watch had changed over for the night, the eight bells having just sounded. The ship, the SS *Aramac*, was gliding across a calm and moonlit sea. A relatively new addition to the fleet belonging to the Australasian United Steam Navigation Company, it had been largely broken in on regular crossings between Sydney and Brisbane and back again. Most of the crew and passengers were sleeping (or on their way to it) when an explosion ripped through the ship; debris crashed into the waves, and flames surged across the deck. Below deck, a steerage passenger who had provided the alias Frederick Howard, according to his own later account, instinctively bolted from his bunk and ran to the deck to see whether he could provide assistance. The mysterious Mr. Howard soon found himself detained and arrested when the ship moored in Brisbane, and he was eventually forced to reveal his real name: Larry Petrie.

Many of the details surrounding Lawrence Petrie (known to friends and enemies alike as Larry) are nebulous and scant. Historians have largely been unable to determine the precise date and location of his birth; the closest anyone has come thus far is Bob James, who claims that Petrie was born in 1859.[1] According to Scottish birth records, a Lawrence Dilnot Petrie was born in Old Machar, Aberdeen, on 2 May 1859. This individual appears to have been the only son of John Petrie and Harriet Eliza Youden, who were married five years earlier in August 1854 in Alness, a small town in the eastern part of Scotland. Old Machar is a parish in southeast Aberdeen that, although well-to-do in comparison to its neighbor Den Burn at the time, had just six years prior to Petrie's birth opened a poorhouse with enough room for some 247 inmates.[2] Petrie was, it seems, lucky at birth; according to details in the biography and reminiscences of the English painter Julian Rossi Ashton (who moved from Surrey to Melbourne in Australia in 1878), Petrie's father may have been a writer employed by the Signet in Edinburgh,[3] so although the family may not have had stable income, it seems unlikely that they were as ravaged by poverty as many others in Scotland were during the latter part of the nineteenth century. Beyond this, almost nothing is known of Petrie's early life in Scotland.

Larry Petrie is now remembered, if he is at all, in connection with Australian history, rather than that of Scotland. At some juncture, Petrie moved to the country with which he would be most associated. As with his birth, the circumstances and details of Petrie's immigration have for many years been overlooked or largely relegated to the background. A search of the unassisted immigration records for Victoria during the period 1852–1923[4] reveals two records for individuals named Laurence and Lawrence Petri, who arrived in Victoria in January 1875 and September 1885, respectively. The former was only sixteen years old and arrived on the ship *Allanshaw*; the latter arrived on the *Sorata*. The latter passenger was twenty-six on arrival, which would indicate a birth year of 1859; however, Petrie was by 1885 a well-established presence in the radical province of Melbourne. Additionally, according to reports in *The Worker*,[5] Petrie confirmed that his birth name was Laurence (not Lawrence, as previously thought), and thus it appears likely that he was only sixteen years old when he arrived in Australia. This raises the intriguing possibility that Petrie may have been a Home Child.

In 1869 a child migration scheme was founded by a Scottish evangelical Quaker named Annie MacPherson. As part of this program, known as Home Children, some 100,000 children from the British Isles were transported to Australia, Canada, South Africa, and New Zealand to alleviate labor shortages. (This practice had roots going back more than a century; in 1757, merchants and magistrates in Petrie's hometown of Aberdeen had been accused of forcing poor Scottish children to immigrate to America.[6]) Many Home Children were either orphaned or from poverty-stricken families.

Larry Petrie

These children were placed with settlers or within industrial settings that were often poorly supervised and regulated. Many of the forced young migrants were exposed to lives of privation and abuses of all kinds thousands of miles away from the support networks that they may have once had access to. The Home Children and other forced child resettlement schemes have left dark marks on the history of Australia and the United Kingdom, and both countries have formally recognized and apologized to the victims. Many Home Children who entered Australia did so as assisted migrants. The sixteen-year-old who stepped off the *Allanshaw*, however, was an unassisted migrant, which may indicate that not only had his passage been paid for, but arrangements had also been made for his arrival. It is worth noting that in the nineteenth century, it was common for children to start working in their teens (if not sooner); indeed, many by the age of sixteen had already begun to establish families of their own. To a modern reader, the concept of a sixteen-year-old traveling many thousands of miles alone to an unknown future may seem shocking, but in 1875 it was probably far more normal (and, for the young man involved, potentially an exciting and heady experience).

Whether Petrie was on board the *Allanshaw* is lost to history; his next confirmed appearance is in connection to the Melbourne Anarchist Club (MAC). In 1885, an American immigrant from Boston who had recently arrived in Melbourne gave a short lecture to a small gathering titled "What is Anarchy?" Although well received by some in attendance, the talk served to irritate representatives from the Australasian Secular Association (ASA). Although the ASA helped shield its members from greater Australian society, which sought to impose an "austere code of nineteenth century social propriety" that was "reinforced by the dominance of the puritan elite and their churches,"[7] Australia during the 1880s was largely divided according to religious groupings; however, for many the widening economic chasms that were opening up (which would eventually lead to a countrywide depression) were of greater concern. On 1 May 1886, dissident members of the ASA (among them David Andrade; his brother Will; John Arthur Andrews; and the recent American lecturer, Frederic Upham) helped establish the MAC.[8] This organization, which still exists today,[9] would play a seminal role in Petrie's early politics. According to one of the few historians who has diligently researched Petrie's life, he was "a late-comer to the Melbourne Anarchist Club (MAC), as Sam Rosa is, leading debates on 9th June 1888 on 'Anarchy,' on 10 August 1888 'the Chinese,' on 3rd November 1888 ('Individualism' the topic) and 8th December 1888 ('Equity')."[10] Just because Petrie was not present as a speaker, however, does not mean that he was disengaged from the political process. Indeed, he was already exhibiting the organizational skills and empathy for which he is remembered, and he was a frequent speaker at the Queen's Wharf, which had been completed in 1842 and by the 1880s was a continuously active (if sometimes dangerous) waterside mooring and warehousing area in Melbourne. Additionally, Petrie could often be found in slum areas, talking to both customers of tea houses and prostitutes, "for whom he had great sympathy,"[11] about worsening social conditions and change.

Social and economic conditions in Australia had been worsening since Petrie arrived, and these problems did not abate until the early twentieth century. As cogently documented by Christopher Lloyd, the Australian gold rush of 1851 had by the 1880s led to "working man's paradise and a triumphant vindication of the egalitarian and democratic rejection of British social class and privilege."[12] Sadly, this "paradise" was little more than an illusion for many. By the 1860s the gold rush had led to a vast depletion in Australia's mineral resources, and international boosters had led to a growing influx of immigrants, fortune hunters, and urban and rural poor. Although employment was available for skilled workers in support of the burgeoning Australian economy, the monopolization and increase of rents, as well as great numbers of readily available workers, led to increased abuses. Half of the Australian population in the 1880s lived in cities such as Melbourne, and although employment was plentiful, so were largely unregulated working conditions and all of the blights associated with too many people pushed together in too little space. This is one of the reasons why the economic downturn of the 1890s was so pronounced (as will be discussed later in the chapter) and why unionization was seen by many on the Australian Left as one mechanism to protect workers from the ravages of government in this supposed paradise.

In addition to engaging in low-level agitation of workers and prostitutes, Petrie was, according to Jack Andrews (as cited by Bob James), instrumental in organizing meetings outside the Golden Fleece Hotel, Russell Street, Melbourne, as well as in establishing the Knights of Labor in Melbourne and campaigning for the six-hour-day movement. The Knights of Labor (KOL) seems a strange organization for an Anarchist to be a part of at first glance. It is worth noting, however, that, like many on the Australian Left, Petrie was not an Individualist Anarchist but largely Socialist in his beliefs and committed to obtaining rights for workers through unionization. When discussing the KOL, labor historians have largely focused on its North American impact, but by the 1880s the group was truly international in scope, with associated branches in England, Wales, Ireland, Scotland, France, Belgium, South Africa, New Zealand and, of course, Australia.[13] The KOL was one organization that campaigned long and hard for the adoption of an eight-hour working day (as opposed to the fourteen-hour day typical for most Victorian industries). Although the KOL was not involved with the stonemasons' strike in Melbourne in April 1856 (wherein masons put down their tools and marched on Parliament in protest) or the conditions that were obtained in 1858 in which the eight-hour day became the norm for much of the building industry, it had by the 1880s become active in seeking universal application of the eight-hour working day. For Petrie, this change did not go far enough, and he agitated for a six-hour day. This difference of opinion may have been one factor that led to his disillusionment with the KOL and may explain why he is not more closely linked with the group beyond a few references scattered across obscure publications.

Although Petrie was involved with the KOL, he was still active in the MAC. As detailed by S. Merrifield,[14] the MAC initially met every Wednesday evening in the ASA rooms on 120 Swanston Street, Melbourne, and Petrie was a regular attendee. By the time the MAC had moved to Room 7 of the Alexandra Theatre, Petrie was also a regular speaker at the docks on Sunday (as detailed by James). Starting in April 1887, the MAC published a monthly paper called *Honesty*, described as an unequivocal and outspoken advocate for social reform. The mood of the MAC was a hopeful one initially, as summarized in the following verse:

The Anarchists

We'll trumpet a note to the heart of men
A note to sound in the darkest den
Where sorrow and sickness and sin are rife,
To peal to the poorest of prostrate souls,
And call them back to their own lost right,
To blare and burst when the war drum rolls,
And riot and ring in the rage of fights.[15]

Regardless of the members' view of themselves, the MAC received its share of criticism. The *Melbourne Punch* went so far as to describe MAC members as "loafers, drunkards, and thieves,"[16] and the MAC was regularly savaged in the pages of *The Liberator*, a periodical associated with the ASA (from which the MAC had splintered). This denigration may have led Petrie to compose a letter to the editor of *The Liberator* that was published on 26 February 1888:

> There seems to be a general belief that we are opposed to all Governments. Certainly we are opposed to all existing forms of government. But you see, the only government we know is a mixture of subjection, roguery, and robbery. Governments of today govern the people whereas our Government is a government of the people, for the people.
>
> We are credited with a passion for destruction but I should like our opponents to note what we would destroy—theft, slavery, misery and starvation of body and mind. The doctrine of Anarchism is almost identical with the doctrine of advanced Socialism, what some people call, scientific Socialism.
>
> Life without Equality and Fraternity is a lie as black as hell. And where is the government in the world where they are supreme. Nowhere and they are only possible under the conditions of Socialism—Anarchists would govern by conscience although they might use and advocate force to ensure an earlier emancipation for all Mankind.[17]

By the 1880s, Petrie had formed associations with the KOL and the so-called drunkards and loafers of the MAC, and he had become a noted firebrand speaker. His early defense of the use of force may have concerned the more conservative members of polite Melbourne society, as well as some in the wider Socialist community (such as members of the ASA). Perhaps this explains why Petrie eventually left Melbourne and drifted toward New South Wales. It may also be that Petrie sensed the unrest that would ultimately lead to the shearers' strike of 1891. Additionally, Melbourne likely became legally uncomfortable for Petrie during the maritime strike.

In mid–1890, Australian maritime workers had been engaged in a bitter and acrimonious series of labor disputes for several months. Beginning on 15 August 1890, leaders of the Mercantile Marine Officers' Association directed their followers to give twenty-four hours' notice to their employers after the breakdown of negotiations with the Steamship Owners' Association of Victoria. This dispute over working conditions and pay spread quickly from seamen to wharf laborers, and it even encompassed the coal miners who provided materials to the ships. By September 1890, more than 28,000 workers associated with the maritime industry were on strike throughout Australia, with more than 80,000 becoming involved during the tenure of the strike.[18] Although the strike was damaged when police and military forces were brought in by maritime employers, the true death blow came when those same employers utilized non-union workers who would work for reduced rates (due in no small part to the economic depression into which Australia was plunged in 1890). The availability of scab labor ultimately led to the union's acquiescence, and the union members returned to work on the employers' terms in November 1890.

The maritime strike of 1890 was particularly bloody, and the military was called out in support of a floundering and overwhelmed police force. The soldiers were there to provide more than just logistical support and, as detailed by Michael Head, were under specific shoot-to-kill orders with regard to both strikers and supporters. Indeed, the following instruction was issued by a Colonel Tom Price (Thomas Caradoc Rose Price CB) to members of a volunteer unit tasked with suppressing the strike:

> Men of the Mounted Rifles, one of your obligations imposes upon you the duty of resisting invasion by a foreign enemy, but you are also liable to be called upon to assist in preserving law and order in the colony.… To do your work faintly would be a grave mistake. If it has to be done effectively you will each be supplied with 40 rounds of ammunition, leaden bullets, and if the order is given to fire, don't let me see any rifle pointed in the air; fire low and lay them out so that the duty will not have to be performed again.[19]

It was not just the state that had turned violent, however. As Bruce Scates notes:

> In Adelaide … women joined men as they broke through the barricades on the wharf … in Sydney, four "riotous" women chased a driver through the streets … shouting "blackleg" and pelt[ing] him with stones. In Kent Street, a crowd of women and children showered specials with blue metal.… In September four blacklegs … were chased through Argyle Cut by over 200 people. By the time the police arrived a single man was surrounded by a crowd of seven hundred, his body battered by a barrage of brick and stone … "large numbers of women and children" took part in the rioting intent (as the Mail put it) "to do some injury to the men" … The Mail reported "the crowd seemed to increase itself in a miraculous fashion, and the lower end of George Street was filled by a surging mass of men, women and children, estimated at from 4,000 to 5,000 persons. For a time these seemed almost to lose their reason, and made a fearful noise, yelling, hooting and shouting as if they were mad."[20]

Given that Petrie was a very public union organizer (and one who had previously stated how it was often necessary to utilize force), and given that the streets of Melbourne were full of trigger-happy representatives of the state, he may well have decided that in this instance discretion was the better part of valor and opted to head out to the country. According to details provided by John Hannan,[21] Petrie drifted through western New

South Wales and was involved in a range of disputes between union and non-union shearers, as well as other bush workers. There is even evidence suggesting that he played a part in agitation that preceded the 1891 shearers' strike. At Berry Jerry Station in New South Wales, things turned physical, as Petrie later detailed for the press:

> That arm I lost was a most unfortunate one. It was broken in three places when I met with an accident some years ago, shunting metal trucks for W. Loud, of Albert Park, Melbourne; on that occasion I also had my ribs crushed. My broken arm was set, and healed but it was of little use to me. A couple of years afterwards when working at Berry Jerry Station (N.S.W.) I had a tussle with a 14-stone non-unionist and it was again broken—this time in two places. The manager of Berry Jerry refused to run in any of the shearers' or roustabouts' horses, and it was only by the kindness of the roustabouts in purchasing a horse from a traveler who happened to be passing that I was enabled to make my way into Wagga, 32 hours after my arm was broken. The doctors found it impossible to save the arm, which was amputated.[22]

Beyond engaging in bloody fistfights with non-union scab laborers and moonlit dashes to hospitals, the amputation of his already withered arm offers a glimpse of Petrie's gentler side. Both Hannan and James note that a nurse at the Wagga station assisted Petrie in his recovery following the operation. According to an account provided by one of the founders of the Australian Labor Party, noted trade unionist William Guthrie Spence, "all women were angels to Larry, and the nurse was one of the best."[23] To thank her for her ministrations, Petrie desperately wanted to give the unnamed nurse a gift. Being banned from doing so by hospital regulations, and probably not wishing to get her dismissed, Petrie found a novel (if somewhat gruesome) solution: he dug up the arm bone that had been removed as part of the amputation and gifted it to the nurse. Her reaction to this unusual gift has not been recorded, but in 1891 Petrie moved to Sydney with only one arm and no nurse.

In 1891 the General Laborers' Union (GLU) opened offices (and an employment bureau) at Castlereagh Street, between the Protestant Hall and McNamara's bookshop, opposite the City Fire Brigade Station in Sydney. Spence appointed Petrie as secretary-organizer and Rose Summerfield as woman organizer. This decision came as a surprise to many who had either known Petrie or heard of his reputation. As his friend Ernie Lane later wrote, "Petrie was in the super class of rebels,"[24] and he was often perceived as being too rambunctious for a position of authority. During his time at the GLU, Petrie and Lane slept in the offices on stretchers in the back room,[25] but Petrie was in his element in this position. He was a natural organizer, according to all available sources, and would frequently take any opportunity on street corners, in saloons, or anywhere else that brought him into contact with workers, calling for them to join him on the barricades. Though initially treated as an entertaining joke by the Sydney police, Lane asserted that they had underestimated Petrie's effectiveness as an organizer. For example, Petrie was well aware of his physical deficits, and he would frequently call workers "to arms" while holding his one remaining arm up in salute. This gesture never failed to get a few laughs from cynical and often uninterested crowds, which Petrie doubtless utilized to his advantage.

Less than a year after the maritime workers had engaged in strike action, 1891 saw the launch of a countrywide shearers' strike. The Australian Shearers' Union had by 1890 many thousands of workers and thousands of unionized sheds. (It was probably while in pursuit of the latter that Petrie injured his arm.) On 5 January 1891, the shearers' strike started in earnest with clear demands (continuation of existing rates of pay, protection of workers' rights and privileges, just and equitable agreements, and exclusion of low-cost Chinese labor) and quickly spread throughout Australia. The military was called upon to protect non-union leaders, and thousands of arrests were made. For a short time (as with the earlier maritime strike) it appeared that Australia was teetering on the brink of civil war. Union camps were set up across rural communities and outside towns to provide economic and social support to the strikers. On May Day 1891, more than one thousand shearers marched in Sydney, meeting with limited resistance. The strikers could not hold out, however, and by the end of the shearing season they had been forced to return to work as a result of non-union labor and increased economic and police pressure. At the end of the acrimonious dispute, thirteen union leaders had been arrested; they were subsequently transported to Rockhampton for trial. Upon conviction, all were sentenced to three years in St. Helena Island Prison. The maritime and shearers' strikes, although devastating for many who worked in the wool trade, were central to the formation of the Australian Labor Party. As for the GLU, it was absorbed into the Australian Workers' Union (AWU), which was itself a precursor of the Labor Party. Possibly as part of a move toward a more centrist position, or as a result of his actions during the shearers' strike, Petrie was temporarily dismissed from his position as an organizer.

The year 1892 found Petrie at loose ends after his dismissal from the nascent AWU, and he left Sydney for the country with an unnamed friend (at least in the account provided by Bob James). There they engaged in a number of odd jobs such as saw sharpening, with Petrie being responsible for drumming up business. Petrie was to prove a better rabble rouser than a country salesman, and he returned to Sydney in September 1892, securing a position as organizing secretary for the AWU.

By 1893, the labor disputes that had previously rocked Australia had flared in earnest. In Minmi, union coal miners fired a homemade cannon at a barracks housing non-union workers, and fourteen women were arrested when they stopped the police from attempting to interrupt.[26] In Melbourne, some 400 Chinese cabinet makers were on strike, seeking pay equal to that of European workers. This year also saw the collapse of several Australian banks, starting with the failure of the Australian Federal Bank on 30 January 1893.[27] The economic depression that commenced in 1890 had by 1893 led to a full-blown economic collapse, the closure of hundreds of private companies, and workers seeking to retain what few employment opportunities were left through industrial disputes that were often met with egregious levels of violence by employers and the state. It was in this environment that, in addition to his involvement in the AWU, Petrie became a member of the Active Service Brigade.[28]

As the name indicates, the Active Service Brigade was an early direct action group that was headquartered in a building on Castlereagh Street in Sydney. To provide cover for the group's activities, and in furtherance of its political ideology concerning equality and fraternity, the building also provided cheap lodging for the poor of Sydney. As J.A. Andrews later wrote:

> The Brigade offered men a dormitory shelter, with stretcher and blanket, and a morning refreshment of tea and bread and butter, for the total sum of threepence, which covered the cost, and even left a margin when dealing with numbers; and nobody was refused on account of inability to pay—a man was in such a case given credit, with the understanding that he would pay if he got in a position to do so. Those, however, who took advantage of this to sponge on the Brigade whilst persistently boozing away what money they got, were blacklisted, and turned out when other men needed the accommodation. They were only a small minority at any time. In numerous cases men stayed on credit for months, and faithfully paid their share when they later on obtained the means.[29]

Far from running a low-cost hostel, however, the Active Service Brigade had a wider purpose. Originally established by the poet Arthur Desmond (who set up the periodical *Hard Cash* on 11 June 1893, and who, ironically, would go on to become a Fascist who would claim that inherent human rights were nonexistent and Christianity was flawed as a concept owing to Hebraic influence), the Active Service Brigade initially focused on disrupting meetings of its political opponents, and its members were not averse to the use of physical force. As Andrews states regarding one of the group's earlier actions, a meeting was "taken possession of by the Brigade, which held its position in a hand-to-hand fight."[30] Although the Active Service Brigade allegedly had no centralized leadership (a striking difference from many of the committee-heavy organizations of the period), it continued to interrupt political meetings regularly during 1893. At this point, things began to take a darker turn, not just for the Active Service Brigade but also for Petrie.

One member of the Sydney radical milieu was Mary Cameron (later known as Dame Mary Gilmore). Although she would later find fame as a poet, in 1893 Mary was a twenty-eight-year-old school teacher employed at the Neutral Bay Public School in Sydney. She was also involved in the increasing radicalism of the day, supporting the maritime and shearers' strikes. She may have been involved with the AWU during this period, which would have brought her into contact with Larry Petrie. According to Anne Whitehead, Mary was approached by Petrie and "hid some dynamite for him, placing it in a bottom drawer at her lodgings in Newtown."[31] This may have been in part of a plan Petrie had to cause an explosion at the Sydney docks.

In her old age, Mary Gilmore claimed in the pages of the *National Times* (6–11 May 1974)[32] that in 1892 Petrie had formulated a plan to set off an explosion at the Circular Quay, which was then the main dock area of Sydney. After finding out about his plans, Mary had served as a lookout while J.C. Watson and the then vice president of the AWU, Arthur Rae, were tasked with retrieving the bomb that Petrie had planted. A man of diminutive stature at only five foot, Rae would go on to be one of the founders of the Australian Labor Party, but on that day in 1892, as Mary waited for him, he slithered up a drain to recover the bomb in order to stop its detonation. As to what had prompted Petrie to place the explosive charges in the first instance, this idea was probably due in no small part to his involvement with the Active Service Brigade and also served as a direct response to the economic depression and deteriorating working conditions for many of the Australian poor.

One particular incident that was to play a role in later events concerning Petrie was the 1893 maritime strike. As in the earlier 1890 strike, the events of 1893 were prompted by employers making use of non-union labor in an effort to not only neuter the unions but also reduce their own operating costs during a time of economic crisis. As before, seamen and wharf laborers engaged in strike activities, and the state responded with increasing violence. For Petrie, who had been involved in union organization and had seen firsthand the impact of non-union labor for more than a decade, this turn of events may have prompted his earlier planned attack against Circular Quay, and it would also have direct bearing on the events that followed.

As reported in the Melbourne-based paper *The Argus*,[33] on the evening of Thursday, 28 July 1893, just before midnight, the SS *Aramac* was approximately seven nautical miles south of Point Lookout near Moreton Bay en route from Sydney to Brisbane. The *Aramac* was, owing to the maritime strike of 1893, a non-union ship, staffed by scab labor. It had been produced by William Denny and Brothers in 1889 at their shipyard, Yard 415, located in Dumbarton, Scotland. That night, Petrie was on board, using one of his familiar aliases, George Frederick Howard. Earlier that evening, Petrie had planted a gelatin-and-dynamite bomb, reportedly eleven inches long, six inches wide and four inches in diameter,[34] in the forecastle (or upper deck) of the *Aramac*. As the *Aramac* neared Point Danger, a large explosion ripped through the ship's forecabin and "flames were seen to issue from the forepart of the ship."[35] Although a number of passengers were injured (some reports refer to two female passengers being hurt; in others the injured parties are a man by the name of Kramer or Krauser and an unnamed female passenger), there were no serious injuries and no fatalities.

Shortly after the explosion, the press was keen to involve Petrie in a larger conspiracy regarding the events that had occurred on the *Aramac*. According to reports in the *Bundaberg Mail and Burnett Advertiser*:

> It is the opinion of the Queensland police that the explosion on the Aramac was arranged in Sydney. Information supplied by passengers bears out this view. About four minutes before the Aramac left the wharf at Sydney a man was observed to leave the fore cabin and past hastily up the companion. This man came from the port side, where no passengers were accommodated. He bore in his hand a small brown leather handbag. His actions were so suspicious that he was followed on deck by some passengers and the fore cabin steward, who thought he was probably a thief. However, the time of the vessel's departure was so near that nothing was done. One of the passengers states that he watched the man walk hurriedly along the wharf, and observed him join another man after he had gone a little distance from the steamer. This man seized the man who had left the steamer by the arm and shook hands with him, as if congratulating him on something he had done and done well. It is considered extremely improbable that the explosion was manipulated by any person travelling on the steamer from Sydney.[36]

However improbable it may have seemed to the skeptical members of the press, the Queensland police, or even the other passengers on the *Aramac*, when the ship arrived in Brisbane, Petrie found himself under arrest for attempted murder. His story about being safe in his cabin and then moving to the deck when he heard the explosion was not believed (it was thought that he had appeared too quickly on deck to have come from his cabin), and he soon found himself exposed to the tender mercies of the Brisbane police force. As he would later reveal, his initial time in custody was far from pleasant:

> I objected to being kept in a solitary cell with no company other than the occasional visits of the warder, they put in my cell an alleged forger named Harris who informed me that he had forged the name of a Sydney firm for £350. This man was persistently worrying me to accept the reward, and I firmly believe was a detective. I was locked up in a separate and dismal cell for four weeks, not allowed to see anyone but the warder who was continually watching me, and fed on bread and water until I complained, when I was allowed one meal from a restaurant for which I paid for a fortnight, when the authorities or someone else, on my complaining paid for it. The other two meals consisted of bread and water.[37]

His dining choices and temporary cell companions aside, Petrie was doing himself no services while detained. Although questioned repeatedly, Petrie refused to admit any guilt or acknowledge his part in any explosion. He did, however, inform detectives that he would tell the premier of Queensland, Sir Thomas McIlwraith, who was responsible for having caused the explosion. When Petrie was transferred from Brisbane to the Boggo Road Gaol (which he apparently found far more suitable), he received a visitor. Incredibly enough, this person turned out to be McIlwraith, whom Petrie accused personally and as a representative of the wider government as being responsible for the explosion owing to the state's abuse of the working classes and its tyrannies. It is not reported how the authorities received this accusation, but Petrie in all probability was amused by it—at least until the inevitable punishment got under way.

Petrie's trial began on Friday, 11 August 1893, and right from the start things did not seem to be going well for him. Appearing undefended, he faced Sub-Inspector Nethercote of the Brisbane police for the prosecution. A witness by the name of Alfred Lancaster, who had been working as a trimmer on the *Aramac*, recognized Petrie from his union work. After seeing Petrie embark on the ship, Lancaster had also observed him on deck shortly after the explosion. Lancaster believed that there was no way for Petrie to have made it from steerage, through a hatchway and out onto deck (where he was reportedly leaning casually on the starboard side of the vessel) following the explosion, which placed him on deck for reasons other than enjoying the quiet midnight air. Petrie, never one to back down from conflict, berated Lancaster about his version of events, and he also engaged in a heated exchange with the prosecutor when he attempted to assist his witness.

Following a week's adjournment, Petrie was back in the courtroom. A number of the *Aramac*'s crew (including the captain, William Armstrong, and the second officer, William Hunter McLellan) and a cast of supporting witnesses all testified that they had not only heard and reacted to the explosion but also witnessed Petrie behaving suspiciously. The steward, William Rosser, further damaged Petrie's defense when he declared that he had not seen Petrie in his cabin in steerage shortly after the explosion. The *Aramac*'s shipwright, George Radcliffe, testified that he knew Petrie and had heard him use the alias of Howard previously and was aware of his union agitation and fiery temperament. Although Petrie fought just as combatively as he had the previous week, the situation was looking increasingly bleak.

Another adjournment followed, and more witnesses were produced. Among them was Robert Fitzpatrick, reportedly a gang master for a railway company in St. Leonards. According to Fitzpatrick's testimony, Petrie had approached him prior to the *Aramac* explosion. Although he knew Petrie only by reputation, Fitzpatrick was allegedly happy to show him how to prime and use dynamite from the railway stores, and he even demonstrated its potency by blowing up some nearby boulders. Petrie then repeatedly asked to purchase some dynamite, but Fitzpatrick refused. At this point, the case against Petrie was once more adjourned for a week. Petrie, proving he had lost none of his wry humor, asked whether he was likely to be detained much longer, "as it is a little hard on my nerves."

When Petrie returned to court the following week, he was represented by his newly appointed counsel, Mr. McCartney. It did not take too long for McCartney to gather evidence of what Petrie already knew: namely, that he had never met Fitzpatrick and thus had never attempted to purchase anything from him. In a turn of events that proved catastrophic for the prosecution, McCartney established that, far from being an innocent foreman demonstrating the use of high explosives, Fitzpatrick was well known to the Sydney police and amenable to suggestion. On hearing of the evidence against Petrie, the diminutive Arthur Rae, who had previously intervened to prevent the Circular Quay bombing, had sponsored McCartney, who had dug deep into Fitzpatrick's background. Although the police had a reasonably strong case against Petrie, and he certainly fit the then conventional portrait of a bomber, they had no evidence as to where and how he had obtained the materials necessary to cause an explosion. Thus they deployed Fitzpatrick to provide the missing link. McCartney was able to obtain proof of perjury and the creation of supposed evidence against Petrie, and the attorney general of Queensland was required to issue a "no true bill" and dismiss the case. In October 1893, Petrie walked out of prison a free man, thanks in no small part to the actions of the state and its use of provably perjured and tainted evidence.[38]

Following his release, and according to his obituary, Petrie made his way to Melbourne, where he "had hard times with poverty and ill-health."[39] He soon discovered that during his time in jail, the radical community of Australia seemed to have found a mechanism to more actively resist economic privations and the waves of repression that had followed labor disputes. This was achieved by the founding of the New Australia Cooperative Settlement Association, or New Australia Movement, as it was more popularly known by William Lane. Lane was an English expatriate who had been active in the Australian movement for years; like many others, he had become disenchanted with his struggles against the state. Starting in 1892, he had begun searching for a parcel of land somewhere in the world where he and likeminded individuals could create an alternative to Australia's rampant nineteenth-century capitalism. On 28 September 1893, Lane and 238 adults and children found what they were looking for southeast of Asunción, the capital of Paraguay. The society that Lane sought to create for himself and others consisted of a number of core doctrines, including common holdings, lifelong marriages, teetotalism, and adherence to Communist principles. More controversial, perhaps, was the holding of the "color-line," which forbade miscegenation and, indeed, even casual contacts between different races. Almost from the start of this effort, relations between the settlers of what was called Colonia Nueva Australia began to fall apart. Lane was seen by many as being dictatorial in his demands, and he (along with 58 others) soon left, traveling seventy-two miles further south to establish the new settlement of Cosme. Among the adherents who followed Lane across Paraguay were Rose Summerfield, a former comrade of Petrie's from his GLU days, and Mary Gilmore, the one-time lookout. Cosme looked like an attractive proposition for Petrie, but he lacked the membership fee that was required of every new settler to support the upkeep of the community. Never one to let simple matters of finance prevent him from fulfilling his ambitions, Petrie soon came up with a solution.

According to later accounts,[40] Petrie decided to work his way to Cosme. In 1894 he managed to stow away on a ship bound for Honolulu. Exactly how he achieved this passage with only one arm is sadly not documented. Far from finding a tropical paradise in Hawaii, Petrie found a series of islands that he later documented as having the dual afflictions of "parsons and slavery," and thus he soon sought passage to San Francisco. In the United States, Petrie became active in the American Socialist Party before making his way to New Orleans. Again short of cash, Petrie traveled from San Francisco to New Orleans by hopping freight trains. After failing to secure employment in New Orleans, Petrie went to New York. Here he attempted to stow away on a number of vessels bound for South America. However, ship crews in New York proved to be more formidable in their detection abilities than their Australian peers, and Petrie was discovered during each of his abortive attempts to make it to the open sea. Eventually he secured paid passage as a crew member of a ship heading south, finally arriving in Cosme on 23 August 1896. Initially ecstatic at having reached his goal, Petrie soon locked horns with Lane, whom he found dictatorial in the extreme. After fellow settlers were expelled in 1898, Petrie packed up his belongings and moved to Nueva Australia.

Upon arriving in the Nueva Australia settlement, Petrie secured employment as a general watchman at the Villarrica train station.[41] On 1 March 1901, the daughter of the station master was playing on the tracks, unaware of an oncoming train. Seeing the imminent danger, Petrie raced to the child, throwing her to safety with his one remaining arm, but in saving her life he lost his own, as the speeding train crushed him to death. His body was claimed by Rose Cadogan (previously Rose Summerfield), who had worked with Petrie in Sydney.[42] Soon afterward, Petrie was laid to rest in an unmarked grave in the cemetery at Na Sarah in Paraguay,[43] more than 6,000 miles from his Scottish birthplace.

Larry Petrie, owing to the nature of his union organization work, often had to utilize aliases so as to avoid detection by agents of the state. For many years he also successfully avoided detection and discussion by historians. The scant details of his life have only been assembled on a limited number of occasions, and there has been no consideration of his place in relation to enacting propaganda of the deed. Petrie's actions were arguably far removed from the Nihilism of Ravachol or the individualism of many of the illegalists, being driven more by his Socialist and pro-union stance, and he displayed not only a healthy sense of humor but also deeply committed principles. Many of Petrie's peers went on to play an active role in the creation of the Australian Labour Party and the creation of modern Australia, and it is regrettable that Petrie is not granted equal consideration. A sympathetic historian may conclude that Petrie's motivation for bombing the *Aramac* was to cause damage (rather than the attempted murder and carnage for which he was subsequently charged) and, in doing so, create economic hardship for the ship owners who had exploited their workers for so long. Both in his death and throughout much of his life, Petrie seems to have been inspired by altruism and consideration of the needs of others. He may have been a brawler and a firebrand, but it is unfortunate that he appears largely as a localized footnote in history. Petrie illustrates the true internationalist reach of the concept of propaganda of the deed, and an application of this concept to further political ambitions through protest (as opposed to assassination). For this reason alone, his actions and details of his life should be better known, investigated, and discussed.

"I Have to Thank the Crows for Saving My Life"— L. De Petrie (M.J.C. [the alias of Mary Gilmore])

Published in *The Worker*, 9 September 1893, page 3

> The crows kep' flyin' up, boys, the crows, kep'
>   flyin' up;
> Rome, he seen, and whimpered, boys, though
>   he was but a pup
> Rome, he seen, and whimpered, as he follered
>   close as wax,
> Hung his head an' dropped his tail, acreepin' in
>   my tracks.
> We seen 'em as we touched the plain, seen 'em
>   as we crost.
> Seen 'em as we hit the Bend where Simpson's
>   boy was lost;
> We cuts out by the crick, boys, an' what was it
>   we found

Lyin' in the scrub, boys, where the crows was
    fly'n' round?

What was it we found, boys, that was lyin'
    there so still?
(The blasted crows could gather an' wait to
    gorge their fill).
A man an' mate we found, boys, alyin' like the
    dead—
Crows aflyin' up, boys, a goanner at, his head!

We didn't go too near him, we didn't go too
    near—
We stood a bit an' waited, but not because of
    fear:
We thought he might be high, boys, with lyin'
    in the sun,
An' didn't care to start a job that couldn't well
    be done.

So we stopped about a minute, boys, an' then
    we, went acrost—
And found that Larry Petrie was the man and
    mate was lost.
Me and Rome we got him round, and took him
    from the place
Where he laid all stunned an' stupid while the
    crows was sayin' grace.

***

We hear that worse than crows is agettin' at
    him now
Worse, than them goanners that dined upon
    the Chow.
We ain't worth much to look at it, but Rome
    an' me will Wait,
An' do whatever we can do for Larry, man an'
    mate.

Prospectus of the Melbourne Anarchist Club, 1886

Source: Quoted by S. Merrifield, "The Melbourne Anarchist Club, 1886–1891," *Labor History*, no. 3 (November 1962): 35–36

To the people of Australasia

The Melbourne Anarchists' Club extends its greetings to the liberty loving citizens of these young colonies and appeals to them to assist its members in their efforts to remove those public sentiments and public institutions, which have been transplanted here from the northern hemispheres, retard social progress and happiness; and to substitute in their place the enabling principles of Liberty, Equality and Fraternity!

The objects of the Melbourne Anarchists' Club are:

1. To foster public interest in the great social questions of the day, by promoting inquiry in every possible way; to promote free public discussion of all social questions; and to circulate and publish literature, throwing light upon existing evils of society, and the methods necessary for their removal.

2. To foster and extend the principles of Self Reliance, Self Help and a Spirit of Independence amongst the people.

3. To uphold and maintain the principles of Liberty, Equality and Fraternity. By Liberty we mean "the equal liberty of each, limited alone by the equal liberty of all." By Equality we mean "the equality of opportunity for each individual." And by Fraternity we mean "that principle which denies national and class distinctions, asserts the Brotherhood of Man and says 'The world is my country.'"

4. To advocate, and seek to achieve, the abolition of all monopolies and despotisms which destroy the Freedom of the Individual and which thereby check social progress and prosperity.

5. To expose and oppose that colossal swindle, Government, and to advocate Abstention from Voting, Resistance to Taxation, and Private Co-operation or Individual Action.

6. To foster Mutual Trust and Fraternity amongst the working people of all ranks, and to turn their attention to their common foes: the Priests and the Politicians, and their co-adjutors, attacking principles rather than individuals.

7. To invite the co-operation of all, who have realised the innate evils of our governing institutions, and desire their speedy dissolution for the general benefit of Humanity.

8. To promote the formation of voluntary institutions similar to the Melbourne Anarchist Club throughout Victoria and the neighbouring colonies, and, with their consent, to eventually unite with them forming the Australasian Association of Anarchists.

Eight

An Outrage in the Park

"England lags. This country is absurd with its sentimental regard for individual liberty."[1]

The afternoon of 15 February 1894 was bracing. The residents of London moved briskly, as they always did in winter, wrapped in whatever clothing they could afford. In Greenwich Park two schoolboys were making their way home close to the observatory that sat on the hill overlooking the River Thames. Their conversation was interrupted when a loud report sounded and a plume of smoke arose from beyond the trees near the zigzag path that led up to the observatory building. Under the smoke lay the twisted and damaged body of a young French immigrant who would go on to be immortalized in literature, though largely neglected by historians.

The immigrant in question was Martial Bourdin, who was either twenty-six or twenty-seven years old at the time of his death. Historians have thus far failed to be more exact about his age, and there remain a number of critical missing and disputed details about Bourdin's brief life. What is known is that he was born in Tours in the center-west of France sometime in 1868, one of eight children; his older brother, Henri, would come to play a large role in later events and, indeed, in the truncated life of his younger brother. It is commonly believed by many historians who have chosen to focus upon the life of Martial Bourdin that Henry Samuels (born Levi Herris Wilchinski) was married to his sister.[2] Even this detail, however, is disputed, with some researchers positing that it was Henri who was married to Samuels' sister, Emmeline Kate (commonly referred to as Kate).[3] Regardless of the later marital relationships, at some juncture in his early history, Bourdin found work as a ladies' tailor, as did his brother Henri, which may indicate that tailoring was a family trade. According to Paul Gibbard's biography, one of the few sources of information regarding Bourdin, by 1884, at the age of sixteen, Bourdin was working as a tailor in Paris and had joined an Anarchist group by the name of L'Aigulle (The Needles). Gibbard[4] claims the young Bourdin was using the alias of J. Allder, and it was under this name that he was sentenced to two months' imprisonment for attempting to organize a public meeting on a crowded thoroughfare. This claim is further supported by an article published in the *Morning Leader* on 19 February 1894 and referenced by Hermja Oliver.[5]

Although the image of Martial Bourdin as a teenage revolutionary so committed to his cause that he was imprisoned by the French state is a romantic one, it is disputed by Mary Burgoyne and others. In addition, there is no record of Bourdin being a member of L'Aigulle in Jean Maitron's *Dictionnaire bio graphique du mouvement ouvrier franfais*

(1964–1990) and *Le Mouvement anar- chiste en France* (1975).[6] That L'Aigulle existed, however, is not under dispute (the noted French Anarcho-Communist and vice secretary of the General Confedera- tion of Labor from 1901 to 1908, Emile Pouget, was a member of this group and "La Sentinelle revolutionnaire" as of 1887/1888)[7]; according to Oliver, the group was established in 1882. Whether Bourdin was a teenage radical and, indeed, what prompted his revolutionary fervor at such a young age remains uncertain. One explanation may lie in Bourdin's fam- ily background. In addition to tailoring, there may well have been a family tradi- tion of active engagement with politics within the Bourdin clan. Following Bour- din's death, *The Standard* reported that his father had been arrested as part of the detention of seven Anarchists in Paris.[8] Whether this is an accurate record or a blatant attempt to shape reality to sell more papers is definitely debatable; how- ever, it is worth considering that tailors

Martial Bourdin

have traditionally played a part in the history of labor—perhaps the Bourdin family car- ried on this custom.

Whether the teenage Bourdin was imprisoned by the French state cannot be known for certain; if he was, it would go some way toward explaining his later actions, as con- ditions for prisoners at the time were deliberately hostile. It is known that in 1887, aged nineteen, Bourdin crossed the English Channel to join his brother in London. In 1886, Henri was married to Kate, who was cohabiting with him at 12 Noel Street, St. James's. By the time Bourdin arrived in London, Henri and his growing family (Burgoyne suggests that the reason for Henri's marriage to Kate was her pregnancy with their first daughter, Adele) were resident in 18 Great Titchfield Street, Marylebone, where Henri was working as a master tailor for ladies in his own workshop. It was here that Bourdin secured piece- work from his older brother and probably first made contact with the Autonomie Club and its membership.

The Autonomie Club was to prove infamous in connection to London's Anarchist history, although, surprisingly, a full history of the club and its members has never been attempted. The club was established by Josef Peukert, a German Bohemian Anarchist, in 1886. Prior to establishing the Autonomie Club, Peukert had been a member of a Socialist League club in Whitfield Street, from which he was expelled by a fellow member, Victor Dave (with whom Peukert had a fierce personal and factional rivalry). The Autonomie is variously described as "the key meeting point for the international colony of anarchists in London"[9] and "an Anarchist 'centre,' in which many European outrages had been planned."[10] Initially, the Autonomie Club was established at 32 Charlotte Street in Fitzrovia. This central London district is situated near London's West End, just north of Soho. Today this neighborhood is one of the most desirable areas in London; in Bourdin's time, however, it was far from ideal. Nearby Charlotte Street were the St. Giles rookery and the oppressive slums of Seven Dials that were a world away from the lights and glamor of the West End. Fitzrovia was filled with immigrants who often lived in crowded and cramped conditions, and the police rarely ventured into this area unless they were in a substantive group. It was perhaps for this reason that the famed Communard Louise Michel established the International School to teach French, German and English to exiled Anarchists and their children at 19 Charlotte Street. A fitting description of the Autonomie Club was provided by Detective Sergeant MacIntyre of the London Metropolitan Police (who would go on to play a role in later events): "Here the malcontents of all nations fraternized and denounced their various governments to their hearts content, mixing with their denunciations the largest possible quantities of lager beer and miscellaneous liqueurs."[11]

By the time of Bourdin's arrival in London, the Autonomie Club had relocated to 6 Windmill Street, nearby Tottenham Court Road. For all of its later impact, the Automonie Club was a "very small place, just two rooms,"[12] which was "composed of a long and narrow room (hall), a small canteen and two or three tiny rooms on the first floor."[13] The complete membership of the Autonomie Club is lost to history, but it definitely included Henry Samuels, a number of the Walsall Anarchists, and also Auguste Coulon. Coulon was a half-Irish, half-French founding member of the Socialist League branch in Dublin in 1885. By 1889, he had surfaced in London and was one of the most inflammatory contributors to the *Commonweal* newspaper, which had been launched in 1885 by the Socialist League and its founder, William Morris. By 1890, Morris had stepped down, and David Nicholl had assumed editorial duties. The relationship between Coulon, Nicholl, and Samuels would form a backdrop for Bourdin's later activities.

During his brief tenure at the Autonomie Club, Martial Bourdin was committed to the cause. As Samuels later wrote, "When a comrade was in danger on the continent, and money had to be sent to pay the expenses here, Martial was always the most energetic in collecting and borrowing the needful: when the funds of the club were run out, when money had to be raised by means of subscriptions lists, concerts, balls, excursions, and what not, Martial always bought in the most money."[14] Bourdin also served as the secretary for the club's French-speaking section. It seems likely, given Bourdin's political viewpoint and his association with the Autonomie Club, that he was present at the Bloody Sunday protest that took place at Trafalgar Square on 13 November 1887. This march against unemployment and coercion in Ireland was violently attacked by the Metropolitan Police and the British army, resulting in the arrest of four hundred people, serious injuries to seventy-five, and the death of a young clerk named Alfred Linnell, who was run down by a police horse and subsequently died of complications from his injuries. This reaction by the authorities to what certainly started as a peaceful protest may have played a part in not just Bourdin's radicalization but also the nascent British Anarchist movement as a whole.

Precisely how long Bourdin spent in London (and his activities aside from occasional piece work on behalf of his brother and others who employed casual tailors at the time, fundraising on behalf of the Autonomie Club, and the occasional protest) is unknown. At some point, Bourdin returned temporarily to France before making his way to America via London. Oddly, there are no immigration records available under the name of Bourdin or his potential alias of Allder, which may indicate that Bourdin had to travel under a secondary alias for some reason. His movements during this period are largely unknown; however, he was, according to all available records, absent from the United Kingdom, possibly working as a women's tailor in New York and the surrounding areas[15] until his return to the United Kingdom in 1893, where he rented rooms at 30 Fitzroy Street, St. Pancras, from Ernest Delebescque, a cabinet maker and then treasurer of Louise Michel's International School.[16] According to reports at the time, Delebescque knew Bourdin for four years prior to the events that were to make him infamous in 1894, perhaps indicating that Delebescque was a colleague from Bourdin's time at the Autonomie Club. However, Anarchists both in the United Kingdom and abroad had been active in Bourdin's absence, and radical London may well have shifted in the time that he was away.

The Bloody Sunday protest had been a radicalizing event for a number of Londoners, among them a poet and Oxford graduate, John Evelyn Barlas. Born to Scottish parents in Rangoon in 1860, Barlas was one of the first Anarchists to engage in individual propaganda of the deed, albeit on a strange and relatively minor scale. According to reports published in *The Times*, on the morning of 1 January 1892, at around 8:20 a.m., a London policeman was making his way along Bridge Street in Westminster when he heard a succession of loud gunshots. He saw Barlas (or Borlos, as press articles called him) repeatedly firing a revolver at the Houses of Parliament. The constable quickly crossed a presumably busy thoroughfare before reaching Barlas, who stated, "I am an anarchist and I intended shooting you, but then I thought it a pity to shoot an honest man. What I have done is show my contempt for the House of Commons."[17] Barlas was quickly subdued and taken to the King Street police station; however, a number of flattened bullets were found on the Speaker's Green, and the walls of the House of Commons were marked where the bullets had struck. The judge at the hearing, a Mr. de Rutzen, asked the question that must have occurred to many of those first hearing of Barlas' "attack" early on New Year's Day: "Mr. de Rutzen.— Was the prisoner sober? Witness.— Perfectly." Bail was posted for a sober Barlas by his friend Oscar Wilde. Unfortunately, taking potshots at the House of Commons may have been more indicative of Barlas' mental state than any deeply held political beliefs; he was declared insane in July 1894 and committed to Gartnavel Royal Asylum, where he died in 1915.[18]

The year 1892 was to prove a fateful one with regard to Anarchism in London (and, indeed, in the wider United Kingdom) for reasons other than poets armed with revolvers and grievances. The year prior, Frederick Charles (born Frederick Charles Slaughter) had traveled from Sheffield to Walsall in search of work. Prior to leaving for Sheffield, Charles had been active in the Norwich branch of the Socialist League. Charles had long been associated with the Socialist movement in Norwich and had previously opened the Gordon Café at 5 Duke Street, which served as a meeting point and social hub in Norwich. Ironically, Charles' work as a special constable was what exposed him to revolutionary ideas, as he was required to police a meeting at which the working-class Communist Anarchist orator Charles Mowbray was speaking.[19] How Charles lost his café and ended up in Sheffield is not known, but while there he met with Dr. John Creaghe and established the *Sheffield Anarchist* paper, which, although it had a limited publishing history (eight issues over four months), led to legal issues from the start. Speaking later of Charles, Creaghe (who would go on to be active in Argentinian Anarchist circles) stated in the pages of *Commonweal*, "I cannot forget the time that Charles who was then out of work started with me the first number of the Sheffield Anarchist. He would do nothing for himself. If his chances of getting a £1000 depended on his keeping an appointment, I am certain he would not be there and I was astonished how actively and steadily he worked for the cause he loved. I cannot say how often I regretted it when he had to leave me, for we spent some happy hours in that anything but sweet smelling den which served us for a club and office at 47 West Bar Green, Sheffield. How we laughed as we scribbled and enjoyed in anticipation the horror and rage of the enemy."[20] Either as a result of spending all his time in establishing the *Sheffield Anarchist* or because of other factors, Charles was unsuccessful in his attempts to secure employment in Sheffield, and he moved to Walsall in the Midlands.

One factor that may have precipitated Charles' move to Walsall was the fact the he knew Joseph (Joe) Deakin, a founding member and secretary of the Walsall Socialist League and Socialist Club. Charles had known Deakin since 1888, when Deakin had requested copies of *Commonweal* and pamphlets on behalf of the Walsall Socialist League; indeed, Deakin composed a report about the speech given by Peter Kropotkin on his second visit to the Midlands, where he spoke at the Institute in Dudley: "Comrades here took advantage of his being in the district for him to pay us a visit the next day and although there was but little time to organize a meeting a capital audience assembled at the Walsall Unitarian Schoolroom and listened to an eloquent address on the Social Problem."[21] Born in 1858, Deakin was a clerk at the Wednesbury ticket office. Owing to his job as a clerk for the London and North Western Railway, Deakin had a privilege ticket that could be employed to travel regularly to London and increase his contacts with Anarchists and others in the capital. Upon arriving in Walsall, Charles joined Deakin as a member of the Socialist Club; he was also able to secure employment as a clerk in a local iron foundry operated by a Mr. Gameson (employment that was to prove significant later in his history and that of Anarchism in the United Kingdom), as well as accommodation in the house and workshop of a fellow club member, William Ditchfield.

Frederick Charles was not the only new member of the Socialist Club. Joining him as a member on 10 August 1891 was Victor Cailes, a French railway man who had recently moved to Walsall with his partner, Marie Piberne. Cailes was known to both Charles and Deakin from contact they had made previously in London via a mutual acquaintance: Auguste Coulon.

Coulon, as previously outlined, had been part of the radical Socialist movement in Ireland since 1885; however, by 1891 he was living in Fitzroy Square in London. Owing to his fluency in several languages, it was Coulon who had suggested to Louise Michel that the International School be opened, and he worked with her as her partner. As noted by Alex Butterworth, "Michel would teach the piano, Coulon classes in French and German."[22] By the time Charles had found his way to Sheffield, Coulon was a well-established fixture among the British Anarchist movement. Unfortunately, Coulon had been in the employ of the Special Branch of the Metropolitan Police since 18 July 1890, when he received a "Special Gratuity to Coulon"[23] for the value of £2, and he continued to receive regular payments for the next thirteen years and three months, under both his own name and that of his alias Pyatt, in whose name all payments were made for his services from January 1891 onward.

Coulon's involvement with the Walsall contingent while being firmly on the payroll of the Metropolitan Police as an informer likely led him to act as an agent provocateur. According to the account provided by John Quail, later events may have been precipitated by a conversation that occurred at the Autonomie Club on the evening of 29 August.

Deakin was on his way back to the Midlands from an International Congress that had recently ended in Brussels, and he had stopped off in London. Here he began "chatting to a group of Anarchists to whom he was known. Someone asked after Charles: 'Oh he's all right,' said Deakin, 'he's at work in an iron foundry.' 'Oh, he will do to make bombs for us,' cried Coulon, who was present."[24] Sometime later Coulon sent a sketch of a bomb to Victor Cailes in Walsall. In addition, Coulon provided introductions between most of all those in Walsall and instructions for the construction of a bomb, and he also involved and incriminated his next-door neighbor in Fitzroy Square, Jean Battola, an Italian shoemaker who barely spoke English. The means of such incrimination could be found in the bomb instructions sent to Cailes, which were signed in the name of Degnai; Metropolitan Police would subsequently claim that this letter had been composed by Battola, despite him not knowing Cailes at the time and only being fluent in French and Italian.

On 2 December, Battola, at the urging of Coulon, traveled from London to Walsall in order to collect "bombs for Russia." Whether he knew the true purpose of his trip is unknown; however, his movements did not go unnoticed. He was followed by Detective Inspector Melville, who, in addition to being one of the founders of the Special Irish Branch that was established in 1882 to combat Fenian dynamitists, was also the officer in charge of the agent provocateur, Coulon. He was joined in Walsall by Chief Constable Charles Taylor.[25] Battola was seen entering the Socialist Club as well as visiting the home of William Ditchfield in Cailes' company. Upon returning from Ditchfield, Cailes and Battola went back to the club, which was visited by Joseph Deakin, Frederick Charles, and John Wesley. Battola, Wesley, and Charles were later observed returning to the Walsall train station, where Battola caught a train back to London. From this point on, all of these suspects were under close observation by the police in both London and Walsall.

According to a later account provided by David Nicholl,[26] it was Cailes who asked Deakin to travel to London on 6 January 1892 in order to provide bomb components to Battola. Although Deakin was supposed to rendezvous with Battola at Euston, the two men failed to meet, and Deakin was tailed to the Autonomie Club by Melville. Here he was arrested and found to be in possession of a bottle labeled "chloroform" in a cigar box filled with white powder, which he could not provide a valid explanation for carrying. Following Deakin's arrest in London, Taylor questioned Ditchfield in his Green Lane home and removed castings, molds, and brass and lead bolts. Ditchfield was detained for further questioning. Afterward, Taylor, Detective Sergeant Cliffe and Detectives Ingram and Smith traveled to the Socialist Club, where they arrested Charles, Cailes, and Marie Piberne. A search of the property revealed more moldings, plaster, fuses, and Anarchist literature. Wesley, who had not been present at the Socialist Club, was arrested later that day when he returned to the Walsall train station. Subsequently, Battola was arrested in London, and both he and Deakin were transferred back to Walsall, where they soon found themselves detained with everyone else (except for Marie Piberne, who had been released) in the cells beneath the Magistrates Court on charges of possessing explosive substances for an unlawful purpose and conspiring to cause an explosion. According to press reports at the time, Charles, when arrested, was in possession of a "loaded revolver and handful of cartridges."[27]

The outlook for the accused bomb plotters was not good; however, in London Coulon also found himself embroiled in controversy. The arrests of a number of known Anarchists in both London and the Midlands created concern at the Autonomie Club. Prior to the arrests, Coulon was residing in Fitzroy Square; here he lived comfortably without having any obvious means of support. At a meeting on Sunday, 10 January, at the Autonomie Club, Coulon was openly accused of being a police agent and having betrayed those arrested in London and Walsall. According to Nicholl,[28] an unnamed member of the club speculated somewhat presciently about Coulon, "You do no work; how do you get your living if you are not a police spy?" Coulon may have been expecting such a line of questioning owing to the very public arrests of his peers, and he attempted to justify himself by replying, "I am a true Anarchist; I live by plunder." This somewhat vague response, unsurprisingly, did little to appease the other members of the Autonomie Club, and Coulon was subsequently expelled from its ranks.

In February 1892, the six accused—described, according to *The Times*, as "Frederick Charles, 27, clerk; Victor Cailes, 33, engine-driver, John Wesley, 32, brush maker; William Ditchfield, 43, filer; Joseph Thomas Deakin, 33, clerk, and Jean Battola, 30, shoe-maker"[29]—were transferred from the cells beneath the Walsall Magistrates Court to the Stafford Assizes. They had already faced a preliminary trial at the Magistrates Court, where they had complained about the treatment, accommodation, and food they had received. These complaints were probably justified; in an article in the *Walsall Free Press and South Staffordshire Advertiser*, Chief Constable Taylor "admitted that the prisoners were only given enough food to keep them alive."[30] The discomfiture of the arrested men continued until their trial commenced on 30 March 1892.

During the trial, evidence was presented by the state, including statements from Colonel Arthur Ford, the home office inspector of explosives, who testified to the probable composition and nature of the device the defendants were constructing. Outside the courtroom, the case had generated a high degree of press hysteria regarding the supposed Anarchist threat of violence. Of particular interest to the press were the pamphlets that had allegedly been discovered at both the Socialist Club and the nearby home of Cailes, most notably "The Means of Emancipation" and "The Anarchist Feast at the Opera." The latter of these documents provided a theoretical discussion of how to wreak carnage at the opera by means of a gas leak and incendiary devices beneath seats. Both Charles and Cailes denied having these materials in their possession when arrested, and, indeed, they may well have found their way into the evidence by other means.

During the sentencing of the accused, Battola pointed the finger of blame (via a translator, owing to his inability to speak English) squarely at Coulon as the instigator and commissioning agent for the supposed bomb plot. Although the presiding judge, Justice Hawkins (who had already earned the nom de guerre of "Hangman" Hawkins), did not believe him, history has since proven Battola correct. On 4 April 1892 the jury retired; following a nearly two-hour adjournment, they returned to pronounce Charles, Cailes and Battola guilty, Deakin guilty but with a recommendation for clemency, and Ditchfield and Wesley not guilty. Following statements from the accused, Justice Hawkins wasted no time in releasing the largely hapless Wesley and Ditchfield; he then sentenced Deakin to five years' imprisonment and Charles, Cailes and Battola to ten years. The Anarchist press and even publications such as *The Times* were quick to decry the severity of the sentences; however, as can be seen elsewhere in this publication, comparatively speaking, the accused fared better than some of their international peers, although penal servitude in Victorian England was far from a pleasant experience.

The mood among the Anarchists in London (and, indeed, throughout the United Kingdom) was still simmering with anger at what many suspected was persecution by the state based on police entrapment when Martial Bourdin returned to the capital in late 1893. How Bourdin spent his time until 1894 and who his associates were are unknown. According to reports that emerged later, at around midday on 15 February 1894, Bourdin visited his brother Henri to inquire about any available piece work and found that none was forthcoming. According to Paul Gibbard, Bourdin was by 2:00 p.m. dining at the International Restaurant in Bennett Street along with two companions (one of whom may have been Henry Samuels). At 3:10 p.m., Bourdin was to board a tram at the Westminster Bridge terminus before traveling to the East Greenwich terminus. Witness statements from the tram timekeeper stated that "Bourdin's overcoat was undone all the way up and looked as if there was something in the left-hand pocket."[31] Additional witnesses described Bourdin as "extremely nervous" and "constantly peering around him."[32] Bourdin may have suspected that he was being followed by the police or agents acting on their behalf, although events later that February afternoon would provide another reason for his nervousness.

What happened when Bourdin finished traveling has remained a puzzle, along with his ultimate destination. Some have suggested that his demise was accidental and that he may have been walking through Greenwich Park either to hand over explosives (most likely the dangerous and volatile nitroglycerine) as part of a wider Anarchist conspiracy or to test them in a secluded area; others claim that his ultimate destination was not in fact the Royal Observatory, but rather the nearby Royal Arsenal.[33] However, the events in which Bourdin found himself involved when he finished his journey (which, if he was traveling with the massively volatile compound of nitroglycerine on a public tram, was a feat in itself) can be gleaned from UK Home Office files and media reports of the period.

At approximately 4:50 p.m. on 15 February 1894, George Frost and Thomas Winter, both aged fourteen, were returning home through Greenwich Park from the nearby Roan Boys School, situated on East Street, Greenwich. According to reports in *The Times*,[34] the two schoolboys heard an explosion and saw blue smoke rising from beyond the nearby tree line close to the Royal Observatory. Because the curiosity and bravado of youth is universal, the two boys ran toward, rather than away from, the explosion. The explosion had also attracted the attention of two park keepers—namely, Patrick Sullivan and his colleague, Wright. As illustrations[35] in Home Office documents show, at the time of the explosion Bourdin was walking down a zigzag pathway away from the main park thoroughfare and toward the observatory building. By the time the curious schoolboys and park keepers had arrived, he was lying on the path, mortally injured, with shrapnel and parts of his body (including the remains of his left hand, in which he was probably carrying the explosive disguised as a parcel) scattered across the path.

Sullivan was quick to react and sent the schoolboys to collect a local doctor, William Willes. As Willes later testified at Bourdin's inquest,[36] the injured man was largely unresponsive, uttering only the phrase "take me home" before lapsing into unconsciousness. Rather than taking Bourdin back to his rooms, Willes had him transferred to the nearby Seaman's Hospital, where he was attended by Dr. Arthur Jarvis, the house surgeon. The injuries Bourdin presented with were severe, including the loss of his left hand, numerous wounds to his lower legs, and (as Jarvis was to testify) an inch-and-a-half oval wound above his navel from which his intestines were protruding. With such significant injuries, it is somewhat surprising that Bourdin had the mental faculties to utter his last words, "I'm cold," prior to dying some fifty minutes after the initial explosion at 5:40 p.m.

As is true in the modern era, an unexpected explosion in a public area sent the press into a feeding frenzy of conjecture and supposition. Over the coming days, events would continue to escalate. In the report concerning the explosion that was published by *The Times* some five days after it had occurred, the anonymous journalists tied Bourdin to the previous Walsall bomb plot, which was still very much at the forefront of public consciousness; even though subsequent research has found no direct or indirect link between Bourdin and the events in Walsall, the *Times* article stated categorically that "one thing is clear, and that is the tendency of every piece of evidence with regard to the manufacture of the bomb in iron to connect Bourdin with the Walsall Anarchists, with whom he is stated to have had more or less intimate relations."[37] Bourdin's inquest (at which Henri reportedly refused to take the oath upon the Bible) was also impacted by politics. Again as reported in *The Times*, following the formal inquest, the coroner for southeast London at the time, Mr. E.A. Carttar, took the jury on a day trip to inspect the scene of the explosion. This outing was, according to the media, interrupted when "a scene was caused by two Anarchists from London, one of whom mounted the fencing close by the spot where Bourdin died and proceeded to harangue the jury and the crowd in support of Anarchist principles."[38] For all of the haranguing, the unnamed Anarchists must have been somewhat peaceable in nature, as they were subsequently removed by the park keepers rather than the police.

Why Bourdin was in Greenwich Park was baffling to many at the time and remains so now, as does the cause of his death. Many assumed that his death had been accidental in nature or that the infernal machine he was carrying had detonated early or been jarred into detonation. However, evidence presented by Colonel Vivian Majendie, HM Chief Inspector of Explosives (who had at that point acquired twenty years of experience in his field, having first come to prominence while combating the wave of Fenian dynamitists who had launched an explosive campaign across London), ran contrary to this accepted wisdom. He stated that "he was also, decidedly of opinion that explosion was not caused by an accidental fall either of the deceased or of the bomb."[39] What, then, if not carelessness, caused the explosion? Prior to the invention of dynamite, one of the common elements used in bomb making was nitroglycerine. The chemical composition of nitroglycerine is a contact explosive in which physical shocks can trigger a detonation. In its undiluted form, nitroglycerine is one of the world's most powerful explosives and incredibly dangerous to both use and transport. Even though the compound may appear stable, it degrades over time, which only serves to increase its instability. Although Majendie refused to provide any details at a public inquest regarding the device that ultimately killed Bourdin, a core of nitroglycerine would go some way toward potentially explaining not only the ferocity of the explosion but also its timing; indeed, the nitroglycerine may well have become dangerously unstable in the time it took Bourdin to reach Greenwich Park.

The mysterious nature of the (probably early) detonation of Bourdin's device was further compounded by a search of his person and rooms. On his body at the time of his death was a membership card for the Autonomie Club, along with £13 (in modern terms, about $1,800–$2,500). This was a large sum of money for a part-time tailor to be carrying, and it led to speculation in the press that Bourdin may have intended to flee the country following a successful detonation. Additionally, among his possessions was a tram ticket to Woolwich Arsenal, which was then one of the UK government's facilities for making guns and explosives. Woolwich would certainly have been a more attractive target for an attack; perhaps this was Bourdin's true destination. Had he grown paranoid on the tram journey? Did he know that the device he was carrying was degrading and becoming unstable? In all likelihood, answers to these questions will never be found. When police searched his rooms in Fitzroy Street a number of bomb-making components (including sulfuric acid and additional chemicals) were recovered along with the ubiquitous Anarchist literature.

Following a search of Bourdin's rooms, the police next turned their attention to the Autonomie Club. As highlighted earlier in this chapter, this meeting place was important to the development of Anarchism and Socialism within the United Kingdom as a whole, and it had been linked to earlier events and actors such as those in Walsall. The discovery of a membership card on Bourdin's body gave the Metropolitan Police the excuse they had been waiting for. On Friday, 16 February 1894, they conducted a raid of the club's premises. As documented in the media of the day, "having installed themselves in the building, the detectives detained the callers as they arrived, and each one was questioned as to his address and other matters. By eleven o'clock no fewer than eighty persons were thus detained, and were grouped together in the hall in the basement. A little later a Frenchman presented himself, and finding the place in possession of the police tried to escape, but after a struggle he was overpowered. About midnight the police were withdrawn from the Club, none of those present being taken into custody."[40] Although no arrests were made at the time, following the police raid, the doors of the Autonomie Club were closed, reopening only briefly. In addition to destroying himself, Bourdin's actions would lead (thanks to the actions of the police) to the destruction of a vital component of radical organization within Victorian London.

Just as Bloody Sunday and the sentences of the accused in the Walsall case had led to discontent among members of the UK Anarchist community, so, too, did Bourdin's untimely death. Thanks in large part to the gruesome and excitable media coverage, many London residents were equally aggrieved. Events surrounding Bourdin's funeral certainly had the potential to become tumultuous. This danger was noted in a letter from the home secretary, H.H. Asquith, to the commissioner of police, Sir Edward Bradford, the day prior to the planned funeral: "With reference to the proposed demonstration at the funeral of Bourdin tomorrow, I desire you to carry out the following instructions. The funeral is to proceed by the shortest and most direct route. No procession of any kind is to be allowed to follow the hearse. If any attempt is made, either at the starting place, or en route, to form a procession it must be at once prevented and broken up by the police. Only the mourning coach and officials of the undertakers shall be allowed to follow. At the cemetery no one is to be permitted to make a speech of any kind. If any one attempts to do so, he shall be stopped and if necessary remanded."[41] Despite the recommended precautions, on the morning of 23 February 1894, Bourdin's funeral descended into near chaos.

As detailed in the *St. James Gazette*,[42] which provided some of the most detailed coverage, Bourdin's body left the undertakers' premises situated on Chapel Street, Edgeware Road, heading toward the East Finchley Cemetery. A large and unsympathetic crowd had gathered, and prior to the body's departure there was already trouble. An hour before the funeral procession got under way, a group had gathered at the top of Chapel Street, carrying red banners edged with black. Dismissed by the police stationed nearby, the mourners were soon set upon by both the police and the crowd, and banners were torn up gleefully. As Bourdin's body was placed into the hearse, the crowd grew even more hostile, with cries of "Go back to your own country!" and so much jostling that mounted police had to be called from the nearby Lisson Street station to provide a phalanx and escort. A further fifty police armed with batons were required to hold back the mob as the hearse reached the cemetery. Here an unmarked grave had already been prepared. As the coffin was being lowered, and while the nearby mob hissed its displeasure, a young woman clad in the traditional black stepped forward and placed a bouquet of white flowers on the lid with the message "With deepest sympathy, from Fanny." Fanny's identity and the nature of her relationship to Bourdin are like so much of his brief life—lost. At this time Charles Thomas Quinn, a member of the *Commonweal* staff, stepped forward in an attempt to provide an oratory for the deceased. No sooner had he commenced with his opening of "Friend and Anarchists…" than he was quickly arrested and bundled from the cemetery, away from a hostile crowd.

The turmoil did not stop once Bourdin was interred. By late afternoon (the hearse having reached the cemetery at 3:30 p.m.) the crowd had turned its attention to the Autonomie Club, which had been widely referenced in the press. Missiles were thrown, windows were broken, and members of the club foolish enough to attend were set upon by an enraged mob. Again, thanks to police intervention (albeit somewhat delayed), no serious harm was done. The troubles of the Autonomie Club did not end there, however, and in the days following Bourdin's funeral it received a number of mailed threats, including the following missive: "I give you full notice that on the first explosion caused by any of your dirty crew in England it shall soon be followed by a second, and the second will be by the firing of a bomb in your club, and I shall take care that there is a full household of you, and that your carcasses shall be blown sky high." Following more police raids and continued harassment, the Autonomie Club was forced to close its doors forever.

Compared to other countries, the British response to the threats presented by Anarchist propaganda of the deed activities was muted. Countries such as Spain and Italy enforced increasingly repressive regimes, and as early as the 1870s, following the Paris Commune, Russia and Germany had led calls for international cooperation regarding the threat of political violence. However, as explained by Richard Bach Jensen, "Britain disliked the idea of political policing"[43] and greatly resisted it. However, that is not to say that the British authorities were unprepared for terrorist acts. By the time of Martial Bourdin's actions, the British legal and extralegal authorities had endured a bruising campaign against acts of Irish Nationalist terrorism.[44] Thanks to this experience, British police were already familiar with the use of covert surveillance, paid informants, and agent provocateurs. Although seen by many as a refuge from the more repressive mechanisms introduced globally, Britain was arguably only accepting of political dissidents as it allowed them to be tracked and surveilled. Indeed, in addition to allowing entry to political dissidents, Britain permitted foreign nations to employ agents on British soil to track these dissidents' movements (with perhaps not the full understanding that such agents would also be tracked by the British). As well as endemic surveillance, the police had other mechanisms at their disposal; for example, police raids against the *Commonweal* offices in 1892 and 1894 caused so much damage to the premises that the paper was forced to stop printing. Add to this illegal detentions and sentences for those arrested that were shaped not by justice but by the demands of the British state, and Britain was clearly not the open society envisioned by many of those attracted to it from around Europe and beyond. However, the British police had their own shortcomings. As an article in *The Times*[45] revealed somewhat embarrassingly, "The death of Bourdin took place on Thursday afternoon of last week. It appears now that official intelligence of the fact that an explosion had taken place in Greenwich Park reached New Scotland Yard, not by telegram, but by letter on Friday."

The probable accidental death of Martial Bourdin and the supposed Walsall bomb conspiracy are some of the most prominent examples of early Anarchist propaganda of the deed in the United Kingdom, but they are not unique. In April 1894, two Italian immigrants (Francesco Polti and an eighteen-year-old acquaintance of Bourdin, Guiseppe Farnara) were arrested in another supposed bomb plot. Their alleged plan was to detonate a device in the London Stock Exchange, which, if successful, could have resulted in numerous deaths. However, Farnara and Polti had accidentally targeted the Royal Exchange instead, which, far from being a hive of the bourgeoisie, was by that time largely unused. Rather than being remembered as Anarchists striking a blow against the dominant system of capitalism, this hapless duo is now considered a historical footnote and largely remembered (if at all) as inept.

As with many of the other individuals included in this book, we cannot truly know what motivated Bourdin or, indeed, any other Anarchists of late Victorian Britain. Given the contemporary focus on their acts, as opposed to the Anarchists as individuals, and the dearth of historical materials that pertain to their specific lives and circumstances, there is not enough information available to provide insight into their choices. In Bourdin's case, this is particularly noticeable. His actions and untimely death influenced the broader culture, most notably in the fictionalized plot of Joseph Conrad's *The Secret Agent* and in the T.S. Eliot poem "Animula" ("Pray for Guiterriez, avid of speed and power, For Boudin, blown to pieces"), and they also had lasting ramifications for Britain's Anarchist community. Following Bourdin's demise, police repression was noticeably increased, *Commonweal* was closed, and the Autonomie Club shuddered to a halt. Rather than a grand gesture causing a popular uprising against the injustices of Victorian Britain, his premature detonation in Greenwich Park resulted in divisions and fractures in the British Left that remain unresolved to this day. Unfortunately for Martial Bourdin, his actions can be best summarized by another of Eliot's poems, "The Hollow Men," as his world ended "not with a bang but a whimper."

Obituary for Martial Bourdin

Source: The Commonweal: A Revolutionary Journal of Anarchist Communism 2, no. 23, New Series (Saturday, 10 March 1894); original text by H.B. Samuels

In Memoriam	
Martial Bourdin. Died Feb. 15, 1894	
Aged 26 Years	
Spurning the name of a slave,	Time shall not rob him of fame;
Fearless of gaol or grave,	Hating the Tyrant, and game
Fighting for Freedom he gave,	In the spirit that rings in his name
His life in the Revolution.	He died for the Revolution.

Our noble comrade lies now beneath the sod. At an early age he risked his future chances of comfort, pleasure, and life itself for the benefit of suffering humanity—ignorant, brutish, suffering humanity—that greeted his funeral cortege with derision, contempt, and hatred, bred from their brutalizing surroundings and prejudices which enable the classes who "toil not, neither do they spin" to live in splendour and voluptuousness upon the degradations and miseries to which the workers are condemned by the present capitalist system, which Martial Bourdin laboured to destroy and for which he sacrificed his life. He was not one of the poorest, the most wretched, the most exploited or oppressed; he earned a tolerably comfortable livelihood, but he had seen enough of the cruelties and injustices inflicted upon the class to which he belonged—the workers—in France, in America, and in London, to make him determined to throw himself entirely into the struggle of the workers against the shirkers.

He was no writer, he had not any oratorical ability; so he contented himself with working in a quieter and more effective way as he considered, rather than do nothing except criticize and waste his time in bickerings and unmanly actions, as some do. His old father and mother, nearly ninety years of age, still obliged to work and still in poverty after working their whole lives and rearing a family of eight to be useful workers in this rotten society: seeing that this is the end that we must, nearly all of us, reach if we are fortunate enough to escape disease, starvation, or the workhouse, he threw himself into the struggle.

Not for the love he bore the contented slaves and cowards who patiently submit to life-long servitude and remorseless tyranny, but because he hated, with a hate as cold as ice and then as hot as the fabled fires of hell, those institutions and conditions, with those who profit by them, that cause so much suffering and anguish, mental and physical, among the many millions of innocent, helpless men, women, and children, victims to the greed and lust of an idle, vicious, useless class, venomous and parasitical: a class of mild and wild beasts that live only upon the blood, muscles, and sinews of our class; who use as tools for their own selfish purposes our strength, our skill, our patience and ingenuity, and who, therefore, must as a class be destroyed or abolished.

Our comrade was not of an affectionate nature (I shall not ascribe to him virtues he did not possess); but one virtue he excelled in, and that was tenacity of purpose; another was his intense heartfelt love for the movement. The movement, not that which comprises a few known men; the movement, not of one party or land, but a holy love for the world-wide movement of the workers towards emancipation, towards Freedom—social and economic; the movement of which we Anarchists are but as the links in the chains encircling the known earth, only visible here and there wherever tyranny and oppression have forced it to the surface; underneath, barely visible even to those who form connecting links, lies dormant yet powerful the natural, potential, forces of human solidarity that, in the course of time—that time which we Anarchists are bringing nearer, with an irresistible force will embrace and entwine the aspirations of a Universal Brotherhood of Labor, when a new era will have commenced and the people will be on the high road to Peace and Harmony and Love.

It is owing to such comrades as Martial Bourdin, with their resolution and tenacity, that the social question has forced itself even so far upon the masters of the race. How droll, and yet how terrible!—a handful of creatures, fellow mortals, social atoms like ourselves, individually weak and helpless, yet masters of the race, with all-powerful influences, holding within their grasp the lives and liberties of millions—blind, stupid, and brutal. But only because of the mental blindness of the masses do the classes manage to retain their power; the blindness that is fostered by all the cursed cliques of priests and politicians, who see in the people's intelligence their own destruction. Martial believed with us that no force outside individual physical force will ever suffice to show our blood-suckers and oppressors how really in earnest we are in our endeavours to win for the workers of the world real Freedom, in order that we should all have the fullest and freest opportunities for the cultivation and development of our highest and best faculties.

We both read the great Wendell Phillips, where he wrote: "Every step of progress that the world has made has been from scaffold to scaffold and from stake to stake. It is no exaggeration to say, that all the great truths relating to society and government have first been heard in the solemn protests of martyred patriotism or the loud cries of crushed and starving labor. The law has always been wrong. Government began in tyranny and force, began in the feudalism of the soldier and bigotry of the priest: and the ideas of justice and humanity have been fighting their way like a thunderstorm, against the organized selfishness of human nature."

Martial was a relative of mine, but there was hardly any affection between us on that score. He had no affection, I believe, for anybody in the ordinary sense; he was too much wrapped up with interest in the growth and development of the revolutionary movement to have time for any display of selfish personal affection or gratification, and although he was always to the fore in any frivolous yet necessary affair, it was for other reasons and with other motives that he seemingly threw off the serious and became the social. Just one or two instances of this dual nature will show what kind of comrade we have lost. Once he went with me to a lecture, and afterwards walked the whole distance back rather than change a sovereign, and then went to bed supperless for the same reason. Some time afterwards a comrade was obliged to leave London on important business, but he had no money for the expenses: he told our comrade so, and with an exhibition of impatience (he was always impatient) Martial took two sovereigns from his purse and gave them over, and the journey was made. I, naturally, was somewhat surprised, knowing his niggardly disposition generally; and on asking for an explanation he said: "I don't require much for myself, but for the movement, and when something has to be done, everything I have would be too little; I can make shift and manage easily for myself, but the work of the movement must be carried on."

On another occasion several comrades had been arrested and their wives and families rendered penniless; he came among the friends and, going to each one separately, soon collected enough for their immediate wants. When a comrade was in danger on the continent, and money had to be sent to pay the expenses here, Martial was always the most energetic in collecting and borrowing the needful: when the funds of the club were run out, when money had to be raised by means of subscriptions lists, concerts, balls, excursions, and what not, Martial always brought in the most money; when a few weeks back the *Commonweal* was without funds and we were obliged to attempt to print the paper by hand on our own antiquated press, Martial (although he did not stand any higher than the machine) was there offering Cantwell to do anything that might be useful in the work on hand; when any suspicious characters entered the club, he was among the first to point them out and urge their expulsion, only on the Saturday before his unfortunate death he shouted the loudest and argued the most against the presence of persons he considered dangerous to the movement and the club. He was not always thanked, rather he was abused, but he was not moved from his uncompromising position or purpose which he carried with him to the end.

Such as comrade was he, and at the age of 26 he undertook the conveyance of dangerous explosive compounds to a secluded spot, where none could have been injured, in order to put to the test a new weapon of destruction that would have furnished the revolutionary armoury with another means of terrorizing those who consciously or unconsciously consign so many innocent lives to destitution and despair. In vain they tell us that force is no remedy: in vain they point out that these acts form the excuse for the most brutal repression: in vain they hang, torture, and imprison: all this has no effect on those who know history, who know human nature, who know how in the past, in spite of persecution and oppression and torture and ostracism, the truth has still made itself heard and felt,—those who know how much the element of fear enters into the spirit that concedes anything whatever. Was it not an English statesman who, speaking at Carlisle, Jan 13th, 1871, said that "Catholic Emancipation was passed through fear of revolution in Ireland; the first Reform Bill was passed by the light of Nottingham and Bristol in flames; Free Trade would not have been carried as it was, if there had not been a famine in Ireland that alarmed our statesmen: the second Reform Bill was in danger of not being passed, until Hyde Park railings came down"? And again: "I am not sure whether the Irish Church would not have been standing still if the Fenians had not blown down Clerkenwell Prison; and as to the Irish Land Bill, I doubt whether we would have got it if the Irishmen had not taken to the fatal practice of shooting their landlords." Believing this, we stand and look the whole world in the face, all those that hate us, misunderstand us, and who show no appreciation for our efforts on their behalf: to those workers who, like worms are content to squirm and grovel under the heel of injustice, those worms who are satisfied with getting enough dust to eat—even among those who knew Martial and who know us—to these and to the workers of the world generally we say, with our eyes fixed on the corpse of our comrade, that come weal come woe, we pledge ourselves to the fallen dead and the living, we make this solemn vow: That we will strive by every means in our power to destroy ignorance and oppression, prejudice and cruelty, fear and falsity, in order that it will be impossible for some men to murder, rob, and dominate millions of their fellows for no other reason than their helplessness and simplicity.

Were the authorities afraid that these words spoken at the graveside on the platform of death, carried over the whole world through the telegraph and telephone by the representatives of a world's press, who had assembled by the graveside to do that work; their very presence being a proof of the fact that the peoples are interested in our principles and practices: were they afraid of the effect our words would have on the minds and hearts of the workers, that they ruthlessly prevented any speaking? Well, our speeches they may prevent, but the very system that they maintain is breeding, in ever increasing numbers, such men as Pallas, Berkman, Ravachol, Vaillant, and Bourdin, who will rather face sudden and violent death than endure the sight of the intense suffering that is the lot of the majority of the workers of the world. Comrades, be of good courage! We have a world to win, and nothing to lose but our chains. Prepare for the Social Revolution.

Martial, in spirit I clasp your hand and vow at all costs to continue the work for Liberty, Equality, and Fraternity. Vive l'Anarchie!

Nine

A Carnival of Revenge

More than a century has passed since the events at the Homestead Steel Works on the Monongahela River near Pittsburgh, but their reverberations are still felt today. Starting with an industrial dispute that led to workers being locked out in 1892, it escalated to a series of ongoing battles between striking steel workers and private security agents employed by the works owners. The Homestead strike stands as one of the most serious labor disputes in U.S. history. On top of the dispute itself, which saw the nascent union movement in the United States flex its muscles, the events at Homestead gave rise to an Anarchist attempt to find some retribution and justice for the nine strikers who lost their lives.

As revealed by Jean Brust, "at a street intersection in Homestead today, a stone plaque stands in honor of the victims slain by the Pinkerton thugs of the ruling class"[1]; however, the events that this plaque memorializes, and the actions taken by an Anarchist in response, are now largely forgotten. The strike that occurred in Homestead, Pennsylvania, saw the organized forces of labor in the form of the Amalgamated Association of Iron, Steel, and Tin Workers (commonly abbreviated to AA) square off against one of the most powerful corporations of the period: the Carnegie Steel Company. Formed in 1876, the AA was initially a craft union that represented skilled iron and steel workers. As the name suggests, the AA was an amalgamation of existing trade bodies that included the United Sons of Vulcan (which had been formed in Pittsburgh on 17 April 1858), the Associated Brotherhood of Iron and Steel Heaters, and the Iron and Steel Roll Hands Union. At the first convention of the AA in August 1876, "an elaborate constitution was adopted"[2]; several years later, the AA secured its first major victory.

More than ten years before the events at Homestead unfolded, the AA was involved in another labor dispute at the Homestead Steel Works. On 1 January 1882, the management of the Homestead plant introduced a new contract containing a "yellow dog" clause. This was a specific mechanism utilized by employers seeking to prevent the unionization of their work force; as highlighted by Steven Danver, "yellow dog contracts were so vile that no decent human being would require even an old yellow dog to sign one."[3] Although such clauses were common in the United States during the nineteenth century, the AA was quick to respond, calling for a work stoppage in March. Eventually management brought in scab labor, which was widely available owing to a countrywide recession. The scabs were met with protest, which eventually turned physical, and "there was violence, and the county sheriff sent deputies to prevent further trouble."[4] By 20 March 1882, the yellow dog contract had been revoked, and work resumed. For the AA, this result marked a victory for its members, and its strength would be remembered. For Scottish American

135

industrialist and self-professed "world's richest man"[5] Andrew Carnegie, this incident was not the last of his problems with the AA in Homestead. In 1889, the AA negotiated a union scale governing both pay scales and shift lengths. Carnegie refused to sign the agreement and, rather than overtly drive out the union, chose instead to implement mass layoffs and wait the situation out. The company chairman, William L. Abbot, was tasked with negotiations while Carnegie was conveniently out of the country, and, as revealed by Jonathan Rees, he "hired re-placements and tried to bring them into the plant under protection of the local sheriff."[6] With the support of the immigrant communities in Homestead, the AA was able to repel scab labor for a second time, and it conducted what Paul Krause (one of the historians who have dedicated much time and effort to studying events surrounding the Homestead dispute) called a "successful reconnaissance"[7] of management practices and responses. The management of the Homestead works was forced to acquiesce to the AA's demands once again; however, workers were forced to accept a reduction in pay scales in return for three-year union-approved contracts.

In 1881, Carnegie placed Henry Clay Frick in charge of operations at the Homestead Steel Works. Originally from West Overton in Pennsylvania, Frick is remembered today not only as an art collector and financier of the Pennsylvania Railroad but also for his union-busting activities. Indeed, it was these actions that first bought him to Carnegie's attention. As Carnegie noted in a letter to Frick, "The mills have never been able to turn out the product they should, owing to being held back by the Amalgamated men."[8] Frick's expressed agenda was to drive out the AA from Homestead. Between 1889 and 1892, the Homestead Steel Works was tasked with increasing production. Rather than being enacted to meet pressing market demands, this production increase was implemented to allow the Carnegie Steel Company to withstand another industrial dispute. In February 1892, the AA and Frick entered into negotiations to discuss contract renewal. The profits yielded by the steel industry during this period were enormous, and the AA, acting in the interests of its members, sought an increase in base wages. Predictably, this request was refused, and negotiations broke down. Indeed, Frick stated that he would no longer recognize the right of the union to negotiate on behalf of its membership.

Frick's high-handed tactics continued, and on the evening of 28 June 1892 he locked workers out of the plant. This action was compounded when the gates of the plant shut on 29 June, and workers found themselves faced with a high barbed-wire fence that had been under construction since January, sniper towers with searchlights situated near each building inside the mill, and high-powered water cannons at all entrance points. The imposing fence "gave the place the impression of a fortress. Homestead residents soon named it 'Fort Frick.'"[9] The militarization of the steel mill did not assuage the concerns of workers or the AA, and it did little to encourage negotiation. Indeed, union members (in conjunction with the Knights of Labor) had begun to patrol the Monongahela River in a steam-powered river launch and several rowboats, and picket lines were hastily erected around the Frick's fortress and throughout the town of Homestead to prevent scab labor and non-union members from entering. However, on 25 June, Frick had already contacted Robert Pinkerton to provide "service at our Homestead mills as a measure of precaution against interference with our plan to start operation of the works on July 26th, 1892."[10] The Pinkertons were infamous for their violent strike breaking, and their activities at Homestead would not deviate from familiar patterns. On 6 July 1892, there were violent clashes between the Pinkertons and striking workers that resulted in the deaths of nine workers. Eventually, after engaging in battles along the shore of the

Monongahela River where the Pinkertons had attempted to land, the outsiders were forced to surrender to the workers. Order was only restored on 12 July 1892, when "8,500 state militiamen descended on Homestead and enforced martial law for over three months."[11] The presence of thousands of heavily armed Pennsylvania state troops suppressed resistance and allowed Frick to relight the mill furnaces on 15 July, operated as they were by non-union members.

Homestead was operational again, the AA had largely been crushed, and Frick likely felt content with the state of affairs. However, his contentment was disrupted when, on 23 July, a young man purporting to be a representative of a New York employment agency came into his office, took out a revolver, and started firing. As it transpired, the young man in question was Russian born, a committed Anarchist, and a companion of Emma Goldman; his name was Alexander Berkman.

Berkman was born on 21 November 1870 and named Ovsei Osipovich Berkman. Born in the Lithuanian city of Vilnius (then called Vilna and part of the Russian Empire), he was the youngest of the four children born to Osip Berkman and Yetta Berkman (née Natanson). The family was far from destitute, and the four children were raised in a "prosperous Jewish merchant family."[12] Following seven years in Vilnius, the Berkman family moved to St. Petersburg from the Pale of Settlement. Established in 1791 by Catherine the Great, the Pale was the region exclusively reserved for settlement by Russian Jews. Life in the Pale environment was, for many, arduous and poverty stricken; the Berkmans were a rare exception to this rule, escaping largely unscathed from the frequent pogroms that devastated the Jewish communities. Officially "the capitals of Moscow and St. Petersburg were off limits to Jews"[13]; however, exceptions could be made for doctors and other desirable occupations. After successfully building a business as a leather merchant, Osip Berkman and his family qualified for relocation, and they were able to leave the harsh conditions of the Pale behind them.

Upon arriving in St. Petersburg, the family sought to acclimate to their new surroundings; in doing so, Ovsei adopted the Russian name Alexander, which he was to use for the rest of his life. Known to friends and family alike as Sasha, young Alexander enjoyed the wealth his father had generated from his business dealings, which had continued to flourish following the family's relocation from the Pale. As Paul and Karen Avrich reveal, "The family acquired a lavish house in the city and a country place in a fashionable suburb, with a staff of servants to attend them. The children were provided with tutors and sent to a classical gymnasium, a school reserved for the private elements of St. Petersburg society."[14] Unlike some of his contemporaries and later comrades in the Anarchist community, Alexander

Alexander Berkman

Berkman was not raised in poverty, nor did he suffer from its privations during his formative years.

However, all was not as idyllic as it first appeared in the Berkman's world. He grew up in a country that was riddled with political disaffection; indeed, "during his childhood and adolescence, Russia went through one of the most turbulent and violent periods of its history, with news of violence from radical movements circulating daily."[15] By the time of Berkman's birth, Nihilism was on the march in Russia, and there would be repeated attempts against the life of the tsar and against other authority figures (including the assassination of the governor-general of Kharkov, Prince Dmitri Kropotkin, the cousin of Russian Anarchist Peter Kropotkin). As Berkman's later lover, Emma Goldman, was to state in her sympathetic biography, "Alexander Berkman, sensitive and idealistic, could not escape the influence of that time."[16]

The shifting nature of Russian politics impacted closer to home when, in 1877, Berkman's uncle was arrested. Involved in student politics while studying at the Medical and Surgical Academy and later the Institute of Agriculture in St. Petersburg, Mark Maxim Natanson rejected the Nihilism of Sergei Nechaev but would later join Narodnaya Volya. Although Natanson was not directly involved in any act of physical terrorism, the very act of associating with Narodnaya Volya was enough for the Russian state to sentence him to exile in Siberia until 1889. When Berkman was twelve, his family received word that, in light of the recent assassination of Tsar Alexander II in 1881, political detainees such as Natanson had been sentenced to death. Ultimately, the sentence was not carried out, and the one-time student radical was transferred to an even bleaker part of Siberia in which to serve his term of exile, but these events arguably had a significant impact on Berkman, then a youth on the verge of puberty. According to Goldman, Berkman shared his early influences with her during conversation, "dwelling particularly on his beloved Nihilist uncle Maxim, and on the shock he had experienced on learning he was sentenced to die."[17] However, it wasn't just shock that had been stirred in Berkman; as he later stated, "The terms Socialist and Anarchist were quite unknown to me then, but 'Nihilist' held a mysterious charm, swaying me with awe and admiration. It was a forbidden word and it conjured up visions of dreaded gendarmes, iron chains, and the frozen steppes of Siberia. Vaguely I felt that these forbidden people, the Nihilists, somehow suffered for the sake of others. I did not know why or how, but my young heart glowed with admiration of them."[18]

In addition to processing the news of the death sentence that had been issued against his uncle, and the wave of repression and anti–Semitism that had been unleashed following the assassination of the tsar, young Berkman experienced two other events at the age of twelve that had a lasting impact on his life. Shortly after his birthday, his father, following a short illness, died. Yetta was then forced by circumstance to sell the assets that had previously belonged to her husband's business and move her family away from the urbane and privileged surroundings of St. Petersburg. Considering later events in Alexander's life, his next childhood home was to prove ironic. Following their relocation from St. Petersburg, where they were no longer legally permitted to reside, the family traveled to Kovno. Now the second largest city in Lithuania, Kovno, at the time of the Berkmans' arrival, was a significant railway hub between the Russian Empire and Imperial Germany in addition to a major industrial center. Kovno was also the birthplace of Emma Goldman. Here, the Berkmans found refuge with Nathan Natanson, Yetta's brother. Conservative in nature and a financier by occupation, Nathan owned real estate, including the second-floor flat where he deposited his sister and her children, situated above the Kovno police headquarters. Although the family had definitely been financially impacted by the death of its patriarch, they were still resolutely middle class, and Berkman was soon enrolled at a local school.

It was at this school that Berkman experienced the second transformative event of his twelfth year. Although he was classically educated, Berkman was also a voracious reader of Russian authors of the period such as Tolstoy. One author who particularly captivated the young Berkman was Nikolai Chernyshevsky. A Russian revolutionary democrat, philosopher, and critic, Chernyshevsky (the son of a priest) was born in 1846 and educated at the local seminary. During his university years, Chernyshevsky renounced his earlier beliefs, declared himself an atheist, and, following graduation, moved to St. Petersburg. Here he became the chief editor of *Sovremennik*, a major Russian literary, political, and social journal. Chernyshevsky was one of the chief proponents of the concept of Narodism and agitated vocally for a revolutionary overthrow of the existing autocratic facets of Russian society and a return to a Socialist society based broadly around the concept of a peasant commune. In the Russian Empire, such demands were far from popular, and Chernyshevsky was carefully monitored by the tsarist secret police; "though Chernyshevsky tried to remain within the boundaries of Russian censorship, he was accused of being connected with student protests in 1862."[19] Chernyshevsky was arrested on largely trumped-up charges in July 1862 and interred in the Peter and Paul Fortress in St. Petersburg. Here he composed in 1863 a novel that was to influence Vladimir Lenin to the extent that he named one of his most famous tracts after it, and it also captivated Alexander Berkman: *What Is to Be Done?* In his novel, Chernyshevsky presents the reader with the character Rakhmetov, a stoic, sincere, and austere revolutionary who works stubbornly toward obtaining revolutionary social ends, subordinating all other aspects of his life to this goal. For Berkman, it was heady stuff, and it directly influenced his own school career. Although by all accounts an excellent student, the twelve-year-old Berkman composed an essay with the provocative title "There Is No God." His literary efforts were not appreciated by the school authorities, and his efforts were said to be exhibiting "precocious godlessness, dangerous tendencies and insubordination."[20] As punishment, Berkman was forced to be educated with younger children, which served only to increase his ostracism and humiliation.

In 1887, Berkman became both an orphan and a ward of his Uncle Nathan when his mother died. Berkman was then a young man, attempting to live up to the image of his revolutionary uncle Maxim Natanson and the fictional Rakhmetov, and the home of a conservative financier was no place from which to launch a revolution. Following an incident in which Berkman was caught red handed attempting to steal copies of the school examination papers, he decided that it was time to leave the comfortable environs of Kovno and immigrate to the United States. However, the attempted theft was not Berkman's only reason for leaving Russia. With a failed school career in his wake, he stood little chance of obtaining a place at university (even though one could have been financially achievable owing to his uncle), and he was rapidly approaching his eighteenth year, which would have made him eligible for military conscription, an unbearable prospect for a nascent revolutionary. For many Russians of the period, the United States presented an attractive vista. With no secret police, no tsar, and (especially important for Berkman) seemingly no widespread and endemic anti–Semitism, it appeared idyllic—at least from a distance. Borrowing his travel costs from his uncle (who may have been relieved that the young revolutionary would be causing problems elsewhere), Berkman left Kovno and arrived by way of Castle Garden in New York on 18 February 1888.

Alexander Berkman arrived in America alone, jobless, and with no friends or family. A further handicap was his inability to speak any English. He soon found that the United States was far from the utopian fantasy he had conjured up in his Russian imaginings, rapidly "discover[ing] the sham of American political freedom and economic opportunity."[21] Berkman gravitated, like so many before him, to the Lower East Side in New York, where he endured a far more proletarian lifestyle than he had enjoyed in Kovno. Work for recent immigrants was scarce, and it often paid little more than starvation wages; as a result, Berkman was forced to endure privations he had not known previously. Also coloring his view of the United States were the events that had unfolded at Haymarket Square in Chicago. As Avrich highlights, it was the events at "Haymarket that bought Berkman to anarchism."[22] On the night of 4 May 1886, at a labor demonstration in support of the eight-hour working day in Chicago, there were violent clashes between protestors and the police. There were scores of deaths and serious injuries, and, at some point during the fray, an unknown party had thrown an explosive. This device ripped through the crowd and resulted in injuries to both the police and the protestors, the former of whom had been firing wildly into the crowd. In the aftermath of these events, the Chicago police (driven by one of the first "red scares" in America) rounded up eight local Anarchists who had no direct involvement in riot. Despite public sympathy for them, and a trial that was rushed through the courts, seven of the defendants were sentenced to death; the eighth man received fifteen years' imprisonment. Although two of the death sentences were later commuted to life imprisonment, one of the remaining condemned men committed suicide, and the other four were executed on 11 November 1887.[23] The injustices suffered by the Anarchists, and their dignity during the trial, garnered much public sympathy at the time; for Berkman, these events ignited a lifelong passion for Anarchism and social justice.

Berkman first got the opportunity to express his newfound political views (having shifted from Nihilism to Anarchism) when he became a member of the Pioneers of Liberty, which, in addition to being formed in direct response to the Haymarket tragedy, was the first Jewish Anarchist group in the United States. Through his contact with other group members, Berkman improved both his Yiddish and his English, and he also came into contact with Johann Most, for whom he was to work as a typesetter for the *Freiheit* paper. Most was an incendiary figure and remains such in the history of Anarchism. Born in Bavaria on 5 February 1846, he had by the age of twelve been expelled from school for organizing a classroom strike against a particularly loathed teacher. As Most aged, he retained a passionate interest in politics. Initially an internationalist and Socialist attracted to the ideas of Karl Marx and Ferdinand Lasalle, in 1874 Most was elected to the German Reichstag as a Social Democrat deputy, a position in which he served until 1878. While serving as a deputy, Most was repeatedly arrested by German authorities, and his political positions hardened. Exiled by the German state in 1878 for advocating direct action and the use of explosives to bring about revolutionary change, Most arrived in London and established the *Freiheit* newspaper. He was arrested in 1881 by the British for expressing his joy in the assassination of Alexander II of Russia; following his release, he immigrated to the United States in 1882. Most soon found himself in trouble with U.S. legal authorities and was arrested on a number of occasions, and in 1885 he published *The Science of Revolutionary Warfare: A Handbook of Instruction in the Use and Prepa-*

ration of *Nitroglycerine, Dynamite, Gun-Cotton, Fulminating Mercury, Bombs, Fuses, Poisons, Etc.* Berkman, like many other radical denizens of the Lower East Side, regarded Most as a hero; indeed, Berkman later described him as the "hero of my first years in America ... my teacher ... the ideal revolutionist."[24]

In 1889, through a fellow member of the Pioneers of Liberty, Berkman met Emma Goldman, with whom he fell passionately in love. The affair between Berkman and Goldman was a turning point for them both, and it remains a love story to rival that of the Japanese Anarchists Kanno Sugako and Shūsui Kōtoku (discussed in a later chapter). Along with sharing a Russian Jewish background, both Berkman and Goldman were committed Anarchists. By the end of the year, they were living together in a communal apartment on 42nd Street with Berkman's cousin, Modest Aronstam (who had arrived in New York in August 1888), and Emma's friend, Helene Minkin, attempting to put the communal vision outlined by Chernyshevsky into practice. Their living situation proved far from peaceful, however, with Berkman often berating Aronstam for spending what little funds he had on bourgeois luxuries and Aronstam resenting his cousin's self-sacrificing ideology. Matters were further complicated when Aronstam and Goldman began an affair, requiring the three to negotiate a ménage à trois, with Goldman frequenting the bedrooms of both cousins.

By 1891, the trio had relocated to Worcester, Massachusetts, where Aronstam briefly operated an art studio by the name of the "French Art Studio." After the failure of this enterprise, he, Berkman, and Goldman opened and ran a successful luncheonette. Although all three were still involved in the Anarchism of the period, it was the incidents at Homestead that galvanized them. Berkman later described his reaction to news of the strike as follows: "I could no longer remain indifferent. The moment was urgent. The toilers of Homestead had defied the oppressor. They were awakening. But as yet the steelworkers were only blindly rebellious. The vision of Anarchism alone could imbue discontent with conscious revolutionary purpose; it alone could lend wings to the aspirations of labor."[25]

On hearing reports from Homestead, the trio decided that the time had come to enact their principles—to engage in a revolutionary display that would precipitate revolution. After purchasing a revolver and fashioning a dagger from a metal file, Berkman made his way to Pittsburgh alone, arriving on 14 July and staying with local Anarchist Carl Nold for a few days. On 21 July he checked into a local hotel, using the name of his fictitious idol, Rakhmetov. By 23 July, he was ready to act and arrived at the office of Frick, posing as an employment agency representative. In Berkman's own words:

> Quickly retracing my steps, I pass through the gates separating the clerks from the visitors, and, brushing the astonished attendant aside, I step into the office on the left, and find myself facing Frick.
> For an instant the sunlight, streaming in through the window, dazzles me. I discern two men at the further end of a long table.
> "Fr—," I begin. The look of terror on his face strikes me speechless. It is the dread of the conscious presence of death.
> "He understands," it flashes through my mind. With a quick motion I draw the revolver. As I raise the weapon, I see Frick clutch with both hands the arms of the chair, and attempt to rise. I aim at his head. "Perhaps he wears armor," I reflect. With a look of horror he quickly averts his face, as I pull the trigger. There is a flash, and the high-ceilinged room reverberates as with the booming of a cannon. I hear a sharp, piercing cry, and see Frick on his knees, his head against the arm of the chair.[26]

Berkman fired on Frick twice and stabbed him repeatedly in the legs after having been wrestled to the floor. Although Berkman was struck on the head by a workman with a hammer, he was only subdued when a crowd (including a deputy sheriff) arrived, attracted by the commotion and the gunshots. Although seriously wounded, Frick survived, returning to his position and his office within weeks of the attack.

Berkman's attempt to assassinate Frick divided the opinions of Anarchists of the period; however, his actions were predictably met with outrage by the press. On the day following the shooting, the *New York Times* described Berkman (incorrectly identified as Simon Bachman) as "a mere crank, a Nihilist whose head was turned by the reading of the Homestead troubles, and who started forth on a mission of destruction."[27] Perhaps the most telling of all the articles published about the attack, however, was from Louisville's *Courier-Journal*. In it the following claim was made: "A remarkable fact in connection with the attempt on Mr. Frick's life was that a number of men, who, by their dress and general mien, showed themselves to be millworkers, looked perfectly aghast, and one was heard to say: 'Good god, this kills our case forever.'"[28] This turned out to be a highly prescient statement.

Even before Frick had returned to work, he made his intentions plain to the strikers. The day following the shooting, he issued a statement in which he declared that under no circumstances would any new hire taken on since the commencement of the strike be dismissed. This decision effectively provided no quarter to the striking workers. The media had also turned against them. Following the attack against Frick, arrests were frequent, and the press grew less and less sympathetic, confirming the fears reported by the *New York Times*, which had determined that "the best thought in Homestead regarding the attempted assassination in but one light, that it was the severest blow the Amalgamated Association had received, for, no matter what the upshot might be, the association would have to bear the responsibility for it in the public mind."[29]

With a Republican presidential administration looking on, repressive troops arresting any supposedly subversive elements, and public sentiments hardening against the workers, the strike all but crumbled. The privations caused by lack of employment and rapidly diminishing financial donations from the public also precipitated the end of the protest. The collapse of the strike by October 1892 was quickly seized upon by the factory owners. As H. W. Brands highlights, in addition to blacklisting members of the workers' strike committee, ensuring that they could never work in the steel industry again, "Carnegie Steel used the Homestead affair as the occasion for a concerted campaign of union-busting; from the summer of 1892 it adopted an unstated but effective policy of hiring only nonunion workers. Carnegie's competitors followed suit. Within a year the Amalgamated union had lost ten thousand members throughout the iron and steel industry."[30] Far from being the spark that lit the fuse of a workers' uprising, the failed assassination ultimately led to a failed strike and had a lasting negative impact on unionized labor in the United States.

The impact on Berkman was negative too. He found himself in jail in Pittsburgh, awaiting trial. During his detention he received support from some in the Anarchist community, particularly Emma Goldman, but also Robert Reitzel, who wrote in the pages of *Der arme Teufel* (The Poor Devil), a popular German-language periodical published in Detroit, that Berkman should be considered "a hero of our time."[31] In other quarters, however, Berkman's actions were less well received; perhaps the most vocal of these critics was his one-time hero, Johann Most. In the pages of *Freiheit*, Most lampooned Berkman and his actions. Worse still, he disputed their very point; as Avrich highlights, Most even went so far as to state that "in the United States, where the anarchist movement had so far found little support, propaganda by the deed would never be understood and would only backfire. The attempt on Frick, [Most] wrote, had proven this. Berkman might have exhibited a certain heroism, Most conceded, but in other respects the effort had been a 'total failure.'"[32] Veering between rage and despondency, Berkman was kept isolated in his jail cell, his future uncertain.

On 19 September 1892, Berkman was instructed to ready himself for court. After dressing, he was escorted from his cell to the Allegheny County Court House. After refusing legal representation, Berkman found himself facing Judge McClung, who warned him of his decision. Rather than present a legal defense, Berkman took the opportunity to read a statement he had prepared in German, which took him two hours to read in its totality. After a further two hours of witness testimony, Berkman found himself at the mercy of the jurors, who quickly found him guilty. Without pausing for a recess, the judge handed down a sentence of twenty-two years (the maximum permissible by law) for a variety of assault charges. As soon as the four-hour trial had concluded, Berkman was transported to the Western Penitentiary of Pennsylvania (commonly referred to as Riverside), where he was to serve his sentence.

Berkman spent the next fourteen years of his life in prison, before his eventual release on 18 May 1906. In 1919, following further brushes with the law (most notably in 1917, when he was arrested for organizing the No Conscription League in New York to resist the carnage of the First World War), Berkman was deported to Russia as part of the Anarchist Exclusion Act, which was established at the height of the Red Scare of the period. Leaving Russia in December 1921, utterly disappointed with the Bolshevik revolution, Berkman found refuge in Saint-Cloud, France, before being forced to move to Nice in search of cheaper accommodations owing to the precarious nature of his earnings as a sometime editor and translator. Suffering from a long-term and debilitating prostate condition, Berkman attempted to shoot himself in the heart on 28 June 1936. However, just as he had previously failed to finish off Frick, his efforts to kill himself met with failure. Paralyzed by the bullet that tore into his spine and lung, Berkman clung to life until the evening of 28 June. Following his death, his funeral was arranged by Emma Goldman, his comrade and love of his youth. Although Berkman had wanted his ashes to be scattered near the graves of the Haymarket defendants who had so inspired him upon arriving on American shores, poverty necessitated that he be buried in a common grave in Cochez Cemetery in Nice. But this was not the end of Berkman's legacy—just as he had been inspired by the events at Haymarket, his attempted assassination of Henry Clay Frick would have a lasting influence on another young proponent of propaganda of the deed, Leon Czolgosz, who would go on to commit a shocking (and, in his case, successful) attack.

By 1901, the United States was encroaching militarily and economically into Latin America. After the brief Spanish-American War of 1898, which resulted in Spain ceding control of Cuba and ownership of Puerto Rico, Guam, and the Philippine islands to the United States (resulting in the collapse of the Spanish Empire), the Republican government of the day and, indeed, much of the American populace were in triumphant mood. This attitude was reflected in the Pan-American Exposition, which opened its doors to the public on 1 May 1901. The expressed purpose of the exposition, held in Buffalo, New York, was to promote U.S. economic interests and highlight recent advances in American technologies. Its stated aims were summarized in the exposition's official slogan, which was to foster and encourage "commercial well-being and good understanding among the

American Republics." Inventors would be granted permission to display their advances; architects would be tasked with creating "stimulating surroundings that embody something like the best ideals and training of American art"[33]; and the public would be invited to witness the Electric Tower and other marvels for a reasonable fee ($7.00 in equivalent currency). The exposition promised a "temporary wonderland on a 350-acre site," where the eight million visitors who were drawn to it could be "dazzled by an array of monumental buildings housing hundreds of exhibits displaying the greatest material, scientific, and technological achievements."[34] Unfortunately for the operators of the Pan-American Exposition Company, which had been formed in 1897, the exposition would be remembered for the events that unfolded owing to the actions of a young and ardent man from Alpena, Michigan.

In the 1870s in Prussia, Paul Czolgosz was a worried man. As a Polish Catholic, he was suffering from the effects of the Kulturkampf policies enacted by the Prime Minister Otto von Bismarck, which sought to oppress and discriminate against Poles resident in Prussia, with the unstated aim of destroying Polish national identity. Indeed, Bismarck's hatred for Poles in Prussia was so pronounced that he even called for their extermination, stating in private letters, "Hit the Poles, so that they break down. If we want to exist, we have to exterminate them."[35] In such an environment, Czolgosz's wife, Mary Nowak, and their sons, Waldeck and Frank, were far from safe. A few years previously, a brother had fled Prussia for the United States and, upon settling in Michigan, had written to Paul, telling him of a place where Poles were not abused and work was plentiful. By early 1873, Paul had also left Prussia and settled in the United States, where he began his life as "an ignorant Pole, who had to fight his way for many years in a land of strangers."[36] Or so the conventional and oft-told history states. In 2008, however, Andrey Dovnar-Zapolsky published an article in *Komsomolskaya Pravda* that quoted findings from Sergei Rybchenok, the chief archivist of the Russian National Historical Archives, which, if substantiated, muddy the origins of Czolgosz as a persecuted Prussian Pole. According to this article,[37] there is documentary evidence to suggest that Paul Czolgosz was actually an impoverished petty nobleman from the Vilna province, now the Grodno region of Belarus. Originally known as Pavel Zholgus, he assumed the name of Paul Czolgosz after immigrating to Germany; rather than being Polish, he was of Hungarian descent. Whether Zholgus or Czolgosz, Hungarian or Pole, by 1873 he was resident in Michigan, and within a few months of finding both work and lodgings, he was joined by his pregnant wife and two young sons. The family grew on 5 May 1873, when Leon Czolgosz was born in the city of Alpena, Michigan.

Like many immigrants of the period, the Czolgosz family went where the work was. Over the years, as Scott Miller reveals, "the growing family would move time and time again, from Rogers City to Alpena, Michigan, to Posen, Michigan, and then back to Alpena; to an area near Pittsburgh, to Cleveland, and finally to a farm in Warrensville, Ohio."[38] For the young Leon, such regular moves around the country may have affected his ability to form lasting friendships of any kind; he was "inclined to remain very much to himself"[39] and was "extremely bashful."[40] His extroversion may have suffered further when Leon was ten years old. Following the birth of his sister, Victoria, his mother took ill. After lingering in an increasingly worsening state for six weeks (and following his frantic father moving his ailing wife to Alpena, where doctors performed increasingly futile examinations), the matriarch of the family passed away. For a quiet, insular boy, easily lost in a boisterous family that now consisted of seven other siblings, this loss was likely pronounced.

Throughout the family's second sojourn in Alpena, Leon Czolgosz received four years of education. He was, according to his older brother Waldeck, "considered the best scholar"[41] of all the students in his small school. His education, however, was cut short when, at the age of fourteen, he secured a job at a glass factory near Pittsburgh, where he had the unenviable task of carrying red hot, freshly cast glass bottles to the factory cooling area. After spending a few years working in this and other positions, Czolgosz (now seventeen) began working at the Cleveland Rolling Mill Company. Opened in 1864, this company converted pig iron into wire and cheap nails; it experienced rapid growth, employing a workforce of 80,00 by its peak in the 1890s, before being absorbed into the American Steel and Wire Company in 1899, which would itself be absorbed into the U.S. Steel Corporation (the successor of the Carnegie Steel Company). In the 1880s, the Cleveland Rolling Mill Company had

Leon Czolgosz

endured a series of strikes due to the falling wages that were a result of the company employing Polish and Czech workers (of whom young Czolgosz was one), and by 1893 the company was embroiled in another labor dispute. Faced with more wage cuts, the union called a strike, and, in keeping with management attitudes of this period, the company owners announced that all workers involved would be both sacked and blacklisted. Czolgosz found that for his involvement, which had been limited to walking out of the factory gates with his colleagues, he had been added to the list; thus, at the age of twenty, he was unemployed and desperate. A few months after the strike, however, the foreman was replaced, and Czolgosz applied for employment under the name of Fred C. Neiman (close to the German word for "nobody," *neimand*, and an alias he would use again) and was rehired.

While employed at the mill, Czolgosz was invited by co-workers to join the Order of the Knights of the Golden Eagle Society. In spite of its somewhat grandiose title, the society was a respectable workingman's association, which was not only staunchly anti–Catholic but also vaguely Socialist in its outlook. As detailed by Walter Channing, "The proclaimed purpose of its founders and the primary of objects of the order are to promote the principles of true benevolence by associating its members together for the purpose of mutual relief."[42] For someone who had been raised Catholic (as Czolgosz was), this choice of club membership seems, on first consideration, somewhat odd. By this time in his life, however, Czolgosz had largely grown disillusioned with the beliefs of his childhood and, roused by industrial disputes and the economic and social disparities inherent in American society during this period, was seeking solutions to them. Although Czolgosz paid his dues regularly and in advance for the Golden Eagle Society, he remained a largely inactive member and was withdrawn during their meetings. The primary reason for this reticence, other than his social awkwardness, may well have been that he "had hoped for more radical solutions to society's ills than the Golden Eagle offered."[43]

It was perhaps due to his time in the Golden Eagle Society (and his disaffection with it) that, in 1894, Czolgosz made the acquaintance of an upholsterer by the name of Anton Zwolinski. At this time, Zwolinski was president of a Polish educational club by the name of Sila ("force" in Polish), which met at Tod Street and Third Avenue in Cleveland. Although Zwolinski later claimed that "Czolgosz made no secret of the fact that he was an Anarchist,"[44] it seems unlikely that he was at the time. While members of Sila discussed Anarchism, "the Cleveland police did not consider the circle an Anarchist organization"[45]; however, it was probably among this group that Czolgosz first started to find answers to some of the questions that had plagued him and driven him away from both organized religion and his co-workers and fellow members of the Golden Eagle Society. Czolgosz also began attending meetings in the Cleveland area where workers let off steam about their harsh working conditions. Although politically naïve, Czolgosz was finding that amid the angry rumblings of a disaffected and abused workforce, there was a thread that led back to Anarchism, which, as a philosophy, offered hope for rectifying the social and economic conditions to which both he and his peers were exposed.

In 1898, aged 25, Czolgosz resigned from his job at the Cleveland Rolling Mill Company for reasons of ill health. Although historians cannot be sure what malady ailed Czolgosz, it affected him deeply. Until his resignation, he had been a steady and focused worker, although he had more than a passing interest in the politics of the period; following his resignation, he became all but a recluse. As Channing details, after Czolgosz left the mill, "he was never able to employ himself at anything steadily."[46] Channing also claims that Czolgosz was possibly epileptic; however, his reported symptoms do not appear to bear this diagnosis out. Czolgosz "had for a long period a cough, took a variety of medicines, consulted several doctors, one of whom gave him certificates to get sick benefits with"; additionally, "he had frequent and peculiar period[s] of somnolence."[47] Impacted by illness, and having witnessed a variety of strikes in Cleveland similar to what occurred in Homestead (albeit ones that ended less violently), Czolgosz sought refuge on the fifty-five-acre farm in Warrensville, Ohio, that his father (through years of saving and scrimping) had managed to acquire.

Now gainfully unemployed, life in the country was anything but peaceful for Czolgosz. He was frequently at odds with his family concerning his perceived indolence and his hardening political views. Czolgosz was an avid reader of both Anarchist and Socialist papers and periodicals of the period, and when news emerged of the assassination of Italy's King Umberto by Gaetano Bresci (as detailed elsewhere in this book), Czolgosz "carefully clipped a newspaper account of the story and placed it in his wallet."[48] Although his interest in Anarchism (and specifically propaganda of the deed) was solidifying during this period, Czolgosz was largely isolated on the family farm. This changed on the afternoon of 5 May 1901, when he traveled to listen to Emma Goldman at the Cleveland Memorial Hall. She remembered him later as "very young, a mere youth of medium height, well built and carrying himself very erect," and when he asked her quietly for reading recommendations before she assumed her speaking position on the platform, "it was his face that held me, a most sensitive face, with a delicate pink complexion; a handsome face made doubly so by his golden curly hair. Strength showed in his large blue eyes."[49] Czolgosz sat entranced as Goldman spoke outlining how even though Anarchism was fundamentally opposed to the violence of the state, it was no surprise that motivated men and women of passion sometimes chose a violent method to stop the abuses of the state. For Czolgosz, these words, like few others, made a lot of sense.

Goldman's appearance in Cleveland was organized in part by the publishers of the Anarchist newspaper *Free Society*. Produced weekly by the husband-and-wife team of Abraham and Mary Isaak, *Free Society* was noteworthy, as it was one of the few Anarchist periodicals to be published in English, rather than German, Russian, or Yiddish, which were the languages favored by other U.S.-based journals of the period. Originally published in Portland in 1895, where it was known as *The Firebrand*, by 1901 operations had shifted to Chicago, and the name had been changed after the Isaaks faced obscenity charges for their defense of both free love and women's rights. As noted by Kenyon Zimmer, the Isaaks were "unlikely revolutionaries,"[50] having turned from Protestant pacifism to Anarchism as a result of their immigrant experience in the United States; however, their home had become "a gathering place for local anarchists and radicals."[51] They would soon be visited by the intense and quiet young Czolgosz, who had recently moved from his family's farm to West Seneca, Buffalo, New York.

Even before his brief meeting with Goldman, Czolgosz was a dedicated reader of *Free Society*. The Isaaks provided a caustic and damning view of American society and politics of the period, with much ire directed at the serving U.S. president, William McKinley. For radicals at the time, McKinley's involvement in the Spanish-American War and the campaign in the Philippines pointed to an expansionist agenda, and the president's defense of the industrial sector allowed the abuses suffered by workers such as those at Homestead to continue unchecked. Although many of the journal's contributors perceived McKinley as being as corrupting an influence as an absolute and unchecked monarch, they were keen to explain that "no anarchist wants McKinley assassinated. He is of more use to us right where he is, an object lesson of the worst results of representative government."[52] Unfortunately, Czolgosz disagreed with this conclusion.

Following Goldman's speech at the Cleveland Memorial Hall, her hectic speaking tour took its toll, and she sought respite at the Isaaks' home in Chicago. Here, on 12 July 1901, she was visited by a man calling himself Fred C. Neiman, who had a few weeks before made such an impression on her. On her way to the train station for the next stop on her speaking tour, Goldman did not have time to engage with Neiman for very long; however, as she was later to write, "Neiman told me that he had belonged to a Socialist local in Cleveland, that he found its members dull, lacking in vision and enthusiasm. He could not bear to be with them and he had left Cleveland and now working in Chicago and eager to get in touch with anarchists."[53]

A few weeks before visiting Goldman, Czolgosz had also paid a visit to the Cleveland home of Emil Schilling, a German Anarchist to whom he had been referred by a contact from Sila. According to interviews that Walter Channing later conducted with Schilling, Czolgosz (who again was calling himself Neiman) did not acquit himself well at this meeting. Schilling's suspicions were raised by Czolgosz's query, "Say do you have any secret societies? I hear the anarchists are plotting something like Breschi,"[54] and by his uninvited guest's general demeanor, which seemed overly curious and pointed. Schilling believed he might be dealing with a police agent or investigator and, following a second visit from Czolgosz, wrote to the Isaaks, warning them of this visitation. The editors of *Free Society* were quick to respond, and on 1 September 1901 the following warning appeared in the journal's pages: "ATTENTION! The attention of comrades is called to another spy. He is well dressed, of medium height, rather narrow shouldered, blond and about 25 years of age. Up to the present he has made his appearance in Chicago and Cleveland. In the former place he remained but a short time, while in Cleveland he disappeared when the comrades had confirmed themselves of his identity and were on the point of exposing him. His demeanor is of the usual sort, pretending to be greatly interested in the cause, asking for names or soliciting aid for acts of contemplated violence. If this same individual makes his appearance elsewhere the comrades are warned in advance, and can act accordingly."[55] Now living in a small room in a boarding house in West Seneca, Buffalo, Czolgosz found himself isolated from the very individuals with whom he had aspired to associate and as solitary as he had been back on the family farm.

What brought Czolgosz to Buffalo in the summer of 1901 will never be known, but "it was likely as good a destination as any for a loner with a few bucks in his pocket,"[56] and it is entirely possible that he was in the city in pursuit of employment. The boarding house he found himself in was run by John Nowak, from whom Czolgosz learned of President McKinley's upcoming visit to the Pan-American Exposition. As Marshall Everett states, "The next day, Czolgosz went to the exposition. He went there on the following day, and the day following. The idea that he might kill the President when he came was in his mind, but the purpose was half formed. At this time it might have been possible to have diverted his mind from the thought of such a mission. But he was alone in the city. He had no friends there. There was nothing to check the fever burning deeper and deeper into his mind."[57] Although Everett is somewhat overwrought in his conclusions, he is accurate inasmuch as Czolgosz found himself isolated in Buffalo. He was not, however, without a plan or an agenda.

President William McKinley arrived in Buffalo, accompanied by his wife Ida, on 4 September; around this time, Czolgosz purchased a 32-caliber Iver Johnson revolver for $4.50 at a local hardware store on Main Street.[58] McKinley planned to attend the exposition on 5 September. Here he gave an address and toured the fair. Everett suggests that Czolgosz made an attempt to assassinate the president on this day during his speech but was prevented from doing so when "a stalwart guard appeared in front of him."[59] On 6 September, the president was due to go on an outing to Niagara Falls, following which he would return to the grounds of the exposition to meet the public at the Temple of Music. This event had been heavily advertised and was being used to swell the gate receipts for the day. The president's personal secretary, George B. Cortelyou, was concerned about security arrangements, but McKinley was untroubled. By nature he was a gregarious man and had relied upon personal interactions to achieve the presidency, famously running for the office from his front porch. Although Cortelyou attempted to persuade the president not to return to the fair, McKinley remained resolute in his determination not to change his plans, responding to the entreaties of his loyal secretary by stating, "Why should I? No one would wish to hurt me."[60] For William McKinley, this would prove a fatal error in judgment.

On 6 September, Czolgosz rose early and headed toward the exposition grounds. He arrived at 8:30 a.m., leaving him plenty of time to make his preparations. A formal reception was to be held for President McKinley that afternoon in the Temple of Music. Designed by the architects August Esenwein and James A. Johnson, the Temple of Music was a concert hall and auditorium with capable of seating up to two thousand exposition visitors. The seating in the hall had been removed for the day, and the doors to the building were flung open in an attempt to combat the sweltering heat. Proceeding down the length of the hall, well-wishers could stand in line to shake the hand of their president before exiting the building. Normal security procedures regarding the public approaching the president with empty hands had been lifted for the day, since many in the line to meet McKinley face to face were forced to wipe their faces with handkerchiefs. Security consisted of Buffalo and exposition police, in addition to Secret Service agents who had the unenviable task of surveying the grounds for danger while their view was obstructed by the police, who all wanted the best view of the unfolding events. At 4:07 p.m., after spending many hours in the line to meet McKinley, Czolgosz stepped forward. Everett details events as follows:

> The President smiled and presented his right hand in a position to meet the left of the approaching man. Hardly a foot of space intervened between the bodies of the two men. Before their hands met two pistol shots rang out, and the President turned slightly to his left.
> The bandage on the hand of the tall, innocent looking young man had concealed a revolver. He had fired through the bandage without removing any portion of the handkerchief.
> The first bullet entered too high for the purpose of the assassin, who had fired again as soon as his finger could move the trigger.
> On receiving the first shot President McKinley lifted himself on his toes with something of a gasp. His movement caused the second shot to enter just below his navel. With the second shot the President doubled slightly forward and sank back.[61]

Czolgosz prepared to fire again at the prostrate body of the president of the United States. However, before he could discharge a third shot, James Parker, an African Spanish American who had been standing behind him in line, slammed into him, reaching for the gun. A Buffalo detective by the name of John Geary joined the fray, and Czolgosz tumbled to the floor beneath a pile of bodies. Other police rushed to the disturbance and began to pummel Czolgosz with fists and rifle butts. Prevented from collapsing to the floor by Cortelyou, McKinley had enough presence of mind to call for the assailants to stop beating Czolgosz. The president was rapidly stretchered away as Czolgosz was ushered from the scene in handcuffs, going first to Buffalo's 13th Precinct house at 346 Austin Street before being moved to police headquarters.

News of the attack against the president spread like wildfire. Initially it was hoped that McKinley would soon recover from his wounds. Sadly, although he endured a number of surgical procedures, McKinley ultimately died owing to complications. At one point, Thomas Edison sent a newly patented x-ray machine to help locate bullet fragments that were still believed to be lodged in the president's body; however, the use of this device was prevented by anxious physicians. In the early hours of 14 September 1901, President McKinley passed away.

The attack against McKinley and his later death would have devastating consequences for Anarchists in the United States. Two days following the shooting, on 8 September, the *New York Times* declared Czolgosz a "rabid anarchist."[62] Czolgosz himself failed to help his position. When initially arrested, he gave his name as Fred C. Neiman, but his true identity was revealed within hours of questioning. During this questioning he also provided a number of details that would later make their way into the pages of the popular press. Czolgosz admitted, "I am an Anarchist. I am a disciple of Emma Goldman. Her words set me on fire."[63] The following day, during an interview with a medical examiner who was tending to the wounds incurred during the incident at the Temple of Music (and very likely during interrogation as well), Czolgosz provided further justification for his actions: "I don't believe in the Republican form of government, and I don't believe we should have any rulers. It is right to kill them." He concluded, "I killed President McKinley because I done my duty. I don't believe in one man having so much service, and another man should have none."[64] For an angry public, it was difficult to believe that Czolgosz had acted alone. As Alix Shulman reveals, this supposition and anger was soon directed into acts of rage and revenge against all Anarchists: "All across the land anarchists were hunted, arrested, beaten, persecuted. Their offices were raided, their papers confiscated. In Wyoming a man thought to be an anarchist was tarred and feathered. In Pittsburgh an anarchist was almost lynched. In New York City a mob had to be forcibly prevented from crossing the Hudson River and burning down the whole city of Paterson, New Jersey, where many anarchist workers lived."[65] The police also believed that they were dealing with a wide-ranging conspiracy, and on 7 September they arrested Abraham and Mary Isaak (along with their son, Abraham Jr., and their daughter, Marie), as well as a number of others who were visiting their house, including Clemence Pfuetzer, Alfred Schneider, Hippolyte Havel, Henry Travaglio, and Julia Mechanic. In Chicago on that same day, Martin Raznik, Maurice Fox, and Michael Raz were likewise taken into custody.[66] Johann Most was also rounded up, and Emma Goldman later turned herself in to the Buffalo police. Eventually, all of those who had been arrested were dismissed, as the state had no evidence to counter Czolgosz's vociferous and consistent claims that he had acted alone.

Following McKinley's death, on 16 September, Czolgosz was transferred to the Erie County Jail prior to being arraigned before County Judge Emery. His trial began in earnest on the same day. Czolgosz's defense was the responsibility of the court-appointed Robert C. Titus and Loran L. Lewis; however, they were unable to do much in this regard, as Czolgosz refused to say a single word to them. The only defense that his lawyers could provide was that at the time of his actions, Czolgosz had not been fully possessed of his faculties. The jury was unwilling to consider this as a defense for shooting the president, and on 24 September 1901 he was pronounced guilty. On 26 September 1901, Judge Emery declared that Czolgosz would be put to death by electrocution. Czolgosz was asked whether he wished to provide a statement to the court; unlike many other proponents of propaganda of the deed, he declined. He was led from court and transferred to the Auburn prison that same day, all the while failing to display any emotion. On 29 October 1901, 45 days after McKinley's death, Czolgosz was walked from his cell in the company of the prison warden toward the chamber containing the electric chair. When asked if he had any last words, he replied defiantly, "I killed the President because he was the enemy of the good people—the good working people. I am not sorry for my crime."[67]

The actions of Berkman and Czolgosz were massively divisive within the Anarchist movement in the United States. In the case of Berkman, opinion was divided as to whether his actions had any positive effect. Certainly for the workers at Homestead, his actions proved disastrous, playing as they did into the hands of conservative factory owners who could then point to the dangers of unchecked unionized labor. Czolgosz's actions, for many, served to discredit the nascent U.S. Anarchist movement. By assassinating a serving president, Czolgosz allowed the popular press to stir up negative feelings concerning the movement, which ultimately led to a reactionary and conservative response resulting in increased harassment and surveillance of Anarchists, as well as the passage of the Immigration Act of 1903 (also known as the Anarchist Exclusion Act). President Theodore Roosevelt (who had previously served as McKinley's vice president) introduced this act, he stated unequivocally that it was directed at addressing the supposed threat of Anarchists and declared, "I earnestly recommend to the congress that in the exercise of its wise discretion it should take into consideration the coming to this country of anarchists or persons professing principles hostile to all government…. They and those like them should be kept out of this country; and if found here they should be promptly deported to the country whence they came."[68] The Anarchist Exclusion Act was the first sedition law to be passed in the United States since 1798, and the first legal statute "in American History to provide penalties simply for belonging to a group."[69] Ironically, Czolgosz's actions, in seeking to oppose the repressions of the state, had only helped to increase them, just as Berkman, who had aimed to prevent the abuse of labor, had ultimately served to worsen conditions. In both instances, the violent actions of individuals were met reflectively with a violent and repressive response by the state and the forces of capitalism.

The Tragedy at Buffalo

Source: Emma Goldman, *Free Society*, October 1901, as referenced by the Anarchist Library, https://theanarchistlibrary.org/library/emma-goldman-the-tragedy-at-buffalo (accessed March 2017)

> For they starve the little frightened child
>   Till it weeps both night and day:
> And they scourge the weak, and flog the fool,
>   And gibe the old and gray,
> And some grow mad, and all grow bad,
>   And none a word may say.
> —Oscar Wilde.

Never before in the history of governments has the sound of a pistol shot so startled, terrorized, and horrified the self-satisfied, indifferent, contented, and indolent public, as has the one fired by Leon Czolgosz when he struck down William McKinley, president of the money kings and trust magnates of this country.

Not that this modern Caesar was the first to die at the hands of a Brutus. Oh, no! Since man has trampled upon the rights of his fellow men, rebellious spirits have been afloat in the atmosphere. Not that William McKinley was a greater man than those who throned upon the fettered form of Liberty. He did not compare either in intellect, ability, personality, or force of character with those who had to pay the penalty of their power. Nor will history be able to record his extraordinary kindness, generosity, and sympathy with those whom ignorance and greed have condemned to a life of misery, hopelessness, and despair.

Why, then, were the mighty and powerful thrown into such consternation by the deed of September 6? Why this howl of a hired press? Why such blood-thirsty and violent utterances from the clergy, whose usual business it is to preach "peace on earth and good will to all"? Why the mad ravings of the mob, the demand for rigid laws to curtail freedom of press and speech?

For more than thirty years a small band of parasites have robbed the American people, and trampled upon the fundamental principles laid down by the forefathers of this country, guaranteeing to every man, woman and child, "Life, liberty, and the pursuit of happiness." For thirty years they have been increasing their wealth and power at the expense of the vast mass of workers, thereby enlarging the army of the unemployed, the hungry, homeless, and friendless portion of humanity, tramping the country from east to west and north to south, in a vain search for work. For many years the home has been left to the care of the little ones, while the parents are working their life and strength away for a small pittance. For thirty years the sturdy sons of America were sacrificed on the battlefield of industrial war, and the daughters outraged in corrupt factory surroundings. For long and weary years this process of undermining the nation's health, vigor, and pride, without much protest from the disinherited and oppressed, has been going on. Maddened by success and victory, the money-powers of this "free land of ours" became more and more audacious in their heartless, cruel efforts to compete with rotten and decayed European tyrannies in supremacy of power.

With the minds of the young poisoned with a perverted conception of patriotism, and the fallacious notion that all are equal and that each one has the same opportunity to become a millionaire (provided he can steal the first hundred thousand dollars), it was an easy matter indeed to check the discontent of the people; one is therefore not surprised when one hears Americans say, "We can understand why the poor Russians kill their czar, or the Italians their king, for think of the conditions that prevail there; but he who lives in a republic, where each one has the opportunity to become President of the United States (provided he has a powerful party back of him), why should he attempt such acts? We are the people, and acts of violence in this country are impossible."

And now that the impossible has happened, that even America has given birth to the man who struck down the king of the republic, they have lost their heads, and are shouting vengeance upon those who for years have shown that the conditions here were beginning to be alarming, and unless a halt be called, despotism would set its heavy foot on the hitherto relatively free limbs of the people.

In vain have the mouthpieces of wealth denounced Leon Czolgosz as a foreigner; in vain they are making the world believe that he is the product of European conditions, and influenced by European ideas. This time the "assassin" happens to be the child of Columbia, who lulled him to sleep with

> "My country, 'tis of thee,
> Sweet land of liberty,"

and who held out the hope to him that he, too, could become President of the country. Who can tell how many times this American child has gloried in the celebration of the 4th of July, or on Decoration Day, when he faithfully honored the nation's dead? Who knows but what he, too, was willing to "fight for his country and die for her liberty"; until it dawned upon him that those he belonged to have no country, because they have been robbed of all that they have produced; until he saw that all the liberty and independence of his youthful dreams are but a farce. Perhaps he also learned that it is nonsense to talk of equality between those who have all and those who have nothing, hence he rebelled.

"But his act was mad and cowardly," says the ruling class. "It was foolish and impractical," echo all petty reformers, Socialists, and even some Anarchists.

What absurdity! As if an act of this kind can be measured by its usefulness, expediency, or practicability. We might as well ask ourselves of the usefulness of a cyclone, tornado, a violent thunderstorm, or the ceaseless fall of the Niagara water. All these forces are the natural results of natural causes, which we may not yet have been able to explain, but which are nevertheless a part of nature, just as force is natural and part of man and beast, developed or checked, according to the pressure of conditions and man's understanding. An act of violence is therefore not only the result of conditions, but also of man's psychical and physical nature, and his susceptibility to the world surrounding him.

Does not the summer fight against the winter, does it not resist, mourn, and weep oceans of tears in its eager attempt to shield its children from the icy grip of frost? And does not the winter enshroud Mother Earth with a white, hard cover, lest the warm spring sunshine should melt the heart of the hardened old gentleman? And does he not gather his last forces for a bitter and fierce battle for supremacy, until the burning rays of the sun disperse his ranks?

Resistance against force is a fact all through nature. Man being part of nature, he, too, is swayed by the same force to defend himself against invasion. Force will continue to be a natural factor just so long as economic slavery, social superiority, inequality, exploitation, and war continue to destroy all that is good and noble in man.

That the economic and political conditions of this country have been pregnant with the embryo of greed and despotism, no one who thinks and has closely watched events can deny. It was, therefore, but a question of time for the first signs of labor pains to begin. And they began when McKinley, more than any other President, had betrayed the trust of the people, and became the tool of the moneyed kings. They began when he and his class had stained the memory of the men who produced the Declaration of Independence, by the blood of the massacred Filipinos. They grew more violent at the recollection of Hazelton, Virden, Idaho, and other places, where capital has waged war on labor; until on the 6th of September the child begotten, nourished and reared by violence, was born.

That violence is not the result of conditions only, but also largely depends upon man's inner nature, is best proven by the fact that while thousands loath tyranny, but one will strike down a tyrant. What is it that drives him to commit the act, while others pass quietly by? It is because the one is of such a sensitive nature that he will feel a wrong more keenly and with greater intensity than others.

It is, therefore, not cruelty, or a thirst for blood, or any other criminal tendency, that induces such a man to strike a blow at organized power. On the contrary, it is mostly because of a strong social instinct, because of an abundance of love and an overflow of sympathy with the pain and sorrow around us, a love which seeks refuge in the embrace of mankind, a love so strong that it shrinks before no consequence, a love so broad that it can never be wrapped up in one object, as long as thousands perish, a love so all-absorbing that it can neither calculate, reason, investigate, but only dare at all costs.

It is generally believed that men prompted to put the dagger or bullet in the cowardly heart of government, were men conceited enough to think that they will thereby liberate the world from the fetters of despotism. As far as I have studied the psychology of an act of violence, I find that nothing could be further away from the thought of such a man than that if the king were dead, the mob will cease to shout "Long live the king!"

The cause for such an act lies deeper far too deep for the shallow multitude to comprehend. It lies in the fact that the world within the individual, and the world around him, are two antagonistic forces, and, therefore, must clash.

Do I say that Czolgosz is made of that material? No. Neither can I say that he was not. Nor am I in a position to say whether or not he is an Anarchist; I did not know the man; no one as far as I am aware seems to have known him, but from his attitude and behavior so far (I hope that no reader of "Free Society" has believed the newspaper lies), I feel that he was a soul in pain, a soul that could find no abode in this cruel world of ours, a soul "impractical," inexpedient, lacking in caution (according to the dictum of the wise); but daring just the same, and I cannot help but bow in reverent silence before the power of such a soul, that has broken the narrow walls of its prison, and has taken a daring leap into the unknown.

Having shown that violence is not the result of personal influence, or one particular ideal, I deem it unnecessary to go into a lengthy theoretical discussion as to whether Anarchism contains the element of force or not. The question has been discussed time and again, and it is proven that Anarchism and violence are as far apart from each other as liberty and tyranny. I care not what the rabble says; but to those who are still capable of understanding I would say that Anarchism, being, a philosophy of life, aims to establish a state of society in which man's inner make-up and the conditions around him, can blend harmoniously, so that he will be able to utilize all the forces to enlarge and beautify the life about him. To those I would also say that I do not advocate violence; government does this, and force begets force. It is a fact which cannot be done away with through the prosecution of a few men and women, or by more stringent laws—this only tends to increase it.

Violence will die a natural death when man will learn to understand that each unit has its place in the universe, and while being closely linked together, it must remain free to grow and expand.

Some people have hastily said that Czolgosz's act was foolish and will check the growth of progress. Those worthy people are wrong in forming hasty conclusions. What results the act of September 6 will have no one can say; one thing, however, is certain: he has wounded government in its most vital spot. As to stopping the wheel of progress, that is absurd. Ideas cannot be retarded by restraint. And as to petty police persecution, what matter?

As I write this, my thoughts wander to the death-cell at Auburn, to the young man with the girlish face, about to be put to death by the coarse, brutal hands of the law, walking up and down the narrow cell, with cold, cruel eyes following him,

> Who watch him when he tries to weep,
>   And when he tries to pray;
> Who watch him lest himself should rob
>   The prison of its prey.

And my heart goes out to him in deep sympathy, and to all the victims of a system of inequality, and the many who will die the forerunners of a better, nobler, grander life.

Ten

Museifu Shugi Banzai!

One of the most overlooked aspects of Anarchist history and propaganda of the deed activities can be found in Japan. Many make the mistake of assuming that Japanese society is an orderly, regimented, and hierarchical system consisting of repressed salary men and the overarching domination of capitalism. Historians view Japan as largely insular in nature, having only comparatively recently turned away from feudal prefectures under the direct control of an imperial system with a divine emperor at its head. Some may have heard of the anti–Vietnam War student protests and the impact they had on wider Japanese society during the late 1960s, and potentially even Shigenobu and the Japanese Red Army of the 1970s. The roots of dissent, however, go much deeper in Japan than many realize, and Anarchist direct action has a long and largely unknown history.

Denjirō Kōtoku was born on 5 November 1871 in the provincial and largely agricultural town of Nakamura in the Kôchi Prefecture, about 430 miles west of Tokyo. His father, Atsuaki Kōtoku, operated an established pharmacy and sake brewery in the town. The youngest of four children, Denjirō was raised by his mother, Tajiko, following his father's untimely death in 1872. The young Denjirō was a sickly child and reportedly suffered from a variety of stomach problems during his childhood. Besides these few fragments, little is known of his childhood or his family background; however, his later actions would ensure that he would feature prominently in any discussion of Anarchism in Japan.

The young Denjirō moved to Tokyo in his mid-teens and graduated from the Tokyo School of English. By 1893 (aged twenty-two), he had commenced a career in journalism and taken the literary pseudonym of Shūsui Kōtoku. In October 1896, the Society for the Study of Socialism (Shakai Shugi Kenkyukai) was founded by Abe Isoo (who later went on to be a parliamentarian and also played a pivotal role in introducing baseball to Japan), Sen Katayama (an early member of the American Communist Party and later a founder of the Japan Communist Party), and Shūsui Kōtoku. Although small, the society was focused upon a study of Communism and Socialism and how best to apply these schools of political thought to Japanese agrarian society.

It is worth remembering that although Japan was supposedly modernized in 1868 with the Satsuma revolution, the fall of the shogunate and the Meiji Restoration, for many in Japan the years that followed these changes were just as brutal as the previous years. From 1868 onward, the chief source of income for most Japanese was working the land, and agriculture remained a core industry, the profits of which were divested and channeled into emerging industries such as factories and shipyards. Because of rising taxes that had been levied in the attempt to modernize Japan, many farmers were forced

155

to sell their land at a loss and become tenant farmers. Many Japanese in the late 1890s were indentured agricultural workers or else had drifted toward cities in hopes of securing work in the developing industrial sector. By 1900, this defection from the country to the cities had become so pronounced that the Japanese government introduced a "public peace police law" that outlawed all workers' organizations and strike actions. The Japan of 1896 (the year in which the Society for the Study of Socialism was established) was thus a deeply divided country, with the vast majority of the population being poor (either in cities or on farms) and ruled over by a powerful elite, at the head of which sat the supposedly divine Emperor Meiji. In such a society, the study of Socialism was a courageous act in and of itself.

In 1898, Shūsui Kōtoku joined the staff of the *Yorozu Chōhō* (Every Morning News) as a columnist. At the time this paper was one of the most widely read, populist, and radical dailies in the country. Possibly in reaction to the government actions of 1900, the Society for the Study of Socialism sought to reorganize into Japan's first Socialist political party, the Socialist Democratic Party (Shakai Minshuto), during May 1901. Two days after the party formation, it was banned by the Japanese government. By 1903, the Japanese and Russian states were locked in a dispute that would devolve into the Russo-Japanese War (with the formal declaration of war being issued by Japan on 8 February 1904). In the buildup to this conflict, the previously left-leaning *Yorozu Chōhō* had become increasingly vitriolic and nationalistic. Although the paper had provided Kōtoku with five years of steady paychecks, its embrace of governmental propaganda and its support for a conflict that would ultimately result in the deaths of thousands was enough to prompt him to resign and, together with one of his peers (Sakai Toshihiko) from the paper, establish *Heimin Shimbun* (Commoners' News) in November 1903. The mandate of the new publication was simple: to provide an alternative to the jingoistic press of the time, oppose the war, and present the news of the day from a libertarian and socialist perspective. During its tenure, multiple weekly issues of the newspaper were banned by the Meiji government because they were deemed politically offensive, and Kōtoku and Toshihiko valiantly provided an alternative news source. But in an issue released in 1904, *Heimin Shimbun* overstepped its bounds, providing the first Japanese translation of *The Communist Manifesto* by Karl Marx and Friedrich Engels. For this and many other infractions, Kōtoku and the then editor, Nishikawa Kojiro, were heavily fined, with the offending issue being banned by the state; eventually the two men were arrested and sentenced to imprisonment terms of five

Shūsui Kōtoku

months and seven months, respectively. The last issue of *Heimin Shimbun* was published on 18 January 1905 in a special red ink format, following which the printing presses were confiscated by the police. Kōtoku began his prison sentence the following February.

Prior to his imprisonment, Kōtoku was a staunch Socialist. During a public meeting in 1902, he was supposedly highly critical of the police for their failure to distinguish between Socialists and Anarchists, and, in keeping with many of his peers, he himself associated Anarchists with bearded bomb-throwing terrorists. However, Kōtoku's opinions underwent a change following his detention, possibly due to his correspondence with an American by the name of Albert Johnson. Johnson has now largely faded into historical obscurity, but he was probably a sailor who had formerly worked between San Francisco and Oakland in California.[1] He may or may not have been an Anarchist himself, but he was pivotal in introducing Kōtoku to Anarchist thought. It is not known when Johnson and Kōtoku first started to correspond, but in 1905 Johnson sent Kōtoku a copy of *Fields, Factories and Workshops* as well as a picture of Peter Kropotkin and his British address (where the Russian was in exile at the time). Kōtoku also received from Johnson a copy of John R. Kelso's *Government Analysed*. After reading *Fields, Factories and Workshops*, Kōtoku wrote a letter of thanks to his American benefactor, claiming that although he had entered Sagamo prison "as a Marxian Socialist," he "returned a radical Anarchist."[2] In addition to reading Anarchist literature in prison, it was here that Kōtoku first began to develop intestinal tuberculosis.[3] This condition may have factored into his later actions (it was essentially a drawn-out death sentence), and it almost certainly played a part in his decision to leave Japan. Following his release from prison and the banning of his latest publication *Chokugen* (Straight Talking), Kōtoku embarked on 14 November 1905 for America, where he hoped to be able to learn from foreign radicals and freely express his opinions on the Japanese empire far from its reach. To accompany him on his long voyage to Seattle, Kōtoku bought with him a copy of Kropotkin's *Memoirs of a Revolutionist*.

Kōtoku was met in Seattle by Sakutaro Iwasa (who would later go on to be one of the most influential Anarchists in Japan), who traveled with him to San Francisco. There Kōtoku met with his mysterious correspondent, Albert Johnson. Although not yet formed at the time of his arrival, Kōtoku was in all likelihood instrumental in establishing the Social Revolutionary Party (Shakai Kakumeito), which was founded by Japanese emigres (including Sakutaro Iwasa following his departure from the United States). During his time in California, Kōtoku was involved in the activist community in Oakland and spent time in meetings with both Socialists and Anarchists on the West Coast. During this period Kōtoku may have been exposed to direct action during the 1901 general strike (and the ensuing police brutality), and he was also present in San Francisco for the earthquake of 1906, which may have helped highlight the state's inability (or unwillingness) to respond to a crisis of need. Also during this time, the Japan Socialist Party (Nihon Shakaito) was organized, and on 5 June 1906 Kōtoku agreed to return to Japan to assist with the preparation and management of a paper that the party members wished to produce. By the time his boat left for Yokohama on 23 June 1906, Kōtoku's views had shifted away from Socialism and were now far more fervent and Anarchistic in nature (indeed, during his time in America he had acquired a copy of Kropotkin's *The Conquest of Bread* in English and commenced translating it into Japanese).

The Japan Socialist Party was established and formally recognized in February 1906. The party was largely accepting of parliamentary democracy and had a central mandate

of Socialism within the limits of the law. As news reached Tokyo that Kōtoku was returning from America, a large public meeting was arranged by the Japan Socialist Party to
welcome him home—and also to allow him to provide a report on the development of
his ideas during his absence. At the meeting held on 28 June 1906, Kōtoku denounced
the parliamentary process and called for a general strike, direct action, and full social
revolution in his talk, titled "The Tide of the World Revolutionary Movement." This was
hardly the message that the organizers had expected, and Kōtoku's incendiary speech led
to a schism within the party, with the moderates represented by Sen Katayama and Kōtoku
leading the radical element. However, party divides were temporarily put aside when the
revived *Heimin Shimbun*[4] (now a daily rather than weekly paper) was first published on
5 January 1907, selling some 30,000 copies in its first issue. The popularity of this publication caused consternation among the police, who called for it to be banned. These
censorious feelings were perhaps further aggravated when news reached Japan of the
Social Revolutionary Party dual-language magazine *Kakumei* (The Revolution) in Oakland; this paper called in December 1906 for the overthrow of emperors, kings and presidents, and the Japanese police saw the interjection of these foreign ideas within Japan.
A central figure appeared to the police to be present in the person of Kōtoku. During
this period, Kōtoku had returned to Nakamura, partially as a result of police harassment
but largely owing to his ongoing ill health thanks to the tuberculosis that had first become
apparent during his detention of 1905.

Perhaps owing to the influence of the newly revitalized *Heimin Shimbun*, on 4 February 1907 some 3,600 farmers attacked the Ashio Copper Mine. From 1880 onward,
people living along the Watarase and Tone rivers downstream of the mine had noticed
the water changing color and the fish dying. Some 3,000 fishermen had been made unemployed owing to the environmental damage caused by the mines, and the miners themselves had by 1907 engaged in strike activities. The attack on the mine nearly destroyed
it and resulted in the loss of much of the heavy mining equipment. However, this populist
uprising was brutally quashed with the arrival of some 600 troops. On 5 February 1907,
the front page of *Heimin Shimbun* featured an article by Kōtoku titled "The Change in
My Thought (On Universal Suffrage)," which was a clear statement of direct action and
a rejection of his earlier Socialist parliamentary views. In the article (which had much
in common with *The Conquest of Bread*), Kōtoku stated, "If I were to put in a nutshell
the way I think now, it would be along the following lines: 'A real social revolution cannot
possibly be achieved by means of universal suffrage and a parliamentary policy. There
is no way to reach our goal of socialism other than by the direct action of the workers,
united as one,'" before concluding that "the workers themselves too must be ready not
to rely on such creatures as bourgeois MPs and politicians but to achieve their aims by
means of their own power and their own direct action. To repeat: the last thing the workers should do is to put their trust in votes and MPs."

A conference of the Japan Socialist Party was convened on 17 February 1907. At this
event, Kōtoku was successful in removing the caveat of "within the limits of the law"
from the party mandate. The reaction from the state was as predictable as it was swift,
and the Japan Socialist Party was outlawed on 22 February, with legal action also taken
against *Heimin Shimbun* for publishing Kōtoku's fiery article. By 14 April 1907, publication
of *Heimin Shimbun* was halted after only seventy-five issues. The schism that had been
created within the Japan Socialist Party eventually led to an outright split, with the creation of rival associations: the Friday Society (Kinyo Kai), which Kōtoku helped form,

and the Comrades Society (Doshi Kai). In addition to helping to establish a new organization more in keeping with his political outlook, 1907 also saw Kōtoku continuing his translation of Kropotkin's work. As autumn turned to winter, events in California unfolded that were to have major ramifications in Japan.

On the same day that the emperor of Japan celebrated his fifty-fifth birthday, 3 November 1907, a letter was pasted to the door of the Japanese consulate and a number of other prominent locations in San Francisco, California. Rather than congratulations, the "Open Letter to Mutsuhito, The Emperor of Japan from Anarchist Terrorists" was an open and incendiary attack. The letter was a rejection of the supposedly divine Japanese imperial line, and it decreed that the emperor, just like everyone else, was descended from "apes" and not from "mythical gods." The anonymous authors also declared that the emperor had only come to power owing to the "evil" and "immoral" actions of his not-so-distant ancestors, and he himself was both a premeditated "murderer" and a "butcher." In addition, the letter stressed the necessity for violence in a rejection of supposed imperial power and rights: "None of us are fond of violence, but when violence is used to suppress us, then we must resort to violence in reply. Moreover, we must resist the present order by shedding our last drops of blood in opposition to the Emperor. We must give up our slow and ineffective methods of talk and agitation and must by all means turn to assassination, willing to butcher without regard for rank or status anyone who suppresses or spies on us."[5]

The source of the open letter (as could probably be guessed) was the Social Revolutionary Party that Kōtoku had helped establish in Oakland; in all probability, the letter had been penned by two of the party's young recruits, Iwasa Sakutaro and Takeuchi Tetsugoro. Where the Japanese authorities had once held Kōtoku in disdain, he was now regarded with outright hostility, even though he could not be held directly responsible for the contents of the letter or its dramatic and public dissemination.

The attitude of the state had begun to harden against Kōtoku, and also against others in Socialist and Anarchist circles. At a meeting of the Friday Society that Kōtoku had helped form in 1907, official police observers and meeting organizers clashed. The topic of the January 1908 meeting was Thomas More's *Utopia*. Several of the organizers were arrested, including Osugi Sakai, an Anarchist and a friend of Kōtoku (Sakai would suffer his own tragic fate at the hands of the Japanese police in 1911, when he and his lover, Noe Itō, along with his six-year-old nephew, Munekazu Tachibana, were arrested and beaten to death, following which the military police disposed of their lifeless bodies in a well). Although the crowd that had gathered for the meeting attempted to resist (and, indeed, subsequently to free the prisoners), their efforts were repelled. Sakai was fortunate to only receive forty-five days in detention, but the leniency of the sentences coupled with the supposed rising tide of subversive foreign ideas set the Japanese police on a collision course with protestors and those seeking to oppose the politics of the day.

Frequent arrests and harassment by the police were common among the small community of Anarchists and Socialists within Meiji era Japan. Sakai was arrested on several occasions, as were Kōtoku and many of their peers. One such was Yamaguchi Kōken (or Gizo). Kōken, like Kōtoku, was a journalist and agitator who was not afraid to express dissenting opinions (he was, however, a Socialist as opposed to an Anarchist). He was also a writer for the daily *Heimin Shimbun* and may have played a part in its downfall when, in April 1907, he wrote an article for the paper in which he advised his readers to "kick their fathers and mothers" and overthrow the Japanese establishment.[6] This article may have led to Kōken's detention; however, it would not have been the first time. In April 1906 a series of rallies had been organized in Hibiya Park in Tokyo to protest against rapid fare increases for city transportation. At one such rally, the crowd left the park and began to smash the windows of both streetcars and government buildings. Following the protest, a number of prominent Socialist and Anarchist organizers were arrested; Kōken was among them.

In the Kanda district of Tokyo, a gathering took place on 22 June 1908 that was to have a lasting impact on Japan and the life of Kōtoku and others in the Anarchist community. Yamaguchi Kōken was due to be released from his latest prison sentence (although the reasons for this detention are unknown), and a reception was planned by all members of the Socialist and Anarchist circles within Tokyo. This reception came to be known as the Red Flag incident (*akahata jikan*). On Kōken's return to Tokyo on 19 June, Socialists had met him with banners and flags bearing Socialist sentiments. Three days later, as the meeting to welcome Kōken back from jail was coming to a close, Anarchists and followers of Kōtoku unfurled banners with "Anarchism," "Revolution" and "Anarchist Communism" written on them. They began to sing revolutionary songs; however, when the moderate Socialists in the crowd failed to join them, they left the meeting hall, where the police were waiting for them. Fourteen arrests were made following confrontations with the police; among those who were arrested were Osugi Sakai and a young woman who had crossed the street to see what was happening, Kanno Sugako. Following the events of June, the relatively liberal Saionji Kinmochi was forced to step down as prime minister of Japan in July 1908, and a wave of repression, harassment, and violence was unleashed on both Socialists and Anarchists in Japan.

Kōtoku was not present during the events connected to the open letter and the Red Flag incident. He had returned to the home owned by his family in Nakamura and was actively engaged in translating Kropotkin. The Japanese state had not forgotten him, however, and his family home was so closely watched that the sake brewery business had begun to suffer. By 21 June 1908 he was back in Tokyo (although he did not attend the welcome for Kōken) and keen to reignite the Heiminsha (Commoners' Society) and *Heimin Shimbun*. Although a police tent was set up next to the building of both the society and the nascent paper, this surveillance failed to deter Kōtoku. It was at this time, and under the watchful eyes of the Tokyo police, that he met the fiery young woman who had been previously arrested by the police as an active participant in the Red Flag incident.

Kanno Sugako (sometimes known by one of her pen names, Kanno Suga) was born in 1881 in the city of Osaka, although the exact date is unknown. However, the Osaka of Kanno's birth was not the same one that she would later inhabit. During the nineteenth century, readers of Edo literature and many of the residents of other Japanese municipalities such as Tokyo believed that residents of Osaka could best be defined in terms of calculation, shrewdness, lack of civic spirit, and the coarseness of the vulgar Osaka dialect. This regionalism probably had little effect or impact on the infant Kanno, but it would play a role in her later life when she was accused of calculation, coarseness, and a lack of public spirit. Until she was eight or nine, Kanno was the daughter of the owner of a successful mining business, Kanno Yoshihige, and his first wife (whose name is lost to history). Kanno was the middle child, having an older sister as well as a younger brother and sister, and during her early years (judging from what records are available) she was seemingly content. However, this happiness would soon be undone by changes within the family and beyond it. In 1889 a government ordinance expanded Osaka substantially. This change had the effect of not only expanding the city boundaries but also creating rapid industrialization and modernization, cementing Osaka as a pluralistic industrial hub and leading to an influx of immigrant workers and those from the surrounding countryside. The government of the day also slashed welfare programs that had been in place, and this period saw the number of slums and exploitative industrial employers increase significantly. During this period, when Kanno was eight or nine years old, her father lost his business. A year later, when Kanno was ten, she also lost her mother. The cause of her mother's death is unknown, but it was likely linked to the levels of disease and poverty rampant during this period. Shortly after the death of his first wife, Kanno's father married a new spouse, who would have an extremely negative impact on Kanno's life.

Kanno was, as previously stated, born in 1881. In Japanese culture of the time, this was in and of itself an inauspicious start, as 1881 (or *kanoto-no-mi*) was the year of the serpent. The characteristics of the serpent are commonly perceived as guile, evil, and cunning, attributes that Kanno's new stepmother reportedly attributed to her. Another seismic event in her life occurred when she was only fifteen, when Kanno was allegedly raped by a miner (possibly a previous employee of her father). Worse still, there is evidence to support the claim that this assault may have been arranged or facilitated by her stepmother,[7] although that claim cannot be proven. However, a number of historians believe that this was the first of many rapes and sexual assaults that Kanno suffered, which are reflected in a number of her later articles and novelettes such as *Days of Remembrance*.[8] Regardless of how many assaults Kanno may have endured, her teenage years were undeniably brutal and destructive.

Kanno Sugako

It was when she was fifteen that Kanno first considered the wider social issues that were to influence much of her later life and writing. At this time, she found and read a timely pamphlet by the Japanese Socialist Sakai Toshihiko, who counseled that rape victims should not be burdened with guilt. This was a divisive opinion at the time, as the patriarchal system assumed that such assaults were the fault and, indeed, the responsibility of the victim rather than the perpetrator. As with so much in Japanese culture during this period, even expressing a self-evident fact, such as imperial families not being divine in nature and survivors of sexual assault not being at fault, was not only controversial but also (for the authors of such opinions) dangerous.

During 1898, when Kanno was seventeen, she married the Tokyo-based merchant Komiya Fukutarō as a means of escaping her brutal home environment in Osaka. Although this marriage was in all likelihood arranged, and Kanno had no interest in being the wife of a member of the mercantile classes (and, indeed, no affection for her new husband), it did allow her to get away from her stepmother and her presumably ineffectual or disinterested father. Regrettably, this escape was to be short lived. In 1902 her father suffered from a stroke, and the stepmother who had blighted so much of Kanno's youth promptly abandoned both her husband and Kanno's siblings. Aged twenty-one, Kanno returned to Osaka to care for her younger brother and ailing father.

At this time, Kanno decided that she would attempt to become a writer. The most famous writer in the Osaka area during this period was Udagawi Bunkai (1848–1930). The exact circumstances under which Udagawi and Kanno were first introduced are a mystery. However, Kanno's younger brother was also attempting to pursue literary ambitions, and he had acquired a patron by way of a local working playwright. In all probability, the introduction between Udagawi and Kanno was made via this source, and it would prove to be a successful one. Although Kanno had only a basic elementary-level education (and her previous employment may have only included being a nurse, a hairdresser, and some factory work), she impressed Bunkai; with his help, she was able to get a writing job at an Osaka-based newspaper, *Osaka Chōhō* (Osaka Morning Report). Whether to secure this employment or because they shared a genuine attraction, Kanno, now in her twenties, and Udagawi, who was in his fifties, soon (according to some historians) began an affair.[9] This was the first relationship in which Kanno was involved that would scandalize her largely prurient peers. It would not be the last.

During 1903, Kanno became involved in the Osaka reform movement. Like many reform organizations during this period in Japan, the Osaka Women's Moral Reform Society was largely influenced by both Christian and Socialist traditions. It is perhaps because of her involvement in this cause that Kanno's relationship with Udagawi ended in May of that year. The Osaka reform movement, in addition to seeking to improve the slum conditions that many industrial transient workers were forced to endure, sought to put an end to the legalized brothels of the period. For many modern readers, the image of the geisha is highly romanticized; however, the reality of geisha houses in Osaka during the late 1800s was very different. The popular notion is that geisha were trained in the arts and used such skills to entertain their patrons. Unfortunately, a seedier side existed in the world of the shōgi. In 1872 the government had passed a law legalizing both geisha (supposedly entertainers) and shōgi (prostitutes) and determining that both groups should be known as geisha. Although his decision was eventually reversed, the connection would prove resilient. However, the semantics of the situation were secondary to the wave of abusive behaviors unleashed owing to the new legislation. Rather that utilizing such legislation to control the abuses of pimps and procurers, these two groups could now operate with impunity. Thus many Japanese women of the period found themselves coerced into prostitution. It was not uncommon for poor families in the countryside to be forced by grinding poverty and widespread starvation to sell female children into prostitution. Such children were not treated well, and many endured years of abuse before suffering violent deaths. Far from being environments based around consensus, many legal brothels throughout Japan were venal and positively charnel in nature. Kanno's participation in campaigning for the closure (or at least regulation) of the brothels pushed her toward religion, and in November 1903 she was formally baptized in Osaka's Tenmabashi. Kanno was also frequently published throughout 1903 in two religious magazines, *Michi no Tomo* (Tenrikyō) and *Kirisutokyō Sekai* (Protestant).

Perhaps as a result of her increasing contact with the Osaka Women's Moral Reform Society and her moral objections to the Russo-Japanese War, 1904 marked Kanno's first contact with *Heimin Shimbun*. Through reading this newspaper, her own political views may have been shaped, and it may also have introduced her to the work of Shūsui Kōtoku and his tussles with the government. In 1905, Kanno moved to Kyoto, where she was able to secure work as a Japanese teacher. While in Kyoto, Kanno was also taking care of her sister, Kanno Hide, who had contracted tuberculosis, and from whom she unfortunately contracted the disease. The profound effects and impact of tuberculosis are familiar in the West, and from 1800 onward the disease ravaged much of the world in line with an increase in industrialization and mechanization. From 1895 onward tuberculosis took a heavy toll on the Japanese population but was largely ignored until the introduction of antibiotics in support of Japan's Second World War efforts. Tuberculosis was typically always fatal in nature, and an excruciating way in which to die. Indeed, in Japan it was common practice to only admit to sanatorium environments those patients who were already on the cusp of death.[10] For Kanno and her sister, along with Kōtoku and millions of others, tuberculosis was a slow, lingering sentence of death.

In 1906, Kanno and her sister moved from Kyoto back to Osaka, largely to allow Kanno to focus on her literary ambitions. The publisher (Mōri Saian) of a local newspaper in the Wakayama district of Osaka, *Murō Shinpō* (Murō News), was imprisoned for writing articles critical of the government. Kanno kept the paper going in his absence after the interdiction of Sakai Toshihiko, who had previously opened *Heimin Shimbun* with Kōtoku. During that year, a young journalist by the name of Arahata Kanson joined the staff (he was 19, whereas Kanno was 25), and he and Kanno entered into a common-law marriage. After the publisher of *Murō Shinpō* was released, Arahata and Kanno moved to Tokyo (joined by Kanno's sister); Arahata went to work for *Heimin Shimbun* with Kōtoku. During this period, Kanno was able to secure employment at *Tōkyō Dempō* (Tokyo Telegram, a paper founded by Kuga Katsunan in 1888, ironically after a previous career in the Japanese Ministry of Justice). Concurrent with this position, Kanno also found writing work for *Sekai Fujin* (Women of the World), one of the few feminist papers of the time, the first issue of which appeared on 1 January 1907. By February, however, Hide was seriously ill, and both Kanno and Arahata watched her die at home; she was twenty-one. Kanno took the death of her younger sister particularly hard; as a result, Kanno and Arahata became increasingly estranged. Later in 1907 this relationship ended, and Kanno took a leave of absence to attend a health spa in Ito in an attempt to recover some of her own flagging health.

Kanno was, unlike Kōtoku, present in Tokyo for the Red Flag incident of 1908, even being arrested, although her level of involvement is uncertain. Some historians place her squarely in fray, with others casting her as a mere passerby who knew some of those arrested and was questioning their arrests. However, at this juncture Kanno was a journalist working for both a populist newspaper and a feminist publication. It is thus probable that not only did she personally know some of those involved (indeed, Sakai Toshihiko had previously helped gain her employment) but she was also politically sympathetic to their cause. After all, the Japanese state viewed Anarchists, Socialists, Christians, and feminists as threats and, in the response to the street car riots in Tokyo and strikes in Ashio, had unleashed a wave of repression against all these groups. Although no official charges were ever bought against Kanno for whatever part she may have played in the Red Flag incident (and there is no historical evidence of her having committed any crime), she spent a miserable two months in jail as the only female arrestee. Not only did her tuberculosis worsen considerably as a result of this imprisonment, but, as a direct consequence of her arrest, she also lost her employment at *Tōkyō Dempō*.

Following the Red Flag incident, Kanno met Kōtoku. Doubtless they were aware of each other prior to this point—indeed, the celebration to mark the inauguration of one of the many iterations of *Heimin Shimbun* was held at Kanno's house—but by 1909 they had become a couple. Kōtoku had been married twice by early 1909; however, he divorced his second wife Chiyoko, and he and Kanno began an affair. This was highly problematic for many members of the Japanese radical community because of Kanno's earlier relationship with Arahata. Indeed, Sakae Ōsugi stated that "Shūsui stole the woman of a comrade in prison, and Kanno abandoned a foot soldier in favour of an officer."[11] Once again, Kanno's desire to live her life according to her own terms rather than complying with the patriarchal demands of her day had raised eyebrows and concerns, even within the supposedly egalitarian radical community.

Despite the constant surveillance that Kōtoku (and now, by extension, Kanno) suffered, and the frequent rumors about them that that permeated the Tokyo radical community, the couple attempted in May 1909 to launch a paper of their own, *Jiyu Shishō* (Free Thought). Obviously the surveillance was effective, as the paper was banned by the Japanese state immediately. For its production, Kanno was fined 140 yen, and Kōtoku 70 yen. On 1 September 1909, Kanno was arrested while attempting to circulate the second issue of the paper and was issued a fine of 400 yen or three months in prison. Having spent their limited funds on previous state-inflicted debts, and being unable to secure any more to enable the payment of a then staggering sum, Kanno found herself imprisoned again. Her detention was not to last long, however.

In May 1910 a plot against the emperor of Japan was discovered by the state. The original progenitor is thought to have been Miyashita Takichi (born 1881), a factory worker who had become a supporter of Anarchism and Socialism and had circumstantial links to both Kanno and Kōtoku. Takichi had hoped to construct a bomb that would be used to kill the emperor, whom he perceived as a tool of the establishment. After constructing the bomb from materials he found at his job as a lumber mill employee in Nagano Prefecture, Takichi and the rest of his group (which consisted of Kanno, the journalist Niimura Tadoa, and potentially one or two others) agreed that the device would be stored with Shimizu Taichirō until it was ready to be used. It was Taichirō who subsequently betrayed the group to the police. Prior to that point, the group had drawn lots to see who would throw the device. Kanno won, and the group determined that such an attempt would wait until after she had been released from prison. The reasons for her involvement in this plot may have stemmed from what she recognized as the fast onset of the final stages of tuberculosis, or a desire to rid Japan of a corrupt emperor under whom Kanno, Kōtoku, and the wider socially conscious class had suffered years of harassment and enforced state penury.

Regardless of her motivations, the plot against the emperor was discovered while Kanno was already serving her sentence in connection with *Jiyu Shishō*. Under orders from Prime Minister Katsura Tarō, the authorities used the plot as an excuse to arrest known dissenters to the Japanese state. In addition to Kanno and Kōtoku, some twenty-four other individuals (four of whom were Buddhist monks) were detained and put on trial. Kanno was the only woman among the defendants. The trial began on 10 December 1910 and was closed to the public.

Throughout the trail, Kanno was vociferous in her own defense, as well as that of the innocents who had been rounded up and detained for nothing more than their opinions:

> Only four of us were involved in the plan. It is a crime that only involves four of us. But this court, as well as the preliminary interrogators, treated it as a plan that involved a large number of people. That is a complete misunderstanding of the case. Because of this misunderstanding a large number of people have been made to suffer. You are aware of this. These people have aged parents, young children, and young wives. If these people are killed for something that they knew nothing about, not only will it be a grave tragedy for the persons concerned, but their relatives and friends will feel bitterness toward the government. Because we hatched this plan a large number of people may be executed. If such an injustice should be the end result.... I may die, but my sorrow will linger on.[12]

Kanno's justifiable outrage did nothing to sway the opinion of a vengeful state. On 24 January 1911, eleven of those involved in what would come to be known as the High Treason incident (*Taigyaku Jiken*) were hanged: Shūsui Kōtoku, Morchika Umpai (former editor of *Heimin Shimbun*), Niimura Tadoa (journalist), Matsuo Uita (journalist), Niimi Uichiro (journalist), Miyashita Takichi (factory worker), Furakawa Rikisaku (gardener), Okuyima Tateyuki (activist), Oishi Seinosuke (doctor), Naruishi Heishiro (shopkeeper), and Uchiyama Gudo (Zen priest). The other defendants who had been convicted on 18 January 1911 had their sentences commuted to life imprisonment on 19 January, with the exception of Kanno. She was scheduled to be executed with Kōtoku on 24 January; however, it was deemed too dark when it came time for her execution and she was temporarily reprieved until the following day. The method used for Kanno's execution was particularly brutal; as reported by the newspaper *Miyako Shimbun*, "She mounted the scaffold escorted by guards on both sides. Her face was covered quickly by a white cloth.... She was then ordered to sit upright on the floor. Two thin cords were placed around her neck. The floor board was removed. In twelve minutes she was dead."[13]

The executions of Kanno, Kōtoku, and the others did not mark the end of the abuses of the Japanese state in connection to the High Treason incident. Of the defendants who were sentenced to life imprisonment, Takagi Kennei died in Chiba prison in 1914, Okabayashi Toramatsu was driven insane in the Nagasaki prison, and many others attempted suicide unsuccessfully. National and international reaction to the sentences handed down to the defendants was muted, and their stories were forgotten, only being rediscovered relatively recently.

Among the many examples of propaganda of the deed that are outlined in this publication, the cases of Kanno and Kōtoku are particularly troubling. Their mutual involvement in the supposed plot to kill the emperor can be disputed. Kōtoku was doubtless a thorn in the side of the Japanese state, as were many of the others who were executed in connection with the High Treason incident, but his involvement with anything other than the initial concept of assassinating an unpopular national ruler is at best tangential. In *Mainichi Shimbun* on 29 January 2010, news broke of a letter that was discovered in the house of the journalist Sugimura Sojinkan. In order to avoid censorship, tiny holes had been poked in the supposed letter, thereby inscribing a message on it. When held up to the light, it turned out to be a letter from Kanno that read, "Because of the bomb incident I and three others will soon be sentenced to death. I do hope you are carrying out an exhaustive investigation. Also I sincerely implore you to provide Kotoku with a lawyer. June 9th. He does not know anything at all."[14]

Kanno's own involvement is more certain. According to witness reports, she was directly involved; indeed, she was selected as the potential bomb thrower owing to the drawing of lots, something she never denied. It is worth remembering, however, that both Kanno and Kōtoku were infected with tuberculosis, and the former had already watched a relative die from this fatal disease. A death from tuberculosis was agonizing and painful, whereas dying for a political cause could potentially achieve actions supposedly less futile.

Other than the bomb materials themselves and the presumption of a plot (and the self-incriminating nature of some of the supposed conspirators), the evidence available to the state to support the High Treason incident was limited. It is almost certainly the case that the state overreached in line with following Prime Minister Katsura's instructions, utilizing the plot as a way to get rid of supposed radicals who posed a threat to the established order of the day. The conviction and execution of Kōtoku, who was a notorious radical under active police surveillance (albeit one who had never engaged in violent actions), allowed the Japanese state to send a very clear and threatening message to its opponents. In addition, executing Kanno in a particularly brutal manner that was not inflicted on her male counterparts allowed a patriarchal state to exhibit the scope and sweep of its power. It should be remembered, however, that beyond participating in a plot that was not enacted and expressing views contrary to those of the state by way of publications, speech, and actions (the fact that Kanno and Kōtoku chose to live together outside of marriage was definitely an affront to the conventional morality of their age), none of the defendants had injured anyone. Instead, it was the Japanese state that chose to inflict harm on its opponents. For this reason, as well as the events of their shortened lives, those involved in the High Treason incident should be remembered by historians, revolutionaries, and lovers alike.

Reflections on the Way to the Gallows (Kanno Sugako)

Source: The Anarchist Library, https://theanarchistlibrary.org/library/kanno-sug-ako-reflections-on-the-way-to-the-gallows (accessed December 2016)

This is written as a record of the period from the time the death sentence was pronounced to the time I mount the scaffold. I shall write things down candidly and honestly in a straightforward fashion without any effort at self-justification.

In the women's prison in Tokyo. January 18, 1911. Cloudy. Needless to say, I was prepared for the death sentence. My only concern day and night was to see as many of my twenty-five fellow defendants saved as possible.

I boarded the prison carriage just before noon. From the window of the carriage I could see in the dim sunlight saber-bearing figures solemnly standing guard en route. They seemed to presage the verdicts of the trial, and I waited impatiently for the court proceedings to start at 1:00 p.m.

The time came. We climbed up to the second floor, then to the third floor, and then down again to the second floor to the courtroom of the Supreme Court. The security measures along the corridors and in the courtroom during the proceedings were extremely tight. The court was packed with people—lawyers, newspaper reporters, and spectators. I tend to get dizzy easily, so I felt a bit faint, having climbed many stairs and because of the stifling presence of the crowd in the courtroom. After I calmed down, I looked around at my fellow defendants. They were all sitting circumspectly, looking worried. They looked as if they were afraid to smile at each other. A pride of hungry lions. Their nails and teeth had been filed and smoothed down. There they sat before me. Twenty-five sacrificial lambs.

Soon the judges entered through the left door at the front of the court-house. Will it be life or death? Many of the defendants' hearts must have beat faster. The clerk read the names of the defendants. Chief Justice Tsuru Jōichirō said a few words of instruction. Then, contrary to the usual procedure, he left the verdicts to the end and proceeded to read the lengthy arguments, sipping occasionally from a glass of water. As he continued to read, it became clear that he was arbitrarily linking even those who were clearly innocent to Article 73 of the criminal code. His sophism became increasingly blatant. My concern increased and finally overwhelmed me like a tidal wave. But until he read the verdict for each defendant, I kept hoping against hope that some, even one person, would receive a minimal sentence. But, ah, it was all in vain.... It was all over. Except for Nitta Tōru, who was sentenced to eleven years in prison, and Niimura Zenbei, who was given eight years, the remaining twenty-four of us were sentenced to death.

From the beginning, I feared that this would be the case, but the trial was conducted in such an unexpectedly meticulous fashion that I began to hope that it would be relatively fair. The verdicts came as a shock. I was so angry and upset that I felt as if my entire body were on fire, and I began to tremble.

My poor friends, my poor comrades! More than half of them were innocent bystanders who had been implicated by the actions of five or six of us. Just because they were associated with us, they are now to be sacrificed in this monstrous fashion. Simply because they are anarchists, they are to be thrown over the cliff to their deaths.

I was not the only person shocked by this unexpected turn of events. All the lawyers, prison officials, and police who had been present during the trial on the sixteenth and were privy to the truth about this affair certainly must have been shocked at these outrageous verdicts. You could read it on the faces of everyone in the court. The defendants remained voiceless and silent; for the moment they were frozen in irrepressible anger. Then cold smirks appeared on their lips.

I wanted to comfort my fellow defendants, but I was so upset and angry I could not think of the right words. I could only mutter to myself, "What a shocking, lawless trial."

Then the straw hat was placed on my head. Because we were marched out in reverse order of our arrival, I was the first to leave. As I stood up I thought of my comrades. Though they will mount the same scaffold as I, we shall never meet again. Some of them must certainly feel bitter toward us. But they are all my comrades.

We stood side by side as fellow defendants. Farewell, my twenty-five friends. Farewell, twenty-five victims. Goodbye!

"Goodbye, goodbye!" That was all I managed to say.

"Goodbye, goodbye," they shouted after me. As I left the courtroom I heard someone shout "Banzai!" No doubt one of the zealous anarchists was shouting for the anarchist cause. As I stepped on the first step of the stone stairway someone shouted, "Kanno-san!"

When I returned to the detention room of the courthouse, I began to cool off and regain my composure. I felt somewhat ashamed of myself for getting so angry. But what an outrageous trial!

However, it should not have surprised me. My past experiences should have prepared me to expect this as a matter of course. We initiated our plot precisely because this kind of outrageous legal system and despotic political authority exist. It was absurdly foolish to hope, even for a moment, that the wielders of power—whose authority I do not acknowledge—might save my comrades simply because the court hearings were meticulously carried out.

Soon the prison carriage arrived. I left the dimly lit detention room. The blood-red face of Takeda Kyūhei, one of the defendants, showed in a small detention-room window. He shouted, "Goodbye!" I replied, "Goodbye!" Someone else shouted "Goodbye!" One word filled with so much emotion. The late afternoon sun hits the prison carriage from the side. The carriage carries me to Ichigaya, on a route that I shall never see again.

January 19. Cloudy. Though I was furious, I must have been exhausted from the strain of the past several days. I slept soundly from early evening, and today I feel refreshed. I have received permission from the prison authorities to leave some of my possessions to my friends as mementos. I will leave my formal silk kimono to Sakai Mābō, the single-layer kimono to Hori Yasuko, the black cloak and the lined garment of striped muslin to Yoshikawa Morikuni.

I wrote postcards to the three lawyers, Isobe Shirō, Hanai Takuzō, and Imamura Rikisaburō, expressing my shock at the verdicts. I also wrote cards to Sakai, Hori, and Yoshikawa, telling them about the mementos.

In the evening, the chaplain, Numanami Masanori, appeared. He told me that one of the fellow defendants, Mineo Setsudō, came to appreciate the value of faith in an external power after he was sentenced to death.

The chaplain said he was impressed that Mineo showed no signs of fear or worry. He then urged me to seek solace in religion. I told him I could not be more at peace with myself than I now was. It is ludicrous for an anarchist who is against all authority to turn to Amida Buddha for peace and security simply because he [sic] faces death. But I can appreciate Numanami's position as a religious leader and as a chaplain. I have, however, my own beliefs and peace of mind.

We had sailed into the vast ocean ahead of the world's current of thought and the general tide of events. Unfortunately, we were ship-wrecked. But this sacrifice had to be made to get things started. New routes are opened up only after many shipwrecks and dangerous voyages. This is how the other shore of one's ideals is reached. After the sage of Nazareth was born, many sacrifices had to be made before Christianity became a world religion. In light of this, I feel that our sacrifice is miniscule.

I told the court these thoughts on the last day of the trial. They are with me constantly. I am convinced our sacrifice is not in vain. It will bear fruit in the future. I am confident that because I firmly believe my death will serve a valuable purpose I will be able to maintain my self-respect until the last moment on the scaffold. I will be enveloped in the marvelously comforting thought that I am sacrificing myself for the cause. I believe I will be able to die a noble death without fear or anguish.

At night Tanaka, director of prison instruction, came to see me. He told me that my fellow defendants were fairly calm and serene. I was pleased to hear this. He also talked about instances in which people condemned to death faced their end admirably. I described the kind of coffin I wanted made for me and how I wanted to be dressed after death. I was afraid that the supporters of the emperor and champions of patriotism might dig up my corpse and hack it to bits. I did not want to look too shabby when this happened. After Tanaka gave me his blessings, Numanami brought me two pamphlets: the *Tan'ishō* and *Outline of the Blessings of Faith.*

January 20. Snow. Snow has settled on top of the pine trees and the dead branches of the cypress trees. The world has been covered in silver during the night. Since the beginning of the year there have been several short flurries, but this storm doesn't look as though it will stop soon. Let it snow, let it snow! A foot, two feet. Pile it up high. Envelop this sinful city of Tokyo in snow, like a city buried in ashes. Level the entire landscape.

I wonder what the defendants in the men's prison are thinking of now as they look out at the cold snow from the three-foot iron windows?

Snow. Full of memories. As I stare out the iron window and observe the gently swirling snow, memories of many years float past my eyes, the many times that I looked up at the same sky with all sorts of thoughts and feelings. A combination of happiness and sorrow quietly presses against my chest. I long for those days, but I realize that all things are ephemeral. Everything now belongs to the past. I don't know what will happen to me tomorrow. Now I do not have time to enjoy reminiscing about the past. Oh, yes, I have the time, but my time is too precious. I must use the time to read, to write. And there are things that I must think about immediately. My mind is preoccupied with thoughts of things that I must take care of. Why do I feel so restless and harried? I don't understand it. Is it because a stack of books is facing me? Is it because I can't see the people I must see to have certain things taken care of? Is it because I haven't written my last words to my younger brother? People tell me that I haven't changed at all, that I am still full of energy. But even though I am busy with all sorts of things, nothing gets done. Still, it doesn't matter. I'll do what I can and whatever's unfinished, I'll leave as it is.

Two or three days ago I got a letter from Sakai. He wrote:

> I saw your letter of the fourth. I hope you will write your prison diary as forthrightly and coura-geously as possible. I admire you for not giving up your English studies. There is a saying that goes something like this: "For each day that a person lives, there is one day's worth of work." We all could die tomorrow, but I am studying German and French bit by bit as if I were definitely going to live till I am sixty. I don't know how many days or months you have left. If we look at our lives from the standpoint of the eternal universe's time and space, they last only a split second. Isn't it wonderful that we can spend part of that moment exchanging lighthearted letters like this?

[Kanno had written Sakai on the fourth: "Now that the trial is over I have nothing at all to do. Since the first of the year I have been keeping a prison diary as a sort of record of my thoughts and feelings. I plan to write candidly about whatever comes to mind. Memories, impressions, confessions, hopes. I expect you will be able to see it some-time in the future..."]

I certainly am calm. Since September of last year I've been playing tug of war with the dictionary, trying to learn English. I go at it with a nervous sense of urgency but am making very little progress. I am only one-third into Reader V.

I had gotten so that I could at least read a [Japanese] magazine without much school-ing. It is only natural that I cannot come up to the hem of those who have a formal edu-cation. However, what bothered me most of all was that I did not know a foreign language, and I wanted at least to be able to read one. Though I started to study on my own several times, poor health or something else always interfered. So I had not been able to do any-thing about this till recently. It was due in part to my lack of will power and patience but also to the circumstances I found myself in that only in mid–September did I decide that the time had come for me learn to read at least some simple English selections. I had to do so before I died. So I started with a Third-level Reader. Now, I don't know when I will be executed. I probably don't have much time left, so I guess I won't be able to master the language. I regret this very much.

This diary will be written without any falsehood or pretense. Sakai need not worry about this. It will reveal the naked Kanno Sugako, just as I am.

- I must copy down two or three poems from my other diary.
- What are we puny things fighting about—in the midst of eternal time and boundless sky?
- Born in a tiny country, I am sacrificing my little body for a glimmer of hope.
- What a nation! It takes pride in spilling the life-blood of a hundred thousand people over one inch of the map.
- Another day spent guarding the shadows created by the sunlight that comes through the barred window.
- I know that the cliff drops one thousand fathoms, yet I rush down the path without turning back.
- I lie motionless in the cold night bed and listen time and time again to the stealthy sounds of sabers.
- I lie on my back for half a day, looking through the three-foot window and watch the leaves of the cypress tree sway in the wind.
- The gingko tree in the winter exudes a sense of reverence. It looks like a holy man coming from the snowy mountains.
- This wretched love. It continues to smolder like the smoke that keeps rising from glowing ashes.
- My last day will soon come. I smile as I think about my life. I can think about it forever. Is the strong, courageous child of revolution the same person as the weak, frail, weeping child? Is this me?
- Don't ask where the seed that dropped in the field is. Wait for the east wind that blows in the spring.
- We lined up by the railing listening to the song of the seashore where Hatsushima Island floated three *ri* off in the waves.
- Deep in the night the wounded person cries. Both the old and new wounds are painful.
- In coming and going, did I see through the straw hat, the pale face in the third window?
- His eyes said "forgive me," but my eyes were as cold as the ice in the northern sea.
- I cursed at the light and darkness that came and went through the iron window for two hundred days.
- The evening crow. It keeps solitary watch over the rain clouds floating slowly across the big sky.
- Autumn afternoon. In the hollow of the cherry tree two tiny frogs are having fun.
- The pillars of words in my heart. They collapse one after the other in the autumn wind.
- I remember when I said "I'm going to end my life at twenty-two" and cut the strings of the violin and wept.

- You and I. We go to our graves feeling as if our hearts are separated east and west by the sea.
- The cherry petals fall on the stone-covered path of the Daihikaku Temple. And the temple bell peals.

In the evening I received cards from Sakai and Tameko, Yoshikawa, and Kōtoku Komatarō. I wanted to jot down my thoughts after reading the cards, but it was more than I could do. As I reread what I've written so far, this diary strikes me as totally disorganized and fragmentary. It's almost as if I'm writing down the mutterings of my dreams. It's distressing. Should I stop altogether?

January 21. Clear. The sun is shining on the snow on the pine tree branches. It looks like a painting by Maruyama Ōkyo [1733–95]. An exquisite scene.

When Sakai started his Baibunsha, the first person to ask for help was a student in a women's college. She wanted the Baibunsha to write her senior thesis. What a comment on our society—comical and disgraceful at the same time.

I hear that Sakai Tameko is attending midwives' school. I admire her courage and initiative to begin studies at the age of forty. And I admire Sakai for helping his wife become independent and self-sufficient. I am sure this entails some inconvenience for him. Not every man would be so willing.

Kōtoku's mother died on December 28. She caught malaria and then pneumonia and died ten days after she got sick. I was told that when she came to Tokyo in November to see Kōtoku, she had planned to visit me too, but because Ochiyo was with her she held back and left without seeing me. Even though Kōtoku and I had broken off relations by then, she and I still saw each other as mother and daughter. When I heard that she had come all the way to Tokyo and did not visit me, I was hurt and felt she was being heartless. Now having heard what happened, I feel guilty to have thought ill of her even for a moment. I think of her with fondness. We were mother and daughter, and then we were no longer members of the same family. Now we have parted, never to see each other again. She had comforted me constantly with her letters and packages. The past is like a dream. Ah, life is like a dream. Time is the graveyard, and everyone is going to be buried eventually. It is only a matter of time. Here I am, weeping over the death of others. But I too will be buried soon.

I seem to have caught a cold. I have a bad headache, but I took a bath anyway. Bathing is one of the few pleasures of prison life. Visits, letters, and bathing. I have no family, am virtually alone, so I seldom have visitors or get letters. The bath we are allowed every five days is my greatest pleasure.

From the clear, blue sky the warm sunlight streams in through the barred window. Sitting before the desk, feeling relaxed after my bath, how happy I would be to simply melt away and fall asleep forever.

Yoshikawa wrote in his letter:

> This day a year ago I was released from prison. Of the three of us who left prison that day, Higuchi Den is doing extremely well. In contrast, I am merely staying alive. Oka Chiyohiko went back to his old nest in Chiba and is struggling with cold weather and hunger.

I wonder why Oka was imprisoned. Are those who are successful right and those in the depths of despair wrong? What about Morioka Eiji, who lost his mind and jumped into an old well in Dairen? What about those people who abandon their principles like worn-out sandals because they fear government oppression and hope to save their skins?

Isn't fate fickle? The human heart is so frail. Let those who want to leave, leave. Let those who must die, die. New shoots sprout only after the mammoth tree falls. In the springtime of the intellectual world, those of us who deem ourselves to be pioneers need not look back to fall and winter. We must look forward. We must rush forward. We must rush toward the light that offers us hope.

It seems that the authorities are watching our comrades in the outside world with even greater vigilance. The trial's shocking and outrageous results show that the government is planning to take advantage of this incident to adopt extreme, repressive measures. Persecute us! That's right, persecute us! Don't you know that for every force there is a counterforce? Persecute us! Persecute us as much as you wish. The old way is fighting the new—imperialism versus anarchism. Go ahead: Take your piece of stick and try with all your might to stop the onrush of the Sumida River.

Chaplain Numanami comes and asks me, "How are you?" I reply, "Same as usual." He says, "You have peace of mind because your life is founded on faith in your ism, your cause. Some people may be chagrined about the whole affair, depending on how deeply they were involved in it. You were involved in the affair from the beginning to the end, so you must have been prepared to face anything." What he said pleased me. It was much better than his trying to convert me.

I am sure many fellow defendants are deeply distressed about what has happened. This incident is unprecedented in history, but the punishment is unprecedented too. This affair should not be labeled a conspiracy by the anarchists. Rather it should be called a conspiracy concocted by the public prosecutors. The invocation of Article 73 in the trial was truly idiotic. The public charges and the truth of the matter were totally unrelated, like a novel written by a third-rate writer. Only the five of us—Kōtoku, Miyashita, Niimura, Furukawa, and I—were involved in the conspiracy, the group that the prosecutor called the "reserves under Kōtoku's direct command." The prosecutors linked the others to the conspiracy simply be-cause of the idle talks we had with them in the past, talks that were as ephemeral as smoke drifting in air.

The prosecution argued that the affair was a conspiracy of the anarchists—so-and-so is an anarchist, or so-and-so is a friend of an anarchist; therefore, they were participants in the conspiracy. Using this kind of outrageous reasoning, they went about arresting people. Rushing to fight for honor and fame, the authorities strove to bring as many as possible to the dock. They resorted to deceit, double-dealing, threats, and, in extreme cases, methods similar to the tortures used in the past. Some were questioned continuously day and night without rest or sleep. The prosecutors latched onto the common complaints that ordinary people, not necessarily anarchists, mouth about the government. They presented these casual discussions as if they were linked in a profound way to the conspiracy.

Even though one were to let them interpret these discussions as broadly as possible and define them as being conspiratorial, they can in no way be linked to Article 73. At most, the prosecutors might prove a plot to stage a civil uprising. But the prosecutors and judges who conducted the preliminary investigation questioned the accused in detail about anarchism. When the ideals of anarchism—and these were merely ideals—were expressed, the prosecutors concluded that because anarchism believes in absolute freedom and equality it perforce also naturally rejects the imperial family. Through such reasoning they managed to get their inferences into the records of the examination. They then used these theories and ideals, which have no relationship with the current affair, to entrap completely innocent people.

The more I think about this the madder I get.

You poor pitiful judges. All you wanted to do was protect your positions. To safeguard them, you handed down these verdicts even though you knew they were unlawful and arbitrary. You went against your consciences. You poor judges, poor slaves of the government. I should be angry at you, but I pity you instead. Here I am bound by this barred window, but my thoughts still spread their wings in the free world of ideas. Nothing can bind my thoughts or interfere with them. You may live for a hundred years, but what is a life without freedom, a life of slavery, worth? You poor slaves.

At 4:00 p.m. I was taken to the visiting room. Four people were there: Sakai, Mr. and Mrs. Ōsugi, and Yoshikawa. Before the visit, I was told by the warden that I was not to speak about the trial. This must have been a governmental directive, based on the fear that if the truth about the outrageous trial got out, our comrades might vent their anger against the government.

I remember how Sakai and Ōsugi looked when we were together during the trial of the Red Flag incident in room 3 of the court of appeals. Today they looked no different. Both are healthy and vigorous. We spoke a word here, a phrase there. I tried to avoid meeting their eyes, which were filled with tears. I tried to laugh and chat casually, but finally when the time came to say farewell, especially when it came time to shake Yasuko's hand, the tears that I had been holding back poured out as if from a broken dam. We both cried and held hands for a long time. Oh, my dear friends, my comrades! When I blurted out "The verdicts were a surprise," Sakai said in anguish, "I expected you and Kōtoku to die for the cause but..." That's all he said—his heart was overflowing with emotion.

Today I wrote a letter to Mr. and Mrs. Ōsugi and cards to Messrs. Sakai and Yoshikawa.

[To the Ōsugis she wrote, "Ōsugi, Yasuko, thank you for visiting me. I was pleased to see Ōsugi, looking so well. I hope both of you will take good care of yourselves and live for many years." To Sakai Tameko she wrote, "Please come and pay me a farewell visit when it is convenient for you. I am grateful for the sash you sent me. Thank you so much." To Yoshikawa she wrote, "I am prohibited from making even the slightest comment in my letters, so I am jotting things down in my diary. Please read it after I am gone."]

January 22. Clear. Last night, for the first time since I was jailed, I felt depressed. The final visit from my friends was nerve-racking. Since June 2, when I heard that our plot was uncovered, I have been convinced that I have to learn to discipline myself. Right now I feel like a worthless person—to be overwhelmed, even for one night, by such irrational feelings. I despair for myself. How could I be such a weakling?

Maybe it is only a natural reaction. Asian heroes say that one's face should not reveal feelings of joy or anger, happiness or sorrow. In a way, this is a highly admirable ideal, but at the same time it is hypocritical. Maybe an idiot or a sage can really transcend joy and anger or happiness and sorrow, but ordinary people are filled with such feelings. Only by lying or pretending can they live without showing feelings. I am a weak person, emotional to the extreme. I hate lies, I dislike pretense. I detest all things unnatural. I cry. I laugh. I rejoice. I get angry. I let my emotions have free play. I don't care how others measure my worth as a human being. I will be satisfied if I can end my life without lying to myself.

Today, however, I feel very good. The sadness of last night has vanished. I wonder why I felt so bad? I was overjoyed to hear that my fellow defendants in the male prison wing are ready to face death, displaying a fortitude worthy of anarchists. When I heard this, I felt as if I were floating on air. Since we are responsible for their plight, I was very worried about how they might react. We are all human. It's only natural that they might find it intolerable to be punished so harshly for the truly tenuous connection they had with the affair. I am really impressed that they have decided to sacrifice all for the sake of their principles. They are worthy anarchists, worthy comrades. I am truly happy. I am proud to be a believer in anarchism. I have nothing more to worry about or regret. The only worry that had been hovering over my thoughts like a black cloud has dissipated completely. Everything is as bright and clear as today's sky.

I wrote letters to Koizumi Sakutarō, Katō Tokijirō, Nagae Tamemasa, and cards to Okano Tatsunosuke and Watanabe Yayoko.

In the evening I received letters from our attorney, Hirade, and from Sakai. Hirade wrote:

> I knew what the verdicts would be before the judge finished reading ten lines of the argument. Like all lawyers who hope for favorable decisions, I had clung until then to the hope that five or six of the defendants would get off with light sentences. But it was in vain. Hard as it was to remain in the courtroom, I did not want the two men I was defending to lose hope. So even though I found it painful, I stuck it out until the end of the proceedings. I even said a few words of encouragement to them. There's nothing that can be done about the application of the law, so let us leave the question of the verdicts' justness to the judgment of history. I don't think that you're the sort of person that requires words of comfort. I am tormented, though, when I think about how those who were not prepared to face the worst must have felt. I haven't been able to do anything since the eighteenth.

Even a lawyer feels this way. Is it any wonder that I feel tormented beyond endurance, me, their comrade, who is responsible for their plight? I wrote a reply to Hirade under the dim light-bulb.

January 23. Clear. I wake up every night at 2:00 a.m. when they come to change my hot-water bottle. Though I am drowsy, I can't fall back to sleep for two or three hours. I lie there thinking about all sorts of things. Last night when I woke up, I thought about a number of things—Sakai who came to see me the day before yesterday, my fellow defendants, my younger sister's grave, which is in Seishunji [in Yodobashi in Tokyo]. When Sakai or Yasuko delivers the money to take care of the grave, as I asked them to, I wonder what that monk whom I detest so much will say. I don't believe in the superstition that the dead will be saved by the power of the sutra, so I tended to neglect sending gifts to the temple. Whenever I visited my sister's grave, the monk always gave me a nasty look. As a result, I stopped going to her grave site to place flowers and incense and instead placed her favorite food and so forth before her photograph. This is just as silly, for, after all, the dead person's body has already turned to smoke or has decomposed and returned to its original atomic particles. I don't believe that the spirit survives and is pleased to receive flowers, incense, or other gifts. I did these things out of habit and for my own psychological satisfaction.

Given my current situation, however, I feel I ought to give the temple at least a little money to care for the grave. If not for me, then certainly for the sake of my younger brother, who is currently in America. When he re-turns to Japan one of these years and asks about our younger sister's grave, he would, without question, be crushed if he found that the grave had been neglected and allowed to deteriorate because it was looked on as the grave of a person without family.

Last night I thought about what should be done with my body after my death. After my last insignificant breath and when I have become a mere lump of flesh, I suppose it doesn't really matter what happens to my remains. But I hate the thought of being squeezed into a coffin in an awkward position with my legs bent under. I want a coffin in which my body can be laid out flat. The day before yesterday, when my friends visited me, I asked Warden Kinose, who was present as an observer, to get me a full-length coffin. I expect the coffin will be finished before long. I had also wanted to be in my good clothes. If by chance someone were to dig up my coffin and expose my body, I didn't want to look too unseemly. Now, however, I've decided it would be more natural for me to be dressed in my ordinary clothes. It doesn't matter if my dress is torn or soiled.

I had also asked Section Chief Iizuka to let me take a bath on the morning of my execution, but this morning I told them to forget about that too. I don't care about the headstone. Truthfully, I really don't care if they burn me and scatter my ashes in the wind, or if they throw my body in Shinagawa River. But I suppose they couldn't do a thing like that. So if I am to be buried, I really want to be buried next to my younger sister. As I said, I don't like that temple, so I have arranged to be buried in the convict graveyard in Zōgegaya. This will be the least trouble. The day before yesterday when Sakai and Yasuko asked me if I had anything I wanted taken care of, I told them where I wanted to be buried.

This morning I wrote cards to the Baibunsha and to our attorney, Hirade. I asked the people at Baibunsha to arrange to have a new wooden tablet set up by my sister's gravestone when they went to the temple.

Thinking about the grave, I was reminded of the prosecutor Taketomi Wataru. I met him three years ago after the Red Flag incident. At the time, we clashed over my request to have the wording of my pretrial statement corrected because there were inaccuracies. We ended up getting angry at each other. Then the following year—that is, two summers ago when I was imprisoned and charged with a violation of the press law in connection with my work with the magazine *Jiyū Shisō*—the same prosecutor tormented me. He was extremely mean and devious in questioning me and pressed the case against me in a merciless fashion.

When the current affair broke out, I was initially examined by him, but I was determined not to say a word, since I disliked him so much. In fact, I even thought of killing him and bringing him along with me to the land of the dead if I got the chance. Later, however, he talked about his life—about his mother and how he had worked his way through school—and I began to feel sympathetic toward him and abandoned any thought of killing him. I, too, shared my feelings with him, and we parted amicably.

Several days later he came to me and said, "I find it interesting that you don't want to say a word to me about the affair. I won't try to make you talk about it. Instead, won't you tell me about yourself? Wouldn't it be a novel idea to have me, whom you detest so much, write your life story? I really would like to do it."

I imagined that this would be his way of repaying me viciously, but no matter who writes about me it's highly unlikely that anything good will be said. I have been a maverick and haven't followed any straight and narrow path. Thanks to my stubbornness and determination not to knuckle under, I succeeded in not becoming a prostitute or a textile-factory worker. But the story of my life would not elicit the sympathies of anyone except, perhaps, kindhearted people concerned with social problems. I have given up any hope of winning people's understanding. My story is bound to be told in a slanted way, and I might as well have it told as unsympathetically as possible. So, in the end, I told my life story to the prosecutor almost as if it were a novel.

When we discussed things unrelated to the current affair, the prosecutor impressed me as a cheerful person, free of sinister intents. I didn't see anything hateful in him. I can vividly recall his face as he listened avidly to my story. He would say, "It really is like a novel," and kept repeating, "You and I must have had some strong ties in our previous existence." In the end, he told me, "If by chance you are executed, or if you happen to die before me, I promise to bring flowers and incense to your grave."

His eyes seemed to say that he was not merely flattering me. So I thought he might visit my grave at least once. When I mentioned this to someone, they laughed and said that he was probably just superstitious about the entire thing.

If I could return as a ghost, there are so many people, beginning with the judge of the Court of Cassation, that I would like to terrify. It would be wonderful to scare them witless and make them grovel.

Early this morning, I had an interesting dream. I was with two or three people whom I can't recall now, and we were walking on a path in a field by a brook. When I looked up, I saw the sun and the moon, about three feet apart, vividly etched in the blue sky. The sun was the same color as the moon, and it was not fully round but was shaded by a third. The moon was about ten days past the new moon. I told my companions that when the sun and the moon appear together it means a great calamity is about to befall the nation. Then I woke up. Maybe my brain is somehow injured, but from way back I've often dreamed all night long. I've never had a dream like that, though. A crescent-shaped sun and moon. I wonder what all this means?

Nowadays, every morning when I get up I think in amazement, "Oh, am I still alive?" That I am still alive feels like a dream.

I heard from Tanaka, chief of moral instruction, that over half of the defendants condemned to death have been given a reprieve. Their sentences were probably reduced one degree to life imprisonment. The verdicts were so unjust that this came as no surprise. Still, it is delightful news. I don't know whose sentences were reduced, but it must be those who had very little to do with the affair; those people who, in my opinion, were completely innocent. They must be overjoyed, since, even though they were condemned unjustly and arbitrarily, they were facing the death penalty.

The authorities first hand down these harsh sentences, then reduce them, touting the action as an act of the emperor's benevolence. They try to impress the people of Japan, as well as those of other nations, that this is an act of justice and mercy. Are we to admire this kind of clever scheming? or condemn it as artful politicking? Still I am really happy that my comrades' lives have been spared. To be fully satisfied I would like to see all others saved except for the three or four of us. If I could take the places of all of them, I would be happy to be broiled to death by being trussed upside down or have my back split open and have molten lead poured into me. I am willing to suffer any kind of torture and punishment.

Someone told me an interesting story about Tanaka who was a samurai of Aizu-han. Tanaka was captured and condemned to death in 1872. On his way to the execution grounds he was unexpectedly given a reprieve. It is a story that intrigues someone in my situation a great deal.

Tanaka is tactful in tailoring his talk to fit the person he is talking to. He does not say anything mentally upsetting but simply comes up with timely and appropriate stories. I am impressed. It is the fruit of years of experience.

Five letters arrived. They were from Sakai Mā-san, Koizumi Sakutarō, Minami Sukematsu, Kayama Sukeo, and Tomiyama. Mā-san's is a beautiful picture-card of flowers and grass. She has written in pencil, "I understand you are giving me something. Thank you very much. Goodbye." I can just see her big eyes, fair face, and adorable figure. She is really a lovable child.

Koizumi wrote, "I am writing this as a farewell missive. On New Year's Eve when I got drunk at Chikushi-kan I wrote the following poem for Shūsui:

> Before I lift the sake cup, I think only of the relationship with beautiful princesses. After I am drunk I understand the bitter search. Tonight my dear friend is in prison. Where will the spirit that haunts his dreams be at the end of the year?

I also started to compose a poem for you, but I failed to do so and completed only one phrase: 'How pitiful. This enlightened age derails the talented lady.'"

He has been of great help to me during the past two or three years. I read his letter over and over, and was overcome with emotion. Please stay well. Live for a hundred years.

I am writing this under the dim electric-light bulb. I can barely move the brush, which is cold as ice. It is difficult. The call for us to go to bed was issued sometime ago. The lonely wind is blowing past the window. I guess I will call it a night.

January 24. Clear. I wrote to Messrs. Sakai and Masuda, and Ma-bō. I asked Sakai to send my younger brother in America some mementos from me.

The court's verdict, consisting of 146 pages, arrived. I plan to send it to my comrades in the United States. Yoshikawa sent me the *Suikodo-Kensō*.

I feel distressed after reading the hyperbolic, twisted reasoning of the verdict. I cannot get my spirits up to write today. A postcard from Yoshikawa arrived.

At night I wrote letters and cards to the four lawyers, Isobe, Hanai, Imamura, and Hirade, and to Messrs. Yoshikawa, Minami, Kayama, and Tomiyama. [In her letter to Yoshikawa she wrote]:

> Yesterday I heard that more than half of my fellow defendants were reprieved. When I heard the verdicts, which were completely unexpected, I was so bitter that the blood in my whole body flared up as if on fire. Now, I am very happy that some of the defendants have been saved. They must be the people who I was certain were innocent. After hearing the news I felt that half the burden on my shoulders had been lifted.

Eleven

Beneath a White Tower

They had been correct, King George I of Greece thought to himself. His advisors had once more proved their worth. The tower of Thessaloniki had previously been a symbol of the Ottomans and their bloody rule—a site of torture, imprisonment, and execution. But with a fresh coat of white paint, it now stood as a symbol of a more benign rule, a unifier in a fractured kingdom that was only now recovering from the wounds of the Balkan War of 1912. The late evening sun glistened and radiated across the tower's surface as the Mediterranean fractured the light across the waves beyond. The king's one nominal nod to personal security—his equerry, Colonel Frankoulis—was close by, and together they were discussing the high points of the recent military victories they had secured, cementing both George I's appointed kingdom and his popularity.

Neither the colonel nor the king saw the hand clutching the revolver that abruptly barked out two shots. On 18 March 1913, at around 5:15 p.m., the king of Greece fell dead, and his assassin was promptly captured. The story of the king's assassin subsequently became as ephemeral and seemingly lost to history as the gun smoke from the barrel of his revolver.

The assassin of King George I was Alexandros Schinas, and the nascent Greek state was keen not to ascribe a political motive to his actions. In the intervening century, many of the details about Schinas and his life have become obscured, and although conspiracy theories abound regarding his motives, little is known of the man. He is understood and defined as a lone Anarchist actor, and his regicide is assumed to be an example of propaganda of the deed. He is described as being of "feeble intellect,"[1] a "criminal degenerate,"[2] and a "victim of alcoholism."[3] Over time, the state-issued narrative has become the accepted understanding of Schinas. As with many narratives, however, this portrait may not be an accurate representation, and in seeking to understand the reasons behind his regicide, it is first necessary to attempt to create a fuller picture of Schinas himself, along with factors that may have precipitated his actions.

Historians are presently unsure when and where Schinas was born. A number of sources (most notably interviews that were conducted with his Greek countrymen and found their way into print in the *New York Times* following his regicide[4]) have indicated that his place of birth was Volos, a coastal port city in Thessaly, situated centrally on the Greek mainland; however, some claim that he was born in Serres, an inland city in the region of Central Macedonia.[5] Regardless of the location of his birth, the accepted history is that Schinas was born sometime in 1870. At this time, Greece was still a divided country, one that had been born out of conflict. Greece had been ruled by the Ottoman Empire from the mid-fifteenth century onward. It was only in 1831, with the launch of the Greek

War of Independence, that the vice-like Turkish grip began to falter. Greece as a modern country was not established until the London Conference of 1832, which sought to establish a stable Greek government as negotiated by Britain, France, and Russia; as a result of the conference, a Bavarian prince, Otto, was declared king. This decision (which, rather than being made by the Greeks themselves, was instead foisted upon them by foreign powers) and the attendant monarchical rule was ratified in May 1832 by the Treaty of Constantinople.[6] Both Volos and Serres were contested territories at the time of Schinas' birth (Volos did not become part of the Greek kingdom until 1881, and Serres was an Anatolian beylik, a Turkish principality governed by a bey), which could be one reason why historians cannot be more exact regarding the location, time, and circumstances of Schinas' birth.

Alexandros Schinas

Little is known of Schinas' life before the assassination. The ages, occupations, and composition of his family background have, for the most part, been lost to history. One article published by the *New York Times* claimed that he was of "mixed parentage."[7] A number of other clues, however, can be found in a dialogue that was took place following the assassination in March 1913 between Schinas and a correspondent by the name of Magrini from the paper *Aionos*.[8] From this source, we can determine that Schinas had at least two sisters, one older and one younger. As to the rest of his family, their names and existence remain presently as mysterious as his supposed motives attacking King George I. One interesting element that emerges from Magrini's the interview is that Schinas began to suffer from a "neurological condition" at the age of fourteen. Details about this medical condition are not provided, but it must have not been immediately life threatening, as Schinas was to endure it until the time of his death some decades later.

The details of Schinas' youth are also obscured by history and the lack of credible and presentable research. By his own admission, Schinas studied medicine in Athens. It is possible that he was a medical student at the National and Kapodistrian University of Athens, which was established by the much-reviled King Otto in May 1837. Schinas may also have been, at one point, "an instructor in the medical department of the University of Athens"[9] It was during this period that Schinas began to take an interest in Socialism (as opposed to the assumed Anarchism that prompted his later assassination of King George I). By the age of twenty-five, Schinas had, according his account as reported by Magrini, graduated. He lacked the funds, however, to obtain his degree (and possibly debts incurred during the course of his studies), for which he required fifty Turkish pounds. Schinas, supposedly an individual with limited intellect, was subsequently able to secure positions for both himself and his younger sister as teachers in the Greek village of Klesoura. Unfortunately, because of familial interference from his older sister, who presumably did not wish her younger sister to have to pay belatedly for Schinas' studies out of her earnings, Schinas was forced to resign from this position.

Following his resignation (again according to his own account), Schinas borrowed seven Turkish pounds from an unnamed friend to purchase medical supplies. These he was able to trade locally, netting a two-pound profit, before moving to Xanthi to practice medicine. Lacking a medical degree (and the associated paperwork), it was not long before the authorities clamped down on Schinas' unregulated practice, and he soon found himself unemployed. At this point, knowledge of Schinas becomes more confused and uncertain. According to later reports that were issued in the *New York Times*, citing the Greek consul general for New York, Demetrios N. Botassi, at some juncture Schinas moved to Volos to open up a school. Botassi was the first Greek consul general, having moved to New York in 1856 and held the position for a period of fifty-eight years[10]; he described Schinas as a "man of education and a confirmed anarchist."[11] This allegation seems somewhat opposed to Schinas' own later protestations and those of others who shared his Socialist beliefs. It is worth considering, however, that during the nineteenth century the terms "Socialism" and "Anarchism" were often used interchangeably. Although there is a significant gulf between ideas of remodeling the state and those that aim to remove it altogether, many public figures and press reports of the time ignored this distinction; indeed, both Socialism and Anarchism were seen as grave social and political threats in the public and media consciousness.

According to a Greek merchant by the name of Mr. Parthanis (who is, like Botassi, referenced in the *New York Times* special supplement), Schinas' school, known as the Centre for Workingmen, was opened by Schinas along with an unnamed doctor and lawyer. Some months after opening its doors, the institution was closed down by the government for "teaching anti-government ideas," and the unnamed doctor and lawyer were sentenced to three months' imprisonment. For whatever reason, Schinas was not detained, and he presumably escaped the attention of the Greek authorities. Also according to Botassi, it was during this period that Schinas unsuccessfully stood as a candidate for the office of deputy from Volos for the Greek legislative body. This abortive attempt to join the ranks of the political class did not meet with success, but, again, it hardly seems consistent with the actions of a supposed Anarchist radical. Botassi's claims are disputed by a letter received by the New York Greek paper *Atlantis* from a Bazil Batznoulis and subsequently reported by the *New York Times*.[12] In this revealing article, Batznoulis claimed that, rather than Alexandros Schinas standing for a position in the Greek legislature, it was George Schinas, a native of Argalatis. This short article also provided many other contrary details of Schinas' scant biography. According to Batznoulis, the actual place of Schinas' birth was the village of Kanalia, and although he fails to mention Schinas' sisters, he does indicate Schinas may have had a brother by the name of Hercules, who owned and operated a chemist shop in Volos. Additionally, Batznoulis rejected Botassi's claim that Schinas operated a school in Volos: "Schinas had nothing to do with any school and had no idea of entering politics. He was known as a man who loved isolation and his backgammon. He wore a beard and was an anarchist."

In articles published internationally following the regicide, Schinas was said to have worked in the United States. This may well have been the mechanism he utilized to escape potential prosecution for his involvement in the Volos institution. According to the *New York Times* special supplement, at some point prior to 1913 Schinas was living in New York, where he was employed in the pantry of the Fifth Avenue Hotel (although he is called Aleko Schinas throughout the article). According to Eratosthemus Charrns, a waiter at the Hotel Belvedere in Baltimore in 1913, he and Schinas worked together for more than a year. Schinas allegedly "had no use for Kings and members of the aristocracy. He was always saying that the poor, uneducated man was as good as the wealthy and learned aristocrat." Schinas was also said to be a persistent reader of Socialist ideas and a regular in East Side radical circles. At some point, Schinas left the Fifth Avenue Hotel for a position at the Plaza Hotel, after which he and Charrns ended their association. An article in the *Dundee Courier* describes Schinas as an admirer of the English Socialist journalist and campaigner Robert Blatchford at this time, and he supposedly distributed copies of *Merrie England* to waiters in the hotel.[13]

How Schinas came to be in New York (and his reasons for doing so other than potentially avoiding arrest) is further confused by a search of U.S. immigration records. Only one immigrant seems to conform to Schinas' profile, assuming that he was traveling under his own identity rather than one he had temporarily employed for the purposes of escape. On 30 October 1905, the ship *La Gascogne* arrived at Ellis Island from Havre. It was carrying a Greek passenger, last resident in Kalavrite, by the name of Athanasios Schinas. At the time of arrival, this Schinas was thirty-six years old (putting his birth at 1869) and listed on immigration records as being married. The passenger who stepped onto the soil and sand at Ellis Island might not have been Alexandros Schinas (who may have traveled under an assumed identity to avoid detection by the Greek police), but the general age of this individual and the time period seem to fit. If indeed Schinas did travel to New York in 1905, it raises some interesting historical queries. The passenger Schinas is said to be married; if so, to whom? Had Schinas found love as well as legal troubles in his travels around Greece? Adding to the confusion, Batznoulis alleges that Schinas' reasons for being present in the United States had to do with a family quarrel with his supposed brother, Hercules, rather than a need to evade the Greek police. The truth of this claim, along with the details of how Schinas came to New York (if indeed he did) and how he lived after his arrival, will probably never be known.

Whether as Athanasios or Alexandros, Schinas did not stay long in the United States. By his own account, as told to Magrini, Schinas was deported from Greece in 1910 (because, in his words, "I was good Greek patriot") before returning in February 1913, a month before the assassination. How Schinas had returned from New York (to say nothing of why), and the reasons behind his deportation from Greece, are not clear, and there is much historical research to be conducted on this and many other facets of his life.

One significant consideration when discussing Schinas, aside from the mysterious nature of his history, is his motivation for assassinating King George I. The accepted position is that he was a homeless alcoholic with Anarchist tendencies. The *New York Times* referred to him as a "feeble intellect, who states that he was driven to desperation by sickness and want."[14] This image is further confirmed by reports in the *Dundee Courier* wherein Schinas is described as having lost his health prior to the attack, in addition to losing "most of his patrimony in debauchery [and] the remainder of his fortune on the Bourse at Salonika."[15] Although an inheritance may well have provided a reason for Schinas to return to Greece following his deportation, it seems unlikely that either a committed Socialist or an avowed Anarchist would invest funds in the unreservedly capitalist stock exchange. Other media sources were just as scathing in their understanding of Schinas and his actions; for example, according to the *Burnley News*, "The fuller accounts of the assassination of King George of Greece show that the crime was committed by a man of unstable mind, who was apparently actuated by a private motive. Schinas, the murderer, is said to be a drunkard who had twice lost a petty post in the public service and had applied to the King for assistance. No political importance is attached to the outrage."[16] The idea that Schinas may have been seeking revenge for having been denied state assistance is supported by an article in the *New York Times*, which claimed that the motivation for the attack was that Schinas had applied for assistance at the king's palace in 1911 but was refused and driven off by palace guards.[17] Given that, by Schinas' own account, he had been deported in 1910 and did not return to Greece until 1913, the assertion that he returned for reasons of speculative pleading for financial assistance seems unlikely. If the regicide was not motivated by revenge or a sense of despair, and lacked political significance or import, what, then, drove Schinas to commit such a drastic act?

Like many European men and women of the period, Schinas was able to move freely not just around Europe but also around much of the rest of the globe. One explanation for the mass movement of humanity that occurred throughout much of the nineteenth and early twentieth centuries was the rise of industrialization. In Schinas' case, it seems that he was unable to work in the profession for which he had been trained owing to personal poverty and family difficulties. As such, he may have had no other choice but to leave Greece in pursuit of employment. However, New York, far from being welcoming, may have been as much of a disappointment for Schinas as it proved for many other hopeful immigrants. Here a trained doctor may well have found himself serving meals to American members of the bourgeoisie or washing their dirty plates. It is possible, given such a fate (however temporary it may have been), that Schinas not only cultivated an already keen interest in social equality but also nurtured considerable resentment. Perhaps these ill feelings influenced in his decision to commit a regicide.

Another theory is that Schinas, rather than acting of his own volition, was actually an agent acting on behalf of the Turks or the Bulgarians.[18] It is worth noting that the Greeks had combined with Bulgaria (as well as Serbia and Montenegro) to defeat the Ottoman Empire during the First Balkan War of 1912. Greek forces successfully captured Thessaloniki on 26 October 1912, hours prior to the arrival of Bulgarian forces; owing to the strategic and economic importance of this port, it was a much-disputed territory. Tensions between the nascent Greek state and Bulgaria erupted fully in June 1913, when Bulgaria, dissatisfied with the gains and territories it had acquired, chose to contest them, and thus the Second Balkan War commenced. Although there is strong historical evidence to support conflict between the Greek and Bulgarian states at the time of King George I's death, such conflict was for the most part political in nature. Indeed, the assassination of the king served to destabilize a delicate and hard-won peace. This conspiracy theory explaining Schinas' actions has several parallels to those pertaining to the assassination of John F. Kennedy (a populist leader with a reduced security detail, supposedly assassinated by mysterious forces acting through a dupe), but its accuracy is questionable. Although many details of Schinas' life are presently unknown (and at the time of the regicide the atmosphere in Thessaloniki was doubtless tense), no evidence that Schinas was acting as an agent for the Ottoman Empire, the Bulgarians, or any other entity has emerged.

The interview conducted with Schinas by the Italian journalist Magrini (from the paper *Aionos*) may hold clues to Schinas' motivation that go beyond personal retribution or political machinations. Indeed, according to Schinas' own words, the reasons behind the regicide may well have been more prosaic in nature: "Half a month ago, I got tuberculosis. A few days before I assassinated the King I got severe high fevers. I had deliriums. During the night I was waking up, like I was being taken over by madness. I wanted to destroy the world. I wanted to kill everybody, because the whole of society was my enemy. Luck wanted that during this psychological condition to meet the King. I would have killed my own sister if I had met her that day."[19]

Regardless of the motivating factors that lay behind the regicide (which were almost certainly not, as commonly presumed, part of a wider campaign of propaganda of the deed), the consequences for Schinas were severe. After firing upon King George, Schinas made no attempt to flee the scene, and he was promptly disarmed and detained by Colonel Frankoulis. Within moments of the shooting the Greek gendarmerie had arrived on the scene; according to New Zealand *Poverty Bay Herald*, Schinas "appealed to the police not to let the crowd molest him." Following his arrest, Schinas was transported to the Thessaloniki police headquarters. During his detention Schinas was "forced to undergo examinations, which failed to elicit any facts to show that other persons were implicated."[20] One can only imagine what such examinations entailed, but given the popularity of his victim and the oppressive nature of the Greek gendarmerie, it is highly probable that coercion, physical torture and beatings were liberally applied to Schinas by the largely conservative and militarized gendarmes of the day.

Little is known of Schinas' time in custody other than the suspected abuse that he likely suffered as part of his interrogations. A few weathered photographs and notes are all that appear to remain of his imprisonment. Even when placed in the custodial system, Schinas remained an elusive and largely undocumented figure. His death is also as shrouded in mystery as his life. As the interview with Magrini reveals, Schinas had contracted tuberculosis prior to the regicide. For a man with medical training (which Schinas may or may not have had), this diagnosis must have been concerning, since even laymen at the time probably considered the white plague with immense fear. Although the sanatorium movement to treat tuberculosis had gained ground during the nineteenth century and treatments were available from dispensaries, these were not widespread, and for many with low incomes, tuberculosis remained a drawn-out death sentence in the early part of the twentieth century. As events transpired, Schinas did not have to wait long for the state to provide a remedy for his condition. In an article published in the *Scotsman* newspaper several weeks after his arrest, Schinas' fate was revealed: "According to further reports from Salonika, it appears that at half past eight this morning (May 6th) Schinas was taken by the gendarmes and a warder to the office of the Examining Magistrate, where the warden removed the handcuffs from the prisoner's wrists, and then went to pay the cabman, the gendarmes remaining outside the office. Schinas was detained in the Magistrate's private room, where there were two officials. One of these diverted for a moment, Schinas dashed to the window, which is over thirty foot from the ground, and threw himself out. Death was instantaneous."[21] Whether Schinas committed suicide as reported or was pushed by the mysteriously absent or distracted guards is another element of his life that remains clouded in conjecture. Following his death, the Greek state disposed of Schinas' remains, with the exception of his ear (which was used for identification purposes) and his hand (used to compare fingerprint records), both of which are still stored and exhibited by the Criminology Museum of Athens.

The assassination of King George I is commonly thought to be an example of Anarchist propaganda of the deed (indeed, Schinas is typically referenced as a follower of this philosophy) or the work of a lone madman, motivated by non-political factors. Schinas has been characterized both as an educated and criminally motivated Anarchist and as a hopeless and mentally unbalanced alcoholic. Little research has been conducted into his family background, his motivations, or his history, partly due to the commonality of his surname, but also due to the disparate record keeping of the early Greek state. Schinas remains an elusive figure and a controversial one. The results of his actions are readily apparent, but what prompted them and, indeed, the details of the man behind them remain ephemeral, drawn as they are from muddled statements provided by multiple sources. What is clear is that the understanding that Schinas acted as a motivated Anarchist attacker is inherently flawed. Rather than being part of a wider conspiracy, whether political or enacted by a state, Alexandros Schinas may have simply been a sick man (both mentally and physically) seeking an escape from the harsh realities of the early twentieth century. Like many of the figures associated with early propaganda of the deed, Schinas remains obscured by history and often ignored by students of politics and history, just as he was marginalized during the course of his short life.

The King's Assassin Explains Himself to the Journalist Magrini

Source: *Aionos*, March 1913, from http://ngnm.vrahokipos.net/index.php (accessed November 2016); translated by Dr. Grigorios Fragkos

The war correspondent Magrini (journalist) from "Aionos" in Milan, found himself in Thessaloniki shortly after the assassination of King George. He got permission from the judge and visited the King's assassin in prison accompanied by a second lieutenant (sub-lieutenant).

He telegraphed back to "Aionos" the following, which is concluded that, the King's assassin after his action—being healthy, having a clear state of mind—focused/worked on putting together his apology.

When entered the prison, according to Magrini's telegram, the assassin leaned on his elbows and he stared at with his big glassy eyes, with an expression asking "who are you?"

He (the assassin) hesitated (like he is strangling to answer) to reply to my questions. When he realised that he had a journalist in front of him, he gained courage. His voice however, remained sad (it sounded like the voice of a person who is mourning someone who died).

He (the assassin) insists by saying that he shot the King while he was in a state "of not realising what he was doing."

He did not know how, nor why. He is not worried about the punishment. He is not asking, neither knows, what may be his sentence. He thinks that his finances (being poor), his physical and psychological state, are potentially enough to be provided as the excuse, or at least explain his madness.

Often he replies with mysterious answers, which could reveal that he is trying to be clever, if they (these answers) weren't being a witness of being thoughtless.

Why did you kill the King? The assassin replies.

"Not me, but the bullet of the gun killed the King."

What made/pushed the gun in such action?

"A big natural force armed my hand against the King, without me knowing. Up to two months ago I was a good Greek, even though since the age of fourteen I suffered from a neurological condition, which was an obstacle to me in working and makes my existence very difficult. I suffered a lot. Half a month ago, I got tuberculosis. A few days before I assassinated the King I got severe high fevers. I had deliriums. During the night I was waking up, like I was being taken over by madness. I wanted to destroy the world. I wanted to kill everybody, because the whole of society was my enemy. Luck wanted that during this psychological condition to meet the King. I would have killed my own sister if I had met her that day."

To the question if he premeditated the assassination of the King, he replied:

"No! I assassinated the King by chance (it just happened). I was walking as a dead man (as a zombie) without knowing where I was going. Suddenly by turning my head I saw behind me the King with his adjutant. I slowed my pace. The King walked by me, very close to me. I let him walk by me and immediately, I fired."

Did you target/point the gun at him before you fired the gun?

"I did not have to. The King was only one metre away from where I was. Once I fired the gun, I was not able to understand anything after that."

"The lead me to a pharmacy and started asking me so many questions. After that they took me to the prison."

Since you did not premeditate the assassination of the King, why were you carrying a gun? Why did you write your biography, which you signed "Alexandros Schinas" and wrote that from the civilised and cultured you will be considered as such, from the heroes a hero and from the villainous and unstable, vile and unstable.

"I always found myself carrying the gun. My biography I wrote it five days before assassinating the King. I wrote it during the night, the moments of the fever, when I wanted revenge and I did not know how I was going to target the society and whom I was supposed to hit."

Are you an anarchist?

"No, no! I am not an anarchist, but socialist. I became a socialist, when I was studying medicine in Athens. I do not know how. One becomes a socialist, without realising it, slowly (one step at a time). All people that are good and educated are socialist. The philosophy towards medicine, for me it was the socialism."

How many sisters do you have?

"Two. These were the reason towards my destruction. I had completed my studies toward medicine, but I did not have the money to receive my degree. Fifty Turkish pounds was needed. I begged my sister to accept a teacher's position. I was also become a teacher myself and with that income I would be able to buy the degree. A friend of mine found two teacher positions at the village of Klesoura. I was happy. But, when my younger sister, motivated by the oldest, refused to provide the funds, I then resigned from the teacher's position. My friend contributed to gave to me medical supplies worth seven Turkish pounds (as credit), which I went to resell in a close by area, which gave me a profit of two Turkish pounds within a month. Then, I relocated to Xanthi to practice medicine, but I was not allowed, as I did not have the degree and started then living here and there. I was twenty-five years old, when the neurological disorder started torturing me. I am now forty-three!"

The King's assassin then says that he abandoned Thessaloniki, three years ago.

"I was deported by the New-Turks, because I was good Greek patriot. I came back one month ago, having been a bad person from the people and due to the illness."

What do you think your sentence is going to be?

"The justice know this. I do not know."

How do you think people will judge you?

"Each and every one will judge me according to their understanding. I was unlucky."

Do you have regrets for what you did?

The King's assassin did not answer. Bending his head, he remains silent.

Do you mind if I take a photo of you?

"I am ready. You may take it."

I asked him to stand and to pose naturally. His face is like a ghosts. His vanity was excited and asks to adjust what he was wearing, and brought his hand at his hair. He sits with his head looking upwards and proud and remains there without moving, facing the camera.

When the photo was taken, the King's assassin went back to his mattress. When I was about to exit, he raised himself, pulls his strength together, and with a deep voice said to me.

"Sir I was good, like Jesus! The whole of Thessaloniki can confirm. The people and the society make the people bad and create the criminals!"

While the door of the prison heavily shuts, his words still come all the way to me; I was good!

Twelve

Teenage Wastelands

In many histories of political violence, there is a concentration upon the desires, wants, and motivations of adults. Younger individuals, however, frequently generate political change, and this is particularly true with regard to the subject of this book. Two such individuals, who have unfortunately been reduced to footnotes in many histories, are Anteo Zamboni and Jean Baptiste Sipido. Although from different time periods and locales, both of these teenagers had an impact on Anarchist application and practice of propaganda of the deed, and their actions (although unsuccessful) had very distinct outcomes.

On 31 October 1926, a gunshot rang out in the streets of Bologna. A young child had stepped out from the crowd and fired on Benito Mussolini at close range. The boy's arm went numb as his pistol fell to the ground. He had missed, and he could only stare at Il Duce gliding past in his car as rough hands grabbed him, punching him repeatedly as he fell to the ground. Anteo Zamboni is a name that is largely forgotten in discussions of propaganda of the deed, but on that day he came close to assassinating Mussolini and preventing years of Fascist abuses within Italy. Sadly, his ill-conceived efforts failed and led to a tightening of state authoritarianism and press censorship. They also resulted in Zamboni's public lynching at the age of fifteen by Mussolini's supporters (the Squadristi, or Italian Blackshirts), as well as the detention of much of his family.

Zamboni was not the first person who attempted to rid Italy of Mussolini; prior to his attack, the nascent dictator had experienced a number of narrow escapes. On 4 November 1925, a deputy from the Partito Socialista Unitario (PSU) and one-time Freemason, Tito Zaniboni, was arrested at the Hotel Dragoni near the Palazzo Chigi in Rome. Sometime earlier in 1925, Zaniboni had purchased a precision sniper rifle that he had set up on a tripod in the hotel room overlooking a balcony in the Palazzo Chigi, from which Mussolini was due to deliver a speech to war veterans. Unfortunately for Zaniboni, he was not acting alone; in addition to General Luigi Capello, the circle of accomplices included a police agent by the name of Carlo Quaglia. According to the account provided by Mussolini's son, Romano, Quaglia informed the police of the plot because he "feared the consequences of the assassination."[1] In all probability, however, Quaglia was a paid agent of the police superintendent, Giuseppe Dosi. The early Fascist movement in Italy was keen to keep the threats posed by political opposition in check; thus it had embedded agents throughout various political and social groupings. For Zaniboni, this close liaison with police agents would prove his undoing, and at eleven in the morning (several hours before the planned assassination was due to be enacted) he was arrested. Zaniboni and General Capello were both sentenced to terms of imprisonment of thirty years, the maximum penalty under Italian law. Capello always denied his involvement, referring to Zaniboni as a "madman"[2]; however his protestations fell on deaf ears, and although he was released from prison after serving only a fraction of his sentence, he died before Mussolini on 25 June 1941. Somewhat amazingly, Zaniboni not only survived his imprisonment but also outlived Mussolini, later becoming president of the Italian armed forces union, UNUCI, before his death of natural causes on 27 December 1960.

The next attempt on Mussolini's life came on 7 April 1926, although it was likely motivated by mental illness (as opposed to politics). The aspiring assassin was a fifty-year-old Irish aristocrat, Violet Gibson, who was a resident of Italy at the time. Born in Dublin on 31 August 1876, Violet had moved to Italy in November 1924, having visited the country eleven years earlier. Involved in the Theosophical movement as a younger woman, by the time she arrived in Italy Violet was an ardent and committed Roman Catholic. On that fateful April day, she traveled from her spartan garret to the Palazzo Littorio, where the party offices for the Italian Fascists were then situated and where Mussolini was to deliver a speech. As Mussolini moved among the crowds in the Piazza del Campidoglio, Violet seized her chance. She fired once at the dictator; however, he moved his head at the final second, and the bullet from her revolver served only to graze his nose. After firing off another bullet that grazed Mussolini's hand, Violet was violently wrestled to the ground. She was saved from an angry crowd that was ready to lynch her by the speedy intervention of the police. Her motives are still disputed, and they confused even the police investigators of the period. As Frances Stonor Saunders details in her fascinating biography of Violet, Chief Superintendent Epifanio Pennetta, who was charged with investigating the shooting, "would concede that Violet was mad: but only partly mad … and not to the extent that she had lost her faculty of reason at the time she shot Mussolini."[3] Whether Violet was driven by religious mania, as part of a conspiracy, or for more obscure reasons will perhaps never be known. After a brief detention in Rome, she was returned to England, where she was confined for the rest of her life in the environs of the St. Andrews Hospital (which served as a mental asylum) in Northampton before her death on 2 May 1956. Although Mussolini was required to wear an oversized facial bandage for several months, the attempt was, in his eyes, a "mere trifle" that had been caused by an "old, ugly, repulsive woman."[4]

Anteo Zamboni

Prior to the Anteo Zamboni's attempt to kill Mussolini, and only months after the abortive shooting by Violet Gibson, another Italian Anarchist, Gino Lucetti, had made an attempt of his own. Little is known about Lucetti today, but he was doubtless committed to his cause. He was born in the Tuscan province of Massa and Carrara on 31 August 1900. How he spent his childhood is not known, but, like many of his peers, he was conscripted as a member of the Italian forces during the First World War. According to Pietro de Piero, by the time Lucetti returned from the war he had been politicized, and although he had only attained "self-procured education he took part in the political struggles of the 1920's, confronting the fascists on many occasions."[5] Following a violent altercation with an Italian Fascist (ironically at a venue by the name of the Napoleon Café), Lucetti was shot in the neck. Italian doctors refused to tend his injury owing to his dangerous politics, and with the legal authorities in hot pursuit, Lucetti sought refuge at Montignoso. Eventually he fled by boat to France, where he was finally able to find a doctor willing to treat his wound. According to reports[6] that emerged later, Lucetti first thought of assassinating Mussolini when he was living in Marseilles (an area of France that had long associations with Anarchism) in 1922, after he read of Italian workers who had been shot on the government's orders. By January 1923, Lucetti had returned to Rome armed with a revolver, which he hoped to aim at Mussolini; however, for some unknown reason, he aborted his plans. By September 1926, he had managed to procure a number of Italian military-issue grenades, a revolver full of explosive dumdum bullets that had been coated with hydrochloric acid (or muriatic acid, as it was referred to in publications of the time), and a dagger. Prior to attacking the dictator, Lucetti stayed with a hotel waiter, Leandro Sorio, in his hotel room and had several meetings with fellow Anarchist Stefano Vatteroni. According to his later testimony, neither of these two men knew of his plans; however, events would end as badly for them as they would for Lucetti. On the morning of 11 September 1926, Lucetti traveled to the Porta Pia in Rome, waiting for Mussolini to speed past in his car. As Il Duce's vehicle drew near, Lucetti withdrew one of the grenades from his pocket and hurled the shell. Unfortunately, his aim was awry, and, as de Piero reveals, the grenade "failed to explode, bounced onto the running board and only exploded when it was some meters away on the pavement."[7] Mussolini had managed another escape; however, eight nearby pedestrians were wounded by the explosion. In the confusion, Lucetti attempted to escape, but he was quickly pursued by the police, who soon caught up with him. Before he could withdraw his deadly arsenal, the police had beaten him unconscious and recovered his implements. Shortly thereafter, Lucetti was placed on trial, and although he vociferously denied the involvement of either Sorio or Vatteroni, and some witnesses denied seeing them on the scene,[8] others claimed that they had seen both men driving Lucetti to the scene of the attack. In the highly politicized climate of Italy at the time, it was clear which claims the court system would choose to believe. On 12 June 1927, Lucetti was sentenced to thirty years' imprisonment and detained in the Santo Stefano prison. Vatteroni and Sorio received sentences of twenty years and nineteen years, nine months, respectively. Vatteroni spent the first three years of his time in prison in complete isolation, as many Anarchists before him had. As for Lucetti, he ultimately served seventeen years of his sentence before perishing on 15 September 1943 in Ischia, where he had been transferred. According to Piero, it is unclear whether Lucetti died during an escape attempt or was killed by German shells that fell on his prison as a result of a U.S. air raid dedicated to defeating the very forces Lucetti had sought to oppose. Lucetti's tale was certainly an unfortunate one; however, worse was to come for Anteo Zamboni.

Anteo was born on 11 April 1911, and his timing could not have been worse. By the December 1914 (when Anteo had barely learned to walk), Mussolini had rejected the

Socialism of his youth and Italy was embedded in the bloody conflict that was the First World War. By the time Anteo was eleven, Mussolini and his Squadristi had engaged in the March on Rome and forced the resignation of the democratically elected liberal prime minister of Italy, Luigi Facta, plunging Italy into one of the darkest periods in twentieth-century history.

Anteo was the son of Viola Tabarroni and Mammolo Zamboni; he also had two older brothers named Hired and Ludovico. Mammolo was a former Anarchist and typographer, who, owing to reasons of economics, had changed his political affiliation. With the rise of Fascism, Mammolo found that he could make more money printing propaganda materials for Bologna Fascists than he could working for Anarchists. According to later reports, although Mammolo had been involved in Anarchist circles in Bologna, he had ceased "subversive activities"[9] following Mussolini's rise to power. Anteo, however, embraced his father's earlier left-wing views, although this choice did not improve his standing among his older brothers. Anteo's family nickname was "the potato"[10] (supposedly due to his presumed lack of intelligence), and he was a solitary and reserved figure. Anteo had absorbed some of the tenets of Anarchist propaganda of the deed, and he envisioned a reaction to a tyrannical Fascist state in direct and unconstrained terms—namely, the removal of the head of such a state, leading to its dissolution.

Mussolini had been in power for four years when, as part of the commemoration of the March on Rome on Saturday, 30 October 1926, he inaugurated the Littoriale Stadium in Bologna. This 40,000-seat stadium was opened to replace the Stadio Sterlino; it provided a new home for the Bologna football club and served as a demonstration of the Fascist architectural aesthetic, which largely consisted of concrete representations of the supposed glories of the Roman Empire. Following the inauguration ceremonies, as Mussolini departed in his car, he was accompanied by the deputy general secretary of the National Fascist Party (PNF) and then mayor of Bologna, Leandro Arpinati. Arpinati had been present (but was never publicly named as being responsible) for much of the carnage of the massacre of Palazzo d'Accursio. During 1920, in the elections for central Bologna, local Socialists had secured 58.2 percent of the votes. Local Fascists (among whom Arpinati was one of the most prominent) took to the streets on the night of 4 November 1920 and viciously beat any "Reds" they could detain long enough. Two weeks later, the same Fascist contingent had sought to prevent the installation of the new Socialist mayor by occupying the Bologna town hall. In the chaos that followed, hand grenades exploded and shots rang out. When the smoke cleared, nine people were dead and more than one hundred were injured. Arpinati was not averse to using violence as a political tool; his writings in the Fascist paper L'Assalto helped legitimize the endemic and persistent violence of the Italian Squadristi that led to more than 1,900 agricultural and industrial workers being attacked (and nineteen killed) in 1921 alone. Mussolini could not have picked a more appropriate and venal traveling companion.

Just before 6:00 p.m. on the evening of 31 October 1926, the car transporting Mussolini and Arpinati arrived at the corner of Via Rizzoli and Independence Street in Bologna. Waiting patiently on the street was the small form of Anteo Zamboni. As the car drew close, Anteo, who was standing close to the barriers protecting the road (which were heavily guarded by local police), withdrew his revolver and, as the flower petals flung by enthusiastic supporters drifted down toward the motorcade, leveled it to fire at both the dictator and the Fascist mayor. However, a police sergeant by the name of Vincenzo Acclavi spotted the would-be assassin and struck Anteo's arm as he lined up his shot. The bullet ricocheted and eventually came to rest in the car door, having missed Mussolini by inches.

Anteo was promptly detained by Carlo Alberto Pasolini (the father of Italian film director and poet Pier Paolo Pasolini, who would go on to direct *Salo*, or *The 120 Days of Sodom*, and play a seminal role in Italian politics in the 1960s). However, before he could be arrested, Anteo was beaten and lynched by Leandro Arpinati, Arconovaldo Bonaccorsi, Albino Volpi and other members of the Squadristi. Following his brutal murder on the streets of Bologna, Anteo's attack against Mussolini was described by Pope Pius XI as a "criminal attack whose only thought saddens us ... and we do give thanks to God for his failure."[11]

The public execution of a fifteen-year-old boy was, sadly, not the end of the consequences in connection to the aborted attempt on Mussolini's life. The local police took advantage of the assassination attempt to conduct investigations into local anti-Fascists and Socialists. As part of their reactive dragnet, Anteo's father, Mammolo, and aunt, Virginia Tabarroni, were arrested for motivating the attack and sentenced to thirty years' imprisonment. His brothers, Ludovico and Hired, although acquitted of any involvement in Anteo's plot, were subsequently imprisoned for five years for being "dangerous elements."

Sadly for Italy, it was not just the Zamboni family that suffered as a consequence of the attack. On the night of Anteo's failed attempt, according to reports[12] at the time, thousands of Fascists took to the streets. By dawn, the mob had completed a night of carnage in which one hundred people had been killed and more than one thousand injured.[13] As Fabio Fernando Rizi points out, the Italian state was just as quick to react as the mob, and "that same night, writing on a piece of paper and in pencil, Mussolini issued Draconian orders to the police for the protection of the Fascist regime, thus contributing to an overwrought atmosphere and almost inviting and sanctioning violence against the leaders of the opposition. Within days, the government approved, and Parliament ratified, almost without discussion, a series of resolutions that destroyed the liberal state and created a dictatorial government."[14] Shortly following the attack, the PNF introduced legislation that dissolved all other political parties, introduced capital punishment, and implemented the Fascist Special Court for the Defense of the State, which ultimately was responsible for the deaths of at least forty-two people and the false imprisonment of many thousands more. In addition to sporadic acts of violence, a more concentrated effort was made by the Fascists to instill fear into the general population. The library of Benedetto Croci was ransacked,[15] as were the homes of other outspoken critics and political rivals of Mussolini, including Amadeo Bordiga, Arturo Labriolm and Roberto Bracco.[16]

Although there are a number of conspiracy theories regarding the earlier attempts to kill Mussolini (particularly with regard to Violet Gibson), the debate about Zamboni's involvement in the events of October 1926 is an ongoing one. Upon first reporting the incident, the *New York Times*[17] noted that Zamboni was at one point a member of Fascist Youth, although by the time of his death he had not attended meetings for more than a year. According to Giovanni Berneri, "many believe that it was one of his own retinue that fired the revolver shot that grazed Mussolini's jacket and that young Zamboni was sacrificed to divert any possible suspicion from the fascists."[18] This theory is further supported by Peter Neville, who states that "there are strong grounds for believing that dissident fascists themselves may have been involved in the attempt."[19] Imagining Zamboni as a patsy taking the fall for someone else's misdeed may seem to stretch the bounds of credulity, but this idea is definitely worthy of consideration. Although testimony at the time[20] stated that Virginia Tabarroni had, at some juncture, in her possession a revolver believed to belong to Ludovico, there is still confusion regarding where Anteo could have obtained his armaments. Unlike Mussolini's previous attackers, he possessed neither financial means nor military experience, and although it would certainly have been possible for him to obtain a weapon, he may not have been proficient in its use. Additionally, in one of the witness statements provided to the court,[21] a soldier named Silvio Piggitore testified that at the time of the attack he had witnessed a man with a dagger standing unusually close to Zamboni. For Mussolini, the attempt on his life brought with it political gains that allowed him to introduce a wave of repression, violence, and measures that allowed for the creation of the Italian Fascist state—benefits that might well have been worth sacrificing a teenager's life to obtain.

Unfortunately, Anteo probably never read the words of Leo Tolstoy: "Understand then all of you, especially the young, that to want to impose an imaginary state of government on others by violence is not only a vulgar superstition, but even a criminal work."[22] Perhaps more unfortunately for the Italian people and many in Western Europe, he also missed his shot, as those who had gone before him had missed theirs. However, Anteo was not the first teenager to enact propaganda of the deed; decades earlier an even younger prospective assassin had fired shots that rang throughout Europe.

Jean-Baptiste Victor Sipido

Jean-Baptiste Victor Sipido was born on 20 December 1885 in Brussels, Belgium. His father, Jean Batiste Sipido, was an independent tinsmith who, along with his wife, would go on to raise ten children, including his infamous namesake. In some accounts[23] it is claimed the Sipido the younger was Italian; however, this confusion is probably due in large part to authors conflating the actions of Sipido with those of Sante Geronimo Caserio, as well as the existence of editorial bias. Little is known of Jean-Baptiste's early childhood, but it can be established that at the time of his later arrest, the family was lodging on Rue de la Forge in Saint Gilles Belgium, some two miles from Brussels. Originally intended for workers of the Linière (a vast linen mill in the district from 1837 to 1875), Sipido's childhood home was cramped on all sides by neighboring properties, just as the household interior was cramped by his relatives. As would later be revealed by his parents, education was emphasized for all the children in the household. One of the few details that can be established regarding Sipido's schooling comes from a report in the Australian newspaper *The Age*: "The family I learn is respected in the neighbourhood. The young woman tells me that two lady teachers who formerly had Sipido as a pupil, had come to express their sympathy and affection. During my visit the Communal schoolmaster of the district and his wife enter, and tell me with what surprise they learn of the deed. Sipido they say had always a very feeling heart."[24] As to Sipido's siblings, their histories have been lost as of the time of this publication.

Although Sipido received some schooling—at least enough to ensure his later literacy—he was the son of a working craftsman in the nineteenth century and, in line with societal attitudes of the time, would have been expected at best to become a craftsman himself. His father's workshop was located in the family home and presumably fabricated utilitarian goods such as coffeepots, cooking utensils, and objects of basic industry such as funnels. Sipido was apprenticed to his father and engaged in developing his own skill set as a tinsmith. According to all available records, there is nothing to indicate that Sipido was in any way aberrant; rather, he appears to have been a sensitive working-class boy who performed unremarkably during his early and necessary schooling before engaging in the same trade as his respectable (if fecund) parents.

How Sipido came to be involved in politics and what prompted his later actions is not known. However, at the time of his actions, Anarchism was not unknown in Belgium. Indeed, the unfortunate Belgian Anarchist Jean Pauwels blew himself up when a bomb he was carrying into the Church of the Madeleine in Paris detonated prematurely on 15 March 1894. Before the formation of the modern Belgian state in 1830 owing to the Belgian revolution, Belgium was dependent on its neighbors in Europe, and (at least politically) it also drew influence from them. As explored by Ernst Zenker,[25] Anarchism in Belgium was well entrenched by 1885. One of the fathers of modern Anarchism and mutualism, Pierre-Joseph Proudhon, sought refuge in Belgium following repeated incarcerations by the French before returning to France in 1863 (after being specifically excluded by the French general amnesty of 1859). Peter Kropotkin also traveled through both Belgium and Switzerland in 1872 and formed close links with the Belgian Anarchists. Although the rise of the Social Democrats within Belgium caused Anarchism to fall out of favor among the working classes, by the time of Sipido's birth German-inspired anti–Socialist laws had been passed in Belgium, leading to a renewed interest in Anarchism, as well as the formation of many formal and informal groups dedicated to the study of Proudhon, Kropotkin, and Bakunin. Indeed, one of the foremost members of the *Commonweal* and the expatriate Anarchist community in London (as discussed elsewhere in this book), Victor Dave, was originally from Belgium, having converted from the Social Democratic cause to Anarchism.

In October 1899 a conflict commenced that was to define Europe just as the First World War would do decades later. The Second Boer War (typically known as the Boer War) commenced in earnest when Great Britain plunged into conflict with the two Boer nations within South Africa: the South African Republic (Transvaal) and the Orange Free State. Initially the Boers (descendants of the Dutch-speaking settlers in South Africa) put up a stiff resistance against the British and successfully besieged the cities of Mafeking, Kimberley and Ladysmith. However, under the leadership of Lord Kitchener, the British soon flooded South Africa with well-armed and rigorously drilled troops and unleashed their vengeance. Although the British were quick to take control of both the Transvaal and the Orange Free State, the Boers refused to surrender and turned instead to a campaign of guerrilla warfare designed to harass and frustrate the British. In retaliation, the British detained civilian farmers (with whom the guerrillas could easily blend) in a network of concentration camps. Conditions in these camps were onerous in the extreme, and numerous inmates (both adults and children) died of communicable diseases. Outside of the British Empire, the actions of the British troops and the internment of innocent civilians prompted a vocal backlash. The international perception of the Boers was that their resistance was heroic, outgunned as they were, and that they were essentially freedom fighters.[26] The Boers were able to draw upon the support of entities as diverse as the Russian state (from which 225 serving army officers sought leave to volunteer on behalf of the Boers) and the nascent Irish Republican Army. Through most of Europe and the wider world, the actions of the British within South Africa were egregious, if not outright immoral, and resistance to such was deeply imbued in much of the politics of the period.

On the afternoon of 5 April 1900, at around 5:30 p.m., Charles Crocius,[27] the station master of the Northern Terminus of the Brussel-Noord railway station in Brussels, stood on the platform observing a locomotive slowly begin its departure. He watched as the train picked up steam and repositioned his hat, which one of the passengers had advised him to place back on his head. Behind him, four young men between the ages of fifteen and twenty had entered the station.[28] One of them had purchased a penny ticket and, squeezing his diminutive body through the crowded concourse, made his way to the platform and the rapidly departing train. Before the station master could react, the youngster engaged in an act that would see him later variously described as an "imbecile"[29] and a "cartoon image of the anarchist as a shaggy-headed Frankenstein's monster with a crazed glint in his eye."[30] Inside one of the train carriages, the Prince of Wales and Earl of Chester, Albert Edward, was sitting next to his wife, Alexandra of Denmark, oblivious to the events unfolding on the platform—at least until a shaky hand entered his carriage, clutching a revolver. Both the hand and the revolver belonged to Sipido. As Crocius raced toward Sipido, who was hanging precariously from the footboard of the royal compartment, the young man fired his cheap revolver four times, resulting in two misfires and two near misses of the British royals. The available reports from the period indicate that all of Sipido's shots were wide of the mark. According to Dulcie M. Ashdown,[31] one bullet lodged between the Prince of Wales and his wife, with another embedding itself in the hair bun of the princess's lady in waiting, Charlotte Knollys (although, in the course of researching Sipido's activities and life, it has not been possible to substantiate this claim). Ashdown also claims that Sipido "was never caught"[32]; however, he most definitely was captured, and on more than one occasion.

Following his abortive attempt to assassinate one of the crown princes of Europe, Sipido was rapidly wrestled to the ground by Crocius and nearby undercover police. He was then detained and transferred away from the scene of the shooting. As it turned out, the major casualty of the day was a student by the name of Van Roy, whom the crowd at the station assaulted in the false belief that he was the assailant.[33] Within hours of Sipido's arrest, news of his assassination attempt spread throughout Europe. For Albert Edward, who would later go on to be King Edward VII of Britain, the incident would provide both an anecdote and a souvenir. As discussed by J. Pendrel Brodhurst,[34] following the shooting the Prince of Wales requested that he be sent one of the bullets that were subsequently dug out of the railway carriage.

Two years before the shooting, in 1898, the Belgian Workmans' Party had commissioned the Brussels-based architect Victor Horta to design and build a new structure on its behalf. According to contemporary accounts, the building was to be "the centre of activities, the focus of mutual interests, the living, animating symbol of Democracy and of Collectivism."[35] On 2 April 1899, the Maison du Peuple (People's Hostel) opened its doors. The building provided rooms for offices, coffee shops, small enterprises, libraries, meeting rooms, and a party hall for the party that had commissioned it in the first place. Later classed as a master work of Art Nouveau architecture prior to its unfortunate and misguided demolition to erect a skyscraper in 1965, the Maison du Peuple provided meeting space for the Workmans' Party as well as more radical groups, from which (according to press reports of the period) Sipido drew his inspiration. As discussed by the *New York Times*,[36] one group that regularly met at the Maison du Peuple was the Young Socialist Guard. Much of this group's actions are unknown, but, as reported in the pages of the *Los Angeles Herald*,[37] in April 1902 there were disturbances in Brussels in which this organization was involved. According to Richard Bach Jensen,[38] it is possible that Sipido was affiliated with the Socialist Advance Guard of St. Gilles. Even though Sipido was publicly accused of being a Socialist, he (by his own admission) was an Anarchist, and the organizations with which he was loosely affiliated had an "anarchical tendency."[39] As discussed elsewhere in this book, the media in the late nineteenth and early twentieth centuries tended to conflate Anarchism and Socialism, using the two terms interchangeably to describe any member of the fractious working classes. During the meetings held at the Maison du Peuple, Sipido allegedly listened to fiery speeches decrying the activities of the British in Boer War, and he also made contact with three other impassioned youths—Meert, Peuchot, and Meire, who would later stand as co-defendants at his trial.

Following his arrest, Sipido displayed some of the stoicism demonstrated by other Anarchist attackers described in this book, but he also revealed his youth. According to accounts in the Canadian press, by 6 April, "his attitude is dejected and he appears very tired, having had little sleep. He continues not to express regret at his crime, but has reportedly requested permission to see his mother"[40]; in a later meeting with his father, however, Sipido "paid no attention to his father's appeals, maintaining his previous declarations."[41] At the time of his arrest, Sipido had declared that the attempt on the life of the Prince of Wales had been enacted as reprisal for British activities during the Boer War and because Edward had "caused thousands of men to be slaughtered in South Africa."[42] Following his arrest and interrogation by the Belgian police, Sipido's supposed accomplices were detained. All would subsequently be charged with involvement in the attack, but, as reported on 8 April,[43] it was Meert who was accused of supplying Sipido with the revolver he had used to attack the prince.

The trial of Sipido and his accomplices commenced on 2 July 1900, concluding three days later on 5 July. How and where Sipido spent the intervening months has been lost to history; however, given the circumstances of his arrest and his self-proclaimed and unrepentant guilt, it cannot have been a pleasant experience. Nineteenth-century prisons and jails were notoriously brutal, and it is highly likely that Sipido was kept in isolation until the date of his trial to ensure his survival so that the state's vengeance could be enacted. One notable event from the intervening period is that Sipido's parents wrote a contrite plea to both Queen Victoria and the Prince of Wales: "Two unhappy parents wish to tell you their despair, and implore your pity. It is a father and mother who beseech your Majesty to pardon an unfortunate son for an attempt whereof he has been guilty. We are poor, even in indigence, but we are honest. Neither of us has ever failed in our duty. Our child who has committed this fearful crime is an innocent lad, acted on by evil incitements. They have taken advantage of his inexperience, but he understands now the character of his act, and weeps with us and implores pardon."[44] The British monarchy's reaction to this plea is unknown, as is the veracity of the claims made about Sipido's contrition and weeping.

Sipido's trial proved divisive throughout Europe, so much so that a member of the Brussels legal bar, a Dr. Speyer (no first name provided), was moved to compose an account for the *Journal of the Society of Comparative Legislation*.[45] Following an earlier appeal to a lower court, La Chambre du Conseil (in which bail was rejected), the Belgian high court, La Chambre des Mises en Accusation, opened the trial of Sipido, Meert, Peuchot, and Meire on 2 July 1900. Sitting in judgment of Sipido and his peers was a panel of three judges. The primary defense of the accused was that the supposed assassination attempt was nothing more than a practical joke that had gone too far. According to the defense testimony, Meert, Peuchot, and Meire had made a wager with Sipido that he would not attempt to claim the life of the future king of England, and, in pursuit of a five-franc bet, Meire had helped Sipido secure a defective revolver for 3.5 francs. This explanation was coupled with the defense that, as Sipido was under the age of sixteen at the time of the attempted assault, he could not be held legally culpable for his actions. Disregarding the assailant's professed motives, his defenders sought to paint him as driven by little more than youthful overexuberance. The representatives of the Belgian public prosecutor's office took a rather different slant, claiming that Sipido had, with malice aforethought and consideration, deliberately attempted to assassinate the Prince of Wales, an act for which he should be held responsible.

Perhaps owing to the pro–Boer feeling that was endemic throughout much of Europe, or perhaps owing to the youth of the defendants, the outcome of this trial was quite different from what typically happened supposed Anarchists faced prosecution. The jury in the case, after only two hours of deliberation, found that the evidence against Meert, Peuchot, and Meire was limited. If convicted, they could have faced sentences of up to fifteen years, but the jury judged that the three months the young men had spent in prison awaiting trial were to be punishment enough. For Sipido, who was fifteen at the time of the attempted assassination, it was determined that he had acted without criminal discernment, and thus he could not be held responsible for his actions. During a historical period in which assassination attempts against serving or future heads of state by Anarchists and Socialists almost always led to either lengthy spells of imprisonment or a brief meeting with an executioner, Sipido had successfully avoided either outcome. His punishment was that he would be interred either in a reformatory or in the Belgian army until he reached the age of twenty-one. To facilitate this proposed solution, Sipido was allowed to leave the custody of the courts to return home for three days under police supervision to say his farewells and gather materials for his coming sentence.

As can be imagined, the British reaction to this highly unusual judgment was far from muted. The press decried the judgment as showing leniency toward radicals. A popular viewpoint of the time was echoed only a few years later by Brodhurst in his assertion that "leniency to an anarchist is like tenderness to a mad bull."[46] The verdict of the Belgian jury even found its way into the British Houses of Parliament with a pointed exchange between Arthur Balfour (who was then in charge of the Foreign Office and First Lord of the Treasury, and who would later become prime minister of a Conservative/Unionist coalition government) and a U.S.-born Conservative Member of Parliament, Sir Ellis Ashmead-Bartlett:

ASHMEAD-BARTLETT: "I beg to ask the First Lord of the Treasury whether Her Majesty's Government made any representations to the Belgian Government in consequence of the result of the trial of the Anarchist Sipido, what was the nature of such representations, and what reply was received from the Belgian Government?"

BALFOUR: "Her Majesty's Government have informed the Belgian Government that they consider the result of the proceedings in connection with Sipido to be a grave and most unfortunate miscarriage of justice, and that they have learned with great surprise and regret that the Belgian Government did not see fit to detain Sipido pending a decision as to the course they should take in view of the verdict of the jury. The Belgian Government have not yet replied."[47]

By modern standards, such an exchange may seem subdued, but a senior representative of a government openly accusing a friendly foreign state of perpetuating a miscarriage of justice was quite significant.

In the British press, the Sipido verdict prompted a more openly hostile response. In an illustration that appeared in the British periodical *Punch* on 15 August 1900, titled "The Stain on the Belgian Flag," before a flag labeled "The Acquittal of Sipido" there stood a muscular, long-haired, wild-eyed, snarling youth shooting a revolver. For many members of the political and media classes, the dismissal of charges against Sipido's fellow defendants and the seemingly inconsequential results of the prosecution against the would-be assassin of a future king were certainly not in keeping with the typical sentences imposed throughout the rest of Europe in response to the threats posed by propaganda of the deed.

Following the imposition of the sentence, Sipido, rather than contritely volunteering to be imprisoned, engaged in actions that would further upset the British. Although his actions during his brief visit home were supposedly being observed closely by the Belgian police, he managed to slip from their grasp. This may have been due to the tacit approval of a state that was largely opposed to the British aggression in South Africa, or it could have been that those officers assigned to such supervision soft-heartedly assumed that Sipido would be making tearful farewells to his family, and nothing more. Instead, Sipido fled across the Belgian border toward France.

News of Sipido's escape emerged on 7 July; however, more details were forthcoming later in the month. As revealed by *Reynolds Newspaper*,[48] Sipido arrived in Paris on Sunday, 8 July. Upon arriving in the French capital, he made his way to the home of his uncle, who resided in the Batignolles quarter and made his living as an artisan cabinet maker; Sipido supposedly intended to learn the trade. As reported in the Belgian *Reforme* newspaper, the authorities commenced proceedings against the gendarmes at the court, who, as it transpired, had allowed Sipido to leave despite having no orders to that effect. According to the available reports, the Belgian authorities claimed that they could not arrest Sipido, as his case could still be lodged for appeal during the three days of his bail, and during that interval he was free from prosecution.[49] The Belgian legal comedy of errors continued when it was also reported that the authorities had established watches for the teenage fugitive at border train crossings as of 13 July, even though it was known that he was already in France, safely ensconced in his uncle's lodgings.

Sipido did not have much time in which to enjoy his tenure as an apprentice cabinet maker; as reported by the *New York Times*,[50] he was arrested by French authorities at his uncle's home on 26 October. According to the same report, Sipido had not spent his entire time in Paris constructing cabinets; he had allied himself with Anarchists in the capital and joined in a number of demonstrations. He also resisted the arresting police but was quickly subdued. In most histories of Sipido, this is where the story closes, and, indeed, for many he has served only as a footnote. As Charles Whibley states, "The attack made in Brussels upon the Prince of Wales might have been a tragedy; it was a solemn farce, and the foolish Sipido's preposterous adventure is only memorable because it reminds us that Anarchy is still a genuine danger to the state."[51] Sipido's youthful attack against the Prince of Wales, however, is arguably of great relevance when considering propaganda of the deed.

As detailed elsewhere in this book, the state's typical response to attacks against it was not only repressive but also downright brutal. Many of the individuals examined in this publication ended their days in miserable conditions either within prison cells or upon the executioner's block. The overarching attitude toward Anarchists, Socialists, or any individual or group concerned with addressing the pronounced social and economic disparities of the late nineteenth and early twentieth centuries was negative. Indeed, the same author who described Sipido's assassination attempt as a solemn farce also described Anarchists thus: "the Anarchist, then, is a ruffian of feeble brain and weak inclination, who is pursued by a spirit of restless discontent."[52] Such a response was not uncommon, and in many cases retaliation against Anarchists was considerably more vociferous and, in all likelihood, deadly. All of this causes one to wonder why Sipido was spared and allowed to seek refuge with his uncle in a separate jurisdiction for several months. One answer may lie in his youth, but youth of itself was no defense. During a time period when life expectancies (especially for the urban poor) were exceedingly low, and working lives began early and involved backbreaking labor, the notion that such sentimentalism would exist in the courts appointed to try a potential assassin seems implausible. As detailed in this chapter, at the time of the incident at Brussel-Noord, Britain was engaged in a conflict that much of the world opposed, and Sipido's actions may have been a reaction to British atrocities in the Boer War. However, even if the majority of the Belgian populace was sympathetic to his position, it is not likely that the courts would be swayed by such considerations. Even more astonishing is the ease of Sipido's escape. At the time of his release on bail, he had been tried and found guilty of an assassination attempt against one of the most public figures in Europe. He had also refused to ask for clemency, and he failed to express a sense of guilt. And yet Sipido could blithely wander from the custody of the Belgian courts and seek refuge with family members in another country. The Belgian state's reaction (or lack thereof) to Sipido's case remains a source of great fascination. Typically Anarchist assassins received a far more brutal end, regardless of the success or failure of their attempts. The lighter punishment meted out to Sipido may be indicative of an enlightened Belgian response to jurisprudence (which might be disputed by Anarchists such as Victor Dave who were forced to leave Belgium) or perhaps of the selective application of justice. If the response was selective, this raises a host of questions that need serious examination and consideration beyond the scope of this book.

Sipido's actions are typically compressed into his failed attempt on the life of the Prince of Wales. In many examinations of early political violence, Sipido becomes a background figure, and he largely remains unknown. It is impossible to determine whether the actions of the prospective teenage assassin were inspired by a foolish bet or genuine political convictions. However, given Sipido's economic background, his association with groups at the Maison du Peuple, and his reported activities in Paris, it seems likely that, at least on some level, Sipido was inspired by propaganda of the deed. As such, his actions, motivations, and history are worthy of further investigation by scholars.

Just as with the start of his life, little is known of the events that occurred following Sipido's arrest. He did spend several years in prison for his attempt to kill the Prince of Wales, as well as his subsequent (and politically embarrassing) escape. Following his release, Sipido found work as the technical and commercial director of the General Society of Belgian Socialist Cooperatives, a position that may lend credence to the theory that his earlier actions were prompted by politics rather than wagers. Sipido died peacefully on 20 August 1959, aged seventy-five. Regarding the activities and relationships in which Sipido was involved between the ages of twenty-one and seventy-five, history largely remains silent. One clue, however, can be found in a genealogical website detailing the history of the Demunter family.[53] Several details appear incorrect, but this resource shows that a Julie Demunter, who was born on 5 July 1881, married a warehouseman by the name of Jean-Baptiste Victor Sipido, who was born on 28 December 1884 (rather than the assumed birthdate of 20 December), in Brussels on 2 May 1908. It cannot be said with any certainty whether this man was the same person as Prince Edward's would-be assassin. However, it is known that Sipido was one of the few to be actively involved in propaganda of the deed activities (to the point of attempting to assassinate a head of state) who went on to live a long life and die a peaceful death at an advanced age. For this reason alone, Sipido should be the subject of greater examination than the typical paragraph he and his actions as a teenager often receive.

Although the cases of Sipido and Zamboni are very different, they highlight similar themes. Both teenagers were accused of attempting to carry out politically motivated assassinations—acts that, to many modern readers, may seem abhorrent. In Zamboni's case, he may have been an active participant or an unwitting dupe; as for Sipido, he may or may not have been politically motivated—given the dearth of available evidence, there is no way to be sure. The fate of Zamboni, although it occurred during the early part of the twentieth century, seems more in keeping with the punitive measures imposed on older Anarchists during the nineteenth century (and, indeed, even into the twentieth century). Sipido, by comparison, seems to have escaped mostly unscathed (barring his brief imprisonment). Sadly, both teenagers have faded into the shadows of history and serve as little more than footnotes in most discussions of Anarchist propaganda of the deed. This is arguably an egregious disservice to history and a fuller understanding of the motivations of political violence. Although many scholars have focused upon the activities of older proponents of propaganda of the deed, few (if any) have focused significant attention on either Sipido or Zamboni. The histories of these teenagers remain largely obscured, and it is this very obscurity that fails to allow for a deeper understanding of their actions. It is hoped that this brief examination will allow others to dissect these histories and the disparate reactions of the state that impacted so differentially upon both young men.

Bella ciao

This morning I awakened
Bella Ciao Bella Ciao Bella Ciao Ciao Ciao (*Good-bye beautiful*)
This morning I awakened
And I found the invader
Oh partisan carry me away
Bella Ciao Bella Ciao Bella Ciao Ciao Ciao
Oh partisan carry me away
Because I feel death approaching

And if I die as a partisan
Bella Ciao Bella Ciao Bella Ciao Ciao Ciao
And if I die as a partisan
Then you must bury me
Bury me up in the mountain
Bella Ciao Bella Ciao Bella Ciao Ciao Ciao
Bury me up in the mountain
Under the shade of a beautiful flower
And all those who shall pass
Bella Ciao Bella Ciao Bella Ciao Ciao Ciao
And all those who shall pass
Will tell you what a beautiful flower it is
This is the flower of the partisan
Bella Ciao Bella Ciao Bella Ciao Ciao Ciao
This is the flower of the partisan
Who died for Freedom
This is the flower of the partisan
Who died for Freedom

Chapter Notes

Preface

1. Mark Twain, *The Wit and Wisdom of Mark Twain: A Book of Quotations*, Dover Publishing, 1998, 22.
2. Carlo Pisacane, *Political Testament in Anarchism: A Documentary History of Libertarian Ideas*, Vol. One, Robert Graham (editor), Black Rose Books, 2004, 68.

Chapter One

1. In Paul Avrich, *Anarchist Portraits*, Princeton University Press, 1990, 13, it is revealed that Cleaver "fell in love" with the words of Nechayev.
2. Milorad M. Drachkovitch (editor), *The Revolutionary Internationals, 1864–1943*, Stanford University Press, 1966, 63.
3. The Catechism is included in full as part of this publication.
4. David C. Rapoport (editor), *Terrorism: Critical Concepts in Political Science Vol. 1*, Routledge, 2004, 92.
5. *Ibid.*, 92.
6. Anna Schur, *Wages of Evil: Dostoevsky and Punishment*, Northwestern University Press, 2013, 27.
7. Steve Phillips, *Lenin and the Russian Revolution*, Heinemann, 2000, 7.
8. Many of the biographical details of Khalturins' life are drawn from *The Great Soviet Encyclopedia*, 3rd Edition. S.v. "Khalturin, Stepan Nikolaevich." http://encyclopedia2.thefreedictionary.com/Khalturin%2c+Stepan+Nikolaevich [accessed November 2016].
9. Alexander Polunov, *Russia in the Nineteenth Century: Autocracy, Reform, and Social Change 1814–1914*, Routledge, 2005, 89.
10. Robert Eugene Johnson, *Peasant and Proletarian: The Working Class of Moscow in the Late Nineteenth Century*, Rutgers University Press, 1979, 101.
11. Bruce Lincoln, *Sunlight at Midnight: St. Petersburg and the Rise of Modern Russia*, Basic Books, 2009.
12. Trudy Ring and Noelle Watson (editors), *Northern Europe: International Dictionary of Historic Places*, Vol. 2, Routledge, 1995, 657.
13. Barbara Alpern Engel and Clifford N. Rosenthal (editors), *Five Sisters: Women Against the Tsar*, Routledge, 1987, 47.
14. Claudia Verhoeven, *Time of Terror, Terror of Time: On the Impatience of Russian Revolutionary Terrorism (Early 1860–Early 1880s)*, Jahrbücher Für Geschichte Osteuropas (Yearbooks for The History of Eastern Europe) 58, 2010, 254–273.
15. Lee B. Croft, *Nikolai Ivanovich Kibalchich: Terrorist Rocket Pioneer*, Institute for Issues in the History of Science, 2006, 70.
16. Richard S. Wortman, *Scenarios of Power: Myth and Ceremony in Russian Monarchy from Peter the Great to the Abdication of Nicholas II*, Princeton University Press, 2006, 237.
17. Lynne Ann Hartnett, *The Defiant Life of Vera Figner: Surviving the Russian Revolution*, Indiana University Press, 2014, 126.
18. Andrew M. Drozd, *Chernyshevskii's "What is to be Done?" A Reevaluation*, Northwestern University Press, 2001, 10.
19. Avrahm Yarmolinsky, *Road to Revolution*, Princeton University Press, 2014, 135.
20. Walter G. Moss, *A History of Russia Vol. 1: To 1917*, Anthem Press, 2003, 434.
21. Yarmolinsky, 138.
22. *Ibid.*
23. Anthony Anemone, *Just Assassins: The Culture of Terrorism in Russia*, Northwestern University Press, 2010, 9.
24. Peter Kropotkin, *Memoirs of a Revolutionist*, Dover Publications, 2014, 518.
25. Yarmolinsky, 136.
26. Adam B. Ulam, *Prophets and Conspirators in Pre-revolutionary Russia*, Transaction Publishers, 1998, 158.
27. Paul Avrich, *Anarchist Portraits*, Princeton University Press, 1990, 35.
28. Yarmolinsky, 138.
29. *Ibid.*
30. Ana Siljak, *Angel of Vengeance: The Girl Who Shot the Governor of St. Petersburg and Sparked the Age of Assassination*, 2009, St. Martin's Press, 79.
31. John Van der Kiste, *The Romanovs: 1818–1959*, The History Press, 1980.
32. Yarmolinsky, 139.
33. Geoffrey A. Hosking, *Russia: People and Empire, 1552–1917*, Harvard University Press, 1997, 347.
34. Yarmolinsky, 140.
35. *Ibid.*, 141.

Chapter Two

1. Bernard Thomas, *Alexandre Jacob: Sailor, Thief, Anarchist, Convict (1879–1954)*, Vol. I, Ardent Press, 40.
2. *Ibid.*, 41.
3. "Il Y Prit Goût Et Sombra Dans L'alcoolisme," Jean-Marc Delpech, Parcours et Reseaux D'un Anarchiste: Alexandre Marius Jacob 1879–1954, Doctoral Thesis, Department of History, University of Nancy, 2006, 19.

4. Richard Parry, *The Bonnot Gang: The Story of the French Illegalists* (2nd Edition), PM Press, 2016.

5. Dr Stephen Gapps, *Australian Pirate Tales*. Signals 97 (Dec 2011–Feb 2012, accessible from the Australian Maritime Museum website, https://anmm.wordpress.com/2014/01/13/australian-pirate-tales/ [accessed December 2016].

6. Alain Sergent, *Un anarchiste de la Belle Epoque: Alexandre Marius Jacob*, Les Editions Libertaires, 24.

7. Thomas, 62.

8. Herbert Butterfield, *The Historical Novel*, Cambridge University Press, 2012, 88.

9. Doug Imrie, "The Illegalists," *Anarchy: A Journal Of Desire Armed*, Fall–Winter, 1994–95.

10. Delpech, 47.

11. Thomas, 133–142.

12. Delpech, 62.

13. Thomas, 147.

14. *Ibid.*, 160.

15. Alexandre Jacob, "l'honnête cambrioleur," http://www.atelierdecreationlibertaire.com/alexandre-jacob [accessed January 2017].

16. George Woodcock, *Anarchism: A History Of Libertarian Ideas And Movements*, Meridian Books, 1961, 214.

17. Marius Jacob, *Why I Was a Burglar*, 1905, as quoted in Jean Maitron, Histoire du mouvement anarchiste en France. Paris, Societé universitaire d'editions et de librairie, 1951.

18. Delpech, 122.

19. *Ibid.*, 77.

20. French National Archives, BB18 2261A, File 2069A03, Amiens, April 23 1903.

21. Ephéméride Anarchiste, 29 mars, http://www.ephemanar.net/mars29.html [accessed January 2017].

22. Clément Duval (translator: Michael Shreve), *Outrage: An Anarchist Memoir of the Penal Colony*, PM Press, 2012, 16.

23. Paul Albert, *An Anarchist on Devil's Island*, KSL: Bulletin of the Kate Sharpley Library No. 13, 1997.

24. Marianne Enckell, *Clément Duval Corrections*, KSL: Bulletin of the Kate Sharpley Library No. 14, 1998.

25. Paul Z. Simons, *Illegalism: Why Pay for a Revolution on the Installment Plan…When You Can Steal One?*, Modern Slavery: The Libertarian Critique of Civilization, Fall–Winter 2013–2014.

26. Alexandra Skirna (translator: Paul Sharkey), *Facing the Enemy: A History of Anarchist Organisation from Proudhon to May 1968*, AK Press, 2002, 289.

27. Bibliography for Internationaal Instituut voor Sociale Geschiedenis (International Review of Social History), Vol. 58, Issue 3, 2013, 549–581.

28. Richard Parry, *The Bonnot Gang: The Story of The French Illegalists* (2nd ed), PM Press, 2016.

29. Paul Avrich, *Sacco and Vanzetti: The Anarchist Background*, Princeton University Press, New Ed edition, 1996, 98.

30. Clément Duval, A Letter from Mazas Prison, October 24 1886, retrieved from https://theanarchistlibrary.org/library/clement-duval-a-letter-from-clement-duval [accessed January 2017].

31. More details of Mazas can be found at http://ecrits-vains.com/ballades/balade16/balade16.htm (French) [accessed January 2017], Les balades parisiennes de l'Oncle Jérôme: Seizième balade Autour de la Bastille, Michel Ostertag.

32. Albert, *An Anarchist on Devil's Island*.

33. Alvan Francis Sanborn, *Paris and the Social Revolution: A Study of the Revolutionary Elements in the Various Classes of Parisian Society*, Hutchinson, 1905, 28.

34. Maxine Arnold Vogely, *A Proust Dictionary*, Whitston Publishing Co., Inc, 1981, 519.

35. Victor Serge (Translator: Mitchell Abidor), *Anarchists Never Surrender: Essays, Polemics, and Correspondence on Anarchism, 1908–1938*, PM Press, 2015, 16.

36. Duval, 194.

37. Ce n'fut pas Toujours Croquignol, a Batignolles… (French) http://www.parisrevolutionnaire.com/spip.php?article2717 [accessed January 2017].

38. Duval, 7.

39. Albert, *An Anarchist on Devil's Island*.

40. Duval, 7.

41. Albert, *An Anarchist on Devil's Island*.

42. Duval, 10.

43. Albert, *An Anarchist on Devil's Island*.

44. Robert Hunter, *Violence and the Labour Movement*, MacMillan, 1914, 77.

45. *Ibid.*, 78.

46. René Belbenoît, *Dry Guillotine: Fifteen Years Among the Living Dead*, Blue Ribbon Books, 1938.

47. Paul Simpson, *The Mammoth Book of Prison Escapes*, Running Press, 2013.

48. Cesare Lombroso, *Gli Anarchici, Fratelli Bocca*, 1895, 42–43.

49. Collezioni Digitali Biblioteca Franco Serantini, http://bfscollezionidigitali.org/index.php/Detail/Object/Show/object_id/1800 [accessed February 2017].

50. Nunzio Pernicone, *Italian Anarchism 1864–1892*, AK Press, 2009, 240.

51. *Ibid.*

52. *Il Ciclone* (Paris), September 4 1887.

53. Pietro Paola, *The Knights Errant of Anarchy: London and the Italian Anarchist Diaspora (1880–1917)*, Oxford University Press, 2013, 59.

54. Doug Imrie, "The Illegalists," *Anarchy: A Journal Of Desire Armed*, Fall-Winter, 1994–95.

Chapter Three

1. Gordon Martel, *Origins of the First World War* (Third Edition), Routledge, 2008, 20.

2. Ernest A.Vizetelly, *The Anarchists: Their Faith and Their Record*, Turnbull and Spears Printers, Edinburgh, 1911.

3. Christlieb G. Hottinger, "The Assassination Attempt Against the German Kaiser Wilhelm," *Volksblatt*, no. 20, 153–155.

4. *Ibid.*

5. Max Schütte, "August Reinsdorf and the Niederwald Conspiracy." An historical account of the planned attack against the Imperial Court train on 28 September 1883, the trial and the execution of the condemned (New Life Magazine, 1983.)

6. Hugo Friedländer, *Das Dynamit-Attentat bei der Enthüllungsfeier des Niederwald-Denkmals*, interesting crime processes of cultural and historical significance, 1911–1921, Vol. 4,1911, Berlin.

7. Der Anarchisten-Prozess: Reinsdorf und Genossen verhandelt vor dem 2. und 3. Strafsenat des Reichsgerichts zu Leipzig vom 15 bis 22 December 1884, Vierte Auflage, S. Werner.

Chapter Four

1. Giuseppe Galzerano, *Giovanni Passannante, La vita, l'attentato, il processo, la condanna a morte, la grazia 'regale' e gli anni di galera del cuoco lucano che nel 1878 ruppe l'incantesimo monarchico*, Galzerano editore, Casalvelino Scalo, 2004, 116.

2. *Ibid.*, 118.

3. *Ibid.*

4. Stefano Recchia and Nadia Urbinati, *A Cosmopolitanism of Nations*; Princeton University Press, 2009, 6.

5. Interview with Karl Marx, head of L'Internationale, R. Landor, *New York World*, 18 July 1871, reprinted Woodhull & Claflin's Weekly, 12 August 1871, http://www.hartford-hwp.com/archives/26/020.html [accessed October 2016].

6. Robert Pearce, Andrina Stiles, *The Unification of Italy*, Third Edition, Hodder Murray, 2006.

7. Biographical details of Melillo are scarce, however he does merit in an entry in the Biographical Archive Labor Movement, http://www.archiviobiografi-comovimentooperaio.org/index.php?option=com_k2&view=item&id=26125:melillo-matteo-maria&lang=it [accessed October 2016].

8. Galzerano, 305.

9. Raffaele De Cesare, *The Last Days of Papal Rome*. Archibald Constable & Co., 1909, 444.

10. This is referenced in *Freniatria e di Medicina legale in relazione con l'antropologia e le scienze giuridiche e sociali*, V, 1879, 176.

11. Christopher Duggan, *The Force of Destiny: A History of Italy Since 1796*, Penguin, 2008, 307.

12. Denis Mack Smith, *Italy and Its Monarchy*, Yale University Press, 1989, 71.

13. Nunzio Pernicone, *Italian Anarchism 1864–1892*, AK Press, 2009, 148.

14. Galzerano, 32.

15. *Ibid.*, 396 and Dibattimento svoltosi innanzi alla Corte Ordinaria d'Assisie [sic] di Napoli, Napoli 1879, 83.

16. George Boardman Taylor, *Italy and the Italians*, America Baptist Publication Society, 1898, 88.

17. Untitled article, *Aberdeen Press and Journal*, 23 November 1878, 3.

18. Piero Bianconi, *Pascoli*, Morcelliana, 1935, 26.

19. Galzerano, 27.

20. David Stafford, *From Anarchism to Reformism: A Study of the Political Activities of Paul Brousse*, 1870–90, Weidenfeld & Nicolson, 1971.

21. Pernicone, 150.

22. Galzerano, 120.

23. *Ibid.*, 500.

24. *Ibid.*, 642.

25. Giovanni Rosadi, *Tra la perduta gente*, Firenze 1908, 313.

26. Salvia was renamed by a Royal decree on 3 July 1879, following a contrite visitation to the King by the then major Giovanni Parrella.

27. For more details of this protest, refer to Pernicone, 261–263.

28. Nunzio Pernicone, "The Case of Pietro Acciarito: Accomplices, Psychological Torture, and 'Raison D'état.'" *Journal for the Study of Radicalism*, vol. 5, no. 1, 2011, 67–104. This remains perhaps the fullest and most seminal document concerning a largely undocumented life.

29. *Ibid.*, 75.

30. *Ibid.*, 81.

31. *Ibid.*, 84.

32. *New York Times*, 28 April 1898, "Bread riots in Bari."

33. *New York Times*, 9 May 1898, "Italy Verging on Anarchy; Bread Rioters in Milan Throw Tiles from the Roofs on the Heads of the Soldiers, Who Retire; 300 Killed And 1,000 Injured."

34. "Continuano I Disordini a Milano," *Corriere della Sera*, 9 May 1898.

35. Brescis' father was the owner of a small farm and a three story house, according to accounts available from http://paolomarzi.blogspot.com/2016/11/gaetano-bresci-un-regicida-nella-valle.html [accessed November 2016].

36. http://www.150.comune.prato.it/?act=i&fid=4481&id=20110221094107640 [accessed November 2016].

37. Candace Falk, *Emma Goldman: A Documentary History of the American Years Made for America*, 1890–1901, University of Illinois Press, 2008, 520.

38. Arrigo Petacco, *L'anarchico che venne dall'America*, Mondadori, 1970.

39. This information is drawn from New York, Passenger Lists, 1820–1957.

40. According to http://www.24emilia.com/Sezione.jsp?titolo=Ernestina+e+Gaetano+Bresci&idSezione=53898 [accessed November 2016] Bresci had a number of acquaintances settled in New Jersey by the time he stepped from the boat, including Nicholas Quintavalle, Antonio Laner, Gino Magnolfi, Mario Grisoni and Pasquale Residao, who he may have known from his exile on Lampedusa.

41. Although some sources claim that Bresci and Kneiland were married, it seems more likely given the politics of Bresci that they were actually co-habiting lovers and companions.

42. Later developments are charted in Paterson's Italian Anarchist Silk Workers and the Politics of Race by Salvatore Salerno available from https://theanarchistlibrary.org/library/salvatore-salerno-paterson-s-italian-anarchist-silk-workers-and-the-politics-of-race [accessed November 2016].

43. *New York Times*, 31 July 1900, "Assassin's Lot Fell Upon Anarchist Here; Gaetano Bresci, the King's Murderer, Lived in Paterson," 1.

44. Richard Bach Jensen, *The Battle against Anarchist Terrorism: An International History 1878–1934*, Cambridge University Press, 2014, 190.

45. Petacco, 33.

46. *Ibid.*, 91, also cited in Jensen, 191.

47. Still on display in the Museo Criminologico in Rome.

48. Jensen, 198.

49. As quoted at http://www.andreagaddini.it/Bresci.html [accessed November 2016].

50. *New York Times*, 24 May 1901, "Bresci Commits Suicide; Murderer of King Humbert Hangs Himself in Prison."

51. Jensen, 191.

Chapter Five

1. Jonas Lippmann, "Ravachol, King of the Anarchists," *New York Times*, 29 June 1919, 82.

2. Details of Ravachols' family are available from Nigel McCrery, *Silent Witnesses*, Arrow, 2014, 18–20.

3. Eugène Sue, *The Wandering Jew* (6 vols.), John C. Nimmo, 1903.

4. John M. Merriman, *The Dynamite Club: How a Bombing in Fin-de-Siècle Paris Ignited the Age of Modern Terror*, Yale University Press, 2009, 70.

5. *Le Gaulois*, 13 July 1892; also quoted in Mitchell Abidor, *Death to Bourgeois Society: The Propagandists of the Deed*, PM Press, 2016.
6. Part of Ravachols' statement, provided in this book.
7. Ernest Alfred Vizetelly, *The Anarchists: Their Faith and Their Record*. Turnbull and Spears Printers, Edinburgh, 1911, 106–127.
8. *Ibid.*, 113.
9. Charles Sowerwine, *France Since 1870: Culture, Society and the Making of the Republic*, Palgrave Macmillan, 2009, 71.
10. Vizetelly, 116.
11. René Dumas, *Ravachol: l'homme rouge de l'anarchie* (Ravachol, The Red Man of Anarchy), Saint-Etienne, Le Hénaff, 1981, 41.
12. As referenced on http://www.atelierdecreationlibertaire.com/alexandre-jacob/2012/04/ravachol/ [accessed March 2017].
13. Henry Brodribb Irving, Studies of French Criminals of the Nineteenth Century, William Heinemann, 1901, 318, Vizetelly, and numerous other sources.
14. Walter Laqueur, *The Terrorism reader: A Historical Anthology*, New American Library, 1978, 97.
15. Robert Hunter, *Violence and the Labour Movement*, MacMillan, 1914, 80.
16. Merriman, 80.
17. Vizetelly, 124.
18. The execution of Ravachol is detailed in "Ravachol Put to Death," *New York Times*, 12 July 1892, 9.
19. As quoted by Tuchman, in Barbara W. Tuchman, *The Proud Tower: A Portrait of the World before the War, 1890–1914*, Bantam, 1965, 79.
20. Hunter, 81.
21. Alex Butterworth, *The World that Never Was: A True Story of Schemers, Anarchists, and Secret Agents*, The Bodley Head, 2010, 304.

Chapter Six

1. *New York Times*, 6 February 1894, *The Guillotine's Sure Work: Details of the Execution of Vaillant, the Anarchist*, 1.
2. Charles Malato, "Some Anarchist Portraits", *Fortnightly Review* 333, New Series, 1 Sept 1894, 327–328.
3. John M. Merriman, *The Dynamite Club: How a Bombing in Fin-de-Siècle Paris Ignited the Age of Modern Terror*, Yale University Press, 2009, 137.
4. "Des Militants Anarchistes, Vaillant, Auguste," https://militants-anarchistes.info/spip.php?article12847 [accessed March 2017].
5. Malato, 327.
6. Ernest.A. Vizetelly, "The Anarchists: Their Faith and Their Record," Turnbull and Spears Printers, Edinburgh, 1911, 146.
7. *Ibid.*
8. *New York Times*, 11 Dec 1893, "The Bomb Thrower Found: Auguste Vaillant Confesses," 1.
9. Merriman, 138.
10. *New York Times*, 11 Dec 1893, "The Bomb Thrower Found: Auguste Vaillant Confesses," 1.
11. *Ibid.*
12. Bernard Thomas, *Les Provocations Policiéres*, Fayard, 1972.
13. Clyde Thogmartin, *The National Daily Press of France*, Summa Publications, 1998, 97.

14. As detailed in *New York Times*, 11 Jan 1894, Vaillant's Doom Pronounced, 5.
15. Vizetelly, 153.
16. As reported in *New York Times*, 14 Feb 1894, Vaillant's Grave Guarded, 5.
17. *New York Times*, May 21 1894, "The Guillotine's Sure Work," 1.
18. Paul Avrich, *Anarchist Portraits*, Princeton University Press, 1990, 85.
19. Johann Hari, "Blood, Rage & History," *The Independent* (London, UK), 12 Oct 2009, 2.
20. Émile Henry Defence Speech as published Gazette des Tribunaux, April 1894 and included in this publication.
21. As detailed by John Harland Hicks and Robert Tucker, *Revolution and Reaction: The Paris Commune 1871*, University of Massachusetts Press, 1973.
22. Merriman, 27.
23. Colette E. Wilson, *Paris and the Commune, 1871–78: The Politics of Forgetting*, Manchester University Press, 2007, 9.
24. Merriman, 29.
25. Daniel Guerin, *No Gods, No Masters: An Anthology of Anarchism*, AK Press, 2006, 395.
26. Malato, 328.
27. As detailed in Jean Maitron, *Ravachol Et Les Anarchistes*, Paris, Julliard, 1964.
28. Merriman, 34.
29. Malato, 328.
30. Ernest Alfred Vizetelly, *The Anarchists: Their Faith and Their Record*, Edinburgh: Turnbull & Spears Printers, 1911, 158.
31. Jules Bertaut, Paris 1870–1935, Vincent Press, 2007 131.
32. A thorough overview of the coal miners dispute of 1892, and the impact upon the Socialist Deputy, Jean Jaurès is provided by Harvey Goldberg, "Jaurès and the Carmaux Strikes: The Coal Strike of 1892," *The American Journal of Economics and Sociology*, January 1958, Vol. 17, Issue 2, 167–178.
33. Merriman, 102.
34. Hermja Oliver, *The International Anarchist Movement in Late Victorian London*, Palgrave Macmillan, 1983, 84.
35. *Ibid.*, 124.
36. A former member of the Royal Netherlands East Indies Army (in which he spent five years in the brig), and later activist and newspaper editor, Cohen was sentenced for treason in his native Holland for shouting at William III, before fleeing from the Netherlands and being expelled from Belgium and France before his arrival in London in 1893.
37. Deaglan O'Donghaile, *Blasted Literature: Victorian Political Fiction and the Shock of Modernism*, Edinburgh University Press, 2014, 148.
38. Merriman, 146.
39. Jean-Denis Bredin, Thierry Lévy, Plutôt la mort que l'injustice: au temps des procès anarchistes (Rather, death than injustice: at the time of anarchist trials), Editions Odile Jacob, 2009, 181.
40. The Courtroom Testimony of Émile Henry translated by Mitchell Abidor in Death to Bourgeois Society: The Propagandists of the Deed, PM Press, 2016.
41. As referenced by Merriman, 150, and in the Courtroom Testimony.
42. Merriman, 188.
43. The Courtroom Testimony of Émile Henry translated by Mitchell Abidor in Death to Bourgeois Society: The Propagandists of the Deed, PM Press, 2016.

44. *New York Times*, 16 Feb 1894, Vast Anarchist Conspiracy, 5.

45. Émile Henry Defence Speech included as part of this publication.

46. *New York Times*, 29 Apr 1894, "Henry Sentenced to Death," 5.

47. *New York Times*, 23 May 1894, "Died Before The Knife Fell," 5.

48. *New York Times*, 25 Jun 1894, "Scene in the Theatre," 1.

49. Eugen Weber, *France: Fin de Siècle*, Belknap Press of Harvard University Press, 1988, 113.

50. Merriman, 149.

51. *New York Times*, Jun 25 1894, "Carnot Killed," 1.

52. Biographical details of Sante Geronimo Caserio drawn from Biblioteca Autónoma Sante Geronimo Caserio (an autonomous Anarchist library collective in Santiago, Chile named after Caserio), https://bibliotecasantecaserio.wordpress.com/sante [accessed March 2017].

53. Fausto Buttà, *Living Like Nomads: The Milanese Anarchist Movement Before Fascism*, Cambridge Scholars Publishing, 2015, 37.

54. http://bfscollezionidigitali.org/index.php/Detail/Object/Show/object_id/1011 [accessed March 2017].

55. Emma Goldman, *Living My Life*, Cosimo Classics, 2011, 150.

56. *New York Times*, Aug 3, 1894, "Santo Caserio and his Crime," 5.

57. P.Gori, Sante Caserio, in The Torch (London), 18 June 1895 as referenced in Sante Caserio: Assassin of French President Sadi Carnot and Avenger of Emile Henry and Auguste Vaillant, Pen & Pistol Press, 2013, 6.

58. Buttà, 38.

59. Barbara Stefanelli (Traanslator), Sante Caserio: Assassin of French President Sadi Carnot and Avenger of Emile Henry and Auguste Vaillant, Pen & Pistol Press, 2013, 7.

60. Referenced in the portrait of Caserio provided by the Franco Serantini Library, http://bfscollezionidigitali.org/index.php/Detail/Object/Show/object_id/1011 [accessed March 2017].

61. *New York Times*, Aug 3, 1894, "Santo Caserio and his Crime," 5.

62. Barbara Stefanelli (Traanslator), Sante Caserio: Assassin of French President Sadi Carnot and Avenger of Emile Henry and Auguste Vaillant, Pen & Pistol Press, 2013, 12.

63. *New York Times*, Aug 4 1894, "Caserio Sentenced to Die," 9.

64. As published in *Anarchism and Other Essays*, Dover, 1969.

65. *New York Times*, Aug 16 1894, "Caserio at the Guillotine," 1.

Chapter Seven

1. Bob James, "Larry Petrie (1859–1901)—Australian Revolutionist?" *Red & Black: An Anarchist Journal*, Summer 1978/79 retrieved from http://www.takver.com/history/petrie.htm [accessed December 2016].

2. http://www.workhouses.org.uk/Aberdeen/ [accessed December 2016].

3. Julian Rossi Ashton, *Now Came Still Evening On*, Angus & Robertson, 1941, Sydney, 133.

4. http://prov.vic.gov.au/index_search?searchid=23 [accessed December 2016].

5. *The Worker*, 14 October 1893, "The Aramac Explosion," 2.

6. National Museums Liverpool, Maritime Archives and Library, Child Emigration, http://www.liverpoolmuseums.org.uk/maritime/archive/sheet/10 [accessed December 2016].

7. F. B. Smith, "Joseph Symes and the Australasian Secular Association," *Labour History*, No. 5 (Nov., 1963), 34.

8. More details of the early days of the MAC and the American connection to Australian anarchism, including the impact of the Haymarket affair that transpire only three days after the club was founded can be found in Tom Goyens, "Anarchy at the Antipodes—Australian Anarchists and Their American Connections," Salisbury University, Maryland, presented at Australian-U.S. Comparative and Transnational Labour History Conference, 2015.

9. Refer to http://mac.anarchobase.com/ for details and current events. The MAC is active in opposing local property developers, as well as fascists of all stripes.

10. James, *Red & Black: An Anarchist Journal*, Summer 1978/79.

11. *Ibid.*

12. Christopher Lloyd, The 1890–1910 Crisis of Australian Capitalism and the Social Democratic Response: Was the Australian Model a Pioneering Regime of Social Democratic Welfare Capitalist Regulation?, 2013 Multilayered Historicity of the Present: Approaches to social science history. Haggrén, H., Raunio-Niemi, J. & Vauhkonen, J. (eds.). Helsinki: Helsinki University Press, 247.

13. An overview of KOL activities in Australia can be found in Steven Parfitt, Completing the Order's History down under: The Knights of Labor in Australia, Labour History, No. 110, May 2016.

14. S. Merrifield, The Melbourne Anarchist Club 1886–1891, Bulletin of the Australian Society for the Study of Labour History, No. 3 (Nov., 1962), 32–43.

15. Poem composed by "Wyvis," originally published in the Bulletin. Merrifield, 37.

16. *Ibid.*, 38.

17. Letter by Petrie to *The Liberator*, 26 February 1888, *Ibid.*, 41.

18. As detailed by the Maritime Union of Australia http://www.mua.org.au/1890_maritime_strike [accessed December 2016].

19. Michael Head, *Calling out the Troops: The Australian Military and Civil Unrest: The Legal and Constitutional Issues*, Federation Press, 2009, 44.

20. Bruce Scates, "Gender, Household and Community Politics: The 1890 Maritime Strike in Australia and New Zealand," *Labour History*, 61, 2006, 83–85.

21. John Grant Hannan, *The New Australia Movement, School of History, Philosophy, Religion, and Classics*, The University of Queensland, 1966.

22. *The Worker*, Saturday 14 October 1893, "The Aramac Explosion," 2.

23. Hannan, 250.

24. *Ibid.*, 251.

25. E. H. Lane, *Dawn to Dusk: Reminiscences of a Rebel*, Brisbane: William Brooks, 1939.

26. Iain McIntyre, *How To Make Trouble and Influence People*, PM Press, 2013, 58.

27. For more details refer to C.R. Hickson and J.D. Turner, "Free Banking Gone Awry: The Australian Banking Crisis of 1893," *Financial History Review* 9, 2002, 147–167.

28. As detailed in Bob James, Anarchism and State Violence in Sydney and Melbourne, 1886–1896, an argument about Australian labor history, 1986, MA Thesis held at La Trobe University Melbourne.

29. J.A. Andrews, "The Active Service Brigade, Sydney," Published in *Tocsin*, May 24, 1900, retrieved from http://www.takver.com/history/aasv/aasv_app1.htm [accessed December 2016].

30. Ibid.

31. Anne Witehead, *Paradise Mislaid: In Search of the Australian Tribe of Paraguay*, University of Queensland Press, 1998, 270.

32. James, *Red & Black: An Anarchist Journal*, Summer 1978/79.

33. *The Argus*, "Alarming Explosion on the S.S. Aramac," 29 July 1893 9.

34. *Wellington Times and Agricultural and Mining Gazette*, untitled Article, 19 Aug 1893, 2.

35. *The Bundaberg Mail and Burnett Advertiser*, "Explosion on the S.S. Aramac," 31 Jul 1893, 3.

36. Ibid.

37. *The Worker*, "The Aramac Explosion," 14 Oct 1893, 2.

38. More details of the contemporary media coverage of Petries' trial can be found in: The Week, Explosion on the Aramac, 11 August 1893, 20, The Week, Explosion on the Aramac, 18 August 1893, 10, The Week, Explosion on the Aramac, 25 August 1893, 9, and The Week, Explosion on the Aramac, 8 September 1893, 9.

39. *The Tocsin*, "Larry Petrie," 6 Jun 1901, 2.

40. Hannan, 252.

41. John Gimlette, *At The Tomb Of The Inflatable Pig: Travels through Paraguay*, Arrow; New Ed edition, 2004, 68.

42. Gavin Souter, *A Peculiar People: The Australians in Paraguay*, TBS The Book Service Ltd, 1969.

43. Anne Whitehead, *Paradise Mislaid: In Search of the Australian Tribe of Paraguay*, St. Lucia, Qld: University of Queensland Press, 1997, 333.

Chapter Eight

1. Joseph Conrad, *The Secret Agent*, Penguin Classics, 2007, 23.

2. Mary Burgoyne, "Conrad among the Anarchists: Documents on Martial Bourdin and the Greenwich Bombing," *The Conradian*, Vol. 32, No. 1, The Secret Agent: Centennial Essays (Spring 2007), 147–185.

3. *The Secret Agent: Centennial Essays*: 1 (The Conradian), Allan H. Simmons, and J. H. Stape (editors), Rodopi, 2007.

4. Paul Gibbard, "Bourdin, Martial (1867/8–1894)," *Oxford Dictionary of National Biography*, Oxford University Press, 2004; online edn, Jan 2008 [http://www.oxforddnb.com/view/article/73217, accessed September 2016].

5. Hermja Oliver, *The International Anarchist Movement in Late Victorian*, London: Palgrave Macmillan, 1983, 102.

6. Jean Maitron (editor), *Dictionnaire biographique du mouvement ouvrier franfais*, 37 vols, Paris: Editions ouvrieres, 1964–90, Te Mouvement anarchiste en France, Paris: F. Maspero, 1975.

7. Dean De La Motte (editor), Jeannene M. Przyblyski, Making the News: Modernity and the Mass Press in Nineteenth-century France (Studies in Print Culture and the History of the Book), University Massachusetts Press, 1999.

8. *The Standard*, 9 March 1894, untitled article, 3.

9. Pietro Paola, *The Knights Errant of Anarchy: London and the Italian Anarchist Diaspora (1880–1917)*, Oxford University Press, 2013, 162.

10. *The Age*, 19 Feb 1894, "Important Discoveries The Autonomie Club a 'Centre' of Anarchy," 3

11. *Reynolds Newspaper*, 7 April 1895, 4.

12. Rudolf Rocker, *The London Years*, AK Press, 2005, 67.

13. Charles Malato, *Joyeusetés de l'exil*, 99–100.

14. *The Commonweal: A Revolutionary Journal of Anarchist Communism*, Vol. 2, No. 22, Saturday March 10, 1894, 1.

15. Gibbard.

16. *The Daily Graphic*, 27 February 1894, 3.

17. *The Times* (London), 1 Jan 1892, 6, Police.

18. For more details about the life of Barlas see Philip K.Cohen, *John Evelyn Barals: A Critical Biography*, Rivendale Press, 2012.

19. Anon., "Charles, Fred, c1860–c1934," 2003, https://libcom.org/history/fred-charles [accessed September 2016].

20. John Quail, *The Slow Burning Fuse: The Lost History of the British Anarchists*, Flamingo, 1978, 108.

21. George J. Barnsby, *Socialism in Birmingham and the Black Country 1850–1939*, Integrated Publishing Services, 1977, 52.

22. Alex Butterworth, *The World that Never Was: A True Story of Schemers, Anarchists, and Secret Agents*, London: Bodley Head, 2010, 292.

23. Lindsay Clutterbuck, *An Accident of History? The Evolution of Counter-Terrorism Methodology in the Metropolitan Police from 1829 to 1901, with Particular Reference to Extreme Irish Republican Activity*, PhD Dissertation, University of Portsmouth, 2002, 317.

24. Quail, 109.

25. Further details of this police surveillance are provided in Ray Wilson and Ian Adams, *Special Branch: A History: 1883–2006*, Biteback Publishing, 2015.

26. David Nicholl, *The Walsall Anarchists: Trapped by the Police: Innocent Men in Penal Servitude: The Truth about the Walsall Plot*, LSE Selected Pamphlets, 1892.

27. *Berrow's Worcester Journal*, 9 January 1892, "Socialists Arrested at Supposed Walsall Bomb Factory," 8.

28. Nicholl, 11.

29. *The Times* (London), 30 Mar 1892, "The Walsall Anarchists' Trial," 14.

30. *Walsall Free Press and South Staffordshire Advertiser*, "The Walsall Anarchists," April 1892, [http://www.historywebsite.co.uk/articles/Walsall/anarchists.htm, accessed October 2016].

31. Olivier, 103.

32. Simon Webb, *Dynamite, Treason and Plot: Terrorism in Victorian and Edwardian England*, The History Press, 2012, 29.

33. *The Sydney Morning Herald*, 19 Feb 1894, "Designs on the Royal Arsenal," 5.

34. HO 144/257/A55660 112747 28, *The Times* (London), 20 Feb 1894, "The Greenwich Explosion."

35. HO 144/257/A55660 112747 9.

36. HO 144/257/A55660 112747 29, *The Times* (London), 24 Feb 1894, "The Inquest of Bourdin."

37. HO 144/257/A55660 112747 27, *The Times* (London), 20 Feb 1894, "The Greenwich Explosion."

38. HO 144/257/A55660 112747 28, *The Times* (London), 20 Feb 1894, "The Greenwich Explosion."

39. HO 144/257/A55660 112747 30, *The Times* (London), 24 Feb 1894, "The Inquest of Bourdin."

40. *Weekly Times & Echo: A Liberal Newspaper of Political and Social Progress*, 18 February 1894, "Fatal Bomb Explosion at Greenwich," 1.

41. HO 144/257/A55660 112747, 21.

42. *St James' Gazette*, 24 February 1894, 9.

43. Richard Bach Jensen, *The Battle against Anarchist Terrorism: An International History, 1878–1934*, Cambridge University Press, 2014, 67.

44. An exhaustive account of which is provided in Niall Whelehan, *The Dynamiters: Irish Nationalist and Political Violence in the Wider Words, 1867–1900*, Cambridge University Press, 2012.

45. HO 144/257/A55660 112747 50, *The Times* (London), 22 Feb 1894, "The Greenwich Explosion."

Chapter Nine

1. Jean Brust, *Defending Principles: Political Legacy of Bill Brust*, Mehring Books, 1993, 135.

2. Carroll D. Wright, *The Quarterly Journal of Economics*, Vol. 16, No. 1, "The National Amalgamated Association of Iron, Steel, and Tin Workers, 1892–1901," November 1901, 38.

3. Steven L. Danver, *Revolts, Protests, Demonstrations, and Rebellions in American History: An Encyclopedia*, ABC-CLIO, 2010, 640.

4. Quentin R. Skrabec, Jr., *Henry Clay Frick: The Life of The Perfect Capitalist*, McFarland, 2010, 69.

5. Merle Curti, *The Enduring Vision: A History of The American People, Vol. II: Since 1865*, Wadsworth Publishing Co Inc, 7th edition, 2010, 539.

6. Jonathan Rees, *Pennsylvania History: A Journal of Mid-Atlantic Studies*, Vol. 64, No. 4, Homestead in Context: Andrew Carnegie and the Decline of the Amalgamated Association of Iron and Steel Workers, 1997, 517.

7. Paul Krause, *The Battle for Homestead 1880–1892*, University of Pittsburgh Press, 1992, 250.

8. George Harvey, *Henry Clay Frick: The Man*, Beard Books, 1928; reprinted 2002, 177.

9. H.W. Brands, *The Reckless Decade: America In The 1890s*, University of Chicago Press, 2002, 131.

10. *Ibid.*, 132.

11. Eric Arnesen, *Encyclopedia of U.S. Labor and Working-Class History*, Routledge, 2006, 613.

12. Gina Misiroglu, *American Countercultures: An Encyclopedia of Nonconformists, Alternative Lifestyles, and Radical Ideas in U.S. History*, Routledge, 2008, 74.

13. Anna Foa, *The Jews of Europe After the Black Death*, University of California Press, 2000, 206.

14. Paul Avrich and Karen Avrich, *Sasha and Emma: The Anarchist Odyssey of Alexander Berkman and Emma Goldman*, Belknap Press, 2012, 8.

15. Arnesen, 153.

16. Emma Goldman, *A Sketch of Alexander Berkman, The Russian Tragedy (A Review and An Outlook)*, Der Syndikalist, 1922.

17. Emma Goldman, *Living My Life*, Cosimo Classics, 2011, 28.

18. Alexander Berkman, "Looking Backward and Forward," *Mother Earth*, Vol. VII, Number 10, December 1912.

19. Douwe Fokkema, *Perfect Worlds: Utopian Fiction in China and the West*, Amsterdam University Press, 2014, 212.

20. Avrich, 14.

21. Goldman, *A Sketch of Alexander Berkman*, 6.

22. Avrich, 23.

23. The Haymarket tragedy is one of the most discussed elements of American labor history and a number of excellent materials have been produced concerning it, most notably, Paul Avrich, *The Haymarket Tragedy*, Princeton University Press, 1986; James Green, *Death in the Haymarket*, Pantheon Books, 2006; and the fictionalized account of the incidents, Frank Harris, *The Bomb*, Feral House, 2006.

24. Alexander Berkman, *Prison Memoirs of an Anarchist* (It should be noted that in the 1912 Mother Earth edition and the iteration published by New York Review Books 1999, the quote dealing with Most, is incorrectly ascribed to Berkman musing about a bridge, Most being translating to such in Russian.

25. Alexander Berkman, *Prison Memoirs of an Anarchist*, New York Review Books, 1999, 8.

26. *Ibid.*, 36–37.

27. *New York Times*, 24 Jul 1892, "Chairman Frick Shot," 1.

28. *Courier-Journal*, 24 Jul 1892, "Shot to Kill: Bold and Desperate Attempt To Slay H. C. Frick," 1.

29. *New York Times*, 24 Jul 1892, "The News at Homestead," 2.

30. H.W. Brands, 144.

31. Robert Reitzel, *Der arme Teufel*, 1892.

32. Avrich, 88.

33. Robert W. Rydell, *All the World's a Fair: Visions of Empire at American International Expositions, 1876–1916*, University of Chicago Press, 2013, 136.

34. Thomas E. Leary and Elizabeth C. Sholes, *Buffalo's Pan American Exposition*, Arcadia Publishing, 1999, 7.

35. Leo Lucassen, *The Immigrant Threat: The Integration of Old and New Migrants in Western Europe Since 1850*, University of Illinois Press, 2005, 60.

36. Walter Channing, "The Mental Status of Czolgosz," *American Journal of Insanity*, Vol. LIX No. 2, 1902, 5.

37. Президента США Уильяма МакКинли застрелил белорус? (U.S. President William McKinley shot by Belarusian?) http://www.kp.ru/daily/24205.4/409486/ [accessed March 2017].

38. Scott Miller, *The President and The Assassin*, Random House Trade Paperbacks, 2011, 40.

39. *Ibid.*, 41.

40. Roger Pickenpaugh, *McKinley, Murder and the Pan-American Exposition: A History of the Presidential Assassination, September 6, 1901*, McFarland, 2016, 18.

41. *Ibid.*

42. Channing, 13.

43. Miller, 59.

44. Chicago Sunday Tribune, 8 September 1901, "Czolgosz Says He Had No Aid," 1.

45. Robert Donovan, "The Man Who Didn't Shake Hands," *The New Yorker*, 28 November 1953, 112.

46. Channing, 31.

47. *Ibid.*

48. Miller, 264.

49. Goldman, *Living My Life*, 290.

50. Kenyon Zimmer, Immigrants against the State: Yiddish and Italian Anarchism in America, University of Illinois Press, 2015, 91.

51. Emma Goldman (Candace Falk and Barry Pateman, Editors), *Emma Goldman: A Documentary History of the American Years: Made for America, 1890–1901*, Vol. 1, University of Illinois Press, 2008, 536.

52. James F. Morton, Jr., "Kings and King Slayers," *Free Society*, September 1900.

53. Goldman, *Living My Life*, 290.

54. Channing, 16.

55. Marshall Everett, *Complete Life of William McKinley and Story of His Assassination* (Memorial Edition), Marshall Everett Publishing, 1901, 87.

56. Miller, 295.

57. Everett, 66.

58. "Leon Czolgosz and the Trial—'Lights out in the City of Light'—Anarchy and Assassination at the Pan-American Exposition," http://web.archive.org/web/20120722023016/http://library.buffalo.edu/libraries/exhibits/panam/law/czolgosz.html [accessed March 2017].

59. Everett, 69.

60. Margaret Leech, *In the Days of McKinley*, Harper & Bros., 1959, 584.

61. Everett, 34–35.

62. *New York Times*, Sep 8 1901, *Assassin Known as a Rabid Anarchist*, 4.

63. Miller, 304.

64. *Ibid.*

65. Alix Shulman, *To the Barricades: The Anarchist Life of Emma Goldman* (Kindle Edition), Open Road Media, 2012.

66. Details of these arrests are provided by Everett, 83.

67. Neil A. Hamilton, *Rebels and Renegades: A Chronology of Social and Political Dissent in the United States*, Routledge, 2014, 157.

68. Congressional Edition, Vol. 4203, U.S. Government Printing Office, 1906, 433.

69. Robert Justin Goldstein, *Political Repression in Modern America: From 1870 to 1976*, University of Illinois Press, 2001, 69.

Chapter Ten

1. Mosaburô Suzuki, *Zaibei Shakaishugisha Museifushugisha Enkaku* (History of the Socialists and Anarchists Resident in America), Tokyo: Shakai Bunko, 1964.

2. John Crump, *The Origins of Socialist Thought in Japan*, Croom Helm, 1983.

3. Stefan Anarkowic, *Against the God Emperor: The Anarchist Treason Trials in Japan*, Kate Sharpley Library, 1994.

4. James L.Huffman, *Modern Japan: An Encyclopaedia of History, Culture, and Nationalism*, Routledge 1997.

5. F.G.Notehelfer, *Kotoku Shusui: Portrait of a Japanese Radical*, Cambridge University Press (Reissue 2011), 1971.

6. Donald Keene, *Emperor of Japan: Meiji and His World, 1852-1912*, Columbia University Press, 2002.

7. Setuchi Harumi, *Toi Koe* (Distant Voice), Tokyo: Shinchosa, 1975.

8. Hélène Bowen Raddeker, *Treacherous Women of Imperial Japan: Patriarchal Fictions, Patricidal Fantasies*, London: Routledge, 1997.

9. Mikiso Hane, *Refections on the Way to the Gallows: Rebel Women in Prewar Japan*, University of California Press, Berkeley, 1988.

10. William Johnston, *The Modern Epidemic: A History of Tuberculosis in Japan*, Harvard University Press, 1995.

11. Kondō Tomie, "Kanno Suga" in Setouchi Harumi, ed., *A Woman's Lifetime: Personalities in Modern Women's History, The Romance of Rebellious Women*, Tokyo: Kōdansha, 1980.

12. Itoya Sumio, *Kanno Suga*, Tokyo: Iwanami Shoten, 1970.

13. Nagabata Michiko, *Honoho no Onna*, Tokyo: Shinhyōron, 1981.

14. Takeda Yoshitaka (2010), *Hidden for 100 Years: Kanno's Secret Message from Prison*, http://www.pmpress.org/content/article.php/20100130162821568.

Chapter Eleven

1. *New York Times*, 19 March 1913, "Died Before Reaching Hospital."

2. *The Times*, 19 March 1913, "The Murder at Salonika," 7.

3. *The Times*, 20 March 1913, "The Murdered King," 6.

4. *New York Times*, 20 March 1913, "The Assassin Lived Here; Worked in a New York Hotel—Well Educated and an Anarchist."

5. *Südosteuropäische Arbeiten*, Vol. 75, Issue 2, 28, German Foreign Research Institute (Berlin), Bartl Gerda.

6. Peter H. Paroulakis, *The Greek War of Independence*, Hellenic International Press, 1984.

7. *New York Times*, 20 March 1913, untitled article, 7 (London, 19 March dateline).

8. The English translation of this article is provided for the first time following this chapter.

9. *New York Times*, 20 March 1913, untitled article, 6.

10. Kenneth T. Jackson, and Lisa Keller, *The Encyclopedia of New York City*, 2nd Edition, Yale University Press, 2010.

11. *New York Times*, "The Assassin Lived Here…"

12. *New York Times*, 21 March 1913, untitled article, 2.

13. *Dundee Courier*, 21 March 1913, "Schinas' Career in New York."

14. *New York Times*, "Died Before Reaching Hospital."

15. *Dundee Courier*, 21 March 1913, "Who is Schinas."

16. *Burnley News*, 22 March 1913, "The Dead King."

17. New York Times, 07 May 1913, "King's Slayer A Suicide; Schinas, Assassin of George of Greece, Jumps Out of a Window."

18. *Poverty Bay Herald*, Vol. 40, Issue 13017, 29 March 1913, "A Callous Assassin."

19. Schinas' interview with Magrini is provided in English translation as part of this chapter.

20. *New York Times*, 20 March 1913, untitled article, 6.

21. *The Scotsman*, 7 May 1913, "Suicide of Greek King's Assassin."

Chapter Twelve

1. Romano Mussolini, *My Father II Duce: A Memoir by Mussolini's Son*, W. W. Norton & Co., 2008, 109.

2. Enzo Biagi, *Storia del Fascismo*, Saeda Della Volpe Editore, 405.

3. Frances Stonor Saunders, *The Woman Who Shot Mussolini*, Faber & Faber, 2010, 184.

4. Darragh McManus, "The Irish Woman who Shot Mussolini," *Independent*, 3 April 2016, http://www.independent.ie/life/the-irish-woman-who-shot-mussolini-34588698.html [accessed March 2017].

5. Pietro de Piero, "Gino Lucetti and the Attempt

on Mussolini's life," *Prisoners and Partisans: Italian Anarchists in the Struggle Against Fascism*, Kate Sharpley Library, 1999, 14.

6. *New York Times*, 10 June 1927, "Lucetti Confesses Attempt on Il Duce," 8.

7. Piero, 14.

8. *New York Times*, 11 June 1927, "Evidence Concluded on Trial of Lucetti," 24.

9. *New York Times*, 3 Nov 1926, "Father Inspired Zamboni," 25.

10. Sandro Gerbi, Perché il "Patata" sparò al Duce. Un ragazzo difficile che agì da solo per protestare contro la figura paterna. Mussolini rimase illeso. L'episodio servì al regime per aumentare la repressione, in Il Corriere della Sera, 15.02.1996, 25.

11. Barbara Baraldi, Alla scoperta dei segreti perduti di Bologna, Quest'italia, 2016.

12. *New York Times*, 2 Nov 1926, "Shouts for Death of Mussolini Foes Roar Through Italy," 1.

13. *New York Times*, 8 Nov 1926, "Fascisti Killed 100 London Paper Hears: 1000 Persons also injured," 4.

14. Fabio Fernando Rizi, *Benedetto Croce and Italian Fascism*, University of Toronto Press, 2003, 113.

15. Rizi, 114.

16. *New York Times*, 30 April 1943, *Bracco's Death Lamented: Dramatist's Fate Reviewed in Light of Fascist History in Italy*, Letters to the Times, 20.

17. *New York Times*, Nov 3, 1926, "Father Inspired Zamboni," 25.

18. Giovanni Berneri, "Gli anarchici nella lotta contro il fascismo," *Volunta*, Year XIV, No.4 1961, 206.

19. Peter Neville, Mussolini (2nd Edition), Routledge, 2014, 73.

20. *New York Times*, 8 Sept 1928, "Two are Convicted in Zamboni Trial," 9.

21. *New York Times*, 7 Sept 1928, "Verdict Likely Today in Plot Against Duce: Twenty Three Witnesses," 4.

22. Leo Tolstoy, *The Law of Love and the Law of Violence* (1908), Rudolph Field Publisher, New York, 1948, 110.

23. Charles Johnston, "The Anarchists and the President," *North American Review*, Vol. 173, No. 539 (Oct., 1901), 437–444, University of Northern Iowa.

24. *The Age* (Melbourne, Australia), 12 May 1900, 13, "Sipido's Crime."

25. Ernst Victor Zenker, *Anarchism: A Criticism and History of the Anarchist Theory*, G. P. Putnam's Sons, 1897.

26. Stuart Anderson, "Racial Anglo-Saxonism and the American Response to the Boer War," *Diplomatic History* 2.3 (1978), 219–236.

27. Crocius is named in *The Age* (Melbourne, Australia), 12 May 1900, 13, "Sipido's Crime."

28. As detailed in *Memoirs of a Scotland Yard Man: Among the King Killers* by Ex-Inspector Harold Burst as published in *The Mail* (Adelaide), 25 Jan 1936, 2.

29. Charles Whibley, "Musings Without Method," *Blackwood's Edinburgh Magazine*, Oct. 1901, v170, n132, 559–69.

30. David DeLeon, *The American as Anarchist: Reflections on Indigenous Radicalism*, John Hopkins University Press, 1978. 4.

31. Dulcie M. Ashdown, *Royal Murders*, The History Press, 2009.

32. *Ibid.*, 188.

33. Van Roy is referenced by name in the account of the incident detailed in *The Guardian*, 5 April 1900, "Attempt to Shoot Prince of Wales," 1.

34. J. Pendrel Brodhurst, *The Life of King Edward VII*, Vol. IV, Virtue & Co., 1902, 122.

35. *The Social Democrat*, Vol. V, No. 2, February 1901, 35–37.

36. *New York Times*, 5 April 1900, Assassin Fires at Prince of Wales, 1.

37. *Los Angeles Herald*, 14 April 1902, "Vigorous Measures," 1.

38. Richard Bach Jensen, *The Battle against Anarchist Terrorism: An International History, 1878–1934*, Cambridge University Press, 2014, 186.

39. *The Times* (London) April 6, 1900.

40. *The Daily Colonist*, 6 April 1900, "Europe Sends Congratulations," 1–2.

41. *Ibid.*

42. *The Guardian*, 5 April 1900, "Attempt to Shoot Prince of Wales," 1.

43. *New York Times*, 8 April 1900, "Ask Mercy for Sipido," 1.

44. *Ibid.*

45. Dr. Speyer, *The Legal Aspects of the Sipido Case*, British Institute of International and Comparative Law, *Journal of the Society of Comparative Legislation*, Vol. 2, No. 3, 1900, 434–439.

46. J. Pendrel Brodhurst, *The Life of King Edward VII* Vol. IV, Virtue & Co., 1902, 122.

47. Hansard Commons Sitting Questions, The Attempt on the Life of the Prince of Wales—The acquittal of Sipido, HC Deb, 2 August 1900, Vol. 87, c451.

48. *Reynolds's Newspaper*, 15 July 1900, "Sipido Escapes," 5.

49. *New York Times*, 4 August 1900, "Belgium's Reply to England," 1.

50. *New York Times*, 28 October 1900, "Sipido Arrested in Paris," 1.

51. Charles Whibley, *Musings without Method: A Record of 1900–1901*, W. Blackwood & Sons, 1902, 42.

52. *Ibid.*

53. Demunter Family History, http://www.demunter genea.org/demunter/pafg10.htm [accessed February 2017].

Bibliography

Abidor, Mitchell (editor). *Death to Bourgeois Society: The Propagandists of the Deed*. PM Press, 2016.

"Alarming Explosion on the S.S. Aramac." *The Argus*, 29 July 1893.

Albert, Paul. "An Anarchist on Devil's Island." *KSL: Bulletin of the Kate Sharpley Library*, No. 13, 1997.

Alexandre Jacob, l'honnête cambrioleur," http://www.atelierdecreationlibertaire.com/alexandre-jacob [accessed January 2017.]

Anarkowic, Stefan. *Against the God Emperor: The Anarchist Treason Trials in Japan*. Kate Sharpley Library, 1994.

Anderson, Stuart. "Racial Anglo-Saxonism and the American Response to the Boer War." *Diplomatic History*, Vol. 2, No. 3, 1978, 219–236.

Anemone, Anthony. *Just Assassins: The Culture of Terrorism in Russia*. Northwestern University Press, 2010.

"The Aramac Explosion." *The Worker*, 14 October 1893.

Arnesen, Eric. *Encyclopedia of U.S. Labor and Working-Class History*. Routledge, 2006.

Ashdown, Dulcie M. *Royal Murders*. The History Press, 2009.

Ashton, Julian R. *Now Came Still Evening On*. Angus & Robertson, 1941.

"Ask Mercy for Sipido." *New York Times*, April 8 1900.

"Assassin Fires at Prince of Wales." *New York Times*, April 5, 1900.

"Assassin Known as a Rabid Anarchist." *New York Times*, September 8, 1901.

"Assassin Lived Here; Worked in a New York Hotel—Well Educated and an Anarchist." Special to *New York Times*. March 20, 1913.

"Assassin's Lot Fell Upon Anarchist Here; Gaetano Bresci, the King's Murderer, Lived in Paterson." *New York Times*, July 31, 1900.

"The Attempt on the Life of the Prince of Wales—The acquittal of Sipido." Hansard Commons Sitting Questions, HC Deb 02 August 1900 vol 87 c451.

"Attempt to Shoot Prince of Wales." *The Guardian*, 5 Apr. 1900.

Avrich, Paul, and Karen Avrich. *Sasha and Emma: The Anarchist Odyssey of Alexander Berkman and Emma Goldman*. Belknap Press, 2012.

Avrich, Paul. *Anarchist Portraits*. Princeton University Press, 1990.

Avrich, Paul. *The Haymarket Tragedy*. Princeton University Press, 1986.

Avrich, Paul. *Sacco and Vanzetti: The Anarchist Background*, Princeton University Press, 1996.

"Baraldi, Barbara. *Alla scoperta dei segreti perduti di Bologna*, Quest'italia, 2016.

Barnsby, George J. *Socialism in Birmingham and the Black Country 1850–1939*. Integrated Publishing Services, 1977.

Belbenoît, René. *Dry Guillotine: Fifteen Years Among the Living Dead*. Blue Ribbon Books, 1938.

Belgium's Reply to England." *New York Times*, 4 August 1900.

Berkman, Alexander. "Looking Backward and Forward." *Mother Earth*, Vol. 7, No. 10 December 1912.

Berkman, Alexander. *Prison Memoirs of an Anarchist*. New York Review Books, 1999.

Berneri, Giovanni. "Gli anarchici nella lotta contro il fascism." *Volunta*, Year XIV, No. 4, 1961.

Bertaut, Jules. *Paris 1870–1935*. Vincent Press, 2007.

Biagi, Enzo. *Storia del Fascismo*. Saeda-Della Volpe Editore, 1964–1965.

Bibliography for Internationaal Instituut voor Sociale Geschiedenis (International Review of Social History), Vol. 58, Issue 3, 2013.

"The Bomb Thrower Found: Auguste Vaillant Confesses." *New York Times*, December 11 1893.

Boyer, Paul S. *The Enduring Vision A History of 5he American People* Vol. II: Since 1865. 7th ed., Wadsworth Publishing Company, 2010.

"Bracco's Death Lamented: Dramatist's Fate Reviewed in Light of Fascist History in Italy." Letters to the Times. *New York Times*, 30 April 1943.

Brands, H.W. *The Reckless Decade: America in the 1890s*. University of Chicago Press, 2002.

"Bread riots in Bari." *New York Times*, April 28 1898.

Bredin, Jean-Denis, and Thierry Lévy. *Plutôt la mort que l'injustice: au temps des procès anarchists*. Editions Odile Jacob, 2009.

"Bresci Commits Suicide; Murderer of King Humbert Hangs Himself in Prison." *New York Times*, May 24, 1901.

Brust, Jean, and Bill Brust. *Defending Principles: The Political Legacy of Bill Brust*. Mehring Books, 1993.

Burgoyne, Mary. *Joseph Conrad among the Anarchists: Documents on Martial Bourdin and the Greenwich Bombing*. The Conradian, Vol. 32, No. 1. "The Secret Agent": Centennial Essays (Spring 2007).

Burst, Harold. "Memoirs of a Scotland Yard Man: Among the King Killers." *The Mail* (Adelaide), 25 Jan 1936.

Buttà, Fausto. *Living Like Nomads: The Milanese Anarchist Movement Before Fascism*, Cambridge Scholars Publishing, 2015.

Butterfield, Herbert. *The Historical Novel.* Cambridge University Press, 2012.

Butterworth, Alex. *The World that Never Was: A True Story of Schemers, Anarchists, and Secret Agents.* The Bodley Head, 2010.

"A Callous Assassin." *Poverty Bay Herald*, 29 March 1913.

Carlson, Andrew. *Anarchism in Germany Vol. I: The Early Movement.* Scarecrow Press, 1972.

"Carnot Killed." *New York Times*, 25 June 1894.

"Caserio at the Guillotine." *New York Times*, 16 August 1894.

"Caserio Sentenced to Die." *New York Times*, 4 August 1894.

"Chairman Frick Shot." *New York Times*, July 24 1892.

Channing, Walter. "The Mental Status of Czolgosz, the Assassin of President McKinley." *American Journal of Insanity*, Vol. 59, No. 2, 1902, 233–278.

Il Ciclone (Paris), 4 September 1887.

Clutterbuck, Lindsay. "An Accident of History? The Evolution of Counter-Terrorism Methodology in the Metropolitan Police from 1829 to 1901, with Particular Reference to Extreme Irish Nationalist Activity." PhD Dissertation, University of Portsmouth, 2002.

Cohen, Philip K. *John Evelyn Barlas, A Critical Biography: Poetry, Anarchism, and Mental Illness in Late-Victorian Britain.* Rivendale Press, 2012.

The Commonweal: A Revolutionary Journal of Anarchist Communism, Vol. 2, No. 22, Saturday 10 March 1894.

Congressional Edition. U.S. Government Printing Office, Vol. 4203, 1906.

Conrad, Joseph. *The Secret Agent.* Penguin Classics, 2007.

Croft, Lee B. *Nikolai Ivanovich Kibalchich: Terrorist Rocket Pioneer.* Institute for Issues in the History of Science, 2006.

Crump, John. *The Origins of Socialist Thought in Japan.* Croom Helm, 1983.

"Czolgosz Says He Had No Aid." *Chicago Sunday Tribune*, 8 September 1901.

The Daily Graphic, 27 February 1894.

Danver, Steven L. *Revolts, Protests, Demonstrations, and Rebellions in American History: An Encyclopedia.* ABC-CLIO, 2010.

De Cesare, Raffaele. *The Last Days of Papal Rome, 1850–1870.* Archibald Constable & Co. 1909.

De La Motte, Dean (editor). *Jeannene M. Przyblyski: Making the News: Modernity and the Mass Press in Nineteenth-Century France* (Studies in Print Culture and the History of the Book). University Massachusetts Press, 1999.

De Leon, David. *The American as Anarchist: Reflections on Indigenous Radicalism.* Johns Hopkins University Press, 1978.

"The Dead King." *Burnley News*, 22 March 1913.

de Piero, Pietro. "Gino Lucetti and the Attempt on Mussolini's Life." *Prisoners and Partisans: Italian Anarchists in the Struggle Against Fascism.* Kate Sharpley Library, 1999.

Delpech, Jean-Marc. "Il y prit goût et sombra dans l'alcoolisme." Parcours et Reseaux D'un Anarchiste: Alexandre Marius Jacob 1879–1954. Doctoral Thesis, Department of History, University of Nancy, 2006.

"Designs on the Royal Arsenal." The Sydney Morning Herald, 19 February 1894.

"Died Before Reaching Hospital." *New York Times*, 19 March 1913.

"Died Before the Knife Fell." *New York Times*, 23 May 1894.

Donovan, Robert. "The Man Who Didn't Shake Hands." *The New Yorker*, 28 November 1953.

Drachkovitch, Milorad M. (editor). *The Revolutionary Internationals, 1864–1943.* Stanford University Press, 1966.

Drozd, Andrew M. *Chernyshevskii's "What Is to Be Done?": A Reevaluation.* Northwestern University Press, 2001.

Duggan, Christopher. *The Force of Destiny: A History of Italy Since 1796.* Penguin Books, 2008.

Dumas, René. *Ravachol: l'homme rouge de l'anarchie (Ravachol: The Red Man of Anarchy).* Saint-Etienne, Le Hénaff, 1981.

Duval, Clément. *Outrage: An Anarchist Memoir of the Penal Colony.* Translated by Michael Shreve, PM Press, 2012.

Enckell, Marianne. "Clément Duval Corrections." *KSL: Bulletin of the Kate Sharpley Library*, No. 14, March 1998.

Engel, Barbara Alpern, and Clifford N. Rosenthal (editors). *Five Sisters: Women Against the Tsar.* Routledge, 1987.

"Ephéméride Anarchiste 29 mars." Ephemanar. http:// www.ephemanar.net/mars29.html. Accessed January 2017.

"Europe Sends Congratulations." *The Daily Colonist*, 6 April 1900.

Everett, Marshall. *Complete Life of William McKinley and Story of His Assassination: Memorial Edition.* Marshall Everett Publishing, 1901.

"Evidence Concluded on Trial of Lucetti." *New York Times*, 11 June 1927.

"Explosion on the Aramac," *The Week*, 11 August 1893.

"Explosion on the Aramac," *The Week*, 18 August 1893.

"Explosion on the Aramac," *The Week*, 25 August 1893.

"Explosion on the Aramac," *The Week*, 8 September 1893.

"Explosion on the S.S. Aramac." *The Bundaberg Mail and Burnett Advertiser*, 31 July 1893.

Falk, Candace. *Emma Goldman: A Documentary History of the American Years Vol. One, Made for America, 1890–1901.* University of Illinois Press, 2008.

Fascisti Killed 100 London Paper Hears: 1000 Persons also injured. *New York Times*, 8 November 1926.

"Fatal Bomb Explosion at Greenwich." *Weekly Times & Echo: A Liberal Newspaper of Political and Social Progress*, 18 February 1894.

"Father Inspired Zamboni." *New York Times*, 3 November 1926.

Foa, Anna. *The Jews of Europe after the Black Death.* University of California Press, 2000.

Fokkema, Douwe. *Perfect Worlds: Utopian Fiction in China and the West.* Amsterdam University Press, 2014.

Franchini, Elena. "Collezioni Digitali Biblioteca Franco Serantini."

French National Archives, BB18 2261A, File 2069A03, Amiens, 23 April 1903.

Friedländer, Hugo. "Das Dynamit-Attentat bei der Enthüllungsfeier des Niederwald-Denkmals (Interesting Crime Processes of Cultural and Historical Significance) 1911–1921," Vol. 4, 1911, Berlin.

Galzerano, Giuseppe. *Giovanni Passannante, La vita, l'attentato, il processo, la condanna a morte, la grazia 'regale' e gli anni di galera del cuoco lucano che nel 1878 ruppe l'incantesimo monarchico.* Casalvelino Scalo, 2004.

Gapps, Stephen. "Australian Pirate Tales." *Signals*, No. 97, 2012. Accessed December 2016. https://anmm. wordpress.com/2014/01/13/australian-pirate-tales/.

Le Gaulois, 13 July 1892.

George Woodcock, Anarchism: A History Of Libertarian Ideas And Movements, Meridian Books, 1961, 214.

Gerbi, Sandro. Perché il " Patata " sparò al Duce. Un ragazzo difficile che agì da solo per protestare contro la figura paterna. Mussolini rimase illeso. L'episodio servì al regime per aumentare la repressione, in Il Corriere della Sera, 15.02.1996.

Gibbard, Paul. "Bourdin, Martial (1867/8–1894)." *Oxford Dictionary of National Biography*. Oxford University Press, 2004.

Gimlette, John. *At the Tomb of the Inflatable Pig: Travels through Paraguay*. Arrow, 2004.

Giovanni Rosadi. *Tra la perduta gente*. Firenze 1908.

Goldberg, Harvey. "Jaurès and the Carmaux Strikes: The Coal Strike of 1892." *The American Journal of Economics and Sociology*, Vol. 17, No. 2, January 1958.

Goldman, Emma. "A Sketch of Alexander Berkman." *The Russian Tragedy (A Review and an Outlook)*. Der Syndikalist, 1922.

Goldman, Emma. *Anarchism and Other Essays*. Dover Publications 1969.

Goldman, Emma. *Living My Life*. Cosimo Classics, 2011.

Goldstein, Robert Justin. *Political Repression in Modern America: From 1870 to 1976*, University of Illinois Press, 2001.

Goyens, Tom. "Anarchy at the Antipodes—Australian Anarchists and their American Connections." Salisbury University, Maryland presented at Australian-U.S. Comparative and Transnational Labour History Conference, 2015.

Green, James. *Death in the Haymarket*. Pantheon Books, 2006.

Guerin, Daniel. *No Gods, No Masters: An Anthology of Anarchism*. AK Press, 2006.

"The Guillotine's Sure Work; Details of the Execution of Vaillant, the Anarchist." *New York Times*, 6 February 1894.

"The Guillotine's Sure Work." *New York Times*, 21 May 1894.

Hamilton, Neil A. *Rebels and Renegades: A Chronology of Social and Political Dissent in the United States*. Routledge, 2014.

Hannan, John Grant. *The New Australia Movement*. Dissertation, The University of Queensland, 1966.

Hari, Johann. "Blood, Rage & History." *The Independent*, 12 October 2009.

Harris, Frank. *The Bomb*. Feral House, 2006.

Hartnett, Lynne Ann. *The Defiant Life of Vera Figner: Surviving the Russian Revolution*. Indiana University Press, 2014.

Harvey, George. *Henry Clay Frick: The Man*. Beard Books, 1928; Reprinted 2002. (Which version did author use?)

Head, Michael. *Calling out the Troops: The Australian Military and Civil Unrest: The Legal and Constitutional Issues*. Federation Press, 2009.

"Henry Sentenced to Death." *New York Times*, 29 April 1894.

Hicks, John Harland, and Robert Tucker. *Revolution and Reaction: The Paris Commune, 1871.* University of Massachusetts Press, 1973.

Hickson, C.R., and J.D. Turner. "Free Banking Gone Awry: The Australian Banking Crisis of 1893." *Financial History Review*. Cambridge University Press, 2002, 147–168.

HO 144/257/A55660 112747.

Hosking, Geoffrey A. *Russia: People and Empire, 1552–1917*. Harvard University Press, 1997.

Hottinger, Christlieb G. "The Assassination Attempt Against the German Kaiser Wilhelm I on June 2, 1878." *Volksblatt: A Weekly Magazine with Pictures*, No. 23, 177–179.

Hottinger, Christlieb G. "The Assassination Attempt Against the German Kaiser Wilhelm." *Volksblatt: A Weekly Magazine with Pictures*, No. 20, 153–155.

Huffman, James L. *Modern Japan: An Encyclopedia of History, Culture, and Nationalism*. Routledge, 1997.

Hunter, Robert. *Violence and the Labour Movement*. The MacMillan Company, 1914.

"Important Discoveries: The Autonomie Club a 'Centre' of Anarchy." *The Age*, 19 February 1894.

Imrie, Doug. "The 'Illegalists.'" *Anarchy: A Journal of Desire Armed*. Fall–Winter, 1994–95.

"Interview with Karl Marx, head of L'Internationale." *New York World*, 18 July 1871.

Irving, Henry B. *Studies of French Criminals of the Nineteenth Century*. William Heinemann, 1901.

"Italy Verging on Anarchy; Bread Rioters in Milan Throw Tiles from the Roofs on the Heads of the Soldiers, Who Retire; 300 Killed And 1,000 Injured." *New York Times*, May 9, 1898.

Jackson, Kenneth T., and Lisa Keller (editors). *The Encyclopedia of New York City*. 2nd ed., Yale University Press, 2010.

James, Bob. "Anarchism and State Violence in Sydney and Melbourne 1886–1896 An argument about Australian labor history, 1986." MA Thesis held at La Trobe University Melbourne.

James, Bob. "Larry Petrie (1859–1901)—Australian Revolutionist?" *Red & Black: An Anarchist Journal*, Summer 1978/79.

Jensen, Richard Bach. *The Battle against Anarchist Terrorism—An International History, 1878–1934*. Cambridge University Press, 2014.

Johnson, Robert Eugene. *Peasant and Proletarian: The Working Class of Moscow in the Late Nineteenth Century*. Rutgers University Press, 1979.

Johnston, Charles. "The Anarchists and the President." *The North American Review*, Vol. 173, No. 539. University of Northern Iowa, October 1901.

Johnston, William. *The Modern Epidemic: A History of Tuberculosis in Japan*. Cambridge: Harvard University Press, 1995.

Keene, Donald. *Emperor of Japan: Meiji and His World, 1852–1912*. Columbia University Press, 2002.

"King's Slayer a Suicide; Schinas, Assassin of George of Greece, Jumps Out of a Window." *New York Times*, 7 May 1913.

Krause, Paul. *The Battle for Homestead, 1880–1892*. University of Pittsburgh Press, 1992.

Kropotkin, Peter. *Memoirs of a Revolutionist*. Dover, 2014.

Lane, E. H. *Dawn to Dusk: Reminiscences of a Rebel*. Brisbane: William Brooks, 1939.

Laqueur, Walter. *The Terrorism reader: A Historical Anthology*. New American Library, 1978.

Leary, Thomas E., and Elizabeth A. Sholes. "Buffalo's Pan American Exposition." *Arcadia Publishing*, 1999.

Lincoln, Bruce. *Sunlight at Midnight: St. Petersburg and the Rise of Modern Russia*. Basic Books, 2009.

Lippmann, Jonas. *Ravachol, King of the Anarchists*. *New York Times*, 29 June 1919.

Lloyd, Christopher. "The 1890–1910 Crisis of Australian Capitalism and the Social Democratic Response: Was the Australian Model a Pioneering Regime of Social Democratic Welfare Capitalist Regulation?" *Multi-*

layered Historicity of the Present: Approaches to Social Science History. Haggrén, H., Raunio-Niemi, J. & Vauhkonen, J. (eds.). Helsinki University Press, 2013.

Lombroso, Cesare. *Gli Anarchici.* Fratelli Bocca, 1895.

Lucassen, Leo. *The Immigrant Threat: The Integration of Old and New Migrants in Western Europe Since 1850.* University of Illinois Press, 2005.

"Lucetti Confesses Attempt on Il Duce." *New York Times,* 10 June 1927.

Maitron Jean. *Histoire du mouvement anarchiste en France.* Paris, Societé universitaire d'editions et de librairie. 1951.

Maitron, Jean (editor). *Dictionnaire biographique du mouvement ouvrier franfais,* 37 vols. Paris: Editions ouvrieres, 1964–90.

Maitron, Jean. *Ravachol et les anarchistes.* Paris, Julliard, 1964.

Malato, Charles. "Some Anarchist Portraits." *Fortnightly Review* 333, New Series, 1 September 1894.

Malato, Charles. *Joyeusetés de l'exil.* Mauléon, 1985.

Margaret Leech, In the Days of McKinley, Harper & Bros., 1959.

Martel, Gordon. *Origins of the First World War* (Third Edition). Routledge, 2008.

Schütte, Max. "August Reinsdorf and the Niederwald Conspiracy: An Historical Account of the Planned Attack Against the Imperial Court Train on 28 September 1883; the Trial and the Execution of the Condemned." *New Life Magazine,* 1983.

McCrery, Nigel. *Silent Witnesses.* Arrow, 2014.

McIntyre, Iain. *How To Make Trouble and Influence People.* PM Press, 2013.

McManus, Darragh. "The Irish woman who shot Mussolini." *Independent,* 3 April 2016.

Merrifield, S. "The Melbourne Anarchist Club 1886–1891." Bulletin of the Australian Society for the Study of Labour History, No. 3 (Nov., 1962.)

Merriman, John M. *The Dynamite Club: How a Bombing in Fin-de-Siècle Paris Ignited the Age of Modern Terror.* Yale University Press, 2009.

Miller, Scott. "The President and The Assassin." Random House Trade Paperbacks, 2011.

Misiroglu, Gina. *American Countercultures: An Encyclopedia of Nonconformists, Alternative Lifestyles, and Radical Ideas in U.S. History.* Routledge, 2008.

Morton, James F., Jr. "Kings and King Slayers." *Free Society,* September 1900.

Moss, Walter G. *A History of Russia Vol. 1: To 1917.* Anthem Press, 2003.

"The Murder at Salonika." *The Times* (London), 19 March 1913.

"The Murdered King." *The Times* (London), 20 March 1913.

Mussolini, Romano. *My Father II Duce: A Memoir by Mussolini's Son.* W. W. Norton & Co., 2008.

Neville, Peter. *Mussolini* (2nd Edition). Routledge, 2014.

"The News at Homestead." *New York Times,* 24 July 1892.

Nicholl, David. "The Walsall Anarchists: Trapped by the police: Innocent Men in Penal Servitude." *The Truth about the Walsall Plot.* LSE Selected Pamphlets, 1892.

Notehelfer, F.G. *Kotoku Shusui: Portrait of a Japanese Radical.* Cambridge University Press (Reissue 2011), 1971.

Nunzio Pernicone. "The Case of Pietro Acciarito: Accomplices, Psychological Torture, and 'Raison d'État.'" *Journal for the Study of Radicalism,* vol. 5, no. 1, 2011.

Nunzio Pernicone. *Italian Anarchism 1864–1892.* AK Press, 2009.

O'Donghaile, Deaglán. *Blasted Literature: Victorian Political Fiction and the Shock of Modernism.* Edinburgh University Press, 2014.

Oliver, Hermja. "The International Anarchist Movement in Late Victorian London." Palgrave Macmillan, 1983.

Paola, Pietro. *The Knights Errant of Anarchy: London and the Italian Anarchist Diaspora (1880–1917).* Oxford University Press, 2013.

Parfitt, Steven. "Completing the Order's History Down Under: The Knights of Labor in Australia." *Labour History,* No. 110, May 2016.

Paroulakis, Peter H. *The Greek War of Independence.* Hellenic International Press, 1984.

Parry, Richard. *The Bonnot Gang: The Story of the French Illegalists* (2nd Edition), PM Press, 2016.

Pearce, Robert, and Andrina Stiles. *The Unification of Italy,* Third Edition. Hodder Murray, 2006.

Penderel-Brodhurst, J. *The Life of King Edward VII Four Vol. Set.* Virtue & Co., 1902.

Petacco, Arrigo. *L'anarchico che venne dall'America.* Mondadori, 1970.

Petrie, Larry. *The Tocsin,* 6 Jun 1901.

Phillips, Steve. *Lenin and the Russian Revolution.* Heinemann, 2000.

Pickenpaugh, Roger. *McKinley, Murder and the Pan-American Exposition: A History of the Presidential Assassination, September 6, 1901.* McFarland, 2016.

Polunov, Alexander. *Russia in the Nineteenth Century: Autocracy, Reform, and Social Change 1814–1914,* Routledge, 2005.

La Presse, No. 1179, 30 August 1891.

Quail, John. *The Slow Burning Fuse: The Lost History of the British Anarchists.* Flamingo, 1978.

Rapoport, David C. (editor). *Terrorism: Critical Concepts in Political Science,* Vol. 1. Routledge, 2004.

"Ravachol Put to Death." *New York Times,* July 12, 1892.

Recchia, Stefano. *Nadia Urbinati: A Cosmopolitanism of Nations.* Princeton University Press, 2009.

Rees, Jonathan. "Homestead in Context: Andrew Carnegie and the Decline of the Amalgamated Association of Iron and Steel Workers." *Pennsylvania History: A Journal of Mid-Atlantic Studies,* Vol. 64, No. 4, 1997.

Reitzel, Robert. *Der Arme Teufel.* Detroit, 1892.

Ring, Trudy, and Noelle Watson (editors). Northern Europe: International Dictionary of Historic Places, Vol 2, Routledge, 1995.

Rocker, Rudolf. *The London Years.* AK Press, 2005.

Rydell, Robert W. *All the World's a Fair: Visions of Empire at American International Expositions, 1876–1916.* University of Chicago Press, 2013.

St. James's Gazette, 24 February 1894.

Salerno, Salvatore. "Paterson's Italian Anarchist Silk Workers and the Politics of Race Continuano I Disordini a Milano." *Corriere della Sera,* 9 May 1898.

Sanborn, Alvan Francis. *Paris and the Social Revolution: A Study of the Revolutionary Elements in the Various Classes of Parisian Society.* Hutchinson, 1905.

"Santo Caserio and his Crime." *New York Times,* 3 August 1894.

Saunders, Frances Stonor. *The Woman Who Shot Mussolini.* Faber & Faber, 2010.

Scates, Bruce. "Gender, Household and community politics: The 1890 Maritime strike in Australia and New Zealand." Labour History, 61, 2006.

"Scene in the Theatre." *New York Times,* 25 June 1894.

"Schinas' Career in New York." *Dundee Courier*, 21 March 1913.

Schur, Anna. *Wages of Evil: Dostoevsky and Punishment.* Northwestern University Press, 2013.

Serge, Victor (translator, Mitchell Abidor). *Anarchists Never Surrender: Essays, Polemics, and Correspondence on Anarchism, 1908–1938.* PM Press, 2015.

Sergent, Alain. *Un anarchiste de la Belle Epoque: Alexandre Marius Jacob.* Les Editions Libertaires.

"Shot to Kill: Bold and Desperate Attempt to Slay H. C. Frick." *Courier-Journal*, 24 July, 1892.

"Shouts for Death of Mussolini Foes Roar Through Italy." *New York Times*, 2 November 1926.

Shulman, Alix. *To the Barricades: The Anarchist Life of Emma Goldman* (Kindle Edition). Open Road Media, 2012.

Siljak, Ana. *Angel of Vengeance: The Girl Who Shot the Governor of St. Petersburg and Sparked the Age of Assassination*, 2009, St. Martin's Press.

Simmons, Allan H., and J. H. Stape (editors). *The Secret Agent: Centennial Essays: 1* (The Conradian), Rodopi, 2008.

Simons, Paul Z. "Illegalism: Why Pay for a Revolution on the Installment Plan.... When You Can Steal One?" *Modern Slavery: The Libertarian Critique of Civilization*, Fall–Winter, 2013–2014.

Simpson, Paul. *The Mammoth Book of Prison Escapes.* Running Press, 2013.

"Sipido Arrested in Paris." *New York Times*, 28 October 1900.

"Sipido Escapes." *Reynolds's Newspaper*, 15 July 1900.

"Sipido's Crime." *The Age*, 12 May 1900.

Skirna, Alexandra (translator, Paul Sharkey). *Facing the Enemy: A History of Anarchist Organisation from Proudhon to May 1968.* AK Press, 2002.

Skrabec, Quentin R., Jr. *Henry Clay Frick: The Life of The Perfect Capitalist.* McFarland, 2010.

Smith, Denis Mack. *Italy and Its Monarchy.* Yale University Press, 1989.

Smith, F.B., "Joseph Symes and the Australasian Secular Association." *Labour History*, No. 5, November 1963.

The Social Democrat, Vol. V No. 2 February 1901.

"Socialists Arrested at Supposed Walsall Bomb Factory." *Berrow's Worcester Journal*, 9 January 1892.

Souter, Gavin. *A Peculiar People: The Australians in Paraguay.* The Book Service, Ltd., 1969.

Sowerwine, Charles. *France since 1870: Culture, Society and the Making of the Republic.* Palgrave Macmillan, 2009.

Speyer, Dr. "The Legal Aspects of the Sipido Case, British Institute of International and Comparative Law." *Journal of the Society of Comparative Legislation*, Vol. 2, No. 3, 1900.

Stafford, David. *From Anarchism to Reformism: A Study of the Political Activities of Paul Brousse, 1870–1990.* Weidenfeld & Nicolson, 1971.

Stefanelli, Barbara *Sante Caserio: Assassin of French President Sadi Carnot and Avenger of Emile Henry and Auguste Vaillant,* Pen & Pistol Press, 2013.

Südosteuropäische Arbeiten–Volume 75, Issue 2, Page 28, German Foreign Research Institute (Berlin, Germany), Bartl Gerda.

Sue, Eugène. *The Wandering Jew*, 6 vols. John C. Nimmo, 1903.

"Suicide of Greek King's Assassin." *The Scotsman*, 7 May 1913.

Suzuki, Mosaburô. *Zaibei Shakaishugisha Museifushugisha Enkaku* (History of the Socialists and Anarchists Resident in America). Tokyo: Shakai Bunko, 1964.

Taylor, George Boardman. *Italy and the Italians.* America Baptist Publication Society, 1898.

Thogmartin, Clyde. *The National Daily Press of France.* Summa Publications, 1998.

Thomas, Bernard. *Alexandre Jacob: Sailor, Thief, Anarchist, Convict (1879–1954)*, Vol. 1. Ardent Press, 2013.

Thomas, Bernard. *Les Provocations Policiéres.* Fayard, 1972.

The Times (London, England), 6 April 1900.

The Times (London, England), 1 Jan 1892.

The Tocsin, 24 May 1900.

Tolstoy, Leo. *The Law of Love and the Law of Violence* (1908). New York: Rudolph Field Publisher, 1948.

Tuchman, Barbara W. *The Proud Tower: A Portrait of the World before the War, 1890–1914.* Bantam, 1965.

"Two are Convicted in Zamboni Trial." *New York Times*, 8 September 1928.

Ulam, Adam B. *Prophets and Conspirators in Prerevolutionary Russia.* Transaction Publishers, 1998.

Untitled article 2. *New York Times*, 21 March 1913.

Untitled article 6. *New York Times*, March 20, 1913.

Untitled article 7. *New York Times*, March 20 1913 (London March 19 dateline.)

Untitled article, Reynolds Newspaper, April 7th, 1895.

Untitled article, The Standard, 9 March 1894.

Untitled article, Wellington Times and Agricultural and Mining Gazette, 19 Aug 1893.

Untitled article. *Aberdeen Press and Journal*, 23 November 1878, 3.

Vaillant's Doom Pronounced. *New York Times*, January 11 1894.

Vaillant's Grave Guarded. *New York Times*, February 14 1894.

Van der Kiste, John. *The Romanovs: 1818–1959.* The History Press, 1980.

Vast Anarchist Conspiracy. *New York Times*, February 16 1894.

Verdict Likely Today in Plot Against Duce: Twenty Three Witnesses. *New York Times* 7 September 1928.

Verhoeven, Claudia "Time of terror, terror of time on the impatience of russian revolutionary terrorism (early 1860s—early 1880s)." *Jahrbücher Für Geschichte Osteuropas* (Yearbooks for The History of Eastern Europe) 58, 2010.

Vigorous Measures, Los Angeles Herald, 14 April 1902.

Vizetelly, Ernest Alfred. The Anarchists: Their Faith and Their Record. Turnbull and Spears Printers, Edinburgh, 1911.

Vogely, Maxine Arnold. *A Proust Dictionary.* Whitston Publishing Co., 1981.

"The Walsall Anarchists." *Walsall Free Press and South Staffordshire Advertiser*, April 1892.

"The Walsall Anarchists' Trial." *The Times* (London), 30 March 1892.

Webb, Simon. Dynamite, Treason and Plot: Terrorism in Victorian and Edwardian England, The History Press, 2012.

Weber, Eugen. *France: Fin de Siècle.* Belknap Press of Harvard University Press, 1988.

Werner, S. "Der Anarchisten-Prozess: Reinsdorf und Genossen verhandelt vor dem 2. und 3." *Strafsenat des Reichsgerichts zu Leipzig*, vom 15, bis, 22 December. Berlin 1884.

Whelehan, Niall. *The Dynamiters: Irish Nationalist and Political Violence in the Wider Words 1867–1900.* Cambridge University Press, 2012.

Whibley, Charles. *Musings without Method: A Record of 1900–1901*. W. Blackwood & Sons, 1902.

Whibley, Charles. "Musings without Method." *Blackwood's Edinburgh Magazine*. Vol. 170, No. 132, October 1901.

Whitehead, Anne. *Paradise Mislaid: In Search of the Australian Tribe of Paraguay*. University of Queensland Press, 1998.

"Who is Schinas?" *Dundee Courier*, 21 March 1913.

Wilson, Colette E. *Paris and the Commune, 1871–78: The Politics of Forgetting*. Manchester University Press, 2007.

Wilson, Ray, and Ian Adams. *Special Branch: A History: 1883–2006*. Biteback Publishing, 2015.

Wortman, Richard S. *Scenarios of Power: Myth and Ceremony in Russian Monarchy from Peter the Great to the Abdication of Nicholas II*. Princeton University Press, 2006.

Wright, Carroll D. "The National Amalgamated Association of Iron, Steel, and Tin Workers, 1892–1901." *The Quarterly Journal of Economics*, Vol. 16, No. 1, November 1901.

Yarmolinsky, Avrahm. *Road to Revolution*. Princeton University Press, 2014.

Zenker, Ernst Victor. *Anarchism: A Criticism and History of the Anarchist Theory*. G. P. Putnam's Sons, 1897.

Zimmer, Kenyon. *Immigrants against the State: Yiddish and Italian Anarchism in America*. University of Illinois Press, 2015.

Index

Acciarito, Pietro Umberto: arrest and trial 58; attempted regicide of Umberto I 58; birth and family 56; blacksmith 57; death 59
Active Service Brigade 112–113
L'Aigulle (The Needles) 120–121
Aionos (paper) 179, 182
Amalgamated Association of Iron, Steel, and Tin Workers (AA) 135–137
Anarchist exclusion Act (United States) 143, 150–151
anti–Socialist laws (Belgium) 193
anti–Socialist laws (Germany) 42, 44, 48
SS Aramac 106, 113
Aronstam, Modest 141
Ashio copper mine strike (1907) 158
Ashton, Julian Rossi 106
Australian depression (1890–1893) 112
Australian Labor Party 111–113
Autonomie Club 88, 90, 121–126, 128,–131
Avrich, Paul 10, 84

Bakunin, Mikhail 1, 5, 43, 193
Balkan War (1912) 178, 182
Bari bread riots (1898) 59
Barlas, John Evelyn 123
Battola, Jean 125–126
Becker, Johann 43
Bellegarrigue, Anselme 16
Berezowski, Antoni 10
Berkman, Alexander (Ovsei Osipovich) arrest 142; attempted assassination of Frick (Henry Clay) 142; birth and childhood 137; death 143; education 138; emigration to United States 139; life in prison and deportation 143; meeting Emma Goldman 141; radicalization 140; trial 143
Berneri, Giovanni 191
Bloody Sunday (London) 123, 129
Boer War (1899) 193, 195, 198
bombs and bombing 1–2, 8, 44–47, 55, 69–72, 82, 115, 117

Bonnot, Jules 30
Bonnot Gang (La Bande à Bonnot) 2, 32
Bourdin, Martial: birth and youth 120; death 127; emigration to London 121; family 121; funeral 129; Greenwich Park explosion 120, 127–128, 131; membership of L'Aigulle 120; in New York 122
Bourgeoisie 6, 10–11, 16, 22, 26–27, 31, 45, 67, 69, 72, 84, 90, 92, 97, 131, 182
Bresci, Gaetano: birth and family 60; emigration to Paterson 61; first arrest 60; regicide of Umberto I 62; trial and death 62
Brust, Jean 135
Bunkai, Udagawi 162
Buttà, Fausto 93
Butterworth, Alex 72, 123

Café Terminus 84, 89, 90, 102
Cailes, Victor 124–126
Cameron, Mary (Dame Mary Gilmore) 113
Carnegie, Andrew 136, 142
Carnot, Marie François Sadi 82, 83, 91, 92
Caserio, Sante Geronimo: arrest and trial 96; assassination of Carnot 92; birth 92; early life 93; execution 96; first arrest 95; life as a fugitive 95
Channing, Walter 145–147
Charles, Frederick (Frederick Charles Slaughter) 123–126
Chernyshevsky, Nikolai 9, 11, 139, 141
Cleaver, Eldridge 5
Commonweal (paper) 122–124, 130–131, 133, 193
Communard 26, 85, 122
Coulon, Auguste 124–126
Creaghe, Dr. John 123
Croci, Benedetto 191
Czolgosz, Leon: as anarchist 146; arrest 149; assassination of Pres. William McKinley 149; contact with Emma Goldman 146; edu-

cation 145; family background and birth 144; ill health 146; imprisonment, trial, and execution 150

Danver, Steven 135
Dave, Victor 121, 193, 198
D'Axa, Zo 87
Deakin, Joseph (Joe) 124–126
demonstrations 26, 54, 59, 79, 94, 129, 140, 197
Ditchfield, William 124–126
Duval, Clément: arrest and trial 28; arson attacks 27; birth 23; death 30; escape from French Guiana 30; first robbery and arrest 25; injury 24; military service 24; stabbing of Rossignol 28
dynamite 7, 8, 11, 26, 31, 44–47, 70, 113–115, 128, 141

Enckell, Marianne 23, 24, 30
Engels, Friedrich 43, 156
expropriation 16, 21, 23, 28, 30, 31, 32

Fenian dynamitists 125, 128
Le Figaro (paper) 83
Fourmies protest (1891) 69, 101, 103
Franco-Prussian War 24–25, 37, 43–44, 65
free love 147
Freiheit (paper) 44, 140, 142
Frick, Henry Clay 136, 137, 141, 142, 143
Friday Society (Kinyo Kai) 158–159
Friends of the Constitution 1

Galleani, Luigi 2, 30
Garibaldi, Giuseppe 30, 51
Gibson, Violet 188, 191
Goldman, Emma 61, 93, 96, 137–138, 141–143, 146–147, 149–150
Gori, Pietro 94–95
Greek War of Independence (1831) 178–179
Grévy, Jules 29

guillotine 29–30, 32, 72, 79, 83, 90–91, 96
Guillotine Society 2, 32

Haymarket demonstration (1886) 140, 143
Heimin Shimbun (*Commoners News*) (paper) 156–160, 163–165
Hell (splinter group of Organizatsiya) 9
Henry, Émile: arrest and trial 90; birth and family circumstances 85; bombing of Café Terminus 89; bombing of Carmaux mining company 88; education 86; execution 90; in London 88; relationship with Élisa Gauthey 86; in Venice 86
Henry, Fortune (father of Émile Henry) 85
Hödel, Emil Heinrich Max: arrest, trial and execution 39; assassination attempt against Wilhelm I 39; Berlin busker 39; birth 37; journeyman plumber 38; Zeitz reformatory 38
Home Children 107
Homestead Steek Works (1892 strike) 135–137, 141–142, 146–147, 150
Hugo, Victor 18

illegalism 16, 23, 30, 32
individualist anarchism 16, 32
industrial revolution 5, 65
informers 44, 87, 89, 124
Irish Republican Army 194
Ishutin, Nikolai 9
Isoo, Abe 155
Iwasa, Sakutaro 157, 159

Jacob, (Alexandre) Marius: arrest and trial 23; asylum and escape 20; birth 16; burglar 19–21; death by suicide 23; family 17; first arrest 19; life as a sailor 18; pirate 18; schooling 17
James, Bob 106, 108, 112
Jensen, Richard Bach 130, 195

Karakozov, Dmitry Vladimirovich: assassination attempt 10; execution and arrest 11; influence of Nikolai Ishutin 9; manifesto 10; student radical 9; suicide attempt 10; youth 9
Khalturin, Stepan Nikolayevich: as agitator and organizer 7; death 9; planning and execution of attack 7; role in assassination of General Strelnikov 8; youth 6
King George I (Greece) 178–179, 181- 183
Knights of Labor 108, 135
Komissarov, Ossip 10
Krause, Paul 136
Kviatkovsky, Alexander 5, 7

Lloyd, Christopher 108
Lombardi, Michele Angiolillo 2
Lucetti, Gino 188–189
Lucheni, Luigi 2

Maison du Peuple 195, 198
Maitron, Jean 73, 120
Malato, Charles 80, 86
Marx, Karl 43, 51, 80, 140, 156
May Day 56–57, 67, 69, 94, 112
Mazzini, Giuseppe 51–52
McKinley, William (US president) 148–150
Melbourne Anarchist Club 107
Michel, Louise 26, 29, 85, 122–124
Milan bread riots (1898) 59
Most, Johann 38, 44, 48, 140, 142, 150
Mussolini, Benito 51, 187–192

Narodism 6–7, 139
Narodnaya Volya (the People's Will) 5, 6, 7, 8, 11, 138
Nechayev. Sergey 5, 12
Negri, Ada 93
Neville, Peter 191
New Australia Movement 116
New York Times (paper) 59, 90, 142, 149, 178–182, 191, 195–196
Nicholl, David 122, 125–126
Nihilists 138; Italian 55; Russian 11
Nihon Shakaito (Japan Socialist Party) 157–158
Nilson, Anton 2
Nobiling, Karl Eduard: attempted regicide of Wilhelm I 41; birth, family, and education 40; death 41; doctor of philosophy 40; links with Hödel 41
Nold, Carl 141

Organizatsiya (Organization) 9
Ottoman Empire 178, 182

Pale of Settlement 137
Pan-American Exposition 143–144, 148
Panama Scandal (1892) 91–92
La Panthere de Batignolles (The Panther of Batignolles) 26–28
Paris Commune (1871) 37, 51, 52, 70, 130
Passannante, Giovanni: adoption by Giovanni Agoglia 50; arrest and trial 54–55; arrest for subversion 52; attempted regicide of Umberto I 54; birth 50; burial (2007) 56; child poverty 50; Croce di Savoia hotel dishwasher 50; death 56; papal statement (Pope Leo XIII) 55; restaurateur 53
Pauwels, Jean 80, 193
Petrie, Lawrence: arrest 114; birth 106; bombing of SS *Aramac* 114; Circular Quay bomb plot 113; death 117; emigration to Australia 106; life in Paraguay 116;

loss of arm 111; membership of Melbourne Anarchist Club 107; as speaker and organizer 109; trial 115
Peukert, Josef 121
Pini, Vittorio: arrest and trial 31; birth and family 30; death 32; as member of the Gruppo Intransigente 31; move to Paris 31; stabbing of Celso Ceretti 31
Pinkertons 136
Pisacane, Carlo 1
Pouget, Emile 26, 121
Prince of Wales 194–196, 198–199
printing 7, 30, 95, 130, 157, 190
prison 8, 19–20, 23, 25, 27, 29, 39, 47–48, 52, 59–60, 62, 69, 72, 79, 83, 85, 90, 94–96, 112, 116, 134, 143, 150, 157, 160, 164–165, 188–189, 195–196, 198–199
proletariat *see* working class
prostitution 103, 162
Proudhon, Pierre-Joseph 16, 80, 193

Quail, John 124

Ravachol, François (François Claudius Koenigstein): alleged murder of Rivollier and Fradel 66; arrest and trial 71; birth and family 65; confession to Lhérot 71; execution 72; first bombs 70; grave robbery 67; murder of Brunel 67; murder of Marcon and daughter 69; supposed suicide and escape 68; unemployment and early criminality 66
Red Flag incident (akahata jikan) 160, 163–164
red scare 140, 143
Reinsdorf, Friedrich August: accusations of being police spy 44; arrest and trial 47; birth and education 42; contributor to Freiheit 44; execution 48; move to Switzerland 44; Niederwald monument attack 45; trade unionist 43; tuberculosis 47
Reitzel, Robert 142
Revolutionary Insurrectionary Army of Ukraine 2
Rizi, Fabio Fernando 191
Rome May Day protest (1891) 56
La Roquette Prison 29, 79, 83, 90

St. James Gazette (paper) 129
St. Joseph Massacre 29
Samuels, Henry (Levi Herris Wilchinski) 120, 122, 127
Saunders, Frances Stonor 188
Schinas, Alexandros: arrest and death 183; birth 178; education 179; family background 179; motivation for assassination of George I 181–183; in New York 180–181; as schoolteacher and politician 180

science 40, 81, 86, 88, 140
Seige of Rome (1870) 52
Shifu, Liu (Chinese Assassination Corps) 2
Shrearers Strike (1891) 111–113
Shūsui Kōtoku (Kōtoku, Denjirō) arrest for High Treason incident 164; birth 155; conversion to anarchism 157; disputed involvement in High Treason incident 165; education 155; execution 165; first arrest 156; life as a journalist 156; meeting with Sugako 164; in the United States 157
Singh, Bhagat 2
Sipido, Jean-Baptiste Victor: arrest and trial 195; attempted regicide of Prince of Wales 194; birth 192; death 199; escape from custody 197; family background 192; marriage 199
Skirda, Alexandre 25
Social Democrats 37–40, 42, 193
Socialist League 121–124
Socialist Revolutionary Union (France) 80
Soloviev, Alexander 11
Spanish-American War (1898) 143, 147
Squadristi (Italian blackshirts) 187, 190- 191
Stirner, Max 16
Strelnikov, General V. S. 8

strikes 7, 17, 31, 47, 59, 87–88, 109–113, 135–136, 140–142, 145–146, 156–158, 163
Sugako, Kanno: arrest for High Treason incident 164; birth and early life 160; early writings and involvement with Osaka reform movement 162; execution 165; first arrest 164; marriage 162; meeting with Kōtoku 164; second arrest 164; teenage years 161

Takichi, Miyashita 164–165
Thomas, Bernard 17, 18, 82
Times of London (paper) 123, 126–128, 130
Tolstoy, Leo 139, 192
Les Travailleurs de la Nuit (The Night Workers) 21
Treaty of Constantinople (1832) 179
Trial of the Thirty 83
Tsar Alexander II 6, 8, 10, 11, 138
Twain, Mark 1

Umberto I of Italy 53–56, 58–62, 146,
Unions 7, 16, 31, 42–43, 80, 110–113, 115, 117, 135–137, 142, 145, 150, 188, 196

Vaillant, Auguste: in Algeria and Argentina 80; arrest 82; attack on French Chamber of Deputies

81; birth and early life 79; embrace of anarchism 80; execution and reaction 83; socialist 80; trial 83
villainous laws (France) 82, 89
Vizetelly, Ernest Alfred 37–39, 41, 66, 68, 70, 80, 83, 87
Volksblatt (paper) 37, 40, 42
Von Bismarck, Otto 37, 41, 144

weapons 23, 97
Wilhelm I (William Frederick Louis of Hohenzollern) 39–41, 44, 47–48, 55
The Worker (paper) 107, 117
working class 6–7, 16, 19–20, 29, 45, 48, 57, 59, 66, 80, 85, 97, 114, 123, 193, 195

Yorozu Chōhō (Every Morning News) (paper) 156

Zamboni, Anteo: arrest and execution 191; assassination attempt against Mussolini 190; birth 189; family background 190
Zaniboni, Tito 187–188
Zemlya i Volya (Land and Liberty) 5, 6
Zenker, Ernst 193
Zhelvakov, Nikolai 8
Zimmer, Kenyon 147